AF650537

HISTORICAL SKETCHES
OF THE
SOUTH OF INDIA

HISTORICAL SKETCHES

OF THE

SOUTH OF INDIA,

IN AN ATTEMPT TO TRACE THE

HISTORY OF MYSOOR;

FROM THE
ORIGIN OF THE HINDOO GOVERNMENT OF THAT STATE TO THE
EXTINCTION OF THE MOHAMMEDAN DYNASTY IN 1799.

LIEUT. COLONEL MARK WILKS

IN THREE VOLUMES
VOL. I

GYAN

Published by

Gyan Publishing House
5, Ansari Road
Daryaganj, New Delhi-110002
Phone: 011-47034999, 9811692060
E-mail: books@gyanbooks.com

Distribution Network
gyanbooks.com
India, USA, Canada, UK, Australia, France

© Publisher

All rights reserved. No part of this work may be reproduced, stored, adapted, or transmitted in any form or by any means, electronic, mechanical, photocopying, micro-filming, recording or otherwise, or translated in any language, without the prior written permission of the copyright owner and the publisher.

ISBN: 978-81-212-8763-0 (Set)
978-81-212-8762-3 (PB)
First Published, 1810

2nd Impression 2023

Printed at: Gyan Press, Delhi.

The book is sold subject to the condition that it shall not, by way of trade or otherwise, be lent, resold, hired out, or otherwise circulated without the prior publisher's written consent.

HISTORICAL SKETCHES OF THE SOUTH OF INDIA (VOL. I)
Author: Mark Wilks

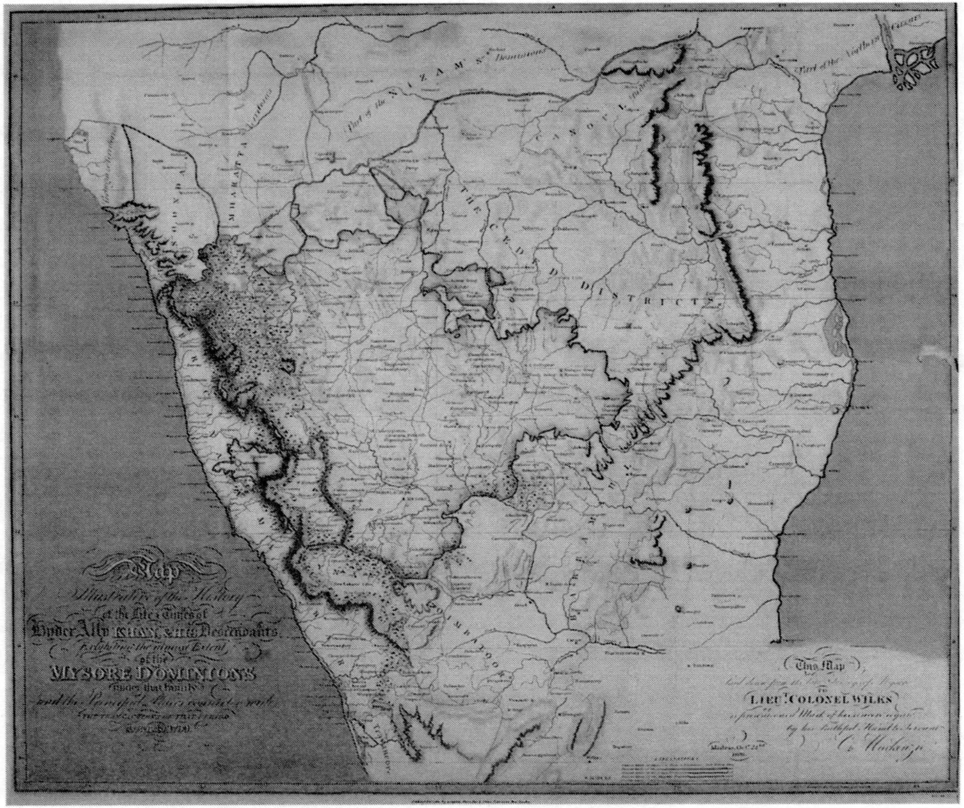
Map
Illustrative of the History
of the Life & Times of
Hyder Ally Khan, & his Descendants
of the
MYSORE DOMINIONS
Part of the NIZAM'S Dominions
Part of the Northern Circars
MAHARATTA
CANOOL
THE CEDED DISTRICTS
This Map
To
LIEU^t COLONEL WILKS

HISTORICAL SKETCHES

OF THE

SOUTH OF INDIA,

IN AN ATTEMPT TO TRACE THE

HISTORY OF MYSOOR;

FROM THE

ORIGIN OF THE HINDOO GOVERNMENT OF THAT STATE, TO THE EXTINCTION OF THE MOHAMMEDAN DYNASTY IN 1799.

FOUNDED CHIEFLY ON INDIAN AUTHORITIES COLLECTED BY THE AUTHOR WHILE OFFICIATING FOR SEVERAL YEARS AS

POLITICAL RESIDENT AT THE COURT OF MYSOOR.

BY LIEUT. COLONEL MARK WILKS.

VOL. I.

LONDON:

PRINTED FOR LONGMAN, HURST, REES, AND ORME,
PATERNOSTER-ROW.

1810.

TO

COLONEL BARRY CLOSE,

THE FRIEND WHOSE INSTRUCTION

AND

AFFECTIONATE ATTACHMENT

HAVE BEEN

THE PRIDE AND DELIGHT OF THE BEST YEARS OF HIS LIFE,

AND THE CHIEF SOURCE

OF WHATEVER HE MAY HAVE DESERVED OR ATTAINED

OF DISTINCTION IN ITS PROGRESS,

THIS VOLUME,

THE EXECUTION OF WHICH

NO ONE IS MORE EMINENTLY QUALIFIED TO APPRETIATE,

IS DEDICATED,

AS A TRIBUTE OF GRATITUDE, RESPECT, AND AFFECTION,

BY

THE AUTHOR.

ADVERTISEMENT.

IT is difficult to devise any plan for the orthography of Asiatic names that shall be entirely free from objection. The scheme of Sir William Jones would be unexceptionable, were it generally known to the English reader, but without this previous knowledge its adoption might tend to mislead. The letter ù in Hindù, for example, would be the correct orthography for Italy; but to convey the proper sound to the mere English reader we must write Hindoo. There is a variety of sounds which different persons, and even the same person at different times, will express by different English letters, and for practical purposes it is unnecessary to be fastidious in our choice. Whether we write Ali, Alee, or Aly, seems to be quite indifferent; the second syllable will probably be pronounced in the same manner. Where it is to be decided whether errors familiarised to the English ear should be rejected or retained, the rule which I have proposed to myself is to retain the error where it has been uniform, and to reject it where the spelling has been various. An example of each will explain this design. 1st. To substitute for the well known name Seringapatam the true orthography of Sreerung-puttun, would not only have the appearance of affectation, but would produce real confusion. There are however some few exceptions to the general rule of retaining the error where it has been uniform. Adoni, for example, instead of Adwanee, is so violent a change, and so absolutely unintelligible to any native of India, that after having noticed the identity of the name where it first occurs, I have generally continued the latter spelling. 2d. In the various readings of the same capital Visapoor, Visiapore, Viziapoor, Bejapoor, Beejapoor, Beejapore, there is already abundant confusion, and this is not increased by restoring the true orthography Vijeyapoor. The same observation applies to Vijeyanuggur, and many other words. Two places named Balapoor, Balipoorum, Balabarum, Balipoor, have been written (as one or the other of the four vernacular languages in common use have been employed) with the prefixes of Burra and Chota, Pedda and Chenna, Dud and Chick, Perri and Chinni. It is more convenient to the English reader that they should be distinguished by the English translation of these terms, Great and Little Balipoor. The names or rather titles of Mohammedan chiefs are generally composed of significant words, and where they can be rectified without causing one name to be mistaken for another, I should unnecessarily incur the charge of ignorance of the language in which they are written, by continuing the wrong orthography. In the name Murzafa Jung, for example, the former is not an Arabic word at all, and I have restored the proper reading, Muzzuffer Jung (victorious in war). There are other cases of names in their ordinary use not intended to be significant, where there is no danger of misleading the reader by endeavouring to convey the original sound. The second syllable of the word Mysore, as it is usually written, was never so pronounced by any native of India, Mohammedan, or Hindoo, and there is no danger that Mysoor should be mistaken for another place. Similar errors, however, in the names Bangalore and Tanjore escaped my observation in the correction of the first sheets, and have, to prevent confusion, been continued throughout. Innes Khan is not a Mohammedan name, and the person intended was called Yoonas (Jonas) Khan. It would be tedious and unimportant to state the grounds of preference in each particular case, but the examples which have been given will explain the general intention.

PREFACE.

THE first materials of the following work were collected for purposes connected with my public duties, without the most remote view to publication. Personal curiosity, and the increasing interest of the subject, induced me to pursue it, without any definite object, beyond that of rescuing from oblivion, before it should be lost for ever, the information possessed by living characters; and the farther examination of written authorities followed as a necessary and almost imperceptible consequence of what had already been done.

The public is little interested to know the gradation of circumstances by which I have been induced to prepare for publication the substance of a mass of materials collected with so little of fixed design, and still less of literary skill: but I may be permitted to observe, that in their existing state they could have been of little use if placed in abler hands, and that the task of translating, preparing, and arranging them for that purpose, would have been infinitely more laborious than that which I have undertaken.

Extensive opportunities of observing the characters and manners of the people whose transactions I describe, have afforded advantages which may compensate for some defects; but I am too well aware, that a person who has passed all but the earliest period of his life far removed from the ordinary opportunities of literary attainment must appear before the public with very humble pretensions. In presenting to my country a narrative of facts, I hope that I apprehend aright the moral obligations which I incur: and the errors of defective judgment, inadvertence, or unskilful narrative, are at the bar of public opinion.

The reference to authorities, so rigidly exacted in the western world, would be useless to the public in an undertaking where few of these authorities are before it; and the absence of all fixed design in writing many of the notes from which the work has been composed would render it a task of infinite labour, if it were of sufficient importance, to retrace the manuscript authorities for every fact: but as many of these manuscripts, and particularly those of the Mackenzie collection, may hereafter be deposited in some public institution, I have, in some cases, where the fact is either remarkable in itself, or liable to be controverted, endeavoured to state the authority where either memory or written reference has enabled me to trace it. For the rest, it may be satisfactory to the public to be furnished with a cursory account of the principal materials which have been employed.

1st. An historical memoir, prepared at my request, under the direction of Poornia, the present able and distinguished minister of Mysoor, and his intelligent assistant Butcherow. The best informed natives of the country who were known to possess family manuscripts or historical pieces were assembled for this purpose; and the memoir is a compilation framed from a comparison of these authorities.

2. A Persian manuscript, entitled An Historical Account of

the ancient Rajas of Mysoor, was found in 1799 in the palace at Seringapatam; it purports to have been "Translated in 1798, at the command of the Sultaun, by Assud Anwar, and Gholaum Hussein, with the assistance of Pootia Pundit, from two books in the Canara language:" this Persian manuscript was conveyed with other works to Calcutta, and I had not the opportunity of perusing it until the year 1807, when my friend Brigadier-General Malcolm obtained a copy from Bengal. A book in the Canara language, of which the contents were then unknown, was given in 1799 by Colonel W. Kirkpatrick, one of the commissioners for the affairs of Mysoor, to Major, now Lieutenant-Colonel Colin Mackenzie, and has since been translated under his direction with scrupulous care. It is the Canara manuscript from which the Persian translation was made, and is entitled "*The Succession of the Kings of Mysoor, from ancient Times, as it is in the Canara Cuddutums, now written into a Book by command by Nuggur Pootia Pundit.* It is divided into two parts, as noticed in the Persian translation: the first contains the historical narrative; and the second, the series of territorial acquisitions. In the first the dates are recorded in the year of the cycle only; and in the second they are reckoned by the number of years which had elapsed from the compilation of the work, or, in the language of the original, *so many years ago.* The apparent embarrassment of fixing the chronology was easily surmounted by Lieutenant-Colonel Mackenzie. By ascertaining a single date, all the rest were at once arranged, and the manuscript was proved beyond all controversy to have been written in the year 1712-13.

The circumstances which regard the discovery of this manuscript are well known. On the death of Cham Raj Wadeyar, the father of the present Raja, in 1796, the family was transferred from the palace to the miserable hovel where they were found on the capture of Seringapatam in 1799. Among the plunder of every thing useful or apparently valuable, which was on that occasion carried off to the stores of the Sultaun, were accidentally thrown two *Cudduttums* *, which attracted his attention nearly two years afterwards, when he ordered them to be examined and translated: and two old Cudduttums, which Lieutenant-Colonel Mackenzie received along with the book in 1799, prove, on examination, to be the actual originals from which it was copied, and are probably the *two books* mentioned in the Persian translation. A short time before the real compilation of this document,

* *Cudduttum, curruttum*, or *currut*, a long slip of cotton cloth, from eight inches to a foot wide, and from twelve to eighteen feet long, skilfully covered on each side with a compost of paste and powdered charcoal. When perfectly dry, it is neatly folded up, without cutting, in leaves of equal dimensions; to the two end folds are fixed ornamented plates of wood, painted and varnished, resembling the sides of a book, and the whole is put into a case of silk or cotton, or tied with a tape or ribbon; those in use with the lower classes are destitute of these ornaments, and are tied up by a common string: the book, of course, opens at either side, and if unfolded and drawn out, is still a long slip of the original length of the cloth. The writing is similar to that on a slate, and may be in like manner rubbed out and renewed. It is performed by a pencil of the *balapum*, or lapis ollaris; and this mode of writing was not only in ancient use for records and public documents, but is still universally employed in Mysoor by merchants and shopkeepers. I have even seen a bond, regularly witnessed, entered on the cudduttum of a merchant, produced and received in evidence.

This is the word *kirret*, translated (of course conjecturally) *palm-leaves* in Mr. Crisp's translation of Tippoo's regulations. The Sultaun prohibited its use in recording the public accounts: but although liable to be expunged, and affording facility to fraudulent entries, it is a much more durable material and record than the best writing on the best paper, or any other substance used in India, copper and stone alone excepted. It is probable that this is the linen or cotton cloth described by Arrian from Nearchus, on which the Indians wrote.—Vincent's Nearchus, p. 15. Art. 717.

the Raja Chick Deo Raj, who died in 1704, had directed an extensive collection to be made of historical materials, including all inscriptions then extant within his dominions, which were added to a library already reported to be voluminous: the above-mentioned work is probably one of the memoirs prepared in conformity to his directions, but it appears to have been presented to his successor, and is a brief but correct record of events up to the year 1712. It is, however, to be regretted that the author furnishes no incidents beyond a mere chronicle of events, after the occupation of Seringapatam by Raj Wadeyar in 1610, probably restrained by prudential motives in respect to living characters. The Sultaun, in removing the Raja's family from the palace, had intended to destroy the building altogether; and gave orders for that purpose, which were afterwards changed. It was reported to him that several large apartments were full of books, chiefly of palm leaf and Cudduttums, and he was asked how they were to be disposed of. "Transfer them," said he, "to the royal stables, as fuel to boil the cooltee (grain on which horses are fed):" and this was accordingly done. A small miscellaneous collection was preserved from this destruction by the pious artifice of a bramin, who begged the apartment might be respected, as containing the *penates* of the family. This room was opened in the confusion of the 4th of May 1799, and a large portion of the contents fell into the hands of a British officer.

I have reason to believe, that through various channels I have had access to copies of most of the historical tracts which this collection contained*, and among these was the record of a cu-

* If the collection of *Shassanums*, or inscriptions, has been preserved, it may be considered as an historical manuscript of great value. A few days before my

rious inquiry into the state of the family about the year 1716, for the purpose of ascertaining which of the branches had preserved the true blood of the house unpolluted by unworthy connections; when, out of thirty-one branches, thirteen were pronounced to be legitimate, and eighteen were excluded from the privilege of giving wives or successors to the reigning Raja.

3. Two manuscripts, corresponding to each other in all material circumstances, preserved in different branches of the family of the ancient Dulwoys of Mysoor*.

4. A great variety of smaller manuscripts and memoirs in different languages, and of various degrees of merit, relative to detached facts: such, for example, as a memoir of the ancestry of the late Mohammedan dynasty, prepared at my request by the officiating priests at the mausoleum of the grandfather of the late Tippoo Sultaun at Colar; characters of Hyder Ally and Tippoo Sultaun, from the pen of my valuable friend Seyed Hussein, Persian secretary to the Rajah of Mysoor, &c. &c.

5. The extensive and valuable collection of grants, generally of a religious nature, inscribed on stone or copper, which are in the possession of my friend Lieutenant-Colonel Colin Mackenzie of the corps of engineers on the establishment of Fort St. George. These ancient documents are of a singularly curious texture;

embarkation from Madras its probable existence was ascertained, and I trust that it has been added to the Mackenzie collection.

* *Dulwoy, general,* from Dul, an army (Canara). The word is translated sometimes minister, but more frequently regent, in the records of Madras, and in Mr. Orme's history. Nunjeraj, the person who commanded the Mysoor troops at Trichinopoly from 1752 to 1755, held also the appointment of minister of finance; or rather, he and his brother had usurped the whole power of the state in all its departments.

they almost always fix the chronology, and frequently unfold the genealogy and military history of the donor and his ancestors, with all that is remarkable in their civil institutions, or religious reforms; and the facts derived from these inscriptions are illustrated by a voluminous collection of manuscripts, which can only be trusted with confidence, so far as they are confirmed by these authentic documents. The manuscript of Pootia, which seemed to deserve a separate description, belongs to this collection, which, at the period of my departure from Madras, amounted to near one thousand seven hundred grants, and six hundred MSS.

The department of ancient history in the East is so deformed by fable and anachronism, that it may be considered an absolute blank in Indian literature. There is no hope that this important defect will ever be supplied, except from an extensive collection of such documents. Lieutenant-Colonel Mackenzie has devoted to this pursuit the leisure which he has been enabled to snatch from a long course of active and meritorious service; and has formed, under numerous discouragements, a stupendous and daily increasing collection of all that is necessary to illustrate the antiquities, the civil, military and religious institutions, and ancient history, of the south of India; and I trust that he will in due time communicate to the public the result of his extraordinary perseverance.

I am obliged to Lieutenant-Colonel Mackenzie for several valuable communications on particular periods of history, written expressly for my aid and information in arranging the materials of the present work: and I cannot acknowledge in terms of too much gratitude how largely I am indebted to an unlimited access to the study of the collection which I have described, and to an intercourse entirely unreserved with its worthy possessor, and, his large establishment of learned native assistants, for whatever knowledge I possess of the ancient history of the south of India: a ground on which I have but slightly touched for the illustration of later events.

6. The fifth chapter of the present work was written at as early a period as possible, for the purpose of subjecting its facts to the most rigorous test. It was accordingly submitted to the examination of numerous friends, well qualified to correct errors, most of them holding the highest situations under the government of Fort St. George. Mr. Francis Ellis, a name which it will hereafter be permitted to quote as authority, has furnished me with a learned note *, on a particular subject of discussion, which will be found in the Appendix; and the reader will join with me in regretting the want of more numerous illustrations from the same pen. Mr. Ellis wrote in pencil, on blank leaves, which were inserted for the purpose, such observations as occurred to him on perusing the manuscript of that chapter, and very kindly gave me discretionary permission to apply the facts which they contain: this is the foundation of those notes on that and other parts of the work which refer to his authority.

This profound and ingenious orientalist had in contemplation a work of great labour and public utility, namely, the translation into modern Tamul and English of the Sanscrit text of the ancient law tract, most esteemed in the south, named Vignyan Ishwar, with notes shewing the variations of doctrine exhibited

* The reader is requested to supply an omission of the printer by referring to this note from p. 128.

in the more modern work of Videyarannea; of which some notices will be found in the fifth chapter of this work: and I advert to the design, in the hope that it may attract the attention of those who ought to patronize and promote it.

7. Notes and extracts from the records of the government of Fort St. George, to which I had unlimited access from the confidential situations which I had the honour to hold under Earl Powis, and by the obliging permission of Lord William Bentinck, and of Mr. Petrie, during their respective governments. These results of a long and laborious examination have been rendered less satisfactory from the very defective state of the earlier records. Of the labour itself, Mr. Orme has correctly observed, that it probably exceeds the conception of any of his readers, excepting the keeper of the records.

The removal from Seringapatam to Calcutta of the official records of the late dynasty of Mysoor, had deprived me of an authentic source of information on a variety of subjects. I had hoped, through the interposition of a friend, and the sanction of Sir George Barlow, when governor general, which was readily given, to procure an examination of these records for certain special purposes. But I am aware that the labour is greater than can be expected from gentlemen fully occupied by their official duties, on whom I have no personal claims. My expectations from this and some other sources are now extinguished; but although I have been compelled by severe ill health to leave India at an earlier period than was consistent with the plan which I had formed for completing the work in that country, I hope that I have been able to authenticate by other means most of the facts for which I was desirous to refer to those authorities: and I have since my arrival in England received from Colonel William Kirkpatrick, who long filled with distinguished ability very important public situations in Bengal, some unexpected lights on the subject of a portion of these records, which will demand a more particular acknowledgment in the second volume, to which they chiefly apply.

Acknowledgments to all who have assisted my researches would include a long and respectable list; but I am particularly indebted to Colonel Close, political resident at the court of Poona, whose observations give light and strength to whatever they approach; to the correct judgment and extensive knowledge of Colonel Agnew; to Mr. Hodgson, and Mr. Thackery, members of the board of revenue, and to Mr. Hurdis of the Sudder Adawlut, for the lights derived from their official labours, and for directing my attention to other valuable records in their respective departments, connected with the discussions of the fifth chapter.

I have some doubt how far I am at liberty to mention my obligations to Sir James Mackintosh, who was so good as to peruse the detached portions of this volume which were written in India*: but I trust that he will receive with kindness this public acknowledgment of the instruction which I have received from his observations.

8. Two military memoirs compiled in the Persian language under my own direction, by Abbas Ali, the field secretary of the late Hyder Ali Khan, from the written memoirs, or oral statements of two distinct assemblies of the oldest and most intelligent military officers of the late dynasty. Over one of these presided Budder u Zeman Khan, an old officer of distinguished talents

* The greater part was written during the voyage from India to England.

and cultivated understanding, well known to the troops of Bombay by his respectable defence of Darwar. The other meeting was directed for a time by Lutf Aly Beg, one of Tippoo Sultaun's embassadors to Constantinople in 1785, and the defender of Nundidroog in 1791. This venerable old gentleman terminated his earthly career before he had finished the compilation, which he had kindly undertaken; and the remainder of the narrative was chiefly directed by Jehan Khan, the officer who repulsed the flower of Sir Eyre Coote's army from the fortified pagoda of Chillumbrum in June 1781, and was desperately wounded in the breach of Seringapatam in 1799; a plain, unlettered old soldier, of clear and distinct understanding, and a memory uncommonly retentive and correct.

9. A history of Coorg, written by the present Raja, whose romantic character and adventures are well known in India. Its pretensions to profound historical research are not extensive, but it presents some characteristic traits of the mountaineers of the west of India, which are singularly curious.

10. Desultory memoranda, containing the results of repeated personal intercourse with every surviving individual, sufficiently well informed for my purpose, who had been employed under the late dynasty in civil, military, or diplomatic situations: and written memoirs from the most intelligent of them on such transactions as were most interesting or important.

11. The last in this enumeration is a work written under the personal direction of the late Tippoo Sultaun himself; and as this circumstance will probably excite some curiosity, I shall here subjoin a short account of this remarkable performance.

The title of the work is *Sultaun u Towareekh* or the *King of*

Histories; the substance was dictated by Tippoo Sultaun himself and the work composed by Zein-ul-ab-u-Deen Shusteree*, brother of Meer Aalum, the late minister at Hyderabad.

The style of the work is an example of the false taste introduced into modern works in the Persian language; but it is the style of a person well skilled in that sort of composition, and accomplished in the literature of Persia.

It begins, as is usual, with the praises of God and the prophet, his descendants and approved associates, in a manner which holds a middle course between the tenets of the Sultaun and his secretary, who were of opposite sects† of the Mohammedan religion. The author then proceeds to a dissertation on the gradations of creation; the dissimilitude and inequality of men in their mental qualities, as well as in their exterior appearance. This inequality, he observes, has existed even in the apostles, sent at different periods by the Almighty to enlighten mankind: it exists also among the inferior orders of men: government is requisite for the protection of mankind, and kings have existed in every age: the same distinctions are observable in the relative characters of kings, as among the apostles above them, and the mass of mankind below them; and the proof of this relative superiority of one king over another is exemplified *in the superiority of Tippoo Sultaun, over all kings, ancient and modern.* The author then goes

* Shusteree; his family name being from Shuster; the Suza of the western geographers.

† Tippoo, although educated, and usually classing himself, as a Soonee, affected a superiority of religious knowledge, which looked down on all the sects, and aspired to the character of inspiration: but his zeal for holy war gave him a particular veneration for the character of *Ali*, the doctrines of whose sect he seemed on many occasions to patronize more than those of Ooner (or the Soonee) in which he had been educated.

on for several pages to compare the Sultaun with the sun, the moon, the stars, and the planets; the prophets and apostles; and the most celebrated kings and philosophers of antiquity; in a style of accomplished extravagance and absurdity.

Such, he proceeds, was Tippoo Sultaun, the author of incomparable inventions and regulations, to be recorded in this work; which is intended for the exclusive instruction of his own descendants: and if any other sovereign should adopt by stealth any of these inventions, "he must necessarily be classed among the said descendants;" that is to say, according to the gross and obscene dialect of this court, hereafter to be noticed, of which the Sultaun could not divest himself even in his literary pursuits, "Tippoo Sultaun must be considered to have embraced the mother of the supposed imitator."

The secretary seems to have been ashamed of this early specimen; for, in the very next sentence, which is more than usually involved and inflated, apparently to conceal his purpose, he takes an opportunity of informing the reader, that many passages of the work are of the express dictation of the Sultaun himself.

The work is proposed to be divided into two volumes; first, the genealogy and life of the Sultaun's grandfather and father; second, the life of *Tippoo Sultaun*.

The first volume proceeds no farther than the early youth of Hyder—a blank ensues; and the second commences abruptly with the accession of Tippoo Sultaun in 1783, and is continued to 1789; after some blank leaves, follows a second edition of the genealogy; both of them are equally remote from the truth: and in the narrative of transactions from 1783 to 1789, although some of his successful military operations are related with a respectable degree of clearness and precision, those in which his arms were unfortunate can scarcely be recognized, in the turgid and fabulous shape which the Sultaun has assigned to them.

On the first mention of the English, and sometimes where they are not opposed to him, he is pleased to call them *Nazarenes* (from Nazareth); but on other occasions they are "*rascally infidels*" and a *runaway* race. In narrating their attacks, they are compared to *wounded wild-boars*, and in other passages they are a *race of dæmons*. Madras has the honourable name of the City of *Hermaphrodites*; and the Nabob Mohammed Ali Khan, the contemptuous designation of *the Christian*.

The French officers are treated by the writer without incivility, until their refusal to continue hostilities at Mangalore, in 1783, after the conclusion of a peace between their nation and the English: from that period Mons. Cossigni is called *Nau Sirdar* (viz. the privative *nau* prefixed to the word *officer*); and the nation *fundamentally faithless*.

The character of the Sultaun's literary taste is displayed throughout the work in a strange selection of terms, and a misspelling of the names of his opponents, for the purpose of giving them a contemptuous or obscene meaning: a few examples to explain this species of wit and illustrate the usual phraseology of the Sultaun, are thrown into shade at the bottom of the page *.

* *Mukaad* is the place where any person sits down, it is also the part of the body on a which a person sits. It suited the chosen dialect of the Sultaun to make use of this term to describe the place of encampment of the enemy.

Soherâb Jung, a *Soherâb* in war; the title of the Nizam's late minister. *Soherâb* was the son of *Rustum*, the Persian hero; it is written *Shoreâb*, which causes it to signify *brackish water*. *Tohuvvur Jung*, *valiant in war*, is converted into *Tehcber*

It was impossible to give any tolerable view of the nature of the performance, and it will be equally impracticable to convey even a faint idea of the manners of the court during the late dynasty, without some offence against delicacy; but the transgressions will, I trust, be found as few and as slight as the nature of the subject could possibly admit. I shall conclude this account of the *King of Histories* with a specimen of the performance.

When Brigadier-General Macleod appeared the second time before Mangalore, he is made to address a letter † to the Sultaun, challenging a combat between equal numbers, for the purpose of deciding the war: the following is the Sultaun's reply:

"It is admitted, by the concurring testimony of all religions, that no apostle, excepting the seal of the apostles, has been invested with the power of the sword: and that the text of 'Slay them wheresover thou canst find them,' has descended from the

Jung, undermost in war. Ootè Naick, the name of a Coorg insurgent, is written *Cootè Naick, Captain Dog. Appa Bulwunt*, one of the Mahratta chiefs, is written *Amma Bulwunt*, Mother Bulwunt: and finally, the word *Mahratta*, or rather Mharatta, which, when written in the Hindoo-Persic character, is properly spelled with the aspirate, and sharp Hindoostanee *Te* with four points, has always the aspirate omitted, and the Hindoostanee is converted into the thick Persian *Te* with *two* points; *Marata;* which new orthography produces a word signifying *Catamite*. A copy of the work was in the house of Zein-ul-ab-u-deen, bound in a splendid cover with a lock and key to secure it. A zealous adherent of the late dynasty, of whose veracity in this instance I cannot doubt, in a visit to Zein-ul-ab-u-deen observed the book, and asked, as matter of conversation, what it was. Zein-ul-ab-u-deen excused himself from giving a direct answer, and referred the enquirer to an indorsement on its cover in the Persian language, of which the following is a verbal translation. "Si quis, sine regis imperio, hunc librum aperiens, in eum intueatur, numinis execratione, et regis ira implicitus erit, ac quod si matris in vulvam inspexisset, idem se crimen commissise censeat." It was generally known that *Zein-ul-ab-u-deen* and the Sultaun were engaged in such a work, and that no other person was permitted to see it.

† The state of the fact will be discussed in its proper place.

almighty Avenger to no other. That holy personage did, in conformity to the command of the great Creator, let loose the *infidel-destroying* sword, without distinction, on the Jews, the Nazarenes, the Sabians, and other idolaters. And the victorious lion of the Lord (Ali), who was the rightful Imaum*, and the absolute vicegerent of the seal of the prophets, removed the darkness of infidelity and association (that is the doctrine of assigning to God associates in power), and sent abundance of associators on the road to the abode of misery.

"But your apostle, the holy Messiah, according to universal admission, was not invested by the Almighty with the power of the sword, and never did undertake a holy war. It is evident, moreover, from authentic books, that you *falsely* arrogate to yourselves the religion of the Messiah; that you support the doctrine of the *trinity*, absolutely associating other persons with God, and thereby enrol yourselves with idolaters; and that you perpetrate forbidden things, such as drinking wine, eating swine's flesh, gaming, usury, and every other act which by the universal consent of mankind is held to be a vice. Therefore God, and the apostle of God, that is the Messiah, and all his elect, abominate and abhor you, and you have incurred the wrath of the throne of God.

"Wherefore, all sects being bound by the laws and precepts of their respective apostles, it follows, that killing and slaying†, and bravery, and heroism, and holy war, and the destruction of infidels, and the arts which belong to the gallant and the brave, have descended as an hereditary right to us from our apostle.

* The Sultaun must have been but a lukewarm *Sunni* to have conceded to his secretary this fundamental doctrine of the Sheea sect.

† These repetitions of synonyms are preserved for the purpose of rendering the translation as close and as verbal as the idioms of the two languages will admit.

"If thou hast any doubt of all this, descend, as thou hast written, from thy ships, with thy forces, and taste the flavour of the blows inflicted by the hands of the holy warriors, and behold the terror of the religion of Mohammed; but on that same condition which thou hast written, that soldier opposed to soldier, and officer to officer, in single combat, with such weapons as they shall choose, shall determine which is the better man.

> "Like a man remove fear from thy imagination,
> Make no more idle evasions *like* a woman *."

General Macleod is then stated to have fled on the same night; and the English are admitted as suppliants to liberal conditions of peace.

Since my arrival in England I have been indebted to the Court of Directors for access to the records and library at the India-House, and I have to acknowledge the most obliging attention from every officer of that house with whom I have had occasion to communicate. These records are still more imperfect than those at Madras; but each contains materials that are wanting in the other. My chief intercourse has hitherto been with Mr. Jackson, the register and keeper of the ancient records, which, although extremely defective, afford some valuable matter for the general historian, and extensive materials for a life of Sevajee, which had escaped the researches of Mr. Orme. It is but common justice to Mr. Jackson to notice his clear and intelligent arrangement of these disjointed materials, and the very laborious process by which he has rendered the reference to every record,

* This also is stated to be a specimen of the taste of the Sultaun, which cannot be explained without the most gross indecency.

whether in the order of the subject or the date, perfectly simple and satisfactory.

In a pursuit which from its nature precludes a recourse to the ordinary means of preventing inaccuracy, I am far from presuming to expect that an ardent desire for truth has in every instance attained its object: and communications, accompanied by the requisite authorities which may enable me to correct errors, will be thankfully acknowledged, if the public should ever call for a second edition.

It was intended that the design of this work should be completed by the publication of the whole at this period; but precarious health has prevented the execution of this intention; and the same cause forbids me to speak with confidence of the very early appearance of a second and last volume. Its preparation, however, shall not be unnecessarily intermitted; but the delay will afford me the opportunity of being governed by public opinion, according to which I shall be prepared to prosecute the design with spirit, or to abandon it without severe reluctance.

CONTENTS

OF

THE FIRST VOLUME.

CHAPTER I.

CHAPTER II.

CHAPTER III.

CHAPTER IV.

CHAPTER V.

CHAPTER VI.

CHAPTER VII.

CHAPTER VIII.

CHAPTER IX.

CHAPTER X.

CHAPTER XI.

CHAPTER XII.

CHAPTER I.

DESCRIBING EARLY EVENTS IN THE SOUTH OF INDIA UP TO 1564.

Reflections on the imaginary happiness of the early ages—Progress of conquest, revolution, and decay among uncivilized nations—No pretension to antiquity among the ruling families of the Indian peninsula—State of that country when the Hindoo dynasty of Mysoor began to emerge from obscurity—Sketch of its former geography—First irruption of the Mohammedans to the south of the river Taptee—to the south of the river Kistna—Plunder of the capital of Carnatic—its interesting ruins—Extent of that empire—Its final destruction—Origin of the empire of Vijeyanuggur—its second dynasty—Conquests—Causes of its rapid increase—Rebellion of the Mussulman chiefs of the Decan, and establishment of an independent sovereignty at Calburga—Efforts of the dethroned Prince of Warankul the ally of Vijeyanuggur—Disunion of the Mohammedans of Decan, and separation into five distinct governments—Patan empire of Hindostan invaded by the Moguls at the exact time that Vasco de Gama doubled the Cape of Good Hope—Confederacy of the five princes of Decan, and fall of the empire of Vijeyanuggur—State of that empire during its decline—Reflections on the despotism of the East.

THE golden age of India, like that of other regions, belongs exclusively to the poet. In the sober investigation of facts, this imaginary æra recedes still farther and farther at every stage of the enquiry: and all that we find is still the empty praise of the ages which have passed.

It must not be denied, that a distant view of the miseries attendant on the half-savage state is relieved on a closer exa-

CHAP. I.

mination by a multitude of minute traits in the manners and habits of a people, which break the force of despotism, or partially compensate, by a spirit of rude but manly independence, for the evils which that spirit must encounter. But if the comparative happiness of mankind in different ages be measured by its only true and rational standard, namely, the degree of peace and security which they shall be found collectively and individually to possess, we shall certainly discover, in every successive step towards remote antiquity, a larger share of wretchedness to have been the portion of the human race. If the savage of early times can boast of any real superiority, it is in his exemption from that querulous spirit which distinguishes modern civilization; it is in the happy but universal error peculiar to his character, that his state, and his alone, is wisest, happiest, and best.

The force of these observations, general in their nature, is perhaps more strongly marked in the history of India than of any other region of the earth. At periods long antecedent to the Mohammedan invasion, wars, revolutions, and conquests seem to have followed each other, in a succession more strangely complex, rapid, and destructive, as the events more deeply recede into the gloom of antiquity.

The rude valour which had achieved a conquest, was seldom combined with the sagacity requisite for interior rule; and the fabric of the conquered state, shaken by the rupture of its ancient bonds, and the substitution of instruments clumsy, unapt, and misapplied, either fell to sudden ruin, or gradually dissolved. If the energies of a new dynasty sometimes preserved, for a few generations, the semblance of wisdom and vigour, still the imperceptible consequences of wealth, by relaxing its force, subverting the allegiance of its subjects and dependent chiefs, or inciting the cupidity of its neighbours, had already undermined the tottering state when it appeared to have attained its highest prosperity.

Whether these revolutions were produced by a sudden or a gradual dissolution of the former government, the consequences were nearly the same. Almost every village became a separate state, in constant warfare with its neighbours; the braver and more fortunate chiefs enlarging their boundaries, and augmenting their force; and thus proceeding by rapid strides to the erection of new dynasties.

From causes resembling those which have been thus slightly sketched, there is perhaps not one ruling family in the south of India that has the least pretension to any considerable antiquity; but the difficulty of tracing their origin is not diminished in proportion to its distance from those remote periods which bury all the tribes of the earth in a common darkness. The insignificance of the rulers contributes in this case equally with the lapse of time to that obscurity which hangs over the early history of every people.

In attempting to trace in an intelligible manner the rise and progress of one of these dynasties, whose later history, and that of its Mohammedan subverters, is inseparably connected with the transactions of the British nation in India; it will be necessary to present a sketch, however imperfect, of the state of the south of India, about the period when that dynasty began to emerge from obscurity.

The name of *Deckan*, *Detchin*, or South, was formerly applied by Hindoo geographers to the whole of those countries which are situated to the south of the river Nermudda or Nerbudda; but the fixed possessions of the Mohammedans having for many centuries after their invasion of the Deckan extended no farther south than the river Kistna, the term Deckan came to signify, in Hindostan, the countries situated between those two rivers only: and such is the popular acceptation of its southern limit at the present day. For the convenience of distinguishing this tract from the more southern regions, this is the sense in which it is proposed to apply the term *Deckan* in the course of this work; and whenever " the south of India" shall be mentioned, it is intended (unless otherwise explained) to describe the regions situated to the south of the river Kistna.

With the exception of the low countries forming the northern extremity of the Deckan, which we shall have little occasion to discuss, the great geographical feature of these united regions of the south is a central eminence, elevated from 3000 to 5000 feet above the level of the sea, separated by wild, abrupt, and mountainous declivities, from the low flat countries to the east and west, which form a belt of small but unequal breadth between the hills and the ocean. This central eminence is usually named the Balaghaut, and the lower belt the Payeen Ghaut: words which respectively signify the countries above and below the passes of the mountains.

Identity of language may safely be admitted to prove identity of origin; and in the absence of more direct evidence constitutes a criterion of political union, less liable to change from the influence of time than any other test that can be proposed.

The ancient divisions of the country may accordingly be

traced with greater probability by the present limits of the spoken languages than by any other guide which is easily accessible; and the names of countries have undergone such extraordinary changes, that some confusion may be avoided by briefly adverting to their ancient designations.

The principality which in later times has been named from the obscure village of Mysoor, was the south-western portion of the ancient Carnatic, frequently named also the country of Canara, or the country in which the Canara language was spoken. According to this criterion, the northern limits of that extensive region commenced near the town of Beder in the latitude of 18° 45′ N., about 60 miles N.W. from Hyderabad; following the course of this language to the S. E. it is found to be limited by a waving line which nearly touches Adwanee (Adoni), winds to the west of Gooti, skirts the town of Anantpoor, and passing exactly through Nundidroog, touches the range of Eastern Ghauts; thence pursuing their southern course to the mountainous pass of Gujjelhutty, it continues to follow the abrupt turn caused by the great chasm of the western hills, between the towns of Coimbetoor, Palatchi, and Palgaut; and sweeping to the N. W. skirts the edges of the precipitous western Ghauts, nearly as far north as the sources of the Kistna; whence following first an eastern and afterwards a north-eastern course, it terminates in rather an acute angle near Beder, already described as its northern limit.

From Beder the Mahratta language is spread over the whole country to the north-westward of the Canara, and of a line, which passing considerably to the eastward of Dowletabad, forms an irregular sweep until it touches the Tapti, and follows the course of that river to the western sea, on which the district of Sedashegur, in North Canara, forms its southern limit.

In the geographical tables of the Hindoos, the name of Maharashtra, and, by contraction, Mahratta dasum (or country), seems to have been more particularly appropriated to the eastern portion of this great region, including Baglana, part of Berar and Candeish: the western was known by its present name of Concan.

The Telinga *, formerly called the Kalinga, language occupies the space to the eastward of the Mahratta, from near Cicacole, its northern, to within a few miles of Pulicat, its southern boundary, with the intervention, however, in a stripe of small dimension, of the savage Tongue of the Goands. This space was divided into the Andra and Kalinga dasums, or countries; the former to the south, the latter to the north of the river Godaveri; but at the period of the Mohammedan conquest, the greater part of these united provinces seems to have been known to that people by the name of Telingana, and Warankul as the capital of the whole.

The Tamul language is spoken in the tract extending to the south of the Telinga as far as Cape Comorin, and from the sea to the great range of hills, including the greater part of the Baramahal, and Salem, and the country now called Coimbetoor, and formerly Kangiam †, along which line it is bounded to

* That which, apparently by a strange modification of the term Gentile, Europeans have thought proper to name *Gentoo*, a word unknown to the Indians.

† In the southern part of Mysoor the Tamul language is at this day named the *Kangee*, from being best known to them as the language of the people of Kangiam. In the central portion of Mysoor it is for a similar reason named the *Drauvedee*; far-

the west by the Canara and Malabar. This whole tract had formerly the name of Drauveda, and is so distinguished at this day by its western and northern neighbours; although in the course of political events the greater part of it is known to Europeans exclusively by the name of Carnatic, of which country it never formed a part *, and was comparatively a recently conquered province: the cause of this misnomer will hereafter be traced; first, to the residence in that province of the fugitive king of Carnatic, after the Mohammedan conquest of the country properly so called; and, secondly, to the partition of the dominions of the Carnatic between the kings of Golconda and Vijeyapoor; who, in the division of a country of which they were grossly ignorant, were satisfied with the sweeping designations of Carnatic above and below the ghauts. The subordinate divisions of Drauveda were named from the three rival dynasties of Cholan †, Cheran,

ther north, by the Telingas, and universally by the Mohammedans, the *Aravee*, a term of doubtful origin. Here we have four Hindoo appellations for the same language, and Europeans have added a fifth, by miscalling it the *Malabar*.

* A Poona Mahratta at this day, when speaking of the Carnatic, means the countries south of the Kistna, which we have described as belonging to the ancient Carnatic, distinctly including Savanoor and Mysoor.

† Coromandel, written *Choramandel* in the records of Fort St. George, until about the year 1779—properly Chola, or Chora-mundul. (See the first document in Appendix, No. II.) In Sanscrit, the primitive meaning of the latter word is orbit, circle, and thence a region or tract of country. " In Tamul, it merely signifies a tract of land" (Ellis). The letter in this word, usually expressed by the English R, is an intermediate sound between the *l*, the *R*, and the French *j*. It may be conjectured by placing the tongue in the position to articulate those several letters, but the sound cannot easily be reached by European organs. To the south of the Coleroon it would strike the ear of an European as the letter *l*; near to Madras he would find no distinct articulation, and after frequent repetitions would probably write the letter *R*. " The *Telegu* and *Canara* have not the letter, and substitute sometimes the *l* and sometimes the *d*" (Ellis).—With regard to the first syllable *Cho*, the sound most usually given would be more nearly approached by *Sho*. The

and Pandian; the former, governing in Tanjore and Combaconum, possessed the northern tract: Pandian had Madura and the south: and Cheran united Kangiam and Salem to the dominions of Kèrala or Malabar. The exact limits of these kingdoms cannot now be traced, and without doubt were in a state of incessant change: it is only known with certainty, that they met near to Caroor (about 40 miles W. of Trichinopoly) a town which alternately passed into the hands of each of the rival dynasties.

Rounding the southern promontory of Cape Comorin, we find on the western coast the Malabar language, which extends over Travancore and Malabar, formerly named Kèrala, as far north as Nilisuram *; from thence to Sedasheghur, south of Goa, we find the Toolava language, and the country of Toolava. In some tables Toolava is considered as a subdivision of Kèrala, which is said to have extended from Gocurn, round Cape Comorin, to the river Tumbrapurni, in Tinnavelley. The tract distinguished in our maps as the province of Canara, by a fatality unexampled in the history of nations, neither is nor ever was known by that name to the people of the province, or of any part of India.

place near Paliacate, supposed by some to give the name to the coast, is stated by a native of that neighbourhood to be *Curri-munnul*—black sand: such being the appearance of the *shore* at that place.

There is great reason to doubt whether the *Arcati regia Sora* of Ptolemy be the modern Arcot. *Chera*, *Cheruu*, or *Cerun* was probably the country stated in the Periplus of the Erythrean Sea to have been governed by *Ceprobotus*, by Ptolemy written *Cerabothus-Cera* or *Chera puttri* the progeny of Chera--the Pandia was unquestionably the *Pandi Mandala* of the Periplus, the *Pandionis Mediterranea* of Ptolemy, and their capital the *Modura regia Pandionis* of the same author.

* From a temple of Siva, under his title of Nil-Ishvar, or Nil Kunt Ishvar, the blue god, or the blue-necked god, so called from one of his fabulous exploits. The latter term coincides with the *Nelcunda* of Ptolemy and the Periplus of the Erythrean Sea.

Voyagers, finding that it was a dependency of the kingdom of Canara, and probably that the officers of government spoke that language, fell into the error which I have thought it necessary to notice, and gave that name to the country of Toolava *.

Of the countries which have been thus briefly noticed, Travancore, Malabar, and South Canara alone escaped Mohammedan conquest, until the two latter were invaded by Hyder in 1763—6. Whenever Ferishta mentions expeditions to Malabar, it will be found, on examining the geographical positions of the places enumerated, that the operations of the troops were con-

* It is still more difficult to trace the name Limurika, as this province is called by the ancient geographers of the west. Captain Wilford, (9th vol. As. Res.) conjectures this name to be derived from the kings of Muru, mentioned in the grant from Conjeveram, translated by Sir W. Jones in the third vol. of that work, with the Arabic article *Al* changed into *Li*: but exclusively of this violent deviation from the genius of a language, Sir William Jones, in a note on this word, expressly warns us against concluding with certainty that Muru was the name of a country. I have not had the opportunity of obtaining a copy of the original grant, for the purpose of having it discussed by the Pundits of the south: but so far as my examination of geographical lists, and discussions of the subject with a great variety of learned natives, enables me to judge, I am disposed to think that no country in the south of India was ever known to the natives by the name of Muru, Lymura, or Lymurika. The latter syllable is considered by Dr. Vincent as the adjective termination, the name of the country being Lymura or Lymyra; and in referring to Strabo and Ptolemy for the description of a town of that name in Lycia, it so exactly corresponds with the geographical position of most of the towns on the western coast of India, ("then follow the mouths of the river Lymyra, and ascending it twenty stadia the town of Lymyra." Strabo, lib. 14.) that a plausible conjecture may be indulged of the name having been applied by a Lycian among the first Greek mariners, from its resemblance to his native place, in the same manner as we find the navigators of the west giving European names to transatlantic stations, and as we know to have been the practice of the Greeks in many remarkable instances recorded by Dr. Vincent; from whose Voyage of Nearchus I transcribe the following example: "Hence it is that the names of *Tyrus* and *Aradus* have "been transplanted from Phœnicia on the Mediterranean into the Gulph of Persia, "as if mariners brought from thence had carried the names of their country with "them."

CHAP. I. fined to the hilly belt along the summit of the ghauts from Soonda to Coorg *, and certainly never descended into the provinces at present designated as South Canara and Malabar; although their conquests from the side of Concan extended as far into North Canara as Mirjan and Ankola, and at one time even to Honaver (Onore). The ancient history of these regions may, I trust, be considered as a province already occupied, and the scope of the present work does not require that we should touch an earlier period than that of the Mohammedan invasion of the Decan.

The first † Mussulman force which ever crossed the mountains south of the Tapti was led by Alla u Deen, nephew and
1293. afterwards successor of Ferose the Patan king of Delhi in 1293. The booty obtained from Deogire, the Tagara of Ptolemy, and the modern Dowlutabad, in this wonderful predatory achievement, was an incentive to future invasion; the place was finally taken, and the Rajah Ram Deo was carried a prisoner to Delhi,
1306. in 1306, by Kafoor, or Melick Naib, the general of Alla u Deen.

The earliest Mohammedan army that ever crossed the
1310. Kistna was led, in 1310-11, by the same Kafoor, against Dhoorsummooder ‡, the capital of Bellal Deo, sovereign of Carnatic.

* The Mysoor stated to have been taken, is a place of that name near the Toombuddra, written Masoor in some of our maps.

† The dates of the accurate Ferishta are verified (with few exceptions) by inscriptions and manuscripts in the Mackenzie collection.

‡ Written as two words, Dhoor and Summund, by the translator of Ferishta, and apparently so intended by the author in the copy which I consulted. Of Maber (if originally intended by this author to describe a separate government) I possess no information. Campula, another capital, is also said to have been taken soon afterwards: it is placed by Ferishta on the Ganges (Gunga); the Godaveri, as I conclude, which is usually called the Gunga Godaveri, but the geography of this author

The curious and interesting ruins * of this place have recently been discovered by Major Mackenzie, and identified by inscriptions near to the modern village of Hallabe, about 105 miles N. W. of Seringapatam. Bellal Deo was defeated in a great battle, and the army of Kafoor returned to Delhi, literally loaded with gold. An expedition, sent by Mohammed III. in 1326, finally destroyed the capital of Doorsummooder †, when the seat of the declining government was removed to Tonoor ‡, 12 miles N. from Seringapatam.

1326.

There is ground for believing that the Bellal dynasty extended its possessions over the central and western portions of the south, including the northern part of Kèrala, or the modern pro-

is not very distinct. Among some recent additions to the Mackenzie collection is a Life of Campula Raja, which will probably throw further light on the history of this period: and a variety of manuscripts, not yet sufficiently examined, will unquestionably shew that many other cotemporary governments existed in the south. The Cheritra, or heroic poem of the Bellal dynasty, mentions an alliance by marriage with the Raja of *Gingee*, which, if authentic, places the origin of that government earlier than the date assigned to it by the annals of Vijeyanuggur.

* The sculpture of these ruins, although sufficiently defective, if compared with the Grecian standard, is yet highly interesting. In examining the Indian hero and his charioteer, mounted on their war chariot, we seem to be viewing the car of Achilles. The costume of the equestrian figures is remarkable; the hair twisted into a knot at the top of the head is its only defence or covering: long boots seem to have defended the legs, and a large net-work to have been the ornament or defence of the horse. The figure of the horseman (contrary to every thing that I have observed in any other sculpture or original in India) is an example of the most graceful seat of modern European horsemanship.—Exact fac similes of the most remarkable parts of this sculpture are in the Mackenzie collection.

† Written also Dwara-Samoodrum. It was built in 1133, and had only subsisted 193 years. But the *Balana Raya Cheritra*, a poetical account of this dynasty, expressly states that the town was built on the site of a city of the same name, which had been long in ruin.

‡ Now generally better known by the name of Motee-Talab, or the Lake of Pearls.

CHAP. I. vince of Canara; but there is no reason to suppose that, like the dynasty of Cadumba *, its conquests had ever extended to the eastern sea.

The extravagant fame of the riches of the south, which was more than verified by the spoils of the expedition of 1310-11, seemed only farther to inflame the cupidity of the northern invaders for the plunder of other capitals. After an unsuccessful attempt to penetrate to Warankul, or Arenkil, the capital of

* The Cadumba dynasty had its capital at Banawassi, near the southern extremity of Soonda, where the ruins may still be traced. Its antiquity may be conjectured from the following circumstance: Canara is the language of conversation, of business, and of modern books, throughout the Carnatic, as above described. The Halla Canara, or ancient Canara, now nearly obsolete, is the language of ancient authors: and a still more ancient language and character, Porvada halla Canara, may be considered on the verge of final extinction, being known at present to very few persons indeed, to none that I could trace, excepting two persons now in the employment of Major Mackenzie: this was the language of Banawassi; and the extent of country down to the eastern coast, including Mahabalipoor usually named the Seven Pagodas, in which inscriptions in that character are found, seems to evince the existence of a great and powerful government. It had apparently been subverted in the second century of the christian æra; as Ptolemy, who inserts Banawassi nearly in its proper place, relatively to the coast of Canara, does not distinguish it as a capital. The dynasties already noticed of the lower country existed about the same period; but the Alexandrian authors, who probably received their information from commercial travellers, although extensively acquainted with the names, had but an incorrect knowledge of the relative positions of places in the south of India. The *Modura regia Pandionis*, and *Caroora regia Cerobothri*, correspond with what is known of the Pandian and Cherun dynasties; and the *Arcati regia Sora* (see note on Choromandell, p. 7), although misplaced, would seem to indicate the modern capital of that name; but the identity of the place is not supported by local investigation, nor has any inscription or authority of any kind yet been discovered to confirm the existence of any capital at the present Arcot previously to the year 1716; the capital of the Sora, Shola or Chola dynasty, having unquestionably been fixed at least for a considerable period of time at Combaconum in Tanjore.

A dynasty named the *Chalokia* was still more ancient than the *Cadumba*, and of course its history is more obscure; the Mackenzie collection, however, contains many inscriptions belonging to that remote æra.

Telingana, by an eastern route through Bengal, and the vigorous repulse of a second expedition, which reached it by the western direction of Maharashtra, the persevering efforts of the Patans terminated, in 1323, in the capture of that capital *, and of the raja and his whole family, and the subversion of a dynasty which had lasted 256 years. This disaster led to the establishment of a more southern Hindoo government, which was destined for upwards of two centuries more to oppose a farther barrier to the progress of the Mohammedan arms.

Two illustrious fugitives, Booka and Aka Hurryhur, officers of the treasury of the dethroned king of Warankul, warned by one of those sacred visions which precedes, or is feigned to precede, the establishment of every Hindoo empire, formed the project of a new government, to be fixed on the banks of the river Toombudra, a southern branch of the Kistna, under the spiritual and temporal guidance of the sage Videyarannea. This capital, named Videyanuggur†, in compliment to their minister and pre-

* Warankul was founded in 1067. One of its monarchs, Pertaub Roodroo, is stated in the manuscript history in the Mackenzie collection to have conquered *Panda-desa*, which is, perhaps, an exaggeration. Some of the dynasties of Drauveda had, at an earlier period, made extensive conquests in what are now called the northern Sircars, where, Mr. Ellis informs me, he found the liturgy of some of the temples in the Tamul language and Telinga character.

† Afterwards Vijeyanuggur, as will be presently explained, (often written *Bisnagur*, Bejanuggur, &c.) The origin of this dynasty is erroneously narrated by Ferishta: the Mackenzie collection affords materials for its history in ample detail.

If a very precise coincidence of names and situations were admitted as evidence, we might conclude that Vijeyanuggur and its suburb of Anagoondy, on the opposite bank of the Toombuddra, or rather the vales and mountains in their immediate vicinity, were the ancient residence of Sogreeva, and Hanuman, his general, (transformed by the poet into a monkey, and by the bramins into a god,) as described in the wild but beautiful poem of the Ramayan, (which is assuming not a very captivating English dress,) but the misfortunes of the captive Sita, and the adventures of Rama and Letchman in their efforts for her recovery, find in every part of the

CHAP. I.

1336.

1378.

ceptor, was commenced in 1336, and finished in 1348. Aka Hurryhur reigned until 1350, and Booka until 1378.

This origin of the new government at once explains the ascendancy of the Telinga language and nation at this capital of Carnatic, and proves the state of anarchy and weakness which had succeeded the ruin of the former dynasty. The government founded by foreigners was also supported by foreigners; and, in the center of Canara, a Telinga court was supported by a Telinga army, the descendants of whom, speaking the same

south of India "a local habitation and a name;" every fountain and stream has its legend, "and not a mountain rears its head unsung:" but, unfortunately, different and distant situations are made the scene of the same adventure, and have evidently been sanctified by pious fraud at periods comparatively modern. The description in the Ramayan of Ravana's banquet may, without much aid from the imagination, be taken as the picture of a drunken European feast, at that period, if such there has been, when ladies indulged in the pleasures of the bottle: and is considered by some as a faint evidence of the existence of an European establishment in Ceylon and the south at this unknown poetical æra. However this may be, *Tapoo Ravana*, the Island of Ravana, may, without any forced interpretation, be considered as the name from which the Greeks derived their *Taprobane*. This island is the *Lanka* of the Indian poets, but not of its astronomers.

"Valmeck's description of the forests of Dunda Caroonium," (says my friend Major Mackenzie, in a note now before me,) "the abode of hermits, of moonees, and rooshees, appears to apply to the wild rude state of the Deckan in the time of Rama, extending at least as far as the Cavery: for thence the country of Janastan seems to commence; which, occupied by the armies of the powerful monarch of *Lanka*, and with the several interesting traces of a nation widely differing in language, arms, and even complexion, seems strongly to indicate a state of subjection to some foreign nation, which had then made such progress in the arts and sciences, that even their enemies acknowledge their superiority: for to the ingenuity of the *rachasas*, (by a perversion of terms not uncommon,) now signifying *demons*, the invention and improvement of some of the most useful arts of life are attributed."

The malignant and super human *rachasas* may, I believe, be not improperly translated *giants*, being supposed by the Hindoos to have been produced by "the sons of God going in unto the daughters of men."

Obscure traces may be found, in many parts of the Mackenzie collection, of an early dynasty of the *Yadava* race at Vijeyanuggur, among the ruins of whose former grandeur the new capital was built.

language, are to be traced at this day nearly to Cape Comorin, in the remains of the numerous establishments, resembling the Roman colonies, which were sent forth from time to time for the purpose of confirming their distant conquests, and holding the natives in subjection. The center and the west, probably the whole of the dominions of the late dynasty, including the greater part of the modern state of Mysoor, were subdued at an early period; but a branch of the family of Bellal was permitted to exercise a nominal authority at Tonoor until 1387, in which year 1387.
we begin to find direct grants from the house of Vijeyanuggur as far south as Turkanamby beyond the Caveri. The last of thirteen rajas, or rayeels of the house of Hurryhur who were followers of Siva, was succeeded in 1490 by Narsing Raja, of the religious sect 1490.
of Vishnoo, the founder of a new dynasty, whose empire appears to have been called by Europeans *Narsinga*, a name which, being no longer in use, has perplexed geographers with regard to its proper position.

Narsing Raja seems to have been the first king of Vijeyanuggur who extended his conquests into *Drauveda*, and erected the strong forts of Chandragherry and Vellore; the latter for his occasional residence, and the former as a place of safe deposit for treasure; but it was not until about 1509 to 1515 that Kistna Rayeel finally reduced the whole of Drauveda to real or nominal subjection.

A variety of causes concurred in the establishment and rapid increase of the government of Videyanuggur "the city of science *," which, by an easy change, assumed in its more prosperous days the name of Vijeyanuggur, "the city of victory †."

* † Ascertained by inscriptions in the Mackenzie collection.

CHAP. I.

The crude attempt of Mohammed III. in 1338 to transfer at once the seat of empire from Delhi to Deogire by a forced emigration of the mass of the inhabitants, and the rash and ill-concerted measures which compelled that prince to direct his subsequent attention to the north, incited the dissatisfaction of the
1347. nobles of the Deckan, and their rebellion terminated in 1347 in the establishment of an independent Mohammedan government, which fixed its capital first at Calburga, and afterwards at Beder. Some branches of the royal house of Teligana threw off the Mohammedan yoke about the same period, and renewing with some energy their efforts for independence at Golconda, and recovering the seat of their ancestors at Warankul, were the natural allies of the kings of Videyanuggur.

The early disunion of the Mohammedans of the Deckan gave farther facilities to the growth of the power of Vijeyanuggur; and the successive inroads of the Moguls from the north left to the Patan kings of Delhi little power to attend to their rebellious subjects in the south, and still less prospect of extending their conquests in that direction. These two causes contributed more than any other to the prosperity of the new government. The Mohammedan power between the Tapti and Kistna had, in 1526, separated into no fewer than five independent principalities*; and in the short period from 1295 to 1326 the empire of Delhi experienced four Mogul invasions; the latter of which, says Ferishta, was bought off by nearly the price of the empire. In the same year, Mohammed the Third, as we have seen, sought to

* First, Adil Shah of Vijeyapoor. Second, Kuttub Shah of Golconda. Third, Ummad Shah of Berar. Fourth, Nizam Shah of Ahmednuggur. Fifth, Bereed Shah of Ahmedabad Beder.

reimburse himself by the plunder of the capital of the Carnatic; and in 1338 to establish the seat of his empire nearer to the sources of his spoliated wealth. It is a curious fact, that the plunder of the south of India was thus transferred by a double process to be buried in the plains of Tartary, and to be presented after an interval of five centuries to the astonishment of the philosophers* of Europe. The Moguls were not less eager for the second part of this process, than the Patans were rapacious in performing the first; but although these golden reservoirs began now to be exhausted, and the political state of Deckan and the south interfered with the projects of each of the plunderers, the Moguls continued to direct their attention to Hindostan. In
1396, preparatory to the invasion of Timoor, they established 1396.
themselves to the south of the Indus; and finally, in 1498, in the 1498.

* Coxe's Travels, vol. II. quarto edition, p. 124—8.

"The surprising quantity," says Mr. Coxe, "of golden ornaments found in the tombs of Siberia, were they not evident to sight, would exceed all belief." Demidoff's account of one of these tombs describes the body of the prince in a reclining posture, upon a sheet of pure gold extending from head to foot, and another sheet of the like dimensions spread over him: he was wrapped in a rich mantle, bordered with gold, and studded with rubies and emeralds. The princess had similar sheets of gold, and her neck chains and bracelets were still more sumptuous. The robes of both looked fair and complete; but upon touching crumbled into dust. Mr. Muller judiciously assigns to the 13th and 14th centuries the accumulation of these immense spoils, by Chengeez (Zingis) Khan and his successors; but neither he nor Mr. Coxe appear to suspect that any portion of them had been brought from *India*. The discovery of copper only in the arms, utensils, and ornaments, of the more ancient tombs of Siberia, confirms the date which has been assigned to the others. Mr. Coxe observes, that "Many of the ornaments are executed with such taste and elegance as is hardly to be accounted for from the state of the arts in the East." There can be no doubt that some European artists had penetrated to the court of the Tartar princes at this period: but those who have examined the golden ornaments of Asia know that some of them are not yet exceeded by the artists of Europe.

CHAP. I. fixed government of Delhi, under the celebrated Baber, the founder of the dynasty usually designated as "The house of Timour;" just three years after Vasco De Gama arrived on the coast of Malabar: the Moguls thus appearing on the northern scene, at the precise period of time that the European intruders first arrived by sea in the south of India.

The success which resulted from the weakness of the enemies of Vijeyanuggur was, in the ordinary course of human arrogance, attributed to its own invincible strength; and the efforts which were made for the extension of its dominions to the north, forced the divided states of the Deckan into the confederacy which accelerated its fall. The dynasty of Narsinga continued to govern
1542. until 1542, when a short usurpation of eight months was subverted by a collateral branch, who established a second usurpation, keeping the lineal heir as a pageant and prisoner of state; but at
1564. length, in 1564, the confederacy to which we have adverted, of the four Mussulman kings of Dowlatabad, Vijeyapoor, Golconda, and Beder, defeated the Hindoo army on the plains of Tellicota, between the Kistna and Toombuddra, in a great battle in which Ram Raja the seventh prince of the house of Narsinga, and almost the whole of his principal officers, fell. The victors marched in triumph to the capital; which they plundered with the most shocking circumstances of cruelty and excess. But the brother and representative of the late sovereign having opened a negociation, which terminated in his agreeing to give up the places which had lately been wrested from the Mohammedans, the victors were satisfied; and taking leave of each other at Rachore, returned to their respective dominions. The places which on this occasion were ceded to the conquerors may afford

some explanation of the limits which were thenceforth assigned to Carnatic in the transactions of Mohammedan princes. The sovereign of Vijeyapoor received the *Doab*, generally, or "the country between the two rivers of Toombuddra and Kistna," Mudcul, Rachoor, Adoni, Aulungpoor *, and Bagreetal. The king of Golconda received Kowilleunda, Bankul (Ongole), and Kunpoor (this may be either Gunpoor or Guntoor). From this enumeration we may conclude, generally, that the northern boundary of Carnatic was thenceforth considered to be the Toombuddra; to the south of which the Mohammedans kept no possession excepting Adoni, and perhaps Nundial; a conjecture which is chiefly grounded on finding this place in a subsequent territorial arrangement excluded from the Carnatic: to the north of that river it was probably also considered to include Sanoor Bancapoor, which we find invaded by the troops of Vijeyapoor some years afterwards.

The apparent moderation which we have noticed was the result of jealousies and fears among the confederates themselves, and by no means arose from lenity towards the unfortunate Hindoos. The capital was depopulated by the consequences of the victory: and the successor of Ram Raja deserting the seat of his ancestors, established at Penconda the ruins of a once powerful dynasty, which continued to cast a lingering look at its former greatness, until retiring from thence to the eastern position of Chandrageri; the last branch whose sovereign title was acknowledged, was expelled from this his last fortress in 1646.

The battle of Tellicota brings us down rather beyond the

* I do not know this place unless it be *Alund*.

CHAP. I.

period from which it is proposed to trace the origin of the dynasty of Mysoor; but it appeared to be most convenient to continue the sketch to that remarkable period, as a point to which we shall again be obliged to revert for the explanation of subsequent events. The whole of the south of India had for a considerable period of time before the battle of Tellicota been comprized in the nominal empire of Vijeyanuggur; but the interior system of revenue and government, which had been established and enforced, while a limited extent of dominion admitted of vigilant control, was now exceedingly relaxed. A provincial viceroy at Seringapatam rather compromised for periodical presents, than exacted a fixed revenue from the Wadeyars, or governors of 33 townships, who now seem to have begun to assume the name of Poligars; a title which properly belonged to the chiefs of Telinga colonies, planted in the neighbouring provinces, for the purpose of overawing the aborigines; to which official designation they added, when they dared, the title of Raja. The external appearance of the general government was brilliant and imposing; its internal organization feeble and irregular: foreign conquest was a more fashionable theme than domestic finance at the court of Vijeyanuggur; and while the final expulsion of the Mussulmans from the Deckan was chaunted by the bards* as

* Bart,—Baut,—Batt, as it is differently pronounced, is a curious approximation to the name of the western *bard*, and their offices are nearly similar. No Hindoo Raja is without his *bards*. Hyder, although not a Hindoo, delighted to be constantly preceded by them; and they are an appendage to the state of many other Mussulman chiefs. They have a wonderful facility in speaking improvisatore, on any subject proposed to them, a declamation in measures, which may be considered as a sort of medium between blank verse and modulated prose; but their proper profession is that of chaunting the exploits of former days in the front of the troops while marshalling for battle, and inciting them to emulate the glory of their ances-

an exploit already achieved; the disorganized state of the distant provinces would have announced to a judicious observer the approaching dissolution of the empire.

In adverting to the incessant revolutions of these countries, the mind which has been accustomed to consider the different frames of polity which have existed in the world as one of the most interesting objects of intellectual enquiry, will be forcibly struck with the observation, that no change in the form or prin-

tors. Many instances are known of bards who have given the example, as well as the precept, of devoting themselves for their king, by leading into the thickest of the battle.

At the nuptials (says the legend) of *Siva* (the destructive member of the Indian triad) with *Parvati*, the deity discovered that the pleasures of the festival were incomplete, and instantly created poets for the purpose of singing his exploits to the assembly of the gods: they continued afterwards to reside at his court or paradise of Kylâsum; and being one day desired by *Parvati* to sing *her* praises, submissively excused themselves, by reminding her of the exclusive object of their creation, namely, "to chaunt the praise of heroes." Parvati, enraged at their uncourteous refusal, pronounced on them the curse of "perpetual poverty;" and the bards remonstrating with *Siva* against this unmerited fate, were informed that nothing human could evade the wrath of Parvati: that although he could not cancel, he would alleviate the curse: that they should accordingly be permitted to visit the terrestrial world, where, although sometimes riches and plenty, and always approbation, would be showered over them by the sovereigns of the earth, the former of these gifts should never remain with them; and that "Poets (according to the decree of Parvati) should be ever poor." The alleged prediction contributes to its own fulfilment, and is the apology of the Indian bards for not being much addicted to abstinence of any kind.

The legend adverts to a *Mundanee Misroodoo*, who in the beginning of the Caly-yoog introduced certain ordinances, among which was the prohibition of animal food; a reform which the bramins consented, but the *bards* refused, to adopt. Major Mackenzie conjectures that the name *Misroodoo* may possibly designate the country of the reformer—*Misr*, Egypt; and that this well known reform may have been introduced into India by the Egyptian priesthood. *Shenker Acharee* is mentioned in the legend as reviving, at a period long subsequent, some of the doctrines of Misroodoo; and Shenker Acharee probably lived about the commencement of the Christian æra.

ciples of government was the consequence either of foreign conquest, or successful rebellion; and that in the whole scheme of polity, whether of the victors or the vanquished, the very idea of *civil liberty* had absolutely never entered into their contemplation, and is to this day without a name in the languages of Asia.

The immemorial* despotism of the East is a fact so familiar to every reader, that it seems to be received, as we receive the knowledge of a law of nature, without any troublesome investigation of the causes which produce an effect so wonderful and invariable.

The philosophy which refers exclusively to the physical influence of climate, this most remarkable phænomenon of the moral world, is altogether insufficient to satisfy the rational enquirer: the holy spirit of liberty was cherished in Greece, and its Syrian colonies, by the same sun which warms the gross and ferocious superstition of the Mohammedan zealot: the conquerors of half the world issued from the scorching deserts of Arabia, and obtained some of their earliest triumphs over one of the most gallant nations of Europe†.

A remnant of the disciples of Zoroaster flying from Mohammedan persecution, carried with them to the western coast of India the religion, the hardy habits, and athletic forms of the north of Persia; and their posterity may at this time be contemplated in the Parsees of the English settlement of Bombay, with mental and bodily powers absolutely unimpaired, after the re-

* The exceptions stated by Dr. Vincent in his Voyage of Nearchus, p. 69 and 123 can scarcely be received without suspicion, and the doctor observes that one of these places described as republics by Q. Curtius and Diodorus, is by Arrian expressly declared to be a monarchy. See also the description of an Indian township in the 5th chapter of this work.

† Spain, the *Andalus* of Mohammedan historians.

sidence of a thousand years in that burning climate. Even the passive but ill understood character of the Hindoo, exhibiting few and unimportant shades of distinction, whether placed under the snows of Imaus, or the vertical sun of the torrid zone, has, in every part of these diversified climates, been occasionally roused to achievements of valour, and deeds of desperation, not surpassed in the heroic ages of the western world*. The reflections naturally arising from these facts are obviously sufficient to extinguish a flimsy and superficial hypothesis, which would measure the human mind by the scale of a Fahrenheit's thermometer.

But if thus compelled to reject the exclusive influence of climate, shall we arrive at more satisfactory conclusions by referring to moral causes? In considering the two great classes of mankind with whose transactions we shall be chiefly conversant, namely, the Mohammedans and the Hindoos, the fixed existence of despotism among them may be accounted for on principles which would seem to be entirely conclusive; but principles to be just should be of universal application; and doubts have been suggested whether those to which we advert are capable of standing this necessary test. The argument shall be stated with

* Sed omnes illacrimabiles
Urgentur, ignotique longa
Nocte, carent quia vate sacro.

The incurious eye of the European traveller passes without observation thousands of monuments, every where erected to the memory of Indian heroes who have fallen in battle. Some few of these monuments have epitaphs. In general they consist of a single sculptured slab placed perpendicularly in the ground: the sculpture is usually divided into three compartments: the lowest describes the battle in which the hero was slain; the centre compartment represents him in the act of being conveyed to heaven between two celestial nymphs: in the uppermost he has arrived at the regions of bliss, and is delineated as seated before the peculiar emblem of his religion—generally the lingum—for the practice of erecting monuments seems chiefly to belong to the sect of Siva.

candor, and the objections to which it seems to be liable shall be proposed without disguise: the subject is of great interest, and some indulgence will be allowed to an attempt, however feeble, to furnish one additional fact or reflection capable of throwing light on a question so much involved in obscurity.

The writings esteemed to be sacred by the Hindoos have produced as many sectaries as the codes of other religions; and polemical controversies, as usual, of greater acrimony in proportion to the minuteness of the difference in opinion; but these disputes have generally been of a speculative nature; the different parties have charged each other with falsifying the texts, but the authority of the code itself has seldom been a matter of discussion.

The political, civil, and criminal code of the Hindoos is interwoven with their theology, and is equally considered to be derived from divine authority. The affairs of government, of judicature and of police, down to the most minute forms of social and domestic intercourse, are all identified with religious observances; the whole is sacred and unchangeable; and, in this case, the ideas attached to improvement and profanation can scarcely be distinguished from each other. Monarchical government is that which is prescribed, and the only one which appears to have entered into the contemplation of the authors of their sacred law: the notion which adulation is so prone to inculcate, that the royal authority is an emanation of the divine power, is a doctrine strictly, emphatically, and perhaps originally, Hindoo*: the Platonic philosophy adopted it without alteration; the opposite sects of the Mohammedan faith acknowledge their Imaum and their

* Menu, 7th chapter, and particularly the 8th verse of that chapter.

Caliph to be the vicegerents of God upon earth: and even the mild and unflattering doctrines of the Christian church have modified and softened the same dogma into the admission of reigning "by the grace of God:" but the broad and prominent distinction between the characters of eastern and western polity, between despotism and regular government, seems to consist in the union, or the separation, of the divine and the human code; in connecting in one case by inseparable ties the ideas of change and profanation, or admitting in the other the legal possibility of improvement; the permission to practise, as well as to learn, the lessons which are taught by the experience of ages. The sacred code of the Hindoos, like the Koran of the Mohammedans, is held to be all-sufficient for temporal as well as religious purposes; they have adopted the regal government, because such is the will of God; they have been passively obedient to this emanation of the divine power so long as no competition has appeared; and they have embraced with facility the cause of rebellion and civil war, because, like the Mohammedans, they believe that kingdoms* are the immediate gift of the Almighty, and that victory is a manifestation† of the divine will.

* For the injunctions to incessant conquest, see Digest of Hindoo Law, vol. 2d, p. 92 (I quote the London edition of 1801), the general tenor of the 7th chapter of Menu, and particularly the following passages: v. 101. "What he (the king) has not gained, let him strive to gain by military strength: what he has acquired let him preserve by careful inspection: what he has preserved let him augment by legal means of encrease, and what he augments let him dispense with just liberality. v. 102. Let his troops be constantly exercised, his prowess constantly displayed, what he ought to secure constantly secured, and the weakness of his foe constantly investigated. v. 103. By a king whose forces are constantly ready for action, the whole world may be kept in awe; let him then by a force always ready, make all creatures living his own."

† The doctrine of fatality is not so unqualified among the Hindoos as the Mo-

CHAP. I.

To the general injunctions of the sacred codes may be ascribed the undeviating continuance of regal government, and to a subordinate branch of the same doctrine the incessant revolutions of the East. The much calumniated law of primogeniture has perhaps contributed more than any other cause to the growth of civilization in European monarchies—A rule, of whatever kind, which defines the right of succession, and has been matured by time and popular opinion, palsies the arm of faction, leaves to the monarch no motive of cruelty, and with the hope of permanence, gives to the subject the leisure and the incitement to improve his condition. In contradiction to the fascinating doctrine of natural equality, and in defiance of the ridicule which is invited by the system of leaving to chance whether we shall be well or ill governed, it may safely be assumed, that whatever portion of tranquillity has been enjoyed by the European world, may chiefly be ascribed to the practical operation of this law, however stigmatized as absurd and unjust by all those specious theorists who would govern the world by the dreams of metaphysical speculation.

Among Mohammedans the estates of individuals are divided

hammedans, but may nevertheless be distinctly traced in all their opinions and modes of action. Victory depends on seizing a fortunate moment offered by heaven, Menu, chapter 9, verse 197; and the conduct of affairs depends on acts ascribed to the Deity, as well as on acts ascribed to Men: ibid, v. 205. It is well known that nothing will induce the Hindoo to commence any matter of importance excepting at the preordained moment determined by judicial astrology, which will be found on examination to be a modified fatalism: this imaginary science may instruct us to avoid entering on an undertaking at an unpropitious time, but having once begun, nothing can prevent the termination which has been preordained. "Bhoo Letchmee (the goddess of territorial dominion) has thrown her arms about your neck, you cannot refuse her embraces;" is a figure of familiar conversation among the Hindoos, which well describes their modes of thinking on the whole subject.

according to fixed rules, but the Koran recognizes no rule of inheritance to kingdoms: and although the succession of the first-born seems among them, as among most other sects, to have been considered as the order of nature, the sword is nevertheless the only legal arbiter universally acknowledged*. The Hindoo system of policy, jurisprudence and religion, affects still more strongly than any European code the rights of hereditary succession; but the sons are all coheirs; and the faint distinction in favour of the eldest son is limited by the express condition, that he shall be worthy of the charge†: but unhappily there is nothing so difficult to determine as the relative worth of opposing claimants; and in the pretensions to royalty, the double question of divine favour and superior merit must, in spite of reason, be decided by the sword. If in the western world we have not escaped the evils of this terrible arbiter, and if with the prospect of permanence which, during the greater part of the last century, at least, might reasonably have been indulged by most European nations, so little progress has been made in the establishment of rational limitations on the abuse of power, and in the prevention of civil and revolutionary wars, we shall not require the aid of climate to explain why despotism has continued, and must for ever continue, to accompany the Hindoo and Mohammedan frames of polity and religion, of which, if it be not a vital member, it is at least an inevitable consequence.

* The sword is his who can use it, and dominion for him who conquers.—Koran.

† In private life the distribution of estates among coheirs depends in some cases on this vague condition. Menu, chapter 9, verse 115, 214; and Jagannatha, after a long and subtle disquisition, determines that kingdoms may, or may not, be divided, and that merit and not primogeniture ought to determine the succession. Digest of Hindoo Law, vol. 2, p. 121 to 123.

An examination of the Jewish history and legislation would add considerable force to these opinions; which may be farther illustrated by observing that the Seiks, when they rejected the Hindoo religion for the doctrines of Nanuck, exhibited the first and only instance in the history of the East of an approach, however imperfect, to republican principles: while every previous revolution, whether leading to the establishment of a great government, or its subdivision into a multitude of smaller states, uniformly terminated where it began, in principles of pure despotism.

Such a knowledge of China as can be considered to penetrate beneath the surface of things, appears to be still a desideratum in literature: and what little is known would seem to afford no illustration of the hypothesis which has been proposed.

But it has been objected to the argument which would ascribe such powerful effects to the union of the divine and human codes, that if we turn from the probable causes of eastern despotism to those which unfolded the spirit of freedom in the west, we shall seek in vain for any confirmation of the principles which have been proposed. The substance of this objection may be stated in the following form.

"The earliest examples of a people rejecting despotism, and substituting in its room a free or a qualified government, are presented in the histories of Greece and Italy. In Greece the human mind had at a very early period attained a high state of refinement, and applied metaphysical reasonings to determine just principles of government. At the period when an insurrection would produce a new form of government, or an amended constitution, philosophy had already begun to legislate; and the freest people were also the most enlightened upon earth. But if from these examples we should be disposed to infer that liberty is the offspring of civilization and knowledge, we must reject a dream so flattering to mental improvement, on remembering that the Romans, however cultivated in after times, were, at the period of the expulsion of their kings *, rude, barbarous, unlettered, and in all respects the reverse of an enlightened and philosophising people. In these great examples of antiquity no illustration is presented of the principles which have been proposed; but on the contrary, we perceive the establishment of civil liberty arising out of moral circumstances altogether dissimilar and opposite."

It may appear on a hasty examination of these objections that we must surrender our explanation of the probable causes of despotism in the East, because we have failed in tracing to an opposite source the uniform growth of civil liberty in the West. But it must be remembered that the removal of a cause simply extinguishes the effect which it had produced, but does not necessarily produce an opposite effect. The shackles imposed on the human mind by the union of the divine and human code have been stated as the efficient causes of despotism: but it is a fallacy to conclude that their removal must produce freedom. The removal of these shackles clears away the impediments to civil liberty, but does not necessarily produce it. The separation of the divine and human code is not in itself the efficient cause of freedom; it merely gives scope for other causes to operate: it renders liberty possible, but not inevitable. Despotism is

* The expulsion of the Tarquins from Rome occurred in the very year succeeding that of the Pisistratidæ from Athens, but I do not know that any author has traced a connexion between these two events either by example or otherwise:

CHAP. I.

simple in its nature and operations; while any scheme of practical liberty is necessarily compounded of various and conflicting particles: and if we have satisfactorily shewn a single cause uniformly (not exclusively) producing despotism, our argument is not weakened by the admission that in the complex operation of moral causes many may concur to the production of civil liberty.

CHAPTER II.

FROM THE ORIGIN OF THE HINDOO HOUSE OF MYSOOR TO 1672.

Romantic origin of the Hindoo house of Mysoor, and change of religion—Foundation of the capital of that name—Vijeya—Arbiral—Betad Cham Raj—Bole Cham Raj—Heera Cham Raj—Betad Wadeyar—Deposition of this chief, and election of his younger brother Raj Wadeyar—Reflections on this fact, and on the interesting characters of the brothers—Incidents characteristic of the times—and of the brothers—Acquisition of Seringapatam—its ancient history—Another change of religion—List of conquests, and reason for adopting this arrangement—Cham Raj—Immadee Raj, uncle of the late Raja, and posthumous son of his predecessor—poisoned by his minister—succeeded by Canty Reva Narsa Raj—anecdote of his chivalrous spirit—Evidence of usurpation in the two preceding reigns—Emancipation of the present Raja by the assassination of the usurping minister—Siege of Seringapatam by a Mussulman army—repulse of the enemy—Arrangements—financial—military—the mint—court—religious establishments—conquests—Dud Deo Raj—Repulse of the Raja of Bednore—and of Madura—Conquests of this reign.

THE tribe of Yedava, which boasts among its eminent characters Kristna, the celebrated Indian Apollo, had its early seats near to Dwaraka in Guzerat, and its probable origin in a more northern region. Innumerable traces exist of vast and successive emigrations of this race of herdsmen and warriors, who carried devastation among the agricultural tribes of the south, and, in process of time, were incorporated with their opponents, or assumed more settled habits of life*.

* Among the Mackenzie MSS. is a poem which relates the wars and negotia-

CHAP. II.

During the period that the dominion of the rajahs of Vijeyanuggur extended really, or nominally, over the greater portion of the south of India, two young men of the tribe of Yedava, named Vijeya, and Kristna, departed from that court in search of a better establishment to the south. Their travels carried them to the little fort of Hadana, a few miles from the present situation of the town of Mysoor; and having alighted, as is usual, near the border of a tank, they overheard some women of the Jungum sect, who had come for water, bewailing the fate of a young maiden of their tribe who was about to be married to a person of inferior quality. The brothers enquired into the circumstances of the case; desired the women to be comforted; and offered their services in defence of the damsel. She was the only daughter of the Wadeyar (or lord of 33 villages), who was afflicted with mental derangement; and in this desolate and unprotected state, the chief of Caroogully, a person of mean cast, had proposed to the family the alternative of immediate war, or the peaceable possession of Hadana by his marriage with the damsel: and to the latter proposition they had given a forced and reluctant consent. The offer of the strangers was made known, and they were admitted to examine the means which the family possessed of averting the impending disgrace. In conformity to their advice no change was made in the preparations for the

tions of the herdsmen and the farmers. The rude and uncivilized character of the former is strongly depicted in the narrative. The farmers had agreed to give them the free range of their woods and pastures, on the condition that they should keep aloof from the cultivated land. Soon after the adjustment of this treaty, a young crop of corn of vast extent is overwhelmed by the main herd. The farmers remonstrate on the breach of compact; and the herdsmen apologize by affirming, with the utmost simplicity and truth, " that they really thought it had been grass."

marriage feast: and while the chiefs of Caroogully were seated at the banquet in one apartment, and their followers in another, the men of Hadana, who had been previously secreted for the purpose, headed by the two brothers, sprung forth upon their guests, and slew them, marched instantly to Caroogully, which they surprised, and returned in triumph to Hadana. The damsel, full of gratitude, became the willing bride of Vijeya, who changed his religion *, and became the lord of Hadana and Caroogully.

Such is the account detailed in various manuscripts, and acknowledged, by general tradition, of the origin of the rajahs of Mysoor. It is proposed to pass rapidly over this obscure period, and to rest lightly on such circumstances only as have a tendency to mark the manners of the times, or the progress of the family to future importance.

Manuscripts are not agreed in regard to the date of this event, nor with respect to the number of generations which intervened between the founder of the family and Cham Raj, surnamed "Arbiral," or the six-fingered, from that peculiarity in his person. His succession is fixed in 1507. A. D. 1507.

* From a disciple of Vishnou he became a Jungum or Lingwunt. He assumed, on this occasion, the title of *wadeyar*, which is uniformly annexed in the manuscripts to the name of every rajah, and still retained by the family after another change of religion, which took place about the year 1687. Wadeyar, or lord, (in the Kalla Canara,) seems, at this period, to have indicated the office of governor of a small district; generally of 33 villages. The term is found, also, in many ancient inscriptions in Drauveda, in the Tamul language, (see the first document in Appendix No. 2.). *Poligar* is clearly a modern term introduced by the Telinga government of Vijeyannuggur; and, so late as the year 1750, the person, since named the *Poligar* of Wodiarpollam, S. W. of Cuddalore, is designated as the *Wadeyar* in the records of Madras. It is the title of respect by which the priests of the Jungum are addressed at this day.

For the religion of the Jungum, see Appendix, No. 4.

A subsequent rajah, named Betad Cham Raj, made, during his life-time, a partition of his little dominions between his three sons. To Appan Tim Raj he gave Hemunhully; to Kishen Raj he gave Kembala; and to Cham Raj, surnamed Bole, or Bald, (an accident said to have been produced by a stroke of lightning,) he gave Mysoor. The precise æra of this partition is not well ascertained; but it was probably at, or about, this period, that the permanent residence of this branch of the family was removed to Mysoor, then called Pooragurry. A fort was either
1524. constructed or repaired in the year 1524, to which the new name was assigned of Mahesh Asoor *, usually pronounced Maheshoor, and now contracted to Mysoor; and the partition above noticed has continued to mark the three principal branches of the family, which have furnished wives for the reigning rajas, and successors to the government, when the direct line has been extinct.

A grant is extant, dated in 1548, from Tim Raj, probably the same to whom Hemanhully was assigned, and the state of the times is well illustrated by an incident in his life. He was desirous of paying his devotions at the temple of Nunjendgode, distant about nine miles; and two wadeyars existed in that short distance, whose permission to pass through their territories was regularly asked and obtained. The splendor of his equipage, and the number of his retinue, not less than three hundred persons,

* *Mahesh Asoor*, "the buffalo-headed monster," whose overthrow is the most noted exploit of Cali, the consort of Siva. This goddess, delighting in blood, was then, and is now, worshipped under the name of *Chamoondee*, (discomfiting enemies,) on the hill of Mysoor, in a temple famed at no very distant period for human sacrifices. The images of this goddess frequently represent her with a necklace of human skulls; and the Mysooreans never failed to decorate their Chamoondee with a wreath composed of the noses and ears of their captives.

attracted the envy of the wadeyars, who were assembled at the feast; a quarrel ensued, in which many lives were lost; Tim Raj was victorious; and he shortly afterwards levied a military contribution on the wadeyar of Ommatoor, his principal opponent at the feast.

Nothing worthy of notice occurs until 1571, when Heere Cham Raj succeeded to the government of Mysoor. 1571.

The government of Vijeyanuggur, which had held an authority over the south, fluctuating in efficiency with the personal character of its head, had recently been too much occupied in resisting its northern enemies, to exercise any vigorous rule over its southern dependants: the subversion of that government, in 1564, by the four mussulman princes of Dowlutabad, Vijeyapoor, Golconda, and Beder; and the relaxed authority of a fugitive government, which made successive attempts to re-establish its power at Penconda, Vellore, Chandergherry, and Chingleput; opened an ample field to ambition, and enabled a succession of enterprising petty chieftains of Mysoor gradually to assume a more respectable rank among the powers of the south.

We accordingly find Heere Cham Raj evading the payment of the revenue or tribute due to the viceroy of Vijeyanuggur, residing at Seringapatam, and obtaining permission to erect some works, probably barriers, on the pretext that the wild hogs destroyed the crops, and disabled him from paying the tribute. The works were no sooner erected, than the collectors of the royal duties were expelled; and such was the imbecility of this local government, that after a fruitless attempt to seize the person of Cham Raj, while performing his devotions at the great temple at Seringapatam, he continued to evade all the demands of the viceroy with impunity.

CHAP. II.

Heere Cham Raj died in 1576, and was succeeded by Betad Wadeyar, his cousin, of the elder branch of Hemunkully.

1576. From the few features which have been preserved of this person's character, he appears to have been mild and brave, but thoughtless and improvident; and in the short period of two years, had thrown the finances into such disorder, that the elders* of the land found themselves obliged to propose to his younger brother Raj Wadeyar to supplant him in the government. The scale of its affairs at this period may be conjectured from the chief objection of Raj Wadeyar to undertake so weighty a charge; viz. that with an empty treasury, an arrear of tribute of five thousand† pagodas was due to the viceroy. This difficulty was removed by a contribution of three thousand from the privy purses of the females of the family, and two thousand from the elders of the land: and Raj Wodeyar was installed.

This deposition of the elder and election of the younger brother, by the elders of the country, is a curious feature of ancient Indian manners, and illustrates the uncertainty of succession which characterises the Hindoo law. We find the power exercised, on several subsequent occasions, of deviating from the direct course of lineal descent, for the dangerous, and generally

* *Hala Pyke*, (signifying literally *old peons*, or *soldiers*,) are the Canara words made use of in all the manuscripts: but the technical meaning is universally admitted to be the ancient adherents of the family of every description; and not exclusively those of the military class. The word *peon*, although borrowed apparently from the Portuguese language, is generally employed by Europeans in India, as the translation of a term for which, perhaps, no single word can be found in any of the languages of Europe: viz. "an armed retainer serving on foot in any department of the government, whether of the revenue, the police, or the military establishment." I have, accordingly, considered it more convenient to adopt this corrupt, but well-known term, than to employ any of the various words which denote that description of persons in the several languages of the south.

† £.1840 sterling.

delusive purpose, of obtaining a more worthy, or a more compliant successor; and terminating, as in other countries, in faction, usurpation, and murder. Various incidents seem to prove, that the characters of the brothers, rather than the manners of the time, are marked in the disposal and subsequent history of the deposed raja. He was neither murdered nor imprisoned: and, on his approaching the hall of audience, where his brother had been just installed, he was informed by the attendants, that the measure had become necessary from the state of the finances; but that he might still be usefully and honourably employed, in representing the family at the court of the viceroy at Seringapatam; or, if he should prefer independent retirement, that also had been provided for him at Mysoor. "I will reside at neither," said he, and departed in anger; but, shortly afterwards, we find him living peaceably at Mysoor.

The chief of Caroogully, whom the manuscripts now describe as a relation of the family, had formed the design of seizing Mysoor by surprise, and appeared suddenly before it. Betad Wadeyar was walking carelessly about, with the air of leaving to the new raja the care of his own defence: "What," said a woman who met him, "is this a time for the blood of the Wadeyar to be inactive?" He instinctively seized a battle-axe, called to the troops to follow, cut through, at a blow, the simple bolt of the gate, sallied forth on the enemy, and completely defeated him; and thenceforth we find this generous and gallant soldier leading the forces of his younger brother, and achieving a variety of petty conquests.

A short time before this incident, a dispute occurred at the court of the viceroy, which may furnish a ground of amusing comparison between the customs of those days and the modern etiquette of the eastern or the western world. Raj Wadeyar, in passing to the court at Seringapatam, accompanied by his usual retinue and rude music, met the wadeyar of Kembala going to court, attended also by music. Raj Wadeyar, on ascertaining whose retinue it was, ordered his own music to cease. On his arrival at court, the viceroy asked him why he had not come into the presence with his usual state: " Music is no distinction," said he, " if my inferiors are also allowed it." The chief of Kembala took fire at this insinuation: " Let us meet," said Raj Wadeyar, " and determine the superiority; and with it the right to the music." The viceroy attempted to appease them, but the next day Raj Wadeyar marched to Kembala*, defeated the wadeyar, and took the place.

The weakness of the provincial government begins at this period to display itself, not only in the farther encroachments of Raj Wadeyar upon his neighbours, but in his being alternately in arms against the viceroy, and received with favour at the court. The town of Kèsara, dependent on Mysoor, was besieged by the troops of the viceroy: Betad Wadeyar attacked and defeated them: among the plunder was an elephant; but Raj Wadeyar sagely reflecting, as the manuscript states, that he could maintain thirty soldiers at the same expense as one elephant, sent the animal as a peace-offering to the viceroy. The next year we find him received with particular favour at the court; and, immediately afterwards, not only refusing to pay his tribute, on pretence of some damage done to his plantations by the people of the viceroy, but receiving a farther grant of land to compensate for the injury.

* Kembala, formerly the portion of an elder branch of the family, is now united to Mysoor.

The power and influence of Raj Wadeyar at the court of the viceroy, and the apprehensions which he had excited in the minds of the ministers at Seringapatam, are evinced by a strange and complicated tissue of conspiracies and intrigues, and even a direct attempt to assassinate him in his own dwelling at Mysoor, which was averted by the caution of a faithful adherent. The opportunity was expected to be obtained by the mission of an officer of the court, attended as usual by a large but select retinue, for security after the perpetration of the murder, and ostensibly charged with a secret and confidential message from the viceroy. The Raja, unsuspicious of treachery, without hesitation ordered all attendants to withdraw; but a more vigilant observer took the precaution of concealing himself behind one of the pillars of the hall of audience, and, on perceiving the officer to grasp his dagger, instantly inflicted on the assassin the fate intended for the Raja. Among the intrigues which threatened the most danger to Raj Wadeyar was one which procured the defection of his brother Betad Raj ,who, on quarrelling with the Raja, and retiring to Seringapatam, attempted to direct the decayed energies and disorganised force of the viceroy to the recovery of his own patrimony. In returning carelessly from one of his expeditions he fell into an ambuscade, prepared by direction of Raj Wadeyar, to whom he was conducted as a prisoner. Raj Wadeyar, at the sight of his brother, actuated by the sudden impulse of natural affection, sprung up with extended arms to embrace him; but the prisoner, mistaking this unexpected movement for an attempt on his life, exerted the athletic force for which he was famed, and dashed his brother to the ground. The rigour of his subsequent imprisonment extended, however, no farther than a prohibition to leave his house: but a relation of the family, named Komar Narsa Raj, for reasons not stated in any of the manuscripts, but probably with the view of doing an acceptable service to the reigning Raja, hired a ruffian to put out the eyes of the unfortunate Betad Cham Raj. The intention was providentially made known to Raj Wadeyar just as he had mounted his horse to proceed on an expedition: he immediately returned, ordered Komar Narsa Raj, accompanied by one of his brothers, to be brought before him; and accosted him by desiring he would instantly put out the eyes of his own brother. He remonstrated by asking what crime his brother had committed to deserve such a punishment: "Wretch!" said Raj Wadeyar, "and what crime has *my* brother committed that you should employ a ruffian to blind him?" The nature of the punishment inflicted on this person is not mentioned; but the Rajah immediately released his brother, presented him with a bag of gold, and begged him to consult his own safety and comfort by retiring for the present from so dangerous a scene. He afterwards lived as a private person at the village of Rung Summooder, in perfect amity with his brother.

Many incidents in the history of this period, exclusively of those which have been related, clearly evince, that the mild and humane conduct of these brothers is referable altogether to personal character, and by no means to the manners of the times.

The acquisition of Seringapatam*, in 1610, which is the most

* Some brief notice of the ancient history of a place, so celebrated in later times, may perhaps be expected.

Popular tradition, and manuscripts now proved to be of modern fabrication, relate that Shevensummooder, an island 50 miles east of Seringapatam, remarkable

important event, not only in this reign but in the history of the family, is related in different manuscripts, with a diversity of statement, which seems only to prove a mysterious intricacy of intrigue beyond the reach of cotemporaries to unravel. The

for the much admired falls of the Caveri, and still exhibiting the ruins of a town and fortress, with two bridges over the branches of the river, was conquered and utterly destroyed by one of the Bellal or Hoisala kings; that the heir of the vanquished dynasty, named *Sree Rung Rayel*, after various adventures, recovered his patrimony; and being struck in passing Seringapatam with its resemblance to the seat of his ancestors, determined to erect a fort on the spot; which he called after his own name. On the approach of his dissolution he retired to Talcaud, and bequeathed his government to one of his ministers named Raj Wadeyar, from whom, after many revolutions, the Rajas of Mysoor were afterwards descended.

Shevensummooder is the only place of any importance connected with Mysoor, the history of which has hitherto not been illustrated by ancient inscriptions, although the ruins have been frequently and minutely explored for that express purpose; but it is evident from those which relate to Seringapatam, that the above popular and generally credited tale has been confounded with the revolution of 1610.

In 1133 a celebrated apostle of the Vishnevite sect, named Ramanachooloo or Ramanjacharee, fled from Drauveda to avoid a confession of faith prescribed by the Chola Raja, to be made by all his subjects, the object of which was to establish the superiority of Siva over Vishnoo. This apostle made numerous converts in the upper countries, and among them the Rajah, thenceforth named Vishnoo Verdana, of the Bellal or Hoisala dynasty, who had before this period professed the Jain religion. This royal convert conferred on his apostle and his followers the tract of country on each side of the river at Seringapatam, still known by the name of Astagram, or eight townships, over which he appointed his own officers, under the ancient designations of Praboos and Hebbères.

In 1454, a person named Timmana, a Hebbere or descendant of the Vishnouvite bramins, who accompanied Ramanjacharee from the East, obtained, by a visit to Vijeyanuggur, and by the aid of a hidden treasure which he had just discovered, the government of the district, and permission to erect a fort; which he called *Sree-Runga-puttun*, or the city of the holy Runga, in honour of that God, to whom also he erected a temple; which was afterwards enlarged by the barbarous demolition of 101 Jain temples at Calaswadi, a town half way between that place and Mysoor, the materials of which were removed for the improvement of the new temple. Grants are extant from this Timmana, now named Dhanaick, or Lieutenant, in the same year (1454) that he laid the foundation of the fort. The names are mentioned in subsequent grants of several of his lineal successors; but I cannot ascertain the

prevailing tale states that the viceroy Tremul Raj, or Sree Rung Rayeel, as he is sometimes called, being afflicted with the rajpôra, or royal boil, the disorder most fatal to opulent and luxurious Indians, retired to the holy temple of Talcaud, with the view of being cured by the interposition of the idol, or breathing his last before the sacred shrine; and that previously to his departure he had selected Raj Wadeyar of Mysoor for the confidential trust of administering the government in his absence; and in the event of his death, of transferring it to his kinsman and heir the Wadeyar of Ommatoor. But on adverting to the animosities and jealousies which had prevailed for many years between these two persons; and the recent attempt of the viceroy, only three years before, to remove Raj Wadeyar by assassination, we must reject as contrary to all probability the tale of this singular bequest of confidence and friendship.

Forty-six years had now elasped since the subversion of the empire, from which the viceroy had derived his original powers. This sinking and fugitive state, foiled in the attempt to re-establish its government at Penconda, had now renewed its feeble efforts at Chundergherry. The viceroy himself was worn down with age and disease: his government, long destitute of energy, had fallen into the last stage of disorganization, faction, and imbecility: it is not improbable that, foreseeing its impending destruction, he concluded the best compromise in his power

exact period when they were displaced by the appointment of a viceroy, with higher powers, and a more extensive government, of whom the last was Tremul Raj, a relation of the family of Vijeyanuggur.

For an explanation of the doctrines of the *Jain* above-mentioned, consult Appendix, No. 5.

with his destined conqueror; and the manuscript of Nuggur Pootia even details the names of the persons, probably of his own court, who had combined (as it is stated, with the permission of Vencatapetty Rayeel, who then reigned at Chundergherry) to compel him to retire. All that can be determined with certainty is, the quiet retirement of Tremul Raj to Talcaud, where he soon afterwards died; and the peaceable occupation by Raj Wadeyar 1610.
of the fort of Seringapatam, which thenceforth became the seat of the government of his family. It is certain that until this period the Rajas of Mysoor openly professed the religion of the Jungum; but many circumstances afford room to conjecture that it was about this time that they adopted the insignia and ceremonies of the sect of Vishnoo; and as the whole of the old court had been of that persuasion, it is highly reasonable to suppose that the real or ostensible conversion of the new Raja was one of the fundamental conditions of their conspiring to depose the viceroy. Many however of the subsequent Rajas of Mysoor are supposed to have secretly professed their ancient religion; and it is known to me that several relations of the house continue to do so at this time. Chick Deo Raj is the first who can unquestionably be stated to have made a public profession of the religion of Vishnoo, about 1687.

The numerous wars and conquests of Raj Wadeyar, before and after this important acquisition, present little to arrest the attention. The date of these successive events is preserved in the records of the respective villages or districts, and in the MSS. of Poornia, and Pootia: and as an illustration not altogether uninteresting to those who may wish to verify the general progress of Indian revolutions which has been noticed, or to

CHAP. II. examine the actual growth of the government of Mysoor, lists of these conquests will be subjoined at the conclusion of this and the successive reigns, adding the names of the former possessors, where they have been ascertained.

The rule of Raj Wadeyar was remarkable for the rigour and severity which he exercised towards the subordinate Wadeyars, and his indulgence towards the Ryots. The Wadeyars were generally dispossessed, and kept in confinement on a scanty allowance at the seat of government; and it was the policy of Raj Wadeyar to reconcile the Ryots to the change, by exacting from them no larger sums than they had formerly paid.

A. D: *The following is a List of his Conquests.*

1584. Conquered Auka Hebbal from Narsing Naick of Narsipoor.

1585. Rung Summooder from Tim Raj: (it is doubtful whether it may not be Tremul Raj); twelve villages were annexed to this acquisition.

1590. Kembala by assault; this is the Wadeyar with whom he fought on the ludicrous contest regarding the more ludicrous music.

1595. Nurmullee.

Ditto. Karoogullee from his relation, imprisoned him, and enriched Mysoor with the plunder of the place.

1600. Arrakerra, stated to have been the *Jaghire* of Jugdeo Row.

1606. Sosilla and Bunnoor from Nunderaj of Talcaud.

Ditto. Canniambaddy from Dudeia *Prabhoo.*

1610. Acquired Seringapatam and its dependencies, then probably much reduced in extent.

Took Seroor, a dependency of Periapatam, which was possessed by a relation of the Wadeyar of Coag. CHAP. II.

Sergoor from Sree Kunt Wadeyar. 1610.

1612.

Turcanambady, a dependency of Seringapatam, which had been dissevered from it under Tremul Raj, by Nunderaj Wadeyar. 1613.

Oomatoor from the same person. Ditto.

Ram Summooder and Hadanaud from Chunder Naick, brother of Nunjeraj. 1614.

Haroohully from Nunjeraj and Sree Kunt Wadeyar. Ditto.

Hardunhully from Nunjeraj Wadeyar. Ditto.

Moogoor from Busswan Raj Wadeyar. 1615.

Kikary from Jugdeo Raj.—N. B. This person was the descendant of the celebrated *Jug Deo.* Ditto.

Hooshullul from the same. 1615.

Manuttoor depending on Periapatam. 1617.

CHAM RAJ.

Six sons of the late Raja, who would seem to have arrived at years of maturity, all died before their father, and only one of them, viz. *Narsa Raj*, left male issue, *Cham Raj*, a youth of fifteen, who immediately succeeded to his grandfather. The second wife of Raj Wadeyar was, however, four months advanced in her pregnancy at the time of her husband's decease, and her posthumous son succeeded to Cham Raj.

During a rule of twenty years, in which the dominions of Mysoor were gradually and very considerably enlarged, no event of importance occurred which falls within the plan of this narrative; and the dates and names of the conquest must conclude the meagre chronicle of the reign, which will however be illus-

CHAP. II. trated by subsequent events. An incident connected with the capture of Hegara Devancota in 1624, seems strongly to illustrate the character of the times. The Mysoorean army attacked the place during the absence of its chief, *Chen Raj* Wadeyar, on a distant expedition, and obtained a great booty. The simplicity of a Vakeel, or negotiator, is preserved by tradition, who on the approach of the army came out to treat. "My master, (said he) is absent with the troops: the Ranee (queen) is in labour, and exceedingly alarmed at your approach: we have only fifty soldiers in the place, and the late rains have made two large breaches in the rampart, one on the southern, and the other on the eastern face. To come at such a time is very improper and ungenerous."

It appears that this Raja followed the example of his predecessor in assuming the direct management of the conquered districts; in keeping the captive Wadeyars at the seat of government, under a greater or less degree of restraint according to circumstances; and in refraining from any additional assessment on the Ryots. He died in 1637, and during his reign the following conquests were made:

1621. Shergoor from Jugdeo Row.

Muddoor from Veetana.

Talcad from Soam Raj Wadeyar.

1623. Arcotar from Balajee Naick.

1624. Sindigut, the capital of Jugdeo Row.

Bokunkerra, belonging to the same.

Sattiagal, then the capital of Keerachooree Nunjeraj of Alembaddy.

1626. Hunganoor from the Prabhoo of Yellandoor.

Cuttamalwaddy from Chen Raj Wadeyar.

Teddoor from Dewar Prabhoo. CHAP. II.

Cenapatam, after a long siege, from a descendant of the celebrated Jugdeo, and immediately afterwards Caunkanhully and 1630. Nagamangul from the same person.

Beloor from *Peram Rawata.*

Took Cheneroypatam after a very long siege. 1633.

IMMADEE RAJ.

The posthumous son of Raj Wadeyar ascended the Musnud 1637. in his 20th year, on the death of his nephew Cham Raj, and was poisoned at the expiration of a year and a half by his Dulwoy (general and minister) Veecrama Raj. It is probable that the meagre annals of the preceding reign would furnish more of incident, if we had access to the *genuine* history of the Dulwoys during that period; but not only the fact which has just been stated, and the assassination of Veecrama under the succeeding Raja, are altogether omitted in the family history of the Dulwoys, but even the name of this personage has been obliterated from their annals.

The preceding Raja had succeeded to the government at the early age of fifteen. We may conjecture from subsequent events that his minister had found him of an easy temper; and in the mode so familiar to Indian courts of modern and ancient date, had, by inciting and corrupting his natural propensities, plunged him into habits of low and licentious indolence; and thus kept him through life in a state of perpetual tutelage. *Immadee Raj* was probably found to possess too much of the energy of his grandfather, and was therefore speedily removed.

CHAP. II.

CANTY REVA NARSA RAJ.

1638. This person was son of the gallant and generous Betad Cham Raj Wadeyar. The government returned in his person to the elder branch, from which it had been wrested by the deposition of his father, whose martial spirit he inherited, without his careless extravagance and incapacity for finance.

An instance is preserved of his chivalrous spirit, which seems to be well authenticated. While living in obscurity in a remote village, during the former reigns, a travelling bramin from Trichinopoly mentioned in conversation a celebrated champion at that court, who had defeated all antagonists from every part of India, and had now proclaimed a general challenge. Canty Reva being desirous of seeing this celebrated personage, requested the bramin to be his guide and companion to Trichinopoly, where, concealing his rank, he presented himself as the antagonist of the challenger; and the broad sword having been determined as the weapon, he defeated and slew the champion, in presence of the whole court, assembled to witness the contest. The Raja of Trichinopoly was desirous of distinguishing and retaining in his service this remarkable stranger; but he absconded in the night, and returned to his humble habitation, where the incident was soon made public.

Such was the character of the man whom an usurping minister had the audacity to *select* for his nominal master.

On his arrival at Mysoor, where it was still the practice to instal the Rajas, the minister ordered that he should be lodged in an exterior apartment: and assigning to him a few personal attendants, announced, in a manner sufficiently intelligible, the condition to which he was destined, by departing on a tour of the neighbouring districts, without going through the form of installing him, or even the decent observance of paying his personal respects. During the tour it was reported to the minister that the Raja appeared to be dissatisfied, and would probably attempt to recover his independence :—" Let him take care," said the minister, negligently, " and remember that *I* have not yet installed him."

The murder of Immadee Raja, and the facts which have just been stated, constitute the grounds of the conjecture which has been hazarded regarding the condition of the two preceding Rajas ; and the open and contemptuous arrogance of the minister's demeanor on the present occasion seems to furnish abundant proof of an absolute usurpation.

During the absence of the minister, two of the attendants appointed to wait on the Raja elect secretly unfolded to him the history of the murder of his predecessor, and offered their services to dispatch the usurper: this was accordingly effected on the very night subsequent to his arrival at Mysoor, after he had gone through the form of paying a visit of ceremony to the Raja.

The detail of this transaction has been preserved in several manuscripts. The two attendants (Peons, or foot soldiers) scaled the walls of the minister's court-yard after dark, and laid in wait for an opportunity to effect their purpose. Shortly afterwards the minister appeared, preceded by a torch-bearer, passing towards a detached apartment. The associates first killed the torch-bearer, and the light happened to be entirely extinguished. " Who are you ?" said the minister. " Your enemy !" replied one of the Peons ; and made a blow. The minister, however, closed with him, and being the more powerful man, threw him to the ground, and held him by the throat, in which situation he called out for aid. The night was so very dark that his companion was afraid to strike at random. "Are you uppermost or undermost?" "Undermost," cried the half-strangled Peon, and this information enabled his associate to strike the fatal blow.

Canterava Narsa Raj was installed on the following day, and in two days afterwards proceeded to the seat of government at Seringapatam. In the first year of his accession he had to defend the capital of his dominions against a formidable invasion of the forces of the Mohammedan king of Vijeyapoor, under a general of reputation, named *Rend Dhoola Khan* *, who besieged Seringapatam; and having effected a practicable breach, made a general assault, in which he was repulsed with great slaughter; and not only compelled to raise the siege, but harassed in his retreat † by successive attacks, in which the Raja obtained considerable booty.

After a number of conquests, which will be stated in the usual
1654. manner, Canterava Narsa Raj returned in 1654 to Seringapatam, where he instituted a deliberate inquiry into the condition of all his dependents, and subjects of every description. It was his first object to reduce to entire subjection the remnant of refractory Poligars and Wadeyars which still existed: and it may be inferred that he assumed the direct government of the whole of his

* The bridegroom of the field of battle. This is the only Mohammedan dynasty that gave Hindovee titles: in general they are exclusively Arabic.

† In the same year we find Rend Dhoola Khan uniting with a multitude of rebellious Wadeyars depending on Bednore, and besieging the Raja of that country in Cowlidroog. The Raja bought off the Mohammedan general, who left the Wadeyars to the consequences of the Raja's indignation.

dominions, from the farther measures which he is recorded to have pursued. He made a detailed and particular scrutiny into the condition of the *gouds*, or heads of villages, and principal farmers throughout his dominions, whom he had found to be the most turbulent of all his subjects: and ingeniously attributing their refractory disposition to a purse-proud arrogance, arising from the excessive accumulation of wealth, he determined to apply a very summary and direct remedy, by seizing at once on the supposed source of the evil.

He accordingly levied on the whole of this description of persons such contributions as, according to the manuscripts, left them only a sufficient capital for the uses of agriculture, and nothing for the purposes of commotion: it does not, however, appear that he ventured to augment the fixed assessment of the Ryots.

He improved and enlarged the fortifications of Seringapatam; and being enriched by his various foreign conquests and domestic plunder, supplied it with provisions and military stores, in a style of complete equipment which had hitherto been unknown.

He was the first Raja of Mysoor who established a mint. The cantyrai hoons* and fanams, called after his name, continued to be the sole national coin until the Mohammedan usurpation; and at this time form a considerable portion of the currency of the country.

He is also noted as the author of a new and more respectful etiquette at his court, and for having first celebrated with suitable

* The coin which Europeans call a *Pagoda*.

splendour the feast of the Maha-noumi*, or Dessara; for having presented to the idol Sree Runga a crown of valuable jewels;

* Maha-Noumi, the Great Ninth, the feast being celebrated on the 9th day of the increasing moon; it is the supposed anniversary of a great event in the history of the celebrated Pandoos. The feast is kept with a creditable degree of splendour by the present Raja of Mysoor, and athletic contests and various sports are exhibited before him during nine successive days. Mysoor, I believe, is the only country in the south of India in which the institution of the athletæ (Jetti) has been preserved on its ancient footing. These persons constitute a distinct cast, trained from their infancy in daily exercises for the express purpose of these exhibitions; and perhaps the whole world does not produce more perfect forms than those which are exhibited at these interesting but cruel sports. The combatants, clad in a single garment of light orange-coloured drawers, extending half-way down the thigh, have their right hand furnished with a weapon, which, for want of a more appropriate term, we shall name a cæstus, although different from the Roman instrument of that name. It is composed of buffalo horn, fitted to the hand, and pointed with four knobs, resembling very sharp knuckles, and corresponding to their situation, with a fifth of greater prominence, at the end nearest the little finger, and at right angles with the other four. This instrument, properly placed, would enable a man of ordinary strength to cleave open the head of his adversary at a blow: but the fingers being introduced through the weapon, it is fastened across them at an equal distance between the first and second lower joints, in a situation, it will be observed, which does not admit of attempting a severe blow, without the risk of dislocating the first joints of all the fingers.

Thus armed, and adorned with garlands of flowers, the successive pairs of combatants, previously matched by the masters of the feast, are led into the arena; their names and abodes are proclaimed; and after making their prostrations, first to the Raja seated on his ivory throne, in a balcony which overlooks the arena, and then to the lattices behind which the ladies of the court are seated, they proceed to the combat, first divesting themselves of the garlands, and strewing the flowers gracefully over the arena.

The combat is a mixture of wrestling and boxing, if the latter may be so named: the head is the exclusive object permitted to be struck. The guards for defence, though skilful, are not numerous: the blows are mere cuts inflicted by the cæstus; and before the end of the contest, both of the combatants may frequently be observed streaming with blood from the crown of the head down to the sand of the arena.

The wrestling is truly admirable; and the exertions of the combatants to disengage themselves from unfavourable positions, in which the head would be exposed to the cæstus, are, as mere specimens of activity, not exceeded by any corresponding exhibition on an European stage.

and for having established munificent endowments for the support of all the principal temples. He is of course the idol of his Bramin historians, whose system of ethics is not disturbed by any troublesome reflections on the simple transfer of property, by which the fruits of industry are transformed into pious plunder. CHAP. II.

It remains to detail the conquests of this reign.

He descended the Caveripooram pass, and took Jambelly, and several other places depending on Goottee Moodelaree, of Caveripoorum. 1641.

Took Humpapoor from Nersing Naick. 1644.

Betadpoor from Nunjend Raj, Wadeyar of Coorg.

Periapatam from Nunjend Raj, whose son, Veer Raj, fell in the defence of the place; established there his own garrison, and carried off the plunder to Seringapatam.

Curb-Culloor, and Miasummooder, from Bheirapa Naick. 1646.

Arkulgoor, depending on Bullum. 1647.

When victory seems to have declared itself, or the contest is too severely maintained, the moderators in attendance on the Raja in the balcony make a signal for its cessation, by throwing down turbans and robes, to be presented to the combatants, who before retiring repeat their prostrations to the Raja and the lattices.

A wistful look towards the balcony is the usual symptom of acknowledged inferiority, or of being, in the phrase of English pugilists, *not game:* and the victor frequently goes off the arena in four or five *somersets,* to denote that he retires fresh from the contest. A pair of fresh combatants is introduced with the same forms, and of such pairs about two hundred are exhibited during the nine days of the great festival.

The Jetti of Mysoor are divided into five classes, and the ordinary prize of victory is promotion to a higher class. There are distinct rewards for those of the first class, and in their old age they are promoted to be masters of the feast. During three years that I attended the Raja at this feast there was one champion who remained unmatched; on the fourth a stripling offered to engage, and was merely permitted to spar with him, and on the fifth year this youth was victorious.

CHAP. II. Coondgull from Kimpe Gour of Maagry.

Rettingherry from Eitebal Row.

1647.

1652. Veerabuddra Droog, Kingeri Cotta, Penagra, and Darampoory, depending on Vijeyapoor, and established his own authority in these four talooks. Fourteen years before this period the capital is besieged by the army of Vijeyapoor, the series of conquests begins now to be reversed, and that once powerful monarchy, threatened from the north and undermined within, now verges towards its close.

Took Dankanicotta from Eitebal Row, and carried a large booty from thence to Seringapatam.

1653. Descended the Gujjelhutty pass, took *Denaikancotta*, Sattimungul, and other places from Vencatadry Naick, brother of the Raja of Madura*, and brought home an immense booty; he also took many talooks from *Veerapa, Naick of Madura.*

*Nagana Naid, described to be head of the bullock department to Acheta Deva Rayeel of Vijeyanuggur, founded the dynasty of the Naicks of Madura about the year 1532, with the aid of a *colony* of Telingas, which seems to have been planted in that country some time before by the government of Vijeyanuggur. The persons known by the general designation of southern Poligars, who have so often resisted the authority of the English government, are the descendants of these foreigners, and preserve the language of their ancestors distinct from that of the aborigines; although the Tamul is so generally spoken by them all as to render the existence of a separate language (now verging to extinction) not very obvious to common observation. The fact is known to me not only from personal communication, but from several domestic memoirs preserved in the Mackenzie collection. I believe that the only genuine Tamul of any consequence concerned in the rebellion of 1800-2 was *Chenna Murdoo,* who, from the mean situation of dog-boy, had supplanted the Poligar, properly the Wadeyar, his master, and usurped the government. The most daring of these Poligars are of the *Totier* cast, among whom may be observed the singular and economical custom which is general throughout Coorg, and may be traced in several other countries from Tibet to Cape Comorin, of having but one wife for a family of several brothers. The elder brother is first married, and

Took Oossoor from *Chender Senker*, and obtained a valuable booty. CHAP. II.

In the same year he engaged the army of Kempe-Goud* of 1654.

the lady is regularly asked whether she consents to be also the spouse of the younger brothers. When the means of the family enable them to afford another wife, the second and successively the other brothers marry, and their spouses are equally accommodating. This custom is traced by tradition to the five sons of Pandoo, the heroes of the Mahabarut. During their expulsion from the government their sister Draupeda went to seek and comfort them in the forests where they secreted themselves. The brother who first met her wrote to his mother in these words. "I have found a treasure, what shall I do with it?" "Share it with your brethren, and enjoy it equally," was the answer: she accordingly became their common wife; and in Hindoo poetry is frequently distinguished by an epithet signifying, "adorned with five nuptial bands."

* The ancestor of Kempe-Goud was a common farmer, or Ryot, in the village of Aloor near Conjeveram in Drauveda, and emigrated with his family to avoid the oppression of the Wadeyar of that place, who wished to seize the daughter of the farmer, celebrated for her beauty. He settled on a waste spot about thirteen miles north of Bangalore, and founded the village of Yellavanca, of which he became the Goud or Potoil.

The first exploit of the farmer (for in his days all farmers were soldiers) was a victory over the Wadeyar of Bangalore. The foundation of the present fortress, and of that on the tremendous rock of Savendroog, is the work of this adventurous family; which extended its dominions over the woody country stretching south towards the Cavery, and to a considerable distance on the plain in every direction, forming upon the whole a large, valuable, and formidable possession. During the government of the 5th in lineal succession from *Veera Goud*, the founder of the family, Rend Dhoola Khan, the general of the king of Vijeyapoor, wrested from him Bangalore and most of his possessions on the plain. This must have been between the years 1644 and 1655, which would place the emigration of the family from Drauveda about the middle of the preceding century. The family was extinguished in 1728 by *Dad Kishen Raj* of Mysoor.

Similar to this was the origin of a far more formidable and rapid progress in the north of India. It will be observed that the northern news-letters inserted in the Appendix to the reports of the committee of the house of commons generally speak of Madajee Sindia as the *Putteel* or *Potail* (the same as goud), and he had a pride in being so addressed by his ancient associates in his public Durbar at Delhi; after having overthrown the house of Timour.

CHAP. II. Maagry at Yelavanca, gained a complete victory, with a large booty, pursued the fugitives to Maagry, and levied a contribution on this powerful Goud, now risen to the rank of Raja.

DUD* DEO RAJ.

1659. The late Raja died without issue. It seems to have been a principle on such occasions to revert to some descendant of an elder branch; but beyond this single consideration we shall seldom find an adherence to any fixed rule of succession. The queen dowager and the general of the forces are stated to have decided on this occasion; but it seems difficult to reconcile their decision to any imaginable rule of descent.

Muppin Deo Raj, the eldest son of *Bole Cham Raj*, left four sons, of whom it is known with certainty that the eldest and youngest, and probably the second and third also, were at this time alive. The eldest son Dud Devaia was an old man, and had a son *Chick Deo Raj* aged 32. The younger or fourth brother of Dud Devaia was also no more than 32, the same age as his nephew. This is the person who was selected, to the exclusion of the three elder brothers, and their male issue; although after his decease they again reverted to the same son of the elder brother at 45, whom they had passed over at 32†. Dud Deo Raj sus-

* Dud—*great;* Chick—*little;* or senior and junior. It was on the accession of Chick Deo Raj that the distinction was made to mark the first and second in the order of succession. The name of Dud Deo Raj, previously to his accession, was *Kemp Devaia*, or Devai the fair or red.

† These details, clearly deduced from the genealogical manuscript, are involved in great obscurity in all the historical pieces, from the confused and loose practice of frequently making no distinction between son and fraternal nephew; brother,

tained, during the first year of his reign, a formidable invasion by the troops of Seopha Naick* the Rajah of Bednore, sanctioned by the name and personal influence of the last of the race of Vijeyanuggur.

In consequence of a succession of revolutions and misfortunes in Drauveda, *Sree Rung Rayeel*, the representative of the house of Vijeyanuggur, fled from that country in the year 1646, and took refuge with the Raja of Bednore, formerly a servant of his family, who availed himself of this useful pageant to extend his own dominions under the semblance of re-establishing the royal house of his liege lord: and now appeared before Seringapatam with an army sufficiently powerful to invest the place.

Dud Deo Raj is accused by the historians of Bednore of having employed bribery as well as military prowess for the purpose of inducing this army to raise the siege, and retreat in confusion and dismay to Bednore. The Mysooreans extended their conquests to the west, and appear to have received from the royal pageant forced grants of conquered districts during this and 1663.
the four subsequent years, after which we hear no more of *Sree Rung Rayeel*, or the house of Vijeyanuggur.

This reign is also distinguished by a serious although less 1667.
formidable attack from another power, which had arisen on the

and cousin-german; and other equally puzzling inaccuracies, resulting from the domestic practices and habits of thinking of the Hindoos: those details also explain with sufficient clearness the reason of a fact incidentally noticed, that Chick Deo Raj with his father were kept as prisoners at Turkanamby during this reign.

* About the middle of the 16th century the ancestor of this Raja from the situation of an opulent farmer was raised to the rank of governor of Bednore. In process of time he threw off his allegiance, and by farther conquests had now become a powerful and independent prince. The practice of a Naib, Nabob or deputy, setting up for himself, is far from being a Mohammedan invention.

CHAP. II. ruins of the house of Vijeyanuggur. Chuckapa, Naick of Madura, had meditated the entire conquest of Mysoor; but the events of the war reversed his expectations, and left the districts of Erroor and Darapoor as fixed conquests in the possession of Deo Raj, after he had urged his success to the extent of levying large contributions on Trichinopoly, and other places of importance.

This Raja does not appear to have conducted in person the military operations of his reign; and although he attended with diligence and ability to the administration of affairs, he is less celebrated by his bramin historians for his civil or military talents, and political skill, than for his excessive devotion and religious munificence. A colossal figure of the Buswa, Nundi*, or holy bull, on the hill of Mysoor, is the most remarkable monument of his religious zeal, being probably the largest and most skilfully executed figure of this kind in the south of India: but he is most extolled for having remitted to the bramins a certain assessment on the possessions of the church; and having been profuse in his grants of land and distribution of money to that holy order.

1672. In a progress through his country for civil purposes, he was taken ill and died at Chickanaickenhully, which is stated to have been conquered during his reign from the Mussulman state of Golconda, although considerably removed from the supposed boundaries of that power.

The conquests of this reign were as follow:

1662. Cheyloor and Biddery from the Poligar of Toomcoor.

* The animal on which *Siva* is mounted in the mythological histories and sculptures of the Hindoos.

Sumpaga from the Raja of Bednore.

Chickanaickenhully from the state of Golconda. 1663.

Hassan, including Sacraputtun and other districts, from Sree Rung Rayeel, the royal pageant above mentioned. 1666.

1667.

Saruckvelly, depending on Honavully.

Hooli Narsapoor from the Wadeyar of that place.

Erroor or Erroad, from the Naick of Madura.

Darapoor from the same.

Hoolioordroog and Koonigull from Kempè Goud of Maagree.

Waumeloor from Gaute Moodelair.

CHAPTER III.

GENERAL RETROSPECT FROM 1564 TO 1677.

Critical period in the affairs of Mysoor—Necessity of a retrospect to the general state of Deckan and the south since the battle of Tellicota—Compact of the victors for separate conquest—their progress in the central and western provinces—in the eastern—Numerous smaller states rise from the ruins of the late empire—An Abyssinian king in Deckan—The prince Aurungzebe appointed viceroy of Deckan—Folly of the Mussulman chiefs of the south—Base treachery of the Hindoos themselves—Conquests of Vijeyapoor—and Golconda—crushed by Aurungzebe, now emperor—Beautiful Hindoo prophecy—applied to Sevagi, the founder of the present Mahratta empire—Origin of this family—Baubajee Bhousla—Maulajee—Shahjee—Whimsical affiance of marriage—enforced—Shahjee elevated to the office of minister—Mogul invasion—Flight of Shahjee to Vijeyapoor—Adventures and capture of his wife—Birth of Sevajee—Second marriage of Shahjee—anecdote of his ingenuity—appointed governor of the conquests in Carnatic and Drauveda—innovations in his administration—separate provision for his first wife and son at Poona—Vicious habits of Sevajee—The robber becomes a sovereign—Evidence of Shahjee's intention to establish an independent government for himself at Bangalore—is seized, and ordered to be executed—reprieve—restoration to confidence and power—Sevajee takes revenge on his father's enemies—is visited by his father—Discussion of dates—Conquest of Tanjore—Sevajee's wonderful irruption into Drauveda—incidents of that campaign—meeting with his brother Eccojee for the first time—undisturbed return to Concan.

CHAP. III.

THE period at which we are now arrived presented a combination of circumstances peculiarly favourable to the growth of the rising state of Mysoor, and its councils were now to be directed by the degree of ambition, enterprise, and prudence, which was suited to its actual situation. But some retrospect will be necessary for the purpose of enabling us to understand the scene by which it was surrounded, and to follow more distinctly the thread of our future narrative. CHAP. III.

After the fatal blow sustained by the empire of Vijeyanuggur in 1564 at the dreadful field of Tellicota, we have seen the con- 1564.
federate Mussulman kings diverted by their own dissentions from following up that decisive action by the conquest of the rest of its dominions; and the representative of the house of Vijeyanuggur establishing himself at Penconda or Bilconda, about 140 miles S. E. of the former capital. The design of farther conquest was not, however, entirely relinquished*; for, taking advantage of a favourable juncture of affairs, the two Mussulman kings of Vijeyapoor and Ahmednuggur held a personal conference, in which it was agreed that they should pursue lines of conquest so distinct, as to preclude interference or jealousy; the latter to the N. E. in the direction of Berar, and the king of Vijeyapoor to the S. W. over the dependencies of Vijeyanuggur. After the capture of Adoni, an achievement which gave reputation to his arms, his conquests were extended to the S. W. down to the sea-coast from near Goa to Barcalore, including the modern provinces of Savanore, Soonda, and North Canara. These successes led to
farther efforts towards the S. E., and an attempt was made on 1575.
Penconda, whence Timma Raja had, however, transferred the chief residence of his government some years before to Chan-

* These transactions are stated from a comparison of the authorities in Scott's two volumes of the Deckan, and in the Historical Memoirs of the Adil Shahee, and Kootub Shahee dynasties, and the various local memoirs in the Mackenzie collection, but chiefly those of Condavir, Adoni and Bellary, as digested by Lieutenant-Colonel Mackenzie himself.

 dergherry. The attack on Penconda was successfully repelled by the heroic efforts of Jug Deo Rayeel, a relation of the Raja, whose services were rewarded by the government of an extensive domain, stretching across a large portion of the peninsula, from Baramahal inclusive, nearly to the borders of the western mountains*; this domain, with some fluctuations, remained in the same family, until finally absorbed in the growing fortunes of the Wadeyars of Mysoor. The check thus sustained by Vijeyapoor was aggravated by the defection of some of its officers, and

1595. by a subsequent minority: at intervals, however, we find the generals of that state levying tribute in two expeditions along the woody and mountainous tract of Soonda, Bednore, Bullum and Coorg.

During this state of the Carnatic Proper, the eastern and southern provinces of the late government did not present a much

1597. more settled aspect. About the year 1597, the last descendant of the ancient Rayeels (as the Rajas of that house are always called) who manifested any symptoms of power, ruled with some degree of magnificence at Chandergherry and Vellore; where he

1597. still held a nominal sway over the principal governors or Naicks; the most considerable of whom appear to have been, at this time,

Naick of Gingee. Kistnapa.
of Tanjore.
of Madura.
of Chennapatam. Jug Deo Rayeel.
of Seringapatam. Tremul Raj.
of Penconda.

* Ascertained by inscriptions and local memoirs.

Of the feebleness of his government, and the general contempt of his authority, we have the evidence of European missionaries, who expressly state that the Naick of Madura was at open war with him. Induced *by the solicitation of the merchants of his country*, he seemed disposed to grant a settlement to the agents of the English East-India Company; but was dissuaded through the influence of the Dutch, who had already established themselves at Pulicat. In their correspondence they observe that his death* "without male issue was expected to be followed by great troubles," as, in fact, it was in the succeeding year. 1597.

While in this interval of forty-three years the progress of the Mohammedan arms had been retarded by the causes which have been noticed, and by other events in the Deckan, which cannot conveniently be embraced by a retrospective sketch; a few aspiring individuals laid the foundation of an intermediate order of things, which in the central districts occupied the place of the late government, composing a series of smaller states, which increased or diminished in power and territory as they succeeded or failed in their alternate usurpations. To the northward of Jug Deo's domain already noticed, the most remarkable of these new states were the Poligars of Chittledroog†, Raidroog, Harponnelly, Tarikera, with many others of inferior note, whose united efforts might have opposed a respectable barrier to Mohammedan encroachment, if united efforts could be expected from restless savages, perpetually occupied by intestine quarrels;

* MSS. translation of Havert's Coromandel in the Mackenzie collection.

† Family annals, and local memoirs of these several places in the Mackenzie collection.

CHAP. III. for most of them were of the lower and hardier cast of the Beder, a race of herdsmen and hunters, who, in their earliest accession to power, exhibited all the ferocious symptoms of their savage origin. The family of Bednore, also, in this interval of confusion extended their possessions, from their first small establishment at Caladee in 1499, down to the sea-coast of Honaver (Onore), and south, to the limits of Malabar, over the dominions of the former queens of Garsopa*; while on the north they successfully opposed the farther advance of the forces of Vijeyapoor along the sea coast. To this period of nearly fifty years of general confusion, through which we are now making a hasty progress, may be assigned the origin or the improvement of most of the droogs or fortified rocks of the Carnatic Proper, and of Baramahal.

Of the causes which, in the complicated events of the Deckan, impeded the general progress of the Mohammedan arms, one is too remarkable to be altogether unnoticed; namely, the temporary government established by an Abyssinian (Mallick Amber), who not only resisted the progress of the Mogul arms, but rendered tributary the kings of Vijeyapoor and Golconda, choosing as the capital of his new state the town of Ghurka, afterwards better known by the name of Aurungabad. The death of his successor in 1626 extinguished the hope of a happier order of things, which might reasonably have been indulged from the high character for moderation and policy which is universally allowed to this warrior and statesman.

1634. In 1634 the strong fortress of Dowlatabad fell into the possession of the Moguls, and a regular government was established

* *The pepper queen* of the Portuguese authors.

in the Deckan, of which, under the prince Aurungzebe, the neighbouring town of Ghurka, now named Aurungabad, became the provincial capital. Every measure of this prince indicated his determination to subdue the Patan kingdoms of Vijeyapoor and Golconda as a necessary preparative to the general subjugation of the south. These princes had arrived at that stage of civilization in which gorgeous and awkward splendor covered the most gross political darkness. Instead of directing their united force against this paramount and obvious danger, they were engaged in idle pomp and pageantry, and in an arrogant and short-sighted project for the partition of the dominions of the south, which by its success only tended to accelerate the ruin of its authors. It was agreed that each should extend his conquests over the countries of the *zemindars* of the Carnatic, as they affected to call them, who were nearest to their respective territories. The general imbecility of the Hindoo government opposed but little resistance to their arms; and it is even stated in Hindoo manuscripts * that they were invited by several of the usurpers, who, under the title of Naicks, Rajas, Wadeyars, Poligars, and even Gouds of single villages, had erected separate principalities, and foolishly hoped to preserve or extend them by the aid of a foreign force.

* The Poligar of Tarikera and Anicul in Carnatic Proper, and in Drauveda, the Naicks of Tripassoor, Tanjour, and Madura, are chiefly accused of this act of *national treachery.* This offence, says my friend Major Mackenzie, like parricide among the early Romans, was considered as unknown, *a crime without a name*, they having no particular term to describe it, like treason against a (Gooroo) spiritual preceptor or (Swamey) temporal master, chief or king. But when we recollect that monarchy was the universal form of government, it was scarcely necessary to distinguish between treason against the nation, and treason against the representative of the nation.

CHAP. III.

Rend Dhoola Khan, general of the forces of Vijeyapoor, over-
1636. ran, in 1636, the whole open country of Bankapoor, Hurryhur, Buswapatan, and Tarrikera, up to the woods of Bednore; and
1638. in 1638 we have seen him repelled from Seringapatam. The line of conquest in which he was more permanently successful passed to the north of the hills of Milgota and Savendroog, towards Bangalore, which he conquered in this year, and rendered his chief residence; the Goud escaping to the rock of Savendroog,
1644. then deemed impregnable. Sera was conquered in 1644, and became afterwards the capital of a large provincial government. From Sera, Bangalore and Colar, the conquests of Vijeyapoor embraced towards the south-east the important fortresses of Vellore and Ginjee*, and those of Golconda the possessions situated to the N. E. of that line, including Chundergherry and Chingleput, the occasional places of residence and nominal capitals of the last nominal Rayeel; who, after long secreting him-
1646. self in Drauveda, escaped in 1646 across the peninsula to claim the protection of the chief of Bednore. These conquests occupied the arms of the Patan kings for a lengthened period of time: the march of Aurungzebe with his best officers and troops into
1656. Hindostan for the purpose of asserting his pretensions to the

* Some of the Mackenzie manuscripts afford room to doubt whether Ginjee did not fall to the share of Golconda, but I imagine it is an error of the transcriber, Ginjee for Gunjee-cota on the northern Pennar, the latter word signifying fortress. It is evident from M. Orme's Fragments, p. 231, that it belonged to Vijeyapoor, and Sevajee certainly found it, in 1677, in the possession of a garrison belonging to that power.

The Kinjee described in Scot's History of the Deckan (vol. 2, p. 84-85) is evidently Kanchee, the Conjeveram of our maps; and the description of the route in p. 84 is remarkably accurate at this day.

throne relieved them for a time from the serious pressure of the Mogul arms, and nearly 48 years were allowed to elapse after the first plan of partition, before their ancient and modern possessions were crushed in one common ruin by the arms of the emperor Aurungzebe *.

Such was the state of the times when a Hindoo author, concluding a succinct chronological account of ancient kings, conveyed under the disguise of a prophecy †, thus denounces the evils which were to ensue: "Omens and Prodigies shall appear. The goddess Calee shall descend on earth, in all her wrathful forms; the proprietors, occupiers, nobles, and all the children of the south shall perish: mankind shall be engaged in incessant war; the demons every where exciting to strife, and arms, in every town and every street: the nobles shall be compelled to obey the command of the Toorks ‡, and be led like sheep to the slaughter." The prophecy concludes with the animating prediction of a deliverer and conqueror, who should relieve the Hindoos from these horrible oppressions: "Then the divine Veera Vasunta shall appear; virgins shall announce his approach with songs of joy: the skies shall shower down flowers, &c." Such a

* To prevent embarrassment to the English reader this name (the ornament of the throne) will be continued instead of *Aulumgeer* (the conqueror of the world) assumed on his accession, and universally employed by Indian authors.

† From the Gutpurtie manuscript in the Mackenzie collection, supposed to have been written about 1646, such prophecies have frequently appeared in subsequent times, and one of them had a wide circulation in the south in the year 1805.

‡ *Mussulmans-Toork* is the name by which they are distinguished in all the languages of the south, written or vernacular, at this day. The earliest *Mussulman* invasion was of *Afghans* or *Patans*, from the Indian Caucasus, and the name seems to point to invasions from Toorkomania at more remote periods. The "kine slaying" is the epithet usually prefixed to the name of Toork in most of the manuscripts.

deliverer in the person of the celebrated Sevagee was shortly afterwards supposed to have appeared; and there is abundant evidence that both he and his adherents directly countenanced the idea of his being under the immediate protection of a deity, by whose inspiration he professed himself to be directed. We shall not permit ourselves to be seduced by the adventures of this extraordinary man far beyond the limits which connect them with the direct object of our work.

We have already had occasion to describe the limits of the Mahratta country and people. For upwards of three hundred years it had been subjected to the domination of strangers: the most obvious maxims of policy, and even of necessity, at first compelled these foreigners to give employment to the military classes of the conquered people; and they continued in aftertimes to fill in different proportions the ranks of the Mohammedan kings of Deckan. The existence, the name, and almost the remembrance, of a Mahratta government had fallen into oblivion: but a bond of union continued to exist, which time and conquest had not been able to dissolve: the religion of the vanquished was still different from that of the conquerors; but above all, the Mahratta language continued to be spoken over the whole extent of the ancient bounds of Maharashtra; and described, by an infallible criterion, who were to be followers of a *heaven inspired* Mahratta prince.

"The first* remarkable person of this house was *Baubaajee*

* Such is the exact commencement of a history of the house of Bhonsla in the Mahratta language, communicated by my excellent friend Colonel Close, without any allusion to the reputed descent of this family from the Rajpoot princes of Oudipoor. The facts, as stated in the text, are chiefly taken from this performance.

Bhonsla, Pateel of the villages of Davulgaw, Heganee and Baradee, &c. belonging to the ancient Talook of Poona." He had issue two sons, Maulojee and Veenaujee, who, quarrelling with the cultivators about the lands, removed from thence to the village of Varoola, near Dowlatabad, where they first settled as farmers; and subsequently entered as foot soldiers into the personal guard of Jadoo Row; a chief who held a considerable command under the dynasty of Nizam Sha. In this situation Maulojee was gradually promoted to an office of confidence about the person of his patron. Maulojee had one son, *Shahjee* *; and his master, Jadoo Row, a daughter, *Jeejavoo.* One day when these children, being respectively of the ages of five and three years, were introduced on the occasion of a great festival, at which all the relations of the family and principal officers were assembled, Jadoo remarked that he had never seen children so beautiful, or so well suited to each other! The observation was seized by Maulojee, and faintly assented to by Jadoo Row, as an affiance of marriage; but the wife of the latter was enraged at the prospect of so unequal an alliance; and Maulojee, insisting on the performance of a pledge thus publicly given, was ultimately discharged from the service. The brothers returned to their former residence at Varoola; where the accidental discovery of a hidden treasure enabled them to enlarge their views, and to retaliate the insult sustained by their dismissal. For this

* The wife of Maulojee having been long childless, made her vows to *Shah Seffer*, a holy recluse at Ahmednuggur, who was celebrated for granting the prayers of such votaries (a Hindoo at a Mohammedan shrine, and to that extent it is not unexampled); and her first child is stated in the manuscript to have been named Shah-jee in gratitude to the saint.

CHAP. III.

purpose they raised banditti, with which they secretly plundered the districts committed to the charge of Jadoo Row; and afterwards proceeded to a more direct and successful system of predatory war. These disturbances attracted the attention of Nizam Sha*, who, on hearing the representation of both parties, declared the daughter of Jadoo Row to be duly betrothed to Shahjee, and the former was reluctantly compelled to permit the solemnization of the marriage, of which, Sumbajee, afterwards killed on service in the south, was the first offspring.

Shahjee had attained the age of twenty-five years when his father died: and having acquired rank and influence by the reputation of superior talents, on the occasion of a minority in the house of Nizam Sha was chosen by the family to be the guardian and minister of the minor. A Mogul invasion immediately succeeded this event; and Jadoo Row, never reconciled to Shahjee, joined the invaders; whom he is accused of having invited for the express purpose of supplanting his son-in-law. Shahjee found it prudent to retire with his charge to the Concan, where he was shortly afterwards besieged, in the fort of Mahooly, by a superior force; chiefly composed of the troops of his father-in-law. Finding it impossible to defend the place, he made overtures of service to Ibrahim Adil Sha of Vijeyapoor, which were accepted; and embracing a favourable opportunity, he left the minor behind in the fort of Mahooly, and, accompanied by his wife and son Sumbajee, cut through the troops of the

* The manuscript states the mode adopted of compelling him to do justice. Two hogs were slaughtered, and in the dead of night silently deposited in the great mosque, with labels tied to their necks explaining the demand, and threatening the same pollution to all the other mosques if justice should be withheld.

besiegers, and proceeded by forced marches to gain the territory of Vijeyapoor. He was closely and rancorously pursued by the troops of his father-in-law for several successive days: and his wife being advanced seven months in a second pregnancy, was unable any longer to endure the fatigue. Shahjee in this extremity left her, with a few trusty attendants, to fall into the hands of her father; escaping himself with the infant Sumbajee. She was kindly received, and placed in security in the hill fort of Seevanaree, where she was delivered of the famous Sevajee on the 17th of May 1626*; and Shahjee, now finally separated from his first wife, arrived in safety at Vijeyapoor, where he was honourably received; and having ineffectually endeavoured to obtain the restitution of his wife and son, married another wife, named Tokabaye, by whom he had issue Eccojee, afterwards Raja of Tanjore.

An instance of the ingenuity of Shahjee is related in the manuscript; from which some conjecture may be formed of the general state of the arts and sciences in the Deckan. The minister Jagadeva Row had made a vow to distribute in charity the weight of his elephant in silver; and all the learned men of the court had studied, in vain, the means of constructing a machine of sufficient power to weigh the elephant. Shahjee's expedient was certainly simple and ingenious in an eminent degree; he led

* The birth of Sevajee is placed by several authorities, and in the "Notes on Mahratta affairs," in 1628: there is an apparent mistake in my copy of the manuscript, as the year of the cycle places it in 1626, and the year of Salivahan in 1627, but I adhere to the former as least likely to be erroneous; the object is not of importance, but I quote the words of the manuscript, in order that if I have committed an error, it may be detected. "In Shakum (year of Salivahan), 1549 in the year of the cycle *Cshaya* in the month Vysaukum on the 5th day of the bright moon."

the animal along a stage prepared for the purpose, to a flat bottomed boat, and marking the water line, removed the elephant, and caused stones to be placed in the boat sufficient to load it to the same line. The stones being brought separately to the scales* ascertained the true weight of the elephant, to the astonishment of the court at the wonderful talents of Shahjee.

In the expedition for the conquest of the Carnatic in 1638, to which we have already adverted, Shahjee was second in command to Rend-Dhoola-Khan, the general of the forces; and on the return of that officer to court, two or three years afterwards, was left as provincial governor of all the conquests of Vijeyapoor in Carnatic and Drauveda; or, as it now first *began* to be named, Carnatic below the ghauts. His first residence was at Bangalore; but he afterwards seems to have divided his time between Balapoor and Colar, when not engaged in military expeditions. It was at this time that a swarm of Mahratta bramins was first introduced into the south for the purpose of establishing, under the direction of Shahjee, a new system of revenue administration; and of suppressing not only the universal anarchy which then prevailed, but with it most of the traces of the former order of

* I have once, and only once, seen the ancient balance of India practically employed, namely in a manufacture of steel in the woods between Cenapatam and Bangalore. It has but one scale, suspended from the small end of a tapering iron rod, and the balance is found by shifting the fulcrum instead of the weight, as in the common steelyard: this fulcrum is nothing more than a piece of thread, or twine, which is shifted until the thing to be weighed is balanced by the thick end of the rod. The thing to be weighed is then taken out of the scale, the loop being carefully kept in its place; and weights (generally pieces of coin) are put into the scale until the same balance is restored. The weight is reckoned by the number of pieces of coin employed. This double operation in the use of the balance probably suggested to Shahjee the device which has been described.

things. Among other innovations the offices and Mahratta names of Deshpondee, Deshmook, Koolkurnee, together with the Persian designations of Canoongoe, Serishtadar, and numberless other novelties, were then introduced. The subordinate details of the revenue and of the whole civil administration in the Deckan had generally continued in the hands of the natives; but when we look back on the subjugation of that country, for upwards of three hundred years, by the most rude and ferocious of all the Mohammedan tribes, and reflect on the numberless revolutions of that terrible period, we shall not be prepared to expect a system of government distinguished for mildness and forbearance. Shahjee was, without doubt, a man of considerable talents; and having formed, as we shall presently see, the design of establishing an independent government, would be desirous of conciliating his Hindoo subjects; and certainly observed in his new system as much moderation as was consistent with the indispensable object of collecting a large and regular surplus revenue; one part of which must necessarily be remitted to court, and the remainder form an accumulating fund to support the charges of future rebellion. Among the more brilliant objects of Shahjee's ambition, he remembered the patrimony from which his grandfather had been expelled, and had obtained in jageer a considerable district, including Poona, where he erected a respectable residence; and when detached to the south, left these possessions in the charge of a confidential dependant, named Dadajee Punt; with directions to procure, if possible, the release of his first wife and her son Sevajee, and establish them, with a suitable provision, in the dwelling which he had prepared; which object was soon afterwards accomplished.

The conduct of Dadajee Punt in this delicate charge appears to have been most exemplary: he remitted to Vijeyapoor the stipulated amount of revenue; and although it is stated, as a compliment to his moderation, that he revived the system of Maleck Amber the Abyssinian, he realized a considerable annual surplus, which was faithfully reserved for his master. For Sevajee he procured all the advantages of civil and military education which the state of the times could afford; but at the age of seventeen the young man began to disregard the admonitions of his guardian, collected a banditti, with which he ravaged all the neighbouring districts, and applied the plunder to the daily augmentation of his band. Dadajee Punt was so deeply affected at this disgraceful conduct, that he put an end to his own existence. Sevajee instantly seized the treasures of his father, which had accumulated by the prudent management of his deceased guardian, and increasing his followers to an extraordinary number, began that career of plunder on a larger scale which induced the European settlers of the time to distinguish him by the appellation of the *robber* Sevajee; and the Mohammedans, by the corresponding term *Ghunneem*, a title to which his descendants and followers have not lost their pretension. It is not our intention to follow this extraordinary conqueror through a series of adventures, which are scarcely to be paralleled in the history of the buccaneers; but some of his most remarkable exploits have a direct relation to the object of our narrative.

When the predatory incursions of Sevajee became of so serious a nature as to foil the arms of Vijeyapoor, and even to bid defiance to the power of the Mogul, Shahjee was called upon by his court, to restrain the licentious conduct of his son; and direct suspicions were avowed, by some of the courtiers, of a secret communication between the son and the father. Shahjee not only disclaimed this supposed connection, but affirmed that he had divorced his first wife and her issue in due form, previously to his second marriage; and that he continued to renounce all relationship with either. Sufficient evidence however appears to exist, not only of the imputed intercourse, but of the deliberate intention of Shahjee to establish an independent government. This evidence is chiefly to be found in two remarkable and notorious facts. First, the existence of grants* and other public documents issued by Shahjee, which bear none of the *usual* formalities of acknowledging a superior government; and

* These curious grants are exclusively in the Mahratta character, and in a strange mixture of the Persian and Mahratta languages, which shews how intimately the forms and technical terms of the conquerors had been received into the language of business. Even the Mohammedan æra of the Hijera under the name of *Soora Sun*, (a term of which I cannot ascertain the origin, unless it has a relation to Soorasena in the geographical lists) is inserted, as well as the year of Salivahan, and recited, not in figures, but in the Arabic names of the numerals, written at length in the manner which is usual in historical works in the Persian language. The introductory part of the grant is nearly pure Persian, with the proportion of Arabic usually incorporated into that language; but with the errors which might be expected from Mahratta transcribers unacquainted with the Persian language. The following is the form of commencement: " Az, rekht-khana, Raujestree, Shah-jee-Rajah, dâm. é. Dowlet. é hoo." One of the grants was sent to my friend Colonel Close at Poona, for the purpose of obtaining a technical explanation of the second and third words; but the form was altogether unknown to official men at Poona; and according to their statement could not be traced in any part of the Mahratta dominions. *Rekht* signifies the apparatus, or equipments, of an individual, a house, or an army; and may thus be translated, dress, furniture, or military equipments. In the latter sense the term *rekht-khana* may be translated, arsenal, park of military stores, or army; and was probably intended to mean the seat of power, the court, as all the Mahrattas of Poona conceive. The translation of the introductory words cited will then stand thus: " From *the court* of the illustrious king Shahjee, may his empire be perpetuated." The grant from which I take this note is dated in 1642.

CHAP. III.

second, the following incident, which is related at length in the manuscript history. The court of Vijeyapoor was so entirely satisfied of the intentions and formidable means of Shahjee, that a plan was secretly formed for securing his person; and was executed by Baajee Gorepora of *Moodul**, a chief of five thousand under his command, who treacherously seized him at an entertainment to which he was invited. The court was not agreed with regard to the disposal of this dangerous prisoner. It was at first imagined that by sparing his life Sevajee might either be reclaimed, or enticed to court; but the discussion ended by despatching an order for the execution of Shahjee; which Gorepora was on the point of obeying, with circumstances of wanton barbarity, when the intercession of Shahjee's friend and patron, the general Rend Dhoola Khan, procured a reprieve. He was accordingly conveyed to court, and soon found means to regain the confidence of the ministers, and an order to return with renewed splendour to his former government; from whence his subsequent message to Sevajee and its consequences shall be exactly stated from the manuscript. "If you are my son you must punish Baajee Gorepora of Moodul. Sevajee Raja accordingly assembled an army, attacked Moodul, and put to death Baajee Gorepora, with his followers of the family of Gorepora, to the number of three thousand; one person only, named Accojee, making his escape to Annola: with this single exception, Sevajee Raja destroyed the whole of them, even the infants in the womb: in this manner did the Raja retaliate." Shahjee on hearing of this exploit was much delighted, and exclaimed, "This is in truth a Vijeya-pootra, the offspring of victory, I must visit him;" and

* Probably Mudkul, between the Toombuddra and Kistna.

the circumstances of the subsequent interview are related with great minuteness. Sevajee went out to receive his father with all the external marks of allegiance from a subject to his sovereign, insisting on attending him on foot for nearly twelve miles till their arrival at Poona; and the state and splendour of Shahjee is said to have approached royal magnificence. When he entered the hall of public audience, after visiting his family, Sevajee took his father's slippers from his servant, and stood submissively behind him until compelled by Shahjee to be seated by his side with suitable demonstrations of affection and respect.

I have omitted to ascertain the date of the death of Shahjee*, and of his son Sambajee†, the elder brother of Sevajee by the same mother. A charitable grant from Sambajee in the district of Bangalore is dated in 1650; and it is understood that Shahjee, on the occasion of his visit to court, with the double object of strengthening his interests, and visiting his jageer at Poona for the express purpose of meeting his son, made a provisional distribution of his southern possessions among his other sons and chief minister. This event, in a note in the Mackenzie collection, extracted from a manuscript of the late Colonel Read, is stated to have occurred in 1674: and if that date be correct, it unfolds the fact of his having adopted at this period the singular policy of affecting submission in his own person, while his sons were assuming on opposite sides of the peninsula the rank of sovereigns. The latest grant which I have seen from Shahjee himself is dated 1642: according to the above date, his death could not have occurred

* It can easily be ascertained in India by reference to the records of any one of the districts which he possessed. I did not notice this blank in my materials until it was too late to repair the omission.

† He was killed in the attack of a place called Kanakagherry.

before late in 1674; and in the intermediate period we find Sambajee in 1650, and Eccojee from 1662 to 1670, at Bangalore, assuming in their grants forms and demonstrations of royalty, still more direct and pompous than those adopted by their father. There are also two small religious grants from *Soorut Sing*, the son of Sambajee, in 1665 and 1666 *; but I can trace no farther this eldest branch of the family.

I hesitate to follow the manuscript which assigns to Shahjee the conquest of Tanjore, which he left under the charge of Eccojee; but from a comparison of authorities I am disposed to suspect that the author confounds this event with some former invasion for the purpose of levying contributions, one of which we know to have occurred in 1656. The terms of the submission of Tanjore on that occasion may have been considered as equivalent to an actual conquest; but the final occupation of that country was probably achieved by Eccojee after the death of his father. This event is placed by a manuscript history of Tanjore in the Tamul language, belonging to the Mackenzie collection, and by several concurring testimonies, in 1675; and the following is an abstract of the narrative of this conquest as stated in the manuscript to which we have adverted.

The Naicks of Tanjore, and Madura (or Trichinopoly, as he is sometimes called, for they were both subject to the same Naick) were at war, and the former being pressed by superior force, sent Vakeels to the king of Vijeyapoor to solicit protection and aid as his vassal. The government of Vijeyapoor was

* I must not, however, leave the English reader to make wrong conclusions on this subject; sons are frequently allowed to make *religious* grants during the life of their fathers.

too much occupied by the invasion of the Moguls, and by the rebellion of other officers, to attend in a direct manner to this complaint; but to preserve the appearance of authority, dismissed the messenger, attended by two Mohammedan Vakeels or agents, with an order addressed to Eccojee at Bangalore, directing him to march for the relief of Tanjore. In the actual state of the times this order might be considered rather as a letter of recommendation: but on due reflection, Eccojee undertook the expedition, probably with a view to conquest on his own account, but under the ostensible authority of the government of Vijeyapoor. On his arrival at the scene of action the Naick of Madura was attacked and completely defeated, and Eccojee made the customary demand of the expences of the expedition; the account of which, as usual, doubled the actual amount, and the Tanjorean was unable or unwilling to defray it. Mutual accusations arose, which the Vakeels of Vijeyapoor in vain endeavoured to adjust: Eccojee complained of an attempt to circumvent him, which, in his own defence, compelled him to guard against the treachery of the Naick, and in the end to take possession of the government "for the good of the state, to protect the good, and to punish the wicked," according to the usual phraseology of conquerors, and to establish his own independent authority in that fertile country.

An officer of five hundred horse, named Ragonad Narrain, dissatisfied with the service of Eccojee, marched across the peninsula, negotiating, according to the custom of those days, for other employment, and was received into the service of Sevajee. This person gave the first hint of the practicability of the celebrated irruption of Sevajee into Drauveda, and furnished the information requisite for carrying it into execution.

Sevajee, who in 1672 had exacted a contribution of nine lacs of pagodas from the king of Golconda, had shortly afterwards, by means of an understanding with Madena Pundit, his Hindoo minister, formed an offensive alliance with that prince against the Mogul, and the natural ally of Golconda, the king of Vijeyapoor. The ultimate and secret object of this treaty is said to have been the final expulsion of all the Mussulman powers from the Deckan, including the prince who was party to the alliance: but we are not told what situation Madena Pundit was to occupy as the price of his treachery. Sevajee having made all his arrangements to guard against the inconvenience of a long absence, directed his march towards Golconda early in 1677, at the head (as stated in the MS.) of forty thousand horse, and an equal number of foot, with a train of artillery. Having arrived in the neighbourhood of Bhagnagur, now called Hyderabad, early in 1677, a month was there consumed in interviews of state with the king, in consultations with the minister Madena Pundit, and in receiving, with a heavy equipment of ordnance and stores, a small auxiliary force, and a pecuniary aid for the present support of the army, of about ten lacs of pagodas in cash and valuables. It is difficult, without the explanations which will ensue, to give a proper designation to the treacherous combination of open and secret compact which, for want of a better term, I have named an offensive alliance. Such was the credulity of the unfortunate prince of Golconda, that he was induced seriously to believe that Sevajee, who five years before had given abundant proof of superiority at the gates of his capital, was now to undertake an offensive war, not merely as a subsidiary ally, but in the direct and avowed capacity of an obedient officer of the state of Golconda; and this deception he continued to practise for several months, until it could be no longer concealed by Madena Pundit and his associates, that instead of the host of Mohammedan dependants who were sent with the army to be provided for, Sevajee uniformly placed his own confidential Mahrattas in the charge of all the conquered places. From Hyderabad he directed his march to Kurnool on the Toombuddra, where he levied a contribution of five lacs on Anund Row, who is named in the manuscript the Deshmook of that place. From Kurnool he ordered the body of his army to move by easy marches in a southern direction to Hundi Anantpoor, while he himself, attended by a select corps, proceeded to the eastward for the purpose of performing his devotions at the celebrated temple of Purwattum, situated in the wild mountains through which the river Kistna forces its passage from the upper countries to the sea. At this temple he is stated by the author of the manuscript to have performed the most austere penances; and to have been seized with a temporary fit of remorse, in which he adopted the habit of a penitent, and professed his determination to renounce the world. Naked and covered with ashes, he assumed the freaks of one of those Indian devotees, who, by the appearance or reality of mental derangement, attract the veneration of the multitude through the strange belief that the soul has been absorbed in the Deity as a peculiar mark of divine favour; and in this new character Sevajee exhibited various acts of folly and apparent insanity, which compelled his attendants to station guards in different directions to watch his proceedings. After acting this farce for about nine days, he suffered himself to be prevailed on to join his army at Anantpoor, and proceeded through the great pass of Damalcherri, by the route of the holy temple of Tripety, into the Payeen ghaut.

The whole country, full of consternation at the unexpected visit of a marauder, whose fame alone had hitherto indistinctly reached it from a distant and opposite coast of the peninsula, waited for events to explain the objects of this extraordinary irruption. Rapidly traversing the country within three leagues of Madras in the first week of May 1677, he approached Ginjee with all the demonstrations of passing through a friendly territory; and, assuring the officers sent to communicate with him by the Killedar, Amber Khan, that he had reconciled his differences with their common master, the king of Vijeyapoor, whose servant he professed himself to be, he prevailed on the old man, accompanied by his sons and relations, to pay a visit of friendship at his tents; where they were all treacherously seized, and the fort of Ginjee fell into his hands without a blow.

This important event explained in the most unequivocal manner his intentions with regard to the king of Vijeyapoor; and the other fortresses possessed in Drauveda by the troops of that power were thus warned to prepare for a vigorous defence. The weaker places fell rapidly into his hands; and the king of Golconda, awakening from his stupor, discovered the gross imposture of which he had hitherto been the dupe. In the records of Madras Sevajee is represented, so late as the 6th of June, as "serving the king of Golconda against Vijeyapoor;" "very honestly hitherto contenting himself with his pay;" but on the 3d of July he is stated to be "baffling Golconda, and putting his own people every where in possession. Golconda stops payment, and

Sevajee begins to cast about for plunder over the whole country;" which, on the 23d of October, is described, in the quaint language of those times, as "peeled to the bones." Sevajee's system of cold-blooded plunder was regulated with a degree of skill and vigilance which suffered not the most minute article of theft or robbery to escape his observation and control. His extensive experience in the discovery of hidden treasure, aided, without doubt, in important cases by secret intelligence, enabled him to direct his detached officers to the most probable places of concealment. The general correctness of his conjectures (readily ascribed by the Hindoos to the supernatural aid which they seriously believed him to possess), was transformed into the belief of his being able to give in all cases an unerring direction to every treasure of every private family; and this tale of wonder has been presented, with little variation, to the credulity of Europe.

After the capture of Ginjee, the object of next importance was the siege of Vellore, which made a respectable defence from the middle of May until the end of September *; and in the details of the siege, which are preserved in the manuscript history, it is observable that the fortified posts on the adjacent hills are distinguished by the Mahratta names which they at present bear, and had probably received from his father Shahjee.

In the intermediate period, however, the conquests of Sevajee did not respect the territories of his brother Eccojee, who, aware of the danger at a very early period, had prepared for defence, by alliances with the Naick of Madura and the Raja of Mysoor; and with their aid opposed an active resistance to the progress of

* I can only ascertain that it fell sometime between the 24th of August and 8th of October, and apparently nearer to the latter than the former date.

CHAP. III.

his brother's arms. But Ragonaut Narain, the guide and counsellor of Sevajee in this expedition, having been sent as an ambassador to the Naick of Madura, succeeded in detaching him from the alliance, and obtaining the payment of a considerable military contribution. It was immediately after this defection, viz. in July 1677, that an interview was proposed and effected between the half-brothers Sevajee and Eccojee for the first and only time in their lives. The conference related chiefly to their respective claims in the division of their father's conquests; and the discussions, although obscurely stated both in the historical manuscript, and in the correspondence of the native agent of the government of Madras, seem to favour the supposition that the conquest of Tanjore was considered to have been effected during the life of Shahjee. However this may be, it is certain that Eccojee was so little satisfied with the apparent intentions of his brother, that he escaped during the succeeding night to Tanjore, and recommenced hostilities. But after the lapse of a few months, and the conquest of every thing north of the river Coleroon, the presence of Sevajee was demanded in another quarter. He appointed a strong force for the protection of his new conquests, and prepared to depart at the head of a select corps of no more than four thousand horse; leaving directions with his generals to embrace the earliest opportunity of surprising the Dutch and English settlements of Paliacate, Sadras, and Madras *: but confirming to the French their possession of Pondicherry, as stated by Anquetil du Perron †, who however dates the letter of Sevajee in July 1630, a time when Sevajee was only four years old.

* Madras records. † L'Inde en rapport avec Europe, Vol. I. p. 130.

I do not regard this error with any suspicion of intentional misrepresentation in that author, whom I have generally found to be scrupulously accurate in his facts, however I may dissent from his opinions.

During the absence of Sevajee in Drauveda, the Mogul army had invaded Vijeyapoor, and the king of Golconda, awaking from his dream of conquest, and roused at length to the conviction of their common interest, sent an aid which enabled the state of Vijeyapoor to make a formidable resistance in the field. These operations, which Sevajee had probably foreseen, prevented that state from succouring its distant possessions in Drauveda, and enabled him, by making a circuit round the greater part of its frontier, to fall unexpectedly on its most remote dominions; and after deceiving equally his friends and his enemies, and involving both in serious hostility, to return undisturbed and lightly attended to the Concan; visiting in his way the possessions held by the different branches of his family in the direct road from Vellore, by Colar, Ouscota, Bangalore, and Great Balapoor, to Sera, and thence proceeding by the accustomed route of Hurryhur, through the province of Savanoor, to his fastnesses in the western range.

The departure of Sevajee was the signal for renewed exertion on the part of his brother at Tanjore, who in the month of December obtained a complete victory over Santajee *, the commander in chief of Sevajee's forces in Drauveda. But this general,

* In the records of Madras he is described as the brother of Sevajee, which must be an error. The name of Santajee Gorepudda, or Gorepora, appears in the records of the same and subsequent year, as the leader of *the Sevajees*, as the Mahrattas are frequently named at that period. If this be the same Santajee, the additional name shews him to have been the ancestor of the celebrated Morari Row of Gooti

stung with the disgrace, assembled his officers on the same night, and proposed a plan for retrieving the fortune of the day, which was unanimously approved; the troops were accordingly ordered under arms after a short refreshment, and returning to the field, where Eccojee reposed in the security of victory, completely surprised his army, and made a dreadful carnage. A small remnant escaped with Eccojee across the river; and early in 1678 a peace was concluded, which restored to him a small portion of the territory he had lost, on the payment of a considerable pecuniary aid, which was ever a prominent condition in all the treaties of Sevajee.

CHAPTER IV.

FROM 1672 TO 1704.

Former exclusion and present accession of Chick Deo Raj—Judicial astrology—means of accomplishing its predictions—New minister—Post-office—Spies—Vigorous but unpopular administration—Religion of the Raja—The minister assassinated by the Jungum—His successor—Policy observed in the exterior encroachments of this reign—Remarkable purchase of Bangalore—Farther conquests—to the north and west—and east—Expedition to Trichinopoly—False policy of Aurungzebe in the apparent conquest and real increase of his enemies—Abuses—and financial difficulties—A Mahratta army invades Mysoor—Recal of the troops from Trichinopoly—Singular victory—Embassy to Aurungzebe—its motives and result—The Raja assumes the dignity of being seated on a throne—New arrangement of the departments of government—Public œconomy and order—Wealth—Extent of territory—Necessity of allotting a separate chapter to the question of landed property.

CHICK DEO RAJ.

1672.

THE remarkable irruption of Sevajee into the countries of Drauveda, which closed our last chapter, carries us to a period six years later than the commencement of the reign of Chick Deo Raj; but no material event occurred within that short period to require an interruption in our retrospective narrative.

We have already noticed that this Raja and his father were passed over in the order of lineal descent in 1659; and he now succeeded to the throne at the mature age of forty-five. His early youth had been passed at the remote town of Yellandoor,

CHAP. IV. 1672. where he had formed an intimacy with *Visha Lacksha Pundit*, of the sect of Jain, who was afterwards more generally known by the appellation of the *Jain Pundit*, or Yellandoor Pundit. When, in the preceding reign, Chick Deo Raj and his father had been placed under restraint at the more obscure fort of Hengul, in the district of Goondul, the Pundit continued his attachment, and followed his friend to the place of his confinement. Among the various branches of literature in which the Pundit was eminently accomplished, he had the reputation of profound knowledge in astrology; an imaginary science, which continues to the present day to be an object of serious study and universal delusion in every part of India; and by the aspect of the stars he had discovered that Chick Deo Raj would certainly succeed to the throne. This prediction had, in their hours of confidence, been frequently repeated; and Chick Deo Raj had been induced to declare, that in such event Visha Lacksha should become his prime minister. Fortified with this assurance, the Pundit set about the accomplishment of his prediction by going to the capital, and secretly announcing to the persons possessed of the chief influence in the government, the future succession of Chick Deo Raj, as an event which was written in the decrees of fate, and could not possibly be averted. The reputed learning of the Pundit gained an easy and general credence to the decision of Heaven; and when Dud Deo Raj died, every one was prepared to receive his inevitable successor. The Pundit had carefully abstained from unfolding that page of the book of fate in which his own elevation was preordained, an event which at first produced considerable surprise and murmurs; but the steady and determined character of the Raja, aided by the vigorous talents of his new minister, quickly suppressed every open symptom of discontent.

Among the earliest measures of the new reign was the establishment for the first time of a regular post throughout his dominions. The post-office was not only, as in England, the passive instrument for conveying intelligence, but the active agent for obtaining it. The postmasters at the several stations were, in addition to their passive duties, what in the modern vocabulary of Europe would be named confidential agents of police; and all the inferior servants of the department were professed spies, who made regular reports of the secret transactions of the district, which were as regularly transmitted to court: whatever therefore might have been the views of the former ministers, they were effectually deterred from carrying them into execution by the activity, purposely exaggerated, of this new and terrible instrument of despotism, which we shall hereafter find improved, and actually organized, under the celebrated Hyder, to a degree which scarcely admitted of farther rigour.

The chief financial measures of this reign will be reserved for a separate chapter, in order to avoid an unnecessary interruption to the narrative of political events; and the conquests, which present little interest, or demand no particular explanation, will be recited as usual at the end of the reign.

The first fourteen years of this reign were occupied in these financial measures, interior reforms, and minor conquests; but these reforms had rendered so unpopular the administration of the Jain Pundit, to whom they were chiefly attributed, that a plan was secretly concerted for his assassination. Chick Deo Raj had, without doubt, in the early part of his life, been educated

CHAP. IV. 1672. in the doctrines of the Jungum*, which was the religion of his ancestors: he had hitherto, since his accession to the throne, shewn no very marked attachment to any form of worship, but was supposed, from particular habits which he had adopted, and from the great influence of the Jain Pundit †, to have conceived the intention of reviving the doctrines of that
1686. ancient sect. The Pundit was attacked and mortally wounded, while returning at night, in the usual manner, from court to his own dwelling; and as, in addition to religious motives, the Jungum had a deep account of revenge to retaliate, for the murder of their priests; an event which will be related in the financial narration to which it belongs; the suspicion of this assassination fell chiefly upon that people, and tended to confirm the alienation of the Raja's mind from the doctrines of their sect. He was much affected at the intelligence of this event, and immediately proceeded to the house of the minister to console him in his last moments, and to receive his advice regarding the choice of a successor. The advice was entirely unprejudiced, and he recommended, as the most able and honourable man of the court, a person of adverse religion, namely, Tremalayangar, a bramin of the sect of Vishnoo. To him the Raja gave his whole confidence; and, in conformity to his advice, soon afterwards made an open profession of the doctrines of that prevailing religion. In other respects, the new administration was conducted on the same principles as the preceding, and with an equal degree of prudence and vigour.

In the first years of this reign, the enterprizes of Sevajee and the pressure of the Mogul arms occupied the kings of Gol-

* For an account of this sect see Appendix, No. 4. † See Appendix, No. 6.

conda and Vijeyapoor. The conquests of Sevajee in Drauveda in the year 1677 had established him in front and rear of his former sovereign of Vijeyapoor; and the communication between those distant possessions was kept up by means of the branches of his family possessing Bangalore and the other south-eastern provinces of Carnatic Proper, and by a good understanding with the petty states which formed a chain across the peninsula immediately to the northward of the territory then possessed by Mysoor. This state was thus placed, as it were, in an angle removed from the line of general military operations; and while the transactions in Deckan and Drauveda became more complicated, the greater powers, namely the Mogul lieutenants, the two Mohammedan kings of Deckan, and Sevajee, found in each other opponents too powerful to admit of their attending, in the manner that their importance required, to the gradual and skilful encroachments of Chick Deo Raj.

Sevajee died in 1680; and in 1684 Aurungzebe returned to the Deckan with an immense army, determined to crush the formidable power of the Mahrattas, and to subjugate the Mohammedan states of Vijeyapoor and Golconda, which two latter states he finally reduced from 1686 to 1688. Eccojee in Tanjore finding his distant dominion of Bangalore to be an expensive and precarious possession, insulated in a great degree by the contending armies which constantly ranged over the intermediate country, wisely determined to sell it to the highest bidder. Chick Deo Raj finally agreed to be the purchaser; at a price (*three lacs of rupees*) which sufficiently marks the public opinion of the instability of all possessions in those days of general convulsion: a detachment was accordingly sent to occupy the new

CHAP. IV. 1687. purchase, and to pay the consideration. But the negotiation having been long protracted had become a matter of notoriety, and attracted the attention of Harjee Raja the Mahratta commander in chief at Ginjee, and of Aurungzebe, who had just raised the siege of Golconda on the condition of receiving a military contribution of two millions sterling. These powers entertaining a high opinion of the importance of Bangalore, sent each a detachment from those distant and opposite stations to anticipate the Raja of Mysoor, and endeavour to seize Bangalore for themselves. Kasim Khan, the officer of Aurungzebe, making forced marches to the westward of the range of ghauts, arrived first, and the place being in the dismantled state which may be imagined when about to be sold, was incapable of making a proper defence, and yielded to Kasim Khan without material opposition. The detachment of Harjee Raja finding itself anticipated, returned without much effort to the lower country. The imperial colours, however, were only hoisted for four days on the ramparts of Bangalore; for Kasim Khan, who had more important objects in view, found that by accepting the price which the Raja was still willing to pay, he should, exclusively of a pecuniary aid, be relieved from the necessity of making a large detachment for the occupation of the place, while its use as a point of communication would still be preserved; it was accordingly delivered in July 1687 to the troops of Chick Deo Raj. It was obviously prudent in the state of Mysoor to abstain from any encroachments which should attract the particular attention of the greater powers: and although Chick Deo Raj observed the general policy of enlarging his dominions in the more unobserved directions, yet as he acquired more confidence in his strength and political address, we find him venturing across the line of general operation which has been described. So early as 1676 and 1677 he engaged in the conquest of the territories of the Hindoo chief of Mudgerry; and previously to the arrival of Kasim Khan in 1687, he had seized most of the principal places necessary for connecting his former frontier with this more northern acquisition. The amicable arrangement by which he obtained possession of Bangalore would render it incumbent on Kasim Khan to represent Mysoor to Aurungzebe as a state which ought to be encouraged as a counterpoise in the south to the dangerous power of the Mahrattas; and although it is known that the conquest of Mysoor was in the direct contemplation of that emperor, it was obviously his interest to postpone it so long as the Raja could be of use by being placed on the flank and rear of his actual enemies. We may on the whole infer, with great probability, the establishment and continuance of a friendly intercourse between Kasim Khan and the Raja, who skilfully availed himself of the confusion of the times, and continued to propitiate, in whatever manner, the court of Aurungzebe. In the succeeding year we accordingly find him wresting Ooscota and some places of minor importance from the connections of the Mahrattas *, and pushing his conquests to the eastward, below the ghauts, in that and the following year over a considerable portion of the Baramahal, and of Salem, as far south as Permetti on the Caveri. In 1690 he turned his arms to the opposite direction; and in the four following years had

1687.

1688.

1689.

1690.

* Ooscota had been assigned by Shahjee, when summoned to court, to his minister Ishwunt Row. I cannot trace with certainty in whose possession it was at this time. Pootia's manuscript says the house of Eccojee.

CHAP. IV.

1694.

extended his dominion to the verge of the western hills of Bednore, with which power he seems to have concluded in the year 1694 an advantageous peace, which left him in possession of most of his conquests. Thus relieved from hostility on the west, his increasing power and resources encouraged him, after a few years of repose, to turn again his attention to the S. E., and to plan the conquest of the dominions of the Naick of Madura, commencing his operations with the siege of the important town of Trichinopoly. In the intermediate period, since the acquisition of Bangalore in 1687, Aurungzebe had found sufficient occupation in the conquest of the Deckan. Neither the destruction of the monarchies of Vijeyapoor and Golconda, the death of Sevajee, nor the capture and cruel murder of Sambajee his son, in 1691, seemed to improve the prospects of that emperor for the general subjugation of the south. From the first appearance of Sevajee as an independent leader, his armies had been recruited with the troops of all casts, which the gorgeous improvidence of the Mohammedan kings of Deckan had compelled them to discharge; or by the direct defection of those in actual employ who were chiefly Mahrattas. The destruction of the two last of these Mohammedan states left two considerable* armies disbanded, unemployed, and seeking for employment. The policy of Aurungzebe, however sagacious in many instances, could not descend to the contemplation of peril from the dregs of a vanquished people: the abuses, now grown too dangerous to be at

* "In the countries dependant on Hyderabad and Vijeyapoor, which before their conquest maintained above two hundred thousand horse, there were not now stationed above thirty-four thousand," says the Bondela officer, when narrating the events of a few years afterwards. Scott, vol. ii. p. 107.

once reformed, which had crept into the payment and mustering of his armies, added to the overwhelming expences of his splendour and state, deprived him of the means of preventing these armies from being again marshalled against him. The necessity of attending to this pregnant source of danger was accordingly merged in the greater necessities of disordered finance; and the whole or the greater part of the armies which had recently been opposed to him were, in a short period of time, united to different bands of Mahratta marauders, who at this period began to swarm in greater numbers than had ever before appeared in almost every part of India; thus presenting to the power of Aurungzebe opposition more abundant, diversified and perplexing, at the very time that he had flattered himself with the destruction of the last of his enemies in the person of Sambajee. On the capture of this chief, ama, the second son of Sevajee, escaped after many perils across the peninsula, and assumed the direction of the Mahratta powers at Ginjee. Zulfecar Khan, with a large portion of the imperial army, had been employed since 1693 in feeble and ineffectual attempts to reduce that strong fortress; although he had extended his conquests over the open country with some degree of vigour, and with fluctuating success; and had exacted contributions from the Zemindars * (as they are uniformly named) of Tanjore and Trichinopoly. It was probably one of the auxiliary Mahratta armies, or reinforcements, under the command of Jugdeo Ghautkee, and Nimbajee Ghautkee, which, passing from the western country for the support of Ginjee and Drauveda, and provoked by the aggres-

* See Scott, vol. ii. p. 81.

CHAP. IV. 1697. sions of Chick Deo Raj, or incited by the hope of plunder, suddenly appeared before Seringapatam, while the strength of the army was employed in the siege of Trichinopoly. An express was instantly sent to the Dulwoy Comareia, directing him to return for the protection of the capital*. He is stated in the fa-

* This is one of the few dates which I have failed in arranging to my satisfaction. Neither the records of districts, nor the otherwise very correct MS. of Pootia, are careful in recording the date of an event, excepting when it has been followed by a change of possession. The memoirs of the Dulwoys have few dates: they place this Mahratta invasion next in the order of events to the occupation of Bangalore. Poornia's compilation, formed on a discussion of authorities, places it after the western conquests from Bednoor; but all are agreed that the Mysoorean army was at the time before Trichinopoly. If we should adopt the former, and conjecture the Mahratta force in question to be that which is discussed by Mr. Orme in 155 to 158 of his Historical Fragments, namely, that which marched for the occupation of Bangalore in 1687, we must conclude that this Mahratta force watched the passage of the Mysoorean army through the pass of Tapoor towards Trichinopoly, and moved rapidly across its rear by Changana, Wodiardroog, and Kaunkanhully, to Seringapatam. The objections to the adoption of this date seem to be nearly insuperable. According to Pootia's manuscript, the flag of Mysoor was hoisted at Bangalore on the 29th of July 1687; the Mahratta troops did not leave Ginjee till August; on the 10th of November they are stated by Mr. Orme to be again at Trinomalee, and they had probably been there for some time before the intelligence reached Madras: a conjecture which is founded on the usual severity of the season, and the ordinary habit of the Mahrattas to be hutted by the 15th of October, when within the influence of the N. E. monsoon. Calculating the longest period that can be embraced between these probable extremes, and adverting to the nature of the country to be passed by these two armies respectively incumbered with the equipments of a siege, it can scarcely be considered possible that the Mysooreans could make their arrangements for the occupation of their new possessions, receive equipments for the siege of Trichinopoly, march to that place, be engaged in the siege, and return to Seringapatam; and that the Mahratta army could have invested Seringapatam and have marched after their defeat to Trinomalee within the supposed period. But independently of the shortness of time, and the disagreement in the names of the leaders, it places the expedition at a time of the year when the river Caveri is full, and when it would be scarcely practicable to undertake the siege of Trichinopoly from the north.

The grounds (which I offer without any positive confidence) for adopting the

mily manuscript "to have made a vow not to appear before his Raja until he had taken Trichinopoly: in consequence of which he permitted his son Dudeia to take the command, and reserving with himself a small force, went afterwards to Ginjee;" a determination which seems to afford strong evidence of treachery, and of some secret intrigues which prevent our having received a more distinct account of this material transaction. Authorities are, however, agreed in stating that his son did proceed by rapid marches for the relief of the capital, and defeated the enemy by

order of time stated in Poornia's MS. are the following. I find in a general letter from Madras in 1695-6 that Zulfecar Khan is outnumbered by the Mahrattas, of whom more were expelled from Concan, and, if not supported, must (in their opinion) either join with the Mahrattas or submit; but that an army was reported to be coming to his assistance. This army under Dunnajee Jadoo Row we know to have arrived in 1696. On the 19th of January 1696-7 in a mutilated paragraph, of which the worms had become the chief possessors, I find the following.

> "11th. Nabob Zulphecar Cawn is gone into the Mizore *country after the* Mahratta army (whether to jo*in them or fight them* uncertain) and hath left a *very small part of his* army in these parts."

The blanks are filled in Italics, and may be varied according to the imagination of the reader: but my inference is, that finding on his arrival in or near Mysoor that the Mahratta army was already defeated and dispersed, he returned immediately into the lower country, from which it is certain that he was not long absent: according to the journal of the Bondela officer, translated by Captain Scott, Zoolfecar Khan received a large reinforcement in 1696, but was compelled to raise the siege of Ginjee in the same year. This expedition to Mysoor is not specified in the narrative of the Bondela officer among the operations of the year 1697; probably from being relinquished almost as soon as undertaken; but the conjecture here submitted is farther strengthened by a paragraph from Madras dated the 7th of August 1697, which states that "there is now no army of Mahrattas in these parts," and I should rather infer an omission in the narrative of the Bondela officer than a misstatement in the letter from Madras, where at this time the transactions around them are generally stated with a degree of accuracy which doubles our regret at the destruction of so large a portion of the records.—N. B. I have been enabled to correct the above blanks in the Madras copy from the records at the India-house.

CHAP. IV. 1697. means of a most unmilitary practice, which we find to have been peculiar to the army of Mysoor so long afterwards as 1751; namely, that of always performing their night marches by the light of numerous torches*. It was impracticable to conceal altogether from the Mahratta army the approach of this relief, and this peculiar practice was made the foundation of a stratagem, which was effected in the following manner. In the evening the Dulwoy sent a small detachment in the direction opposite to that on which he had planned his attack; and in the probable line by which he would move to throw his force into the capital. This detachment was furnished with the requisite number of torches and an equal number of oxen, which were arranged at proper distances, with a flambeau tied to the horns of each, in a situation where they could not be observed by the enemy. At an appointed signal the torches were lighted and the oxen driven in the concerted direction, so as to indicate the march of the army, attempting to force its way through the besiegers by an attack on the flank of their position. So soon as it was perceived that the enemy were making a disposition to receive the army of torches, Dudeia silently approached their rear, and obtained an easy but most sanguinary victory. The two Gautkees and most of their officers were killed, and the action terminated in the capture of the whole of their ordnance, baggage, and military stores of every description; and the disorder and flight of the remnant of their army. The Raja on the following day ordered his general and principal officers to be presented to him in public durbar, in the same military habits in which they had

* See Mr. Orme's account, vol. i. p. 211.

fought, "covered with the blood of his enemies;" and in this state rewarded them with dresses and ornaments of honour, and munificent presents proportioned to their respective rank and exploits. 1697.

Kasim Khan, the friend and protector of the Raja at the court of Aurungzebe, who had for many years held some of the highest offices of the state, died in the following year; and this 1698.
event had probably a considerable influence in determining Chick Deo Raj to send a splendid embassy with valuable presents to the imperial court. His various conquests had excited combinations against him among his powerful neighbours, and a 1699.
certain degree of jealousy in the mind of the emperor himself. It was necessary that he should establish a fresh interest at court, and, if possible, obtain the recognition of his authority in its present enlarged extent. Some motives of vanity were probably also mixed with those of policy, and his late signal victory over the Mahratta enemies of the empire afforded solid ground for expecting a favourable reception. The splendour of the embassy does not, however, appear to have made much impression at the imperial court; and if we may judge from the trifling sum* recorded to have been expended in the entertainment of the ambassadors, the Zemindar of Mysoor (as he is called) was not held to be a person of very high consideration. Whether Aurungzebe actually conferred the high honours which were pretended to be received, would perhaps be a balanced question if it were of sufficient importance to merit a separate discussion. It is sufficient to our present purpose to state that they were publicly as-

* Two hundred rupees. Notes on the Asophia Dufter, communicated by Colonel W. Kirkpatrick to Major Mackenzie.

CHAP. IV. sumed, and as far as is known were never questioned; although
1699. a similar assumption on the part of the Raja or Zemindar of Bednore (namely, that of sitting on a throne), attracted the ven-
1700. geance of Aurungzebe some years afterwards. The embassy which departed in the year 1699 found the imperial court at Ahmednuggur, and returned in the year 1700. The Dulwoy and other great officers of state were sent out in due form to receive the supposed letter, presents, and insignia of honour despatched by the emperor, which were carried in solemn procession through the town; and after being exhibited in the great temple at the feet of the idol *Sree Runga*, were brought in similar state to the palace. Among the presents was a new signet prepared by the emperor's direction, bearing the title of Jug Deo Raj, which was thenceforth employed; and part of the ceremonial was the new dignity alleged to have been conferred by the emperor of being seated on an ivory throne. This was afterwards used by his successors, and is the same which, in the year 1799, was found in a lumber-room of Tippoo Sultaun's palace; was employed in the installation of the present Raja; and is always used by him on occasions of public ceremony.

It was soon after the return of this embassy that he is also stated, in some manuscripts, to have distributed the business of the government into eighteen cutcheries or departments, in consequence of learning from the ambassadors that such was the practice of the imperial government, and consequently fit to be adopted by so great a prince as Jug Deo Raj (the sovereign of the world); but this arrangement is referred by others to an earlier period. I incline to the former supposition, from being unable to trace any good reasons for the establishment of so many departments for the transaction of business, which might with greater simplicity and convenience be allotted to less than half that number: the reader who has sufficient curiosity to form his own judgment on a subject of so little importance, will find these departments detailed in the subjoined note*.

* 1. Neroop Chaouree cutchery or department, or the secretary's department, to which he appointed one *Daroga* or superintendant, and three Dufters, registers or books of record (N.B. every thing was recorded in each of the three in exactly the same manner); all letters or orders despatched to be previously read to the Raja. 2. Eikut Chaouree, whose business it was to keep the general accounts of revenue, treasury, and disbursements civil and military; this seems to approach our office of accountant-general. 3 and 4. Obeik Vichar, or *two-fold enquiry*. He divided his whole possessions into two portions; that north of the Cavery he called the *Puttun Hobly*; that south of the Cavery was named the *Mysoor Hobly*: to each of these cutcheries he appointed one Dewan and three Dufters. 5. Seemé Cundachar: it was the duty of this cutchery to keep the accounts of provisions and military stores, and all expences of the provincial troops, including those connected with the maintenance of the garrisons: one Buckshee and three Dufters. 6. Bakul Cundachar (bakul, a gate or portal): it was the duty of this department to keep the accounts of the troops attending at the *porte*, that is to say, the army, or disposable force. 7. Soonka Dé Chaouree, or *duties and customs*: it was their duty to keep the general accounts of customs levied within his dominions. 8. Pom Chaouree: in every talook where the *soonka* was taken there was another or second station, where a farther sum equal to half the former amount was levied; for this duty he established a separate cutcherie. 9. Tundaia Chaouree; tundaia, half, i. e. half of the pom: this was a farther *fourth* of the first duty, levied in Seringapatam only. 10 and 11. In the Obeik Vichar was not included the *Sree Rung Puttun* and *Mysoor Astagrams*, (eight townships): for each of these he had a separate cutchery; besides the business of revenue they were charged with the provisions and necessaries of the garrison and palace. 12. Bennea Chaouree: benné, butter (the butter department): the establishment of cows, both as a breeding stud, and to furnish milk and butter for the palace: the name was changed by Tippoo to *Amrut Mahal*, and then to *Keren Barick*. Amrut, the Indian nectar. Kerenbarick, an Arabic term, may be translated almost verbally *Cornu Copia*. 13. Puttun Chaouree: this cutchery was charged with the police of the metropolis, the repairs of the fortifications and public buildings. 14. Beakin Chaouree (the department of expedition), or the post-office: the business of espionage belonged also to this department. 15. Sammooka Chaouree: the officers of the palace, domestics, and personal servants of every

CHAP. IV.

1701.

It is certain that the revenues were realized with great regularity and precision, and this Raja is stated to have established a separate treasury to provide for extraordinary and unexpected disbursements, of which he himself assumed the direct custody. It was his fixed practice, after the performance of his morning ablutions, and marking his forehead with the upright insignia of Vishnoo, to deposit two bags (thousands) of pagodas in this treasury from the cash despatched from the districts, before he proceeded to break his fast. If there were any delay in bringing the money he also delayed his breakfast, and it was well known that this previous operation was indispensable. By a course of rigid œconomy and order, and by a widely extended and well organized system of securing for himself the great mass of plunder obtained by his conquests, he had accumulated a treasure, from which he obtained the designation of Nou-kote-Narrain, or the lord of nine crores (of pagodas), and a territory producing a revenue calculated on the estimate of the schedules annexed to the treaties of 1792 and 1799, of Canterai pagodas 1,323,571; a sum which is no farther remarkable than in its near coincidence with the value of territory assigned to the revived state of Mysoor after the lapse of another century in 1799, when the minister of one of the confederates objected to its amount, as being (notoriously, according to him) much greater than the Hindoo state of Mysoor

description belonged to the charge of this cutchery. 16. Deostan Chaouree kept the accounts of the lands allotted to the support of religious establishments, the daily rations of food to the bramins, lighting the pagodas, &c. 17. Cubbin Chaouree, iron cutchery: this article was made a monopoly, and its management was committed to a separate cutchery. 18. Hooge Suppin; *the smoking leaf* or tobacco (in Telinga it is *Pookakoo)*, another monopoly by the government, which in Seringapatam was the exclusive tobacco merchant.

had even possessed. The curiosity of many of my readers may be gratified by referring to the annexed map descriptive of the actual extent of Mysoor at this period, and noting the powers by which it was surrounded. Such of them as may desire to investigate the valuation to which I have adverted, will find it detailed in a convenient form in Appendix, No. 6.

Before proceeding to relate the remarkable change in the actual condition of the landholders of Mysoor, which was introduced by Chick Deo Raj, and forms the chief feature of his interior administration, it seems necessary to take an extended view of the question of proprietary right, in order that these changes may be more clearly understood. The local regulation alone might be comprised, or rather dismissed, in a short superficial narrative; but the subject involves considerations which I am unwilling to pass over in that manner: I shall, therefore, in a separate chapter, discuss the nature, and, as far as is practicable, trace the history of landed property in India; and as in the investigation of this subject I have arrived at conclusions materially differing from those which have hitherto been received as authentic, it is necessary that I should submit to my readers the grounds from which those conclusions are derived.

CHAPTER V.

ON THE LANDED PROPERTY OF INDIA.

Preliminary observations—The term "landed property" not sufficiently distinguished from the mode of possessing it under the feudal law—Objection to the employment of feudal terms—Origin of "landed property" according to Menu—the Mohammedans—the Roman lawyers—meaning attached to the term in this work—Earliest opinions regarding the state of landed property in India derived from the companions of Alexander—and embassy of Megasthenes—collected by Strabo—and Diodorus—their imperfect information—later voyagers and travellers—servants of the East-India Company—authors of "The Husbandry of Bengal"—of "Plans for British India"—of digest of Hindoo law—all deny the existence of private landed property—Reasons for dissenting from these authorities—Description of an Indian village or township—Kingdoms composed of these elements—their interior constitution and relation to the government liable to no change—examination of ancient authorities—Menu—digest—contradictions in the commentary—examination of the text—person designated as proprietor—limitations regarding hereditary descent—and public contributions—Proof of hereditary and entailed landed property as an universal principle of Hindoo law—neither king nor zemindar the proprietor—Amount of land tax—objections—viz. fines for neglecting to cultivate—and the land itself granted by the king—answered by reference to the text of the law and the terms of the grants—Reference to the ancient state of landed property in other countries—Judea—Egypt—Spartan fables—Athens—Information doubtful regarding Greece—more ample and perfect in Italy—inference from this examination—Attempt to trace the state of landed property in India, from the earliest periods till the present day—Conquests—of Hindoos—Huns-Toorks—Afghans or Patans—Moguls—interrupted by natural impediments—central regions first over-run—Eastern and western tracts separated by precipices and a burning climate—Examination of the latter from the eastern coast at 13¼ north latitude, round Cape Comorin to 15 N. on the west coast—Canara—one-sixth of the crop the ancient land-tax—increase of 10 per cent. on its conquest by a Pandian in 1252 —conquest by the house of Vijeyanuggur in 1336—law tract composed by the minister of that state still extant—taxes conformable to Menu, and the ancient authorities on Hindoo law—that law dexterously applied to the calculations of the conqueror—raises the revenues 20 per cent.—farther assessment by the rebel governors in 1618—Rate at which lands were then sold—hereditary rights in land indefeasible in Canara—subsequent exactions up to and after the conquest by Hyder in 1763—under Tippoo Sultaun proprietors begin to disclaim their property—inference from this fact—Malabar—fabulous—and real history—landed property of this coast perfect to a degree unexampled in any other country ancient or modern—Travancore—eastern coast, or Drauveda—beginning with the northern limit—conquered by the house of Vijeyanuggur in 1490 to 1515—by the Mussulman states of Vijeyapoor and Golconda in 1646—frequent incursions under Shahjee—Sevajee—first fixed Mohammedan government about 1698—its detestable character—these barbarians acknowledge in the very technical terms they employ the existence of private hereditary property in land at that time—discussions on this subject on the records of Madras—their result—sale of the lands—and creation of Zemindars, in the Jageer Salem, &c.—suspicion of the propriety of that measure—its farther operation suspended—State of property in Tanjore—Madura—Tinevelly, &c. &c.—inferences—The territorial policy of Madras derived from Bengal—Errors in the permanent settlement of that country—Inferences from the whole.

CHAP. V.

THE three persons whose relations to each other, and to the property of the soil in India, have been discussed in former publications, are, the Sovereign, the Zemindar (a proprietor according to some, and an officer of revenue according to others), and the Ryot, or cultivator of the ground: and it has been objected to the whole discussion, that as the relative claims of each of these persons on the produce of the soil, and the extent of certain prescriptive rights which cannot be infringed without the imputation of injustice, are admitted without much variation by all parties; the argument for determining who is the actual proprietor of the soil is rather a dispute about words than a discussion concerning things. This objection would indeed be fatal to any farther agitation of the question, if the premises from which it is derived were fully admitted: it is therefore indispensable to the hope of obtaining a patient perusal of the following observations, that I should protest *in limine* against the definition, in substance as well as in form, of the whole of these claims and rights, regarding which the contending parties are supposed to be agreed.

"Landed property" is a form of speech so familiar to the English ear, that the ideas annexed to it would seem to require but little explanation: and yet the very word *tenure*, by which we express the manner of possessing the right to such property, not only intimates a diversity in the meanings attached to the term "landed property," but also conveys the direct admission of holding such property from a superior on certain conditions. It is natural that an idea so entirely identified with the received notions of landed possession in England, should introduce itself with facility into all our discussions on the same subject in other countries; but those authors who have found in the incidents of landed property in India the whole system of the west, to the extent of applying the technical terms of the feudal law indiscriminately to both, appear to me to have made the same approach to correct investigation as the poet, who, in a happy simile, has discovered a fanciful and unexpected resemblance between things really unlike. I refrain for the present from the proof of this position, because I think it will abundantly unfold itself in the course of the investigation. An elaborate comparison of these two systems would lead to discussions of great length, and perhaps of little importance; and I am neither qualified nor disposed to enter the lists with those *learned men* who have investigated the origin of the feodal institutions; who are not agreed whether feod be a stipendiary property *, or simply glebe or land; whether the system of allotting landed property, in the descending scale of military subordination, as a payment for military service, was imported from the woods of Germany by a people among whom no landed property had previously † existed; or whether the highest of authorities ‡ has solved the difficulty, by making the feofs of the German chiefs to consist in arms, horses, dinners, or other valuable things, according to which explanation every government on earth is feodal.

These diversities of doctrine seem to shew, that a fixed object of comparison will not easily be discovered in the feodal system; but in the investigation of the state of landed property in India, I object to the employment of feodal terms, because they beg the question, by implying a chain of facts which, at least, remain to he proved: and I shall avoid the comparison altogether, because I should only expect to be led by it to the discovery, not of what that property is, but of what it is like: a mode of reasoning which has, perhaps, been the source of most of the errors on this subject which have hitherto been promulgated.

The explanation of the origin of landed property which is delivered by Menu § is not exceeded in correctness by any of the

* Blackstone, Vol. II. c. 4. and the authorities there quoted.

† Tacitus de Mor Germ. c. 26. Cæsar de bello Gall. b. vi. c. 21.

‡ Spirit of Laws, b. xxx. c. 3.

§ Menu, c. 9. v. 44. This is the allodial property of the west, or what may not inaptly be termed property *without tenure*.

writers * of the west. "Cultivated land is the property of him who cut away the wood, or who first cleared and tilled it;" and the exact coincidence of this doctrine with that of the early Mohammedans is worthy of particular remark. "Whosoever † cultivates waste lands does thereby acquire the property of them; a Zimmee (infidel) becomes proprietor of them in the same manner as a Mussulman." The general idea of property, delivered by the Roman lawyers ‡, and adopted into all the codes of Europe, is that of simple, uniform, and *absolute* dominion; but it is manifest that the notion of absolute dominion is to be understood with considerable limitations. The idea of *absolute* dominion over any thing which we possess, is altogether incompatible with the existence of society, which necessarily renders all our possessions *conditional:* property, whether moveable or immoveable, even the disposal of our time, and of our personal labour, the most valuable of our property, and the most unquestionably our own, are all of them liable to the conditions and restrictions prescribed by the community to which we belong, or by the person or persons representing or governing that community. At the very period when Justinian was employed in the compilation of the laws to which we have adverted, many of these persons described as possessing immoveable property in absolute dominion were compelled to relinquish § their lands, because they were insufficient to satisfy the

* Blackstone, Vol. II. c. 1, and the authorities there quoted, together with the civilians quoted by Gibbon, c. 44, and Ayliffe passim.

† An oral authority of Mohammed, quoted in the Hedaya.

‡ Gibbon, chap. 44. Ayliffe passim.

§ Procopius, quoted by Gibbon in chap. 40. There is reason to suspect exaggeration in the statement of Procopius in all that could convey a satire on Justinian; but the fact, though highly coloured, is still entitled to credit.

demands of the treasury. The government must not only have absorbed the share of the produce belonging to the proprietor, but the profit derivable by a tenant before the proprietors could have been driven to relinquish their lands. This case of extreme oppression more than extinguished the property: but if we deny the existence of property merely because it is subject to contributions for the service of the state, we shall search in vain for its existence in any age or nation. In England a proprietor of land who farms it out to another, is generally supposed to receive as rent a value equal to about one-third of the gross produce; this proportion will vary in different countries according to circumstances; but whatever it may be, the portion of it which remains, after the payment of the demands of the public, may safely be described as the proprietor's share of the produce of his own land: that which remains to him, after defraying all public taxes, and all charges of management. Wherever we can find this share, and the person entitled to receive it, him we may, without the risk of error, consider as the proprietor; and if this right has descended to him by fixed rules from his ancestors, as the hereditary proprietor. Property may be limited by many other conditions; but "dominion so far absolute as to exclude all claims, excepting those of the community which protects it," conveys a general idea of the most perfect kind of property that is consistent with the restrictions incident to a regulated society: always supposing, in the case of land, the existence of the proprietor's share which has been described. There is perhaps no single criterion by which the existence of such share is so distinctly ascertained as by the fact of land being saleable. When unoccupied land is abundant (as it is in most parts of India), and all lands are

CHAP. V.

taxed in proportion to their value, we do not hear of men purchasing the privilege to become tenants; to obtain that which is open to all, and even courts the acceptance of all: men do not give a valuable consideration for a thing of no value; the fact of purchase shews that there is something to sell, that there is a proprietor's share. If the demands of the government become so heavy as to leave no such share, the sovereign may then be named the proprietor, or the usurper, or any other more imposing or more gentle term which eastern courtesy shall invent: it is plain that the former proprietor is reduced to the condition of a tenant; he may cling for a time to the possession of his fathers, and this attachment may survive the existence of that which created it; but he is in effect no longer a proprietor of land, it is no longer saleable; there is no proprietor's share, the value and the property have ceased together; and there is no longer a question about exclusive dominion, because no person will contend for that to which no value is attached.

Before dismissing this branch of the subject, it is worthy of remark, that according to the Roman lawyers * the power of

* Adams's Antiquities, p. 56. Ayliffe, p. 282. It is true that the Roman lawyers sometimes consider usufruct as "*a species of dominion or property* (Ayliffe, p. 315.) Dominium, according to this explanation, is to be considered as a *totum*, or *genus*, containing under it as two *species*, a *nude* property, and an usufruct; the *plenum dominium* being the union of both these species of property. But this mode of considering *usufruct* seems to be scarcely compatible with the broad distinction constantly preserved between *it* and *property* by themselves, and is liable to the serious objection of unnecessarily employing the same word (viz. property) to signify two distinct and different things, than which nothing can be more fatal to precision in expressing our thoughts. Thus in the very explanation of this fanciful genus and species, "a nude property (say they) is one thing, and a plenum dominium is another; for a nude property is when the proprietor has the property of a thing the usufruct being in another, and thus *usufruct is distinct and separate from the*

alienating land was the criterion of property; possession without such power being described as merely the usufruct. The inference appears to be irresistible, that the fact of land being saleable ascertains the existence of property, and that the right to sell identifies the proprietor. The reader is requested to bear in mind the definition which has been offered of property, and of the circumstances which ascertain its existence or extinction in the case of land; because, without aspiring to deliver abstract definitions not liable to objection, these are the meanings which will be uniformly attached to the term whenever it shall be found in the course of this discussion. It is hoped that these preliminary explanations will enable us to enter with some advantage into the nature of landed property in India.

The earliest opinions on this subject received by the western world may chiefly, if not wholly, be traced to the narratives of those persons who accompanied the expedition of Alexander, and of the embassy of Megasthenes, who shortly afterwards penetrated still farther into India as the ambassador of Seleucus; the substance of their information, as well as of all that had been

property of a thing." (Ayliffe, p. 315.) It is probably this application of the same term to dissimilar things which has given rise to the indistinct notions to be found on the records of Madras of two properties in one thing. Nothing can be more simple and intelligible than the explanation of usufruct given by the Roman lawyers, without reference to this confusion of two things declared to be distinct and separate, viz. "the right of using the profits arising from *a thing belonging to another person*, without any prejudice or diminution to the substance or property thereof." (Ayliffe, p. 313.) I accordingly adhere to this definition of usufruct, in the persuasion that no confusion of ideas can possibly arise from distinguishing in all cases whatever, between the right to the substance of a thing, and the right to its temporary use, or from always employing different words to express these very different things.

obtained in the intermediate periods, has been collected in the works of Diodorus, a native of Sicily, who flourished at Rome about 44 years before the christian æra, and of Strabo, an Asiatic Greek, who lived in the subsequent century: both of them authors of deserved celebrity, who are said to have visited most of the countries which they described, with the exception, however, of India, as is evident from their works. Strabo complains that the modern voyagers whom he had consulted, who sailed from the Red Sea to India (some few of them even to the Ganges), were so rude and ignorant as to be incapable of making or communicating useful observations. The companions of Alexander are stated by the same author to have given different and opposite accounts of what they had seen; "and if (adds he) they differ thus regarding what they saw, what opinion shall we form of what they only heard?" The means of communication which were possessed by the philosophers who accompanied Alexander are happily described in the quaint but acute answer of Mandanis the sophist, to Onesicritus, when sent by the conqueror to be instructed in the philosophy of India: "I may well be excused (said Mandanis), if conversing with you through the medium of *three* interpreters, ignorant of every language but that of the vulgar, I should find it impossible to unfold the principles of our philosophy. To form such an expectation would be as unreasonable as to demand that I should transmit water in a limpid state through a medium of mud." The imposing reputation of antiquity has, however, given great weight to the information derived from these sources. It seems to have been scarcely noticed, that Strabo, on the authority of Nearchus, assures us *, that the

* Strabo, book 15.

husbandman of India carried home just as much of his crop as was sufficient for the subsistence of the year, and burned *all the rest*, in order that he might have an incentive to labour in the succeding year; that Diodorus affirms famine to be unknown in India; that Arrian and Strabo affirm slavery, which is universal in every part of India, to have no existence there *; and, finally, that Strabo himself stigmatizes as retailers of fables Nearchus, Onesicritus, and Megasthenes, whom in other places he cites as his authorities: while Diodorus and Strabo are carefully quoted to shew that the whole † property of the soil was vested in the king, who received as proprietor a fourth part of the produce. With the aid of more direct and perfect modes of interpreting the pompous phraseology of the east, which styles its monarchs the lords, and its priests the gods of the earth, the inference of these authors, whether strictly correct or otherwise, was very fairly deducible from the translations which they would probably receive of these terms; and a stranger who should receive from an English lawyer an explanation of the king's fictitious rights under the feudal system, without enquiry into the substantial fact, would probably receive a similar impression regarding the property of land in England ‡. It will be seen hereafter, that in conformity

* Vincent's Nearchus, Prel. Dis. page 15.: ibid. p. 57.

† Diodorus, book ii. Strabo, book xv.—In this, however, they are not consistent with each other, for Strabo affirms that the cultivators pay a fourth of the produce *as rent*, while Diodorus states that they pay a fourth of the produce *besides the rent*.

‡ The reader who has not perused the observations of Algernon Sydney on this subject (chap. 3. sect. 29), will be amused and instructed by referring to them, and to the doctrines of his opponents, very similar indeed to the doctrines now held regarding landed property of India; and he will naturally be led to conjecture

to what is stated by Strabo and Diodorus, the king was really entitled to exact one-fourth of the crop in times of public distress. The voyagers * and travellers of later times, without any exception, that has fallen within the scope of my limited reading, and the authors (when they have condescended to notice temporal affairs) of that very strange collection the "Lettres Edifiantes," have all echoed the same doctrine: and † the European travellers who visited the court of Aurungzebe in the latter part of the 17th century are unanimous in denying the existence of private landed property in India. The whole of Asia, indeed, seems to be condemned to the same interdict: and a late ‡ author broadly pronounces that in Syria there is no property, real or personal; an assertion which he might at any time have discovered to be erroneous, by the purchase of a farthing's-worth of greens in the bazar. It is thus that men of genius confound the real with the imaginary consequences of despotism; and because there is no efficient and equal protection for property, conclude at once on its absolute extinction.

When the English government became the sovereign of a vast territory in India, the question of landed property was investigated with warmth, and two opposite parties arose, respectively affirming the right of the sovereign and of the Zemindar, to the property of the soil. The reasonings on this subject were not

what the practical doctrines regarding the property of land in England might have been at this day, if such men as Algernon Sydney had not dared and died for the benefit of posterity.

* I have not been able to procure the work of Cosmas Indicopleustes, who wrote in the age of Justinian.

† Bernier, Thevenot, Chardin, Tavernier, and I believe Manouchi.

‡ Volney, vol. ii. p. 402. I quote the page from Patton.

only recorded on the official proceedings of the company's government, but were submitted to the judgment of the public by men of respectability and talent, personally conversant with the department of Indian revenue: and a decision on the whole case has been pronounced by the high authority of a lawyer, a statesman, and a minister; and generally confirmed in an anonymous work * of merit on the husbandry of Bengal, attributed to an author of still greater authority on subjects of this nature. As this decision appears at present to govern the public opinion, I shall quote it at length.

† " On the subject of the rights of Zemindars the reasonings continued for years in extremes. On one hand it was asserted that the Zemindar had been merely an officer or collector of revenue; on the other, that he had been a feudatory prince of the empire. It has required the most laborious investigation to discover the fact, viz. that the Mogul was the lord superior or proprietor (terms ‡ equivalent in their meaning) of the soil; that the Zemindars were officers of revenue, justice and police in their districts, where they also commanded a kind of irregular body of militia; that this office was frequently hereditary, but not necessarily so; that on the failure of payment of the rents, or of fulfilling the other duties of his office, he could be suspended or removed from his situation at the pleasure of the prince; that the rents to be paid to him were not fixed, but assessed, at the will of

* Husbandry of Bengal, p. 68. † Plans for British India, p. 470.

‡ This is a notable instance of the employment of feodal terms, which, with due submission, appear to me to be rendered *equivalent* by confounding fiction with substantial fact: and at all events cannot, without begging the whole question, be so applied in India.

the sovereign: and that the Ryot or cultivator of the soil, though attached to his possession, and with the right to cultivate it, yet was subjected to payments, varying according to particular agreements and local customs; that, in general, he continued on the spot on which his labours were directed to raise the means for his own subsistence, but that the proportion to be paid to the state was to be judged of by the Zemindar; that the rights of the Ryot had been gradually abridged, and the proportions he paid increased, during the successive revolutions through which his country had to pass before and after the fall of the Mogul empire."

I shall close this formidable list of authorities in favour of the proprietory right of the sovereign, with a reference to a *Digest of Hindoo Law* *. The ingenious author Jagganatha †, with a courtesy and consideration for opinions established by authority which is peculiar to the natives of India, has, in his Commentary, pronounced the earth to be the "protective property of powerful conquerors, and not of subjects cultivating the soil:" they are, however, admitted to acquire an *annual property*, on payment of annual revenue, until a greater revenue be offered by another person! The general object of a commentary is supposed to be the elucidation of the text; and as a curious and in-

* London Edition, vol. i. p. 460.

† I am aware that some other commentators have maintained the same doctrine before Jagganatha, influenced, without doubt, by the same courtesy; but they have produced no text that any man of plain understanding would acknowledge as authority. Jagganatha, as will presently be seen, combats the opinion of *a large class of commentators*, who affirm the *husbandman* to be the proprietor. It will be seen hereafter that the word Cshetra-Carta, translated husbandman, is literally *landlord*.

structive example of inference, the reader is here presented with the text from which this conclusion is drawn.

"Thrice seven times exterminating the military tribe, *Parasu Rama* gave the earth to *Casyapa* as a gratuity for the sacrifice of a horse." I feel it necessary to assure the reader that this is a serious quotation of the whole text: to which is prefixed a short introduction by the commentator, intimating, not inelegantly, if fable alone were intended, that "this earth, created by God, became the wife of *Prithu* (the Cecrops of India, who first invented agriculture), and by *marriage* and otherwise became the property of several princes." The learned and highly enlightened translator of this work truly informs us, "that* much of the commentary might have been omitted without injury to the context," but that he undertook a verbal translation as a public duty, and could take no freedoms with either: a restriction which probably many readers will regret, when apprized on the same respectable authority that the work is intended to serve "as† a standard for the administration of justice among the Hindoo subjects of Great Britain."

I have endeavoured to marshal, without any disguise, the mighty phalanx of opinion which is concentrated against me, and I shall now proceed to examine the authorities which have led me to a different conclusion.

Every Indian village is, and appears always to have been, in fact, a separate community or republic; and exhibits a living picture of that state of things which theorists have imagined in the earlier stages of civilization, when men have assembled

* Preface, p. 24. † Preface, p. 25. London Edition.

in communities for the purpose of reciprocally administering to each other's wants: 1. the Goud, Potail, Muccuddim, or Mundil (as he is named in different languages), is the judge and magistrate; 2. the Curnum, Shanboag, or Putwaree, is the register; 3. the Taliary or Sthulwar, and, 4. the Totie, are severally the watchmen of the village and of the crops: 5. the Neerguntee distributes the water of the streams or reservoirs in just proportion to the several fields; 6. the Jotishee, or Joshee, or astrologer, performs the essential service of announcing the seasons of seed time and harvest, and the imaginary benefit of unfolding the lucky or unlucky days and hours for all the operations of farming: 7. the smith, and 8. carpenter, frame the rude instruments of husbandry, and the ruder dwelling of the farmer; 9. the potter fabricates the only utensils of the village; 10. the washerman keeps clean the few garments which are spun, and sometimes woven, in the family of the farmer, or purchased at the nearest market; 11. the barber contributes to the cleanliness, and assists in the toilet of the villagers; 12. the silversmith *, marking the approach of luxury, manufactures the simple ornaments with which they delight to bedeck their wives and their daughters: and these twelve officers (Barra bullowuttee, or Ayangadee), or requisite members of the community, receive the compensation of their labour, either in allotments of land from the corporate stock, or in fees, consisting of fixed proportions of the crop of every farmer in the village. In some instances the lands of a village are cultivated in common, and the crop divided in

* In some parts of the country the silversmith is not found included in the enumeration of twelve, his place being occupied by the *poet*, a less expensive member of the community, who frequently fills also the office of schoolmaster.

the proportions of the labour contributed, but generally each occupant tills his own field; the waste land is a common pasture for the cattle of the village; its external boundaries are as carefully marked as those of the richest field, and they are maintained as a common right of the village, or rather the *township* (a term which more correctly describes the thing in our contemplation), to the exclusion of others, with as much jealousy and rancour as the frontiers of the most potent kingdoms. Such are the primitive component parts of all the kingdoms of India. Their technical combination to compose districts, provinces, or principalities, of from ten to a hundred thousand villages, has been infinitely diversified at different periods by the wisdom or caprice of the chief ruler, or by the vigour and resistance of those who, in every age, country, and condition, have coveted independence for themselves, and the power to govern the greatest possible number of their fellow creatures. Menu's * arrangement places a lord over one town with its district (which is precisely the township above described); a lord of ten, of twenty, of a hundred, and of a thousand, in a scale of regular subordination, reporting and receiving commands successively from the next in gradation; and fixes with precision the salaries and perquisites of each. His scheme of government recognizes none of those persons who, in these days, are known by the several designations of Wadeyars, Poligars, Zemindars †, Deshayes, &c. (all in

* Chap. 7. p. 115. &c.

† In the work of Tippoo Sultaun, who affected new names for all objects, they are called *Boomeean*, the plural of a Persian word nearly synonymous with Zemindar. He, however, applies it not only to the Indian chief of a district which he is reducing to subjection, but frequently (and with more propriety) to the inhabitants of the district generally; apparently intending to convey the idea of their being the aborigines. *Boom*, country, region, *boomee*, belonging to a region; a person who has never left home.

their respective jurisdictions assuming, when they dare, the title of Raja or king: all the officers enumerated by Menu have, in their several scales, at different periods, simply acted as agents of the sovereign; as farmers of revenue contracting with the sovereign for a certain sum, and levying what they can, as partisans or chiefs of troops, receiving an assignment on revenues managed by another, or the direct management themselves, for the purpose of defraying the pay of the troops. In these several capacities they may have continued obedient to the sovereign who deputed them; they may have obtained from his favour, or from his fears, a remission of a part of the sum to be accounted for; they may have rebelled and usurped the whole government, or have established a small independant principality, or a larger: but with regard to the villages or townships of which the principality is composed, they have appeared but in one character, viz. the government, the sovereign: a person exercising the sovereign authority on his own account, or by delegation on account of another. The interior constitution and condition of each separate township remains unchanged; no revolutions affect it; no conquest reaches it. It is not intended to assert that the village in our contemplation may not have produced the Cæsar of his little world; the rights of the inhabitants may have been invaded by the Potail, by the Poligar ruling over twenty, by the Wadeyar ruling over thirty-three, by the collector over two hundred, or by the sovereign of twenty thousand townships: each or either of these persons may have attempted, or have succeeded, or have failed, in persuading or forcing an augmentation of the proportion of money or of grain paid by the township to the state; but conquests, usurpations, or revolutions, considered as such, have absolutely no influence on its condition. The conqueror, or usurper, directly or through his agents, addresses himself as sovereign or representative of the sovereign to the head of the township; its officers, its boundaries, and the whole frame of its interior management remain unalterably the same *; and it is of importance to remember that every state in India is a congeries of these little republics.

The most ancient and authentic authorities accessible to the English reader are the institutes of Menu translated by Sir W. Jones; and the texts from a great variety of books of sacred law, which are collected and arranged in the digest of Hindoo law already mentioned. The author of that work informs † us in his Commentary, that *Chandeswara and others* explain the word *husbandman* as *owner of the field*, and endeavours to remove the difficulty of reconciling these authorities with his own courtly opinion, already mentioned, by a series of quibbles which I will not attempt to discuss, because I profess myself unable distinctly to comprehend them. This author has not thought proper to quote a text of which he could scarcely be ignorant, viz. "‡ cultivated land is the property of him who cut away the wood, or

* "Every village, with its twelve Ayangadees as they are called, is a kind of little republic, with the Potail at the head of it; and India is a mass of such republics. The inhabitants, during war, look chiefly to their own Potail. They give themselves no trouble about the breaking up and division of kingdoms; while the village remains entire, they care not to what power it is transferred: wherever it goes the internal management remains unaltered; the Potail is still the collector and magistrate, and head farmer. From the age of Menu until this day the settlements have been made either with or through the Potails." Report from Anantpoor, 15th of May, 1806, by my friend Lieutenant-Colonel Munro, to whose excellent reports on revenue I am proud to acknowledge the most extensive obligations.

† Vol. i. p. 463. London Edition. ‡ Menu. c. 9. v. 44.

who first cleared and tilled it;" a passage which distinctly establishes the existence of private property in land in the days of Menu. It may possibly be objected that this passage occurs not in a disquisition concerning land, but for the purpose of illustrating a question of filiation, by comparing the respective claims of the owner of seed, and the owner of the land in which it is sown: but this apparent objection, as I conceive, materially strengthens the authority: we illustrate facts which are obscure, by reference to facts of general notoriety; and it is manifest that this origin of landed property, so consonant to the dictates of reason, and to the general opinion of mankind, must have been familiarly known and acknowledged as a practical rule of society at the period * when the code of Menu was compiled (for it professes to be a compilation), viz. about 880 years before the Christian æra, and 553 before the expedition of Alexander.

The passages *from the Digest itself*, which prove beyond the possibility of cavil the existence of private property in land, crowd upon me in such numbers that I am only at a loss which of them to select; but in order that we may not be disturbed by the claims of the fabulous husband of the earth, in the form of Raja or Zemindar, it may be proper to commence with shewing that the laws of Menu, and of the Digest, with regard to the sale, the gift, the hereditary descent, and other incidents of land, can by no possibility be forced to apply to either Raja or Zemindar, or any other person than the individual occupant and proprietor. †Six formalities for the conveyance of land are enumerated in

* Preface to the Translation. † Vol. ii. p. 161.

the Digest, viz. 1. the assent of townsmen; 2. of kindred; 3. of neighbours; 4. of heirs; 5. the delivery of gold; and 6 of water*: to which six formalities the commentator is pleased to add a seventh, not mentioned in the text, the assent of the king, or the officer of the king residing in the town. I shall, however, be satisfied with his own explanation of this very passage in another place, when he had probably suffered his recollection and his courtesy to be off their guard. "† The assent of townsmen, of heirs, and of kindred, is there required for the publicity of the gift; the assent of neighbours for the sake of preventing disputes concerning the boundaries. Publicity is required that the townsmen and the giver's own kinsmen may be witnesses." The land which is here given or conveyed as private property is a portion, and apparently a small portion, of one of the townships, which we have described; townsmen, neighbours, and kindred, assemble not only on account of the publicity of the gift, but to ascertain *how much* is given. ‡ Menu prescribes the mode of adjusting disputes concerning boundaries, not only between two villages, but between two § fields, and determines that in the latter case the testimony of next neighbours on every side must be considered as the best means of decision. "‖ Let the *owner* of a field inclose it with a hedge. Whatever man *owns* a field,

* The sale of immoveable property cannot be effected without the formalities of donation, vol. iii. p. 432. The delivery of gold and water (which is the usual formality of a gift) is on this account necessary to conveyances of every description.

† Vol. iii. p. 432.

‡ C. 8. v. 243.

§ C. 8. v. 262.—"The bounds of arable fields."—"Should the neighbours say any thing untrue when *two men* dispute about a landmark," &c.

‖ Ibid. v. 239.

if seed conveyed into it should germinate," &c. &c. These are but a few of very many texts which might, if necessary, be adduced to prove a fact no longer to be deemed doubtful; namely, that the land intended is neither a province, nor a kingdom, nor an empire; but simply a field, or an estate, a portion of the lands of a township. This fact will be farther illustrated in treating of the restrictions under which the land was possessed; first with regard to hereditary descent, and secondly with regard to taxes or public contributions, or, in other words, to the claims of the king.

A distinction is made between the * title to land which a man has acquired himself, and that which has descended to him from an ancestor. A man may give or sell at his pleasure what himself has acquired, even though he should leave his family destitute: † "A man's own gift is valid, because he has property which is the established cause of validity, but it is not admitted that the religious purpose is attained," &c. &c. "‡ *Property is equally devested by the voluntary act of the owner in sale as in gift, and it occurs a hundred times in practice;*" but what has descended from an ancestor cannot be alienated without the consent of the heir, or heirs (that is, all the sons equally), who have § a lien equally in the immoveable heritage, whether they be divided or undivided," *i. e.* whether they live under the paternal roof, or have removed to other habitations. "Land, or ‖ other immoveable property, and slaves employed in the cultivation of it, a man shall neither give away nor sell, even though he has acquired them himself, unless he

* Digest, vol. iii. p. 131. † Vol. iii. p. 132.

‡ Vol. iii. p. 452. The words quoted are those of the *Commentator*.

§ Vol. ii. p. 131, text. ‖ Vol. ii. p. 113, text.

convene all his sons." The authorities are not agreed with regard to independent power over what he has acquired himself. "The validity (says Jagganatha) of a gift of land, whether inherited from ancestors, or acquired by the donor himself, being admitted, because the incumbent has ownership, the same would be established in regard even to the whole of a man's state, for the ownership is not different:" and again, "Be it any how in regard to the whole of a man's estate acquired by himself, the gift of what has descended from an ancestor, by a man who has a son living, is void, because he has not independent power over that property *." Such are the commentaries of a man who has pronounced in another place that subjects have no landed property at all: the reader will, however, unquestionably have observed, that we have here not only every requisite character of hereditary landed property, but the actual recognition of † *entailed* landed property as an universal principle of Hindoo law. Without farther waste of time in accumulating the volume of authorities which remain, we pass to the rights of the king.

The author of the Digest ‡ cites an authority for the succession to kingdoms in favour of *one* son, who must be "consecrated to the empire," in opposition to the rule of equal division to all the sons §, *as in the case of private landed property;* but he

* Because the heirs have a lien.

† It is not intended to intimate that landed property is rendered more absolute by entail. He who can sell and devise without restriction has the most absolute property in land. In this case the property is more perfect as it regards the individual; in the case of entail it is more perfect as it regards the family.

‡ Vol. ii. p. 119.

§ The gift of a kingdom is valid, as it is of landed property. Commentary, vol. ii. p. 126.

CHAP. V. affirms the text to relate to the rule in a particular family. The commentator is of opinion that kingdoms may be divided; because they have not been pronounced indivisible by direct sacred authority. It is of little importance to examine the force of this negative argument, because he admits the *king* "may * give *the whole to one*, and that this is in conformity with the practice of former kings." This fact alone, which is of too much notoriety to require illustration, as it regards Rajas and Zemindars † equally would be sufficient, if others were wanting, to prove that the king, although the ‡ "regent of the waters, and the lord of the firmament," and "a powerful divinity who appears in a human shape," never was, in the contemplation of Hindoo law, the proprietor, whose land *must* be divided equally among all the sons. In the former case it *may* be given to one, in the latter it *must* descend in equal shares to all.

The taxes of various kinds which may be levied by the king are detailed by Menu § with great minuteness. Of the produce of land a sixth is the largest share which can be taken in ordinary circumstances, and a ‖ fourth in times of urgent distress; but the whole tenor ¶ of the institutes and the digest shew that the sixth part of the crop is the king's share, which is constantly in the contemplation of all Hindoo lawyers. This share is confirmed

* Vol. ii. p. 118.

† We have already taken occasion to remark that it is the character of all Hindoo institutions to render *offices* as well as property the objects of inheritance. The reader has had the opportunity of understanding the nature and origin of the Zemindars of the south. I am entirely satisfied that those of Bengal were not different, and incidental illustrations of this opinion will be found in the sequel.

‡ Menu, cap. 7. v. 7 and 8. § Cap. 7. v. 127 to 132. ‖ Cap. 10. v. 118.

¶ Cap. 8. v. 304, 308. Digest, vol. ii. p. 168, passim.

by the elegant Hindoo drama of *Sacontala** written,† probably, two centuries after the expedition of Alexander; it is universally recognized in all writings, and of general notoriety among Hindoos of every description: in one word, I have never met with a Hindoo farmer of ordinary capacity that was ignorant of the fact‡; and we shall hereafter find that it was promulgated as the law of the south of India in the sixteenth century.

The public officer who, in a luminous and most able report, has assured us § that "the lands of Canara have for ages been private property, and that the landed property of that province is both more ancient and more perfect than that of England, has stated with equal confidence that || "private property *has never* existed in India, excepting on the Malabar coast." The reasons applying to ancient authorities on which this opinion is founded appear to be, 1st. that if only a sixth were taken as the share of the government, the property would be so perfect that the fine prescribed by Menu for a proprietor neglecting to cultivate his

* Act v.

† I state this from memory. I think this is the æra assigned to it by the learned and accomplished translator. I know that there is reason for placing the age of Calidas considerably later.

‡ I dissent absolutely from the opinion of those who describe the Indian husbandman as destitute of knowledge, observation, and understanding. I have uniformly found them the most observant and intelligent of all the classes with whom I have conversed, and fond of discussing the rationalè of all the operations of their husbandry. To the question whether the broad-cast or the drill husbandry required the greatest proportion of seed, a farmer of Mysoor answered me that he could not state from actual experiment, for that he had never been so slovenly a farmer as to try the broad-cast, as some of his more indolent and poorer neighbours had done, but concluded that a large saving must be made by the drill.

§ Lieutenant-Colonel Munro's Report, dated 9th November, 1800.

|| Ditto, 15th August, 1807.

land would be unnecessary and absurd, and that therefore the sixth was the nominal and not the real share; 2d. that in ancient royal grants of land in Canara and Malabar, the revenue, or king's share, is specified to be the thing given; in other parts of India *the land itself* is given. I am perfectly aware how great an authority I have here to encounter; and the objections which he has urged shall be discussed with every consideration of personal respect and public deference to his eminent talents and extensive knowledge *.

1st. It is necessary to adduce the whole text to which this objection refers.

† "If land be injured by the fault of the farmer himself, *as if he fails to sow it in due time*, he shall be fined ten times as much as the *king's* share *of the crop that might otherwise have been raised;* but only five times as much if it was the fault of his servants without his knowledge."

The owner of the field, who is enjoined six verses before to enclose it, would appear from the translation to be a distinct person from the *farmer* mentioned in this text. The report admits that Ryots, according to Menu, rented their lands to under-tenants; and I will observe in passing, that this very admission necessarily involves the existence of a proprietor's share, and consequently of private property. I notice this distinction, however, of *owner* and *farmer* more on account of a difficulty which will presently be

* My valuable friend Colonel Munro has perused in England the manuscript of this and the succeeding chapter; and I have the satisfaction to know that our difference of opinion is now but slight and unimportant.

† Menu, cap. 8. v. 243.

noticed in comprehending the text, than of any real importance which I ascribe to any interpretation of which it is susceptible.

The words printed in * Italics are the gloss of *Culluca*, a commentator comparatively modern, whose exact æra is unknown; and according to the text (including that gloss), the fine paid to the king for neglecting to sow, is ten times the king's share; or, as the reader will perceive by the most simple calculation, 66$\frac{2}{3}$ per cent. *more than the whole crop* which could have been produced on the field. The text without the gloss merely states that he shall be fined ten times as much as *the share*, without specifying whose or what share, and is absolutely silent with regard to the condition on which the whole objection is founded, namely, that he is fined for "failing to sow it in due time." The naked text, however, merely states, that "if land be injured by the fault of the farmer, he shall pay ten times as much as *the share*:" what this share may be I do not pretend to decide; and will only venture to conclude, that the commentator must necessarily have erred in explaining it to be the *king*'s share: for it is manifestly absurd to have recourse to the monstrous supposition of a tenant's being fined for any neglect whatever, 66$\frac{2}{3}$ per cent. more than the possible gross produce of his farm. However this may be, the naked text of the passage does not justify the assertion that a Ryot is fined for neglecting to sow: but admitting the whole gloss and translation, we proceed to examine whether the fact of being so fined disproves the existence of private property in the land.

The existence of private landed property under the government of Rome, from the earliest periods of its history, will

* Preface to the Institutes, p. 13.

scarcely be questioned; and yet * "Numa Pompilius appointed magistrates over the pagi, or villages, whose business it was to inspect the lands, and to take an account of those which were well or ill cultivated, and the king reprimanded and FINED the slothful, and excited them to cultivate their lands."— The lands in question were not the public domains cultivated by captives, in which case we should not have heard of the mild punishment by fine; but are distinctly stated to have been the allotment of land made to the people by tribes and curiæ as private property. From this apparent reluctance to cultivate, and the punishment which it incurred, I perceive no grounds for denying the existence of private property, but abundant ground to conclude that a proportion of the crop was paid to the king as a branch of public revenue; and this fact we shall afterwards find confirmed. This mode of raising a revenue for the service of the state, would most obviously present itself to all nations in the early stages of civilization: in a small and simple society it is apparently the most equitable rule of public contribution: and some progress must have been made in the study of government before its gross injustice, as a tax on industry, should be ascertained and admitted. When the amount of the sovereign's revenue depends on the amount of the lands which shall be cultivated, he will unquestionably exert all the powers which he possesses to compel the extension of culture; but if his revenue is not to be increased by such extension, his fines and punishments are without an object. We shall probably find no one instance in history, of a government punishing or reprimanding husbandmen for neglecting to cultivate, without finding a revenue raised from a share of the crop; nor any instance of a revenue so raised

* Dionysius Halicarnass. Lib. 2.

without finding the husbandman goaded to extend his cultivation. It is not my intention to affirm, that in the age of Menu, under a government uniformly despotic, the proprietor of the land never suffered oppression. Menu himself decides this question in a remarkable injunction *. "Since the servants of the king, whom he has appointed guardians of districts, are generally knaves, who seize what belongs to other men; from such knaves let him defend his people:" and an author † cited in the Digest classes very quaintly together, as objects of a similar nature, the danger to be apprehended from *fire*, from *robbers*, and from the *king:* but I infer on the ground of the authorities which I have quoted, that the sixth part of the crop was the regulated share payable to the sovereign; and that the property expressly implied by the right to the remaining five-sixths is not invalidated by the existence of a fine for neglecting to cultivate, even if the existence of such a fine had been more clearly made out.

2d. In the royal grants of Canara the revenue is given: in all others *the land itself.*

An examination, more or less close or cursory as the subject attracted my attention, of nearly seventeen hundred grants of land in the Mackenzie collection, enabled me to observe that their forms differ very materially, in various parts of the country: those in the central parts of the peninsula correspond pretty exactly with those found in Hindostan; probably because both countries were subjected to the same conquerors from the north before the Mohammedan invasion, and at periods antecedent to the conquest of the eastern and western tracts. Throughout Drauveda,

* Menu, cap. vii. v. 123.

† Vol. ii. p. 13.

or the eastern country below the Ghauts, now erroneously named the Carnatic, abundance of ancient inscriptions exist, in which revenue is bestowed by the king; and very many, indeed, in which land is bestowed on a temple by the *individual proprietor*. In several remarkable documents, which will hereafter be particularly described, the whole detail is related of the purchase of land at a public auction from a proprietor who is named; and according to the exact injunction of the institutes and digest, of assembling the whole of the township to recognize the validity of the sale, and the amount of the thing sold. I shall be ready to admit that the royal grants in Hindostan and the centre of the southern peninsula confer the land, whenever the advocates of regal proprietary right shall be prepared to concede that they confer the *sky* also, for both are specially given in a hundred instances; to one of which, as being open to public reference, I shall confine my observations. * "I give the earth and the *sky* as long as the sun and the moon shall last:" but the very same grant, in the preceding part of that paragraph, details the things given to be, as I conceive, the rights which the king derives from the village or township described; closing the enumeration with the words, and "*all that has been possessed by the servants of the Raja.*" In a succeeding paragraph the thing given is placed beyond all doubt. "Let all his neighbours, and all who till the land, be obedient to my commands. What you have formerly been accustomed to perform and pay, do it unto him in all things." The thing alienated was the revenue, or the royalties; nothing else could be alienated by the king. In the grant which we have noticed, he alienates the revenues of a township; and I

* Asiatic Researches, vol. i. p. 157.

have never seen an ancient royal grant (which are always for religious purposes), excepting of one or more townships, or of a portion of a township, whose limits on every side are exactly described: in short, of land already in culture, and paying revenue. The Bramin grantee would reject as a meager compliment the gift of waste land, destitute of inhabitants to till it, of which abundance may be procured without obligation: he would accept what we see given in this instrument, the right to a revenue already existing, payable by the inhabitants of a township or part of a township; and indeed, on a close examination of all the possible beginnings of regal proprietary right, we shall find it not only difficult to prove, but equally perplexing distinctly to imagine, the existence of landed property in a king, that had not previously been the landed property of a subject. I shall conclude this branch of the subject with an extract from a Mohammedan law authority, which shall be hereafter quoted at greater length. "Inheritance is annexed to property; and he who has the tribute * from the land has no property in the land: hence it is known that the king has no right to grant the land which pays tribute, but that he may grant the tribute arising from it."

Before proceeding to trace what can yet be discovered of the history of landed property in India from the age of Menu to the present day, in which the invalidity of these two objections will be farther illustrated, it may be useful in a rapid sketch to examine whether any thing exists relative to the condition of the occupants of land, in the early history of other countries, so materially differing from that described in the institutes and the digest, as to justify the conclusions which have been drawn, indi-

* "Omnia tenes Cæsar imperio sed non dominio," say the Roman lawyers.

cating the nature of landed property in India to be distinct from that of all other regions of the earth.

In the most ancient and authentic of all histories, although we find distinct * records of the sale and purchase of the land of individuals in Judea, and of the † partition of the lands of a conquered people as the private property of the victors, I have not been able to trace with any certainty the nature and amount of the contributions which were paid for the service of the state, unless we are to consider the interests of the priesthood and of the sovereign to be united, and a portion of the ‡ tithes in peace, and of the slaves § and cattle taken in war, which was paid to the Levites, as intended to be applied to the public expences of the state ||. The tythe itself is of the exact nature of the Indian contribution; and the inference that this or some separate portion of the crop was payable in kind to the sovereign, appears to be supported by the existence of a special officer for superintending the tribute ¶, and another for " the storehouses in the fields**, in the cities, in the villages, and in the castles;" an enumeration which seems to shew that a portion of the crop was laid up for the sovereign in every field, village, and city.

In Egypt we have the most distinct evidence that one fifth was the land-tax, or the sovereign's share of the crop. †† Pharaoh

* Genesis, chap. xxiii. v. 16 and 17. † Joshua, chap. xix. v. 51.

‡ Leviticus, chap. xxvii. v. 30. § Numbers, chap. xxi. v. 26 to 30.

|| This supposition is strengthened by observing that Mohammed, who borrowed so much from the Jewish institutions, levied a tenth as head of the church, but applied a large portion of it to the services of the state; and it would also seem that this was the portion exacted from Judea after its conquest by the Romans. See Burman. De vectigalibus populi Romani, p. 25 and 26.

¶ 1 Kings, chap. iv. v. 6. ** 1 Chronicles, chap. xxvii. v. 25.

†† Genesis, chap. xlvii. v. 13 to 27.

took up "the fifth part of the land of Egypt in the seven plenteous years." The fifth must consequently have been his established share: and after the supposed purchase by Pharaoh of all the lands and all the people of Egypt, in return for food during the famine, the fifth only was the share which he continued to exact. I hope to be pardoned by biblical critics for the presumption of offering a short observation on this transaction. The learned Blackstone* is of opinion that Pharaoh in this instance, like the feudal sovereigns of later days, acquired the *allodial* rights, and granted back the land as a *beneficium* or *feud:* and the very acute investigator of the principles† of Asiatic monarchies thinks, that by the latter part of the transaction, Joseph had only bound the husbandmen more strongly to the obligation of paying the established tax to the sovereign. If the passage is to be literally interpreted, the people of Egypt were free men and proprietors of the land: by this transaction they divested themselves of their property and became *slaves* to the king. Can any man seriously believe, that so fatal a revolution had taken place in the personal liberty and fixed property of a whole people, and yet that their relation towards the sovereign remained unaltered in all its essential characters? They paid the same taxes as before; and as far as the sacred text informs us, possessed their land virtually on the same conditions as before. Sovereigns do not usually enslave their subjects, and acquire their property, without a more substantial object in view than to restore their liberty and property. The chief difficulty appears to me to be solved, by adverting to the figurative language in which the most fa-

* Com. book 2. chap. 4.

† Patton, p. 29.

miliar, as well as the most important, ideas are conveyed in holy writ, and in all the dialects of the eastern world. "You have purchased me as a slave," is the most common form of speech throughout the peninsula of India at this day, to express permanent gratitude for an important favour: "*You have purchased my house, my family, my lands, my flesh,*" is a form of speech which I have recently heard applied with great warmth, and I believe with perfect sincerity, by a man who meant exactly to say, "I am for ever obliged and devoted to you;" and however strong the expressions may appear in the biblical history of this transaction, all difficulty vanishes if we may be permitted to suppose that Joseph only inculcates, and the people only admit, in figurative language, the important benefits conferred by Pharaoh, and the consequent gratitude due by his subjects. It must however be admitted that the fact of the fifth having been the previous land-tax, as stated by Blackstone, is only inferred from the context, and not positively asserted in the biblical history. At that period the lands of the priests were alone exempted, but in the time of Herodotus and Diodorus the allotments to the military were also free lands: and many other changes had taken place, which forbid any inference being drawn from their works regarding the actual state of more ancient institutions. Egypt was subjugated by the Romans about the time that their own republican government wasfinally extinguished; and we find the emperors retaining the direct management of Egypt as one of their own provinces, and restraining the access of their subjects: the former circumstance indicating a prosperous revenue; and the latter, that there was something to conceal. It is certain, that in the other portions of the Roman empire, one tenth of the crop of corn was the usual tax, and that one fifth was absolutely unknown *in any other province.* A tax is seldom lowered under a despotism, and not very often under any government; and all these circumstances combined give some colour to the hypothesis, that the fifth may have been exacted for the first time under the plea of an expected famine, and that Joseph, like a skilful financier, availed himself of the means which afterwards occurred to perpetuate the tax.

In attempting to trace the state of landed property in Greece, a ground to which I return as a stranger, after a long and unbroken absence, I can discover nothing but the features of splendid fable in many of those institutions which historians and philosophers have held up as sober truths to the admiration of posterity. That the lands of Sparta were equally divided among the citizens, and were free from all public impositions, is the only law of Lycurgus which seems to have a direct relation to the state of landed property in that republic; and it will be necessary, however adventurous the attempt, to offer a few short remarks on the general nature of these institutions, for the purpose of shewing that this representation of the fact is absolutely incredible. The Spartan legislator himself never permitted his laws to be committed to writing: and it cannot be surprising if nothing distinct or certain has descended to posterity regarding that which never had a distinct or fixed existence. Subsequent writers seem to have been chiefly guided by the authority of Xenophon; but whether his treatise on the Lacedemonian Republic (a work which I have only seen in quotation) ought, like the Cyropædia, simply to be considered as an eloquent political romance, is a question which I only venture to suggest on account of the insurmountable contradictions to be found in those authors who appear to have followed its authority.

The state of Sparta had no treasure*; the lands as well as the other property of the Spartans being free from all impositions. One of the means of occasional contribution evinced their extreme poverty; a general fast of all the citizens saved a small sum, which the state conferred on an ally in distress: yet the ingenious and learned author who assures us of this fact, and every where cites his authorities, informs us † that the king or general appeared in the army with great splendour: that the state provided for his maintenance, and that of his household, consisting, besides his usual guard‡, of one hundred select men, of the two pythians or augurs, the polemarchs or principal officers, and three inferior officers who attended on his person (not a very mean staff in those days of simplicity, equality, and poverty). The state, it seems, provided for all these expences, and necessarily for very much more, without taxes, without revenues, and without treasure. §If the land allotted to the king during peace could by any violence of construction be forced to signify the fund provided by the state for the exigencies of war; if the state might be said to have no treasure, although it existed in the hands of their principal officer; and if we should consent to pass, without observation, the express evidence of public revenue in-

* Travels of Anacharsis, vol. iv. p. 157. † Ibid. vol. iv. p. 132.

‡ Herodotus, B. 6. C. 56.

§ The fact of the allotment of land I observe is from Xenophon: the heroes of the Iliad had their separate domains, and so must the kings of Sparta: yet animals, meal, and wine, were sent to them periodically by the state: whence did these supplies come?

volved in the demand of tribute * from *Helos*; and, without comment, the brutal and unmanly conduct of these admired republicans towardsits unhappy citizens, and to the slaves who, in after times, were named *Helots* as a term of ignominy; still it will be altogether impossible to reconcile to the supposed prohibition of money, and equal division of land, a few facts incidentally related by Herodotus, who wrote near a century before Xenophon, and was not composing a political romance. In speaking of a female infant of plain and disagreeable features, he simply narrates that it was a source of great affliction to her parents, who were people of †great affluence in Sparta. A Milesian deposited a large sum of money with a Spartan, exacting an oath for its restitution when demanded: the ‡Spartan, it appears, found that the precious metals were more valuable than the iron currency of Lacedemon in a state of perfect equality; and refused to return it, until he should consult the oracle whether he might avail himself of a quibble of the law to cheat the man who had reposed confidence in him. The king, on a march §, might take for his own use as many sheep as he thought proper. ‖ Notwithstanding the celebrated obligation of dining at the frugal table, to which every citizen subscribed his twelve medimni, private entertainments did exist; and persons were found sufficiently affluent to invite the king to partake of them. ¶ Themistocles paid a visit to Sparta, where he was splendidly entertained; on his departure they gave him the handsomest chariot in Sparta (is it possible that there were handsome chariots in this land of poverty?); and three hundred knights escorted him

* Lempriere in vocem. † Book 6. c. 61. ‡ Ibid. c. 86.
§ Herodotus, book 6. c. 56. ‖ Ibid. c. 57. ¶ Book 8. c. 124.

to the frontier, regarding whose particular quality the annotators seem only to be so far agreed, that none *but those who were wealthy possessed horses* *. The very fact, indeed, which has been so often adduced to illustrate the perfect equality of the citizens of Sparta; namely, that those who had no chariots or horses were entitled to demand the use of these conveniences from such of their neighbours as possessed them; is in itself an incontrovertible proof of open and distinguished inequality. That Lycurgus, like other enthusiasts, may have indulged in the dream of perfect and permanent equality; that, aided by a faction of armed adherents, he † accomplished the forcible plunder of his respectable fellow citizens for the purpose of dividing the spoil among the needy; and even that all this may have been honestly intended, is not absolutely incredible; but those who believe in the reality and the permanence of institutions so evidently contrary to the nature of things, and, as I think, to a fair examination of historical facts, must possess either a grasp of comprehension, or an extent of credulity, which I am altogether unable to reach.

The unsatisfactory result of our enquiries regarding the state of landed property in Sparta is not much relieved by a superior degree of information with respect to Athens. Solon found it necessary by sundry edicts to force ‡ the people to till and cultivate their lands which lay neglected. For the reasons which have formerly been assigned, it is probable that the state received a proportion of the crop; but the fact is not positively confirmed by any thing which I have been able to discover in the subse-

* Beloc, vol. iv. p. 439. † Anacharsis, vol. iv. p. 119.

‡ Beloc's Notes on Herodotus, vol. iv. p. 168.

quent plan of taxation, which, as Athens became a commercial and maritime state, would chiefly depend upon its duties and excise, and latterly upon a sort of property-tax for the construction of ships of war, levied on the possessors of land and other property indiscriminately. We pass to more distinct information in Italy.

Under the Roman empire, through every change of government, a portion of the produce of the lands was paid in kind. The fines imposed by Numa Pompilius for neglecting to cultivate are the earliest evidence of this fact: by subsequent regulations, whoever neglected to till the ground was liable to the animadversion of the censors *; and the imperial † magazines for the reception of a portion of the produce in the various articles of wine or oil, wheat or barley, wood or iron, continued to the latest periods of the empire to be the deposit of this branch of the public taxation.

In the history of a people who rose from the condition of a band of robbers without territory, to be the conquerors of the world, the incidents of landed property must be traced in that branch of the ancient international law of Greece and Italy, by which the vanquished people not only forfeited their territory and personal property, but became the predial or domestic slaves of the conquerors. Under this principle the conquered lands were, of course, disposed of as appeared to be most for the interest of the conquerors. Whilst the territory was very limited, the lands reserved for the state admitted of the same management as the lands of an individual, and would probably be cultivated

* Adam's Antiquities, 533. † Gibbon, chap. 17.

by public slaves: but as the state extended its bounds, this mode would become extravagant or impracticable. The whole conquered territory was sometimes confiscated, as in the case of *Campania*, which was reserved exclusively for the exigencies of the state, and became the great granary * of the city during a considerable period of its history.

Sometimes the conquered people submitted under a sort of capitulation † to pay an aggregate fixed tribute (stipendium or tributum); and others, as in the case of Sicily, were confirmed in their ancient privileges, or were fined in a certain ‡ portion of their land. As the Roman territory farther enlarged, colonies were frequently sent out, as well to provide for distinguished soldiers, as to form a sort of garrison to keep the vanquished in subjection. The conditions of these establishments necessarily varied with circumstances; but the lands allotted to the *coloni* § generally paid as a tax a certain portion of the produce, which never exceeded one tenth || of the crop of grain, and one fifth of the produce of trees. The conquered people were usually ad-

* Pulcherrima populi Romani possessio, subsidium annonæ, horreum belli, sub signo claustrisque reipublicæ positum vectigal.—*Cicero.*

† Inter Siciliam cæterasque provincias hoc interest, quod ceteris aut impositum est vectigal certum, quod stipendiarium dicitur, ut Hispanis et plerisque Pœnorum quasi victoriæ præmium et pœna belli, aut censoria locatio constituta est, ut Asiæ lege Sempronia: Siciliæ civitates sic in amicitiam fidemque recepimus, ut eodem jure essent, quo fuissent, eadem conditione populo Romano parerent qua suis ante paruissent. Cic. 5. Verr.

‡ Burman, p. 8.

§ I use the term *colonus* as I find it uniformly employed by Burman, p. 10, 12, 19, &c. &c. *a proprietor cultivating the lands assigned to him in a new establishment:* the term *coloni conductores* and *partiarii,* apparently *stewards* and *tenants working for a share of the crop,* are sufficiently distinguished by those epithets.

|| Hyginus et Appian, apud Burman, p. 20.

mitted to rent the lands rejected by the *coloni*; and the remainder of the land fit for cultivation, which was left unoccupied (probably by the slain and by the slaves carried off to the old territory, or appropriated by the coloni on the spot) was either rented for a share of the crop, or converted into public pasture (scriptura), which formed a separate branch of revenue. In many cases these lands were sold (redeemable by the state) for a period of one hundred years *; a practice which was supposed to have produced many irregular and corrupt alienations.

The farmers of revenue, generally of the equestrian order, formed a very remarkable corporation, governed by particular laws; and, as far as regarded their influence in the state, may in many respects be compared to the monied interest of England. In the collection of the revenue it must be concluded, that exclusively of the important difference of proprietor and tenant, (which however seems to have been obliterated in Italy when the cities were admitted to the privileges of Roman citizens) a distinction was made between the coloni and common husbandmen (aratores) in the amount of their payments. One material preference consisted in the selection of the best lands. One tenth of the crop was the tax usually exacted from both †; a proportion which is obviously a much heavier tax on poor than on rich land. The farmers of revenue (publicani or socii) divided the business of their department into three branches, corresponding with the three principal heads of Roman revenue; the customs (portorium), the public pastures (scriptura), and the landed

* Hyginus apud Burm. p. 14.

† Burman, p. 23.

revenue; and the very name *decumani* *, by which the persons employed in this latter department were universally distinguished (the two others being called portitores and pecuarii), furnishes abundant evidence that one tenth part was the most common portion † of the crop exacted as a tax. Spain paid one twentieth only of corn, and one tenth of the produce of trees; whether by compact or in consideration of its inferior fertility, does not ‡ seem to be entirely certain. But the distinction between the coloni and aratores, so strongly marked in their first establishment, evidently varied in subsequent periods; and we even find the whole of the pnblic lands of Italy not only confirmed to their actual possessors, as good policy most strongly demanded, but altogether exempted from taxes by the law of the tribune Thorius, so justly reprobated by Cicero. Previously to that period, it seems probable that a distinction existed similar to that of the fixed rent which is noticed by Cicero in his account of the Sicilian revenue, where he attributes to Verres, as an iniquitous innovation, the decree by which he required each farmer to register the number of acres which he annually cultivated; a decree which was obviously no otherwise iniquitous than as it was contrary to the laws of Hiero, the preservation of which constituted the main condition of the compact by which the Sicilians submitted to the

* The term was also applied to those who *paid* a tenth, and the distinction must be determined by the context.

† A tenth is the *traditional* share paid in India, before the institution of the sixth; it is the portion paid in the little principality of Coorg at this day, and the Dutch found and continued that tax in Ceylon.

‡ Burm. p. 26. and 29. and his authorities. Livy, d. l. lib. 43. c. 2. and Cicero.

government of Rome, and these laws exacted not the actual tenth, but a fixed land-tax estimated to be one tenth; thus we find, that some of the cities which had been disfranchised as the punishment of revolt were subject to other conditions *. The publicani, who rented the revenues of a province by public auction at the spear of the censor for a fixed sum (merces), were, in ordinary cases, at perfect liberty to make their own bargains with the husbandmen, subject only to the conditions and restrictions previously promulgated in the tabulæ †, or leges censoriæ, public advertisements of the censor; and the decumani made their annual settlements with the husbandmen for a certain quantity of grain, or of money, *on each acre* ‡ to be cultivated; calculating in the former case the amount of the produce, and agreeing for the estimated tenth, generally at the rate of one medimnus for an acre of good land, which was supposed to produce ten medimni. The coloni, if this explanation be correct, held their lands at a fixed estimate of the probable tenth, and the aratores were subject, like the Ryots of India, to an annual settlement, increasing with the augmentation of their industry. The coloni (or decumani, from whatever cause,) were the proprietors at a fixed land-tax; the aratores were (where the distinction continued) the tenants of lands which were the property of the state, paying in

* Burm. 141. et passim "Qui agros publicos arant, certum est quid ex lege Censoria dare debeant, cur iis quicquam præterea ex alio genere imperavisti." Quid decumani? numquid præter singulas decumas ex lege Hieronica debent. Cic. 7. Verr.

† Burm. p. 133. I do not know whether any of the tabulæ censoriæ have been preserved; they would probably convey a more intimate knowledge of the details of Roman revenue than can be obtained from any other source.

‡ Burm. p. 26.

CHAP. V.

proportion to the quantity of land which was annually tilled. The object of the Agrarian laws, which so much agitated the public mind at different periods of the republic, was not a general division of all the lands, but of those confiscated (publicati) which in Italy were afterwards, by the conflicting meanness and ambition of plebeian and imperial demagogues, not only rendered private property, but with the whole territory of that country exempted from all taxes whatever; leaving to the unfortunate provinces the whole burden of the requisite expenses of the state, and of an institution* which is entitled to hold a more distinguished place than has usually been assigned to it among the causes of the decline of the Roman empire, namely, the gratuitous distribution, first of corn, and afterwards of pork†, bread, and oil, to the licentious and depraved populace of the city. After the impolitic and unjust exemption which has been noticed, the means of making these distributions were necessarily drawn from the provinces; and the idleness and poverty which so high a premium encouraged and ensured, naturally augmented the evil; until, after the lapse of a century and a half from the period of the exemption, Augustus and his successors were obliged to restore the revenues of Italy, through the medium of a complex system of customs, excise, and income-tax; and to revive neglected agriculture by restricting the culture ‡ of the vine.

* This institution is rivalled by the English poor laws alone. To the advocates of this system may be recommended the grave consideration of the humorous answer of a Prætorian prefect to the emperor Aurelian (A. D. 275.) when he was desirous of adding wine to the other gratuitous distributions: "Si et vinum popûlo damus, superest ut et pullos at ânseres demus." Vopisc. c. 47. Burm. p. 53.

† Burman, p. 53.

‡ Italy was covered with pleasure grounds and vineyards, and Domitian, in

The history of the details of revenue under the emperors cannot be easily traced. The canon Frumentarius, which is ascribed to Augustus, seems to have fixed the proportions * of corn and other supplies in kind to be furnished by the several provinces; and the mode in which these proportions and other payments were distributed into *capita* is amply and clearly described by Mr. Gibbon, without enabling us to judge by farther detail whether any material changes were introduced in the later periods of the Roman empire with regard to the proportions of the crop paid by the individual husbandman. It is not credible that the payment of so small a portion as one tenth of the crop could have excited the grievous complaints of oppression which were re-echoed from all the provinces: the right of inspection and interference to ascertain the extent of cultivation which the decumanus unquestionably possessed, involved, under the loose government of the Roman provinces, the power to do more; and the direct interest of the farmer or officer of the revenue to use compulsory means for the extension of culture, is a source of oppression which, exclusively of other exactions †, must every where produce similar effects. The husbandman of Italy or India, whether proprietor or farmer, whether, like the Roman, paying a tenth, or, like the Indian, a sixth, would be incessantly goaded

the early and promising part of his reign, was elegantly complimented as the person,

> Qui castæ Cereri diu negata
> Reddit jugera *sobriasque terras*.

* When these were not sufficient for the supply of the city and the army, the provinces were compelled to *sell* at *rates* fixed by the fiscal officers, which rates, the exemptions allowed to aged persons and men of large families prove to have been considered as oppressive. Burman, p. 42.

† The *cella*, a tax to furnish provisions for the tables of the prætors and proconsuls, would necessarily involve great abuses.

to cultivate, so long as the power and the interest were united which we have described to exist. We find the English husbandman, whether proprietor or farmer, frequently declining to raise corn on his tytheable land: he would be compelled to do this if the person intitled to receive the tythe possessed the power and influence of the decumanus. Fines for neglecting to cultivate can only illustrate the ruinous principle of the tax, without furnishing any conclusive inference for or against the existence of private property in the land.

The barbarous principle of international law, which has been above described, seems to have continued during every period of the Roman history; and a remarkable example occurs under the eastern empire so late as A. D. 536, when the soldiers of Africa, under Solomon the general of Justinian, having married the wives and daughters of the vanquished Vandals, claimed the lands also which formerly belonged to their new spouses, and mutinied to obtain them. Solomon replied, "that he did not refuse slaves and moveables as spoils to the soldier; but the lands he alleged to belong to the emperor and the state which fed them, and gave them the quality of soldiers; not to conquer for themselves the lands taken by barbarians from the empire, but to recover them for the treasury from which they were paid *."

It may hence be fairly risked, as an apology for the errors of those ancient † authors who affirm all land in India to be the property of the state, that they came to the consideration of the subject with minds familiarized and predisposed to the doctrine,

* Procopius, lib. 2. chap. 10.

† It is quite unnecessary to quote examples in Greece; the history of the Helots is all sufficient.

and only found in the supposed institutions of that country an extension of the principle long established in their own. A conjecture may be supported by some traditionary traces, that it was an ancient practice of India to reduce the vanquished to the condition of slaves, and to confiscate their lands; but without discussing the wild chronology of that country, we have abundant evidence that the principle, as well as the practice, if they ever did exist, had ceased many centuries before the expedition of Alexander; that private property in land was then distinctly recognized by law, and that the conqueror was enjoined to respect and maintain the rights and customs of the vanquished. In other respects we find the ancient principle of taxation, namely the payment of a portion of the crop, to have been the same in every country upon earth; and we may now proceed to examine the few faint traces of its history which exist in India from that period to the present day.

Hindoo conquerors are enjoined * to confirm the established laws and customs of the conquered nation; but they are too good casuists not to discover that any additional tax †, however recently imposed by the former sovereign, is, relatively to the period of conquest, an established thing; and consequently to be confirmed. The more northern barbarians, under the designation of Huns ‡, Toorks, Afghans, or Patans, who followed in the same

* Menu, chap. 7. v. 203.

† The Shasters, however, commend as a meritorious act the reduction to one sixth of the taxes of a conquered country which may have been higher.

‡ Toork is the name by which a Mussulman is known in all the vernacular dialects of the south of India at this time. Hun or Hoon is a term chiefly confined to inscriptions and books. The white Huns of Bochara had extended their con-

career, were in this single respect certainly more unmerciful than their Hindoo predecessors. In India, as in Europe, the conquerors and the conquered, successively impelling and impelled, rolled forward, wave after wave, in a southern direction; and whoever will attentively examine the structure and the geography of that portion of India usually called the Southern Peninsula, may infer, a priori, that the countries below the Ghauts, separated by a barrier scarcely penetrable from the central regions, and forbidding approach by a burning climate, always formidable to the natives of the north, will have been the last visited by those invaders, and will have retained a larger portion of their primitive institutions. We shall accordingly find, that in the central regions the existence, and with it the remembrance, of private property in land has been nearly obliterated; while throughout the lower countries it can every where be distinctly proved, and in many places in as perfect a state and as fondly cherished as in any part of Europe. I shall confine my observations on this subject to the tract which, commencing near to Madras in the latitude of about thirteen and a half north, comprises the extent between the sea and the hills from thence to Cape Comorin, and round that promontory, extending north to the latitude of nearly fifteen N. a belt of various breadth, of from sixty to an hundred and sixty miles, and in length near nine hundred English miles.

From the causes which have been noticed, and from circumstances which the limits of this discussion do not permit us to

quests to the Penjab, and probably farther, and were expelled by a king of *Gour* in Bengal. Vide Asiatic Researches, vol. I. p. 136. Europeans are named *Hoons* at this time.

examine, the country known in our maps by the name of Canara * has preserved a larger portion of its ancient institutions and historical records than any other region of India. An early event recorded in poetic numbers may in India well be classed as a traditionary tale; and I only advert to the conquest of this country by one of a dynasty of seventy-seven kings who ruled at Banawassee † about 1450 years before Christ, for the purpose of observing, that according to the tradition, he reduced *Hoobasica*, a *Hullia* ‡ or *Pariar* king, and all his subjects, to a state of slavery, in which their descendants continue to this day. The fact is worthy of note from the ground which it affords for a conjecture which many circumstances will support, that these unhappy outcasts were the aborigines of India; and that the establishment of casts was not the effort of a single mind, but the result of successive expedients for retaining in subjection the conquests of the northern Hindoos; for they, also, are confessedly from the north. Among the various lists of dynasties and kings, real or imaginary, which I have examined in the Mackenzie collection, is one which records the names of the monarchs who successively established the distinctions of the priesthood, the military, the agricultural, and servile classes.

Without further noticing events which have no immediate

* I derive my information on this subject from the able reports above alluded to, from the Mackenzie manuscripts, and from the personal aid in examining them of a most intelligent and learned native of that country named Ramapa.

† Noted by *Ptolemy*, who has a wonderful proportion of the names of places in the south of India, but, as might be supposed, little information regarding their latitudes and longitudes.

‡ The name by which they are known in Canara and in Mysoor at this time.

CHAP. V. relation to our subject, it is only necessary to state, that one sixth of the crop is the share which is said to have been exacted by the government from time immemorial until A. D. 1252, when a nephew of the Pandian *, taking advantage of a civil war, invaded the country in ships, and conquered it. Before his time the sixth had been received in the rough grain; but he imposed on his subjects the task of delivering it deprived of its husks † in a state fit for food, thereby increasing the revenue about ten per cent. which is the estimated expense of this operation. This mode of payment continued until the establishment of a new government at Videyanuggur or Vijeyanuggur, founded by fugitives

* The Pandian race long had their capital at Madura (the Pandionis Mediterraniæ and Madura regia Pandionis of Ptolemy). This invader, from his wonderful success, is fabled to have been attended by an army of demons, *Bootum*, and was thence called *Bootè Pandè Rajà*: he was son of the king's sister, and from that circumstance is said to have established the line of hereditary descent in the conquered country in nephews by the sister's side. The Pandian dynasty must have made conquests on that coast at an early period; for at the æra, whatever it may be, of the "Periplus of the Erythrean sea," *Nelcynda* (Nelisuram), was subjected to that dynasty: *Musiris* to *Ceprobotus*, written by Ptolemy *Cerabothus*, perhaps *Cerun* or *Cherun Puttri* or *Chera Puttri*, *the Progeny of Cherun*, the dynasty which long ruled over Malabar. The *Chaldest* to which, according to Mr. Duncan's paper in the fifth volume of the Asiatic Researches, Malabar was afterwards subject, is no doubt *Chol* or *Chola Desh* (as I since find it was written by Mr. Duncan, the present reading being an error of the press); the latter syllable being a termination signifying country or region; the third of the rival dynasties of the lower south. The remains of an ancient fortress close to the temple of Calliarcoil in the woods of Shevagunga, or the lesser Marawar country, as it is sometimes called, still bear the name of Pandian Kota, *Pandian castle*; and a family claiming a direct descent from the house of Pandian is still said to exist in the neighbouring country.

† The calculation of increase stated in the Shasters is twelve fold; the former rulers of course received as revenue *two measures* for every measure sown. To reduce paddy to rice, it loses exactly one half its bulk; the rate of the Pandian accordingly was one measure of rice for every measure of paddy sown.

from the subverted government of Warangul when the Pandyan dynasty of Canara, having already reached the period of its decline, readily yielded to the rising state in 1336. The minister and spiritual preceptor *Vedyaranya* *, under whose auspices the new dynasty was erected, composed a work on law and government, which is still extant in many hands, and easily procurable: it was intended as a manual for the officers of state; is founded on the text of Parasara, with a copious commentary by Videyaranya, assigning as usual to the king one sixth, as the royal share of the crop, and very rudely pronouncing the king who takes more to be infamous in this world, and consigned to (Nareka) the infernal regions in the next. This share he was desirous of converting from a grain to a money payment, and established fixed rules for the conversion, founded on the quantity of land. the requisite seed, the average increase, and the value of grain. The result literally conforms to the law of the Digest; viz. one sixth to the king, one thirtieth to the bramins, one twentieth to the gods, the rest to the proprietor. It is unnecessary to enter farther into this detail, than to state that thirty is the whole number on which the distribution is made: of which it is calculated that fifteen, or one half, is consumed in the expenses of agriculture, and the maintenance of the farmer's

* *Forest of Science*, a new title; his former name was *Madava Acharee*, and the title of the work to which I particularly allude is *Parasara Madaveeun*, sometimes also called *Videyaranya Smirti.* He also composed another work, sometimes known by the latter title, but generally called *Videyaranya Sungraham*, which treats exclusively of religious duties. The Pundit of the court of Seringapatam informs me that he considers the text of Parasara as the most clear and comprehensive, and the commentary of Videyaranya the most ample and satisfactory, of all the authorities which he possesses.

 family. The distribution of the remaining fifteen stands thus.

To the sovereign one sixth of the gross produce,	5
To the bramins one twentieth,	1½
To the gods one thirtieth,	1
Remains proprietor's share, which is exactly one fourth,	7½
	15

The share payable to the bramins and the gods was received by the sovereign, and by him distributed; so that the sum actually received by the sovereign and by the proprietor were equal. Instead of satisfying himself with leaving things as they were, and taking from this province a smaller revenue on account of its remote situation, as suggested in the report (it is, in fact, not remote compared with many other parts of the dominion), it is evident that Hurryhur Roy called in the aid of the Shasters for the purpose of raising the revenue; and did actually raise it exactly twenty per cent, by his skill in applying that authority to his calculations; the result of the whole detail being that he received one ghetti pagoda for two kauties and a half of land, the same sum only having formerly been paid for three kauties. From 1336 until 1618, when the hereditary governors of the province began to aim at independence, this rate continued unaltered, but soon after this latter period an additional assessment * of fifty per cent. was levied on the whole revenue,

* The rate established by Scopa Naik is still considered to be the highest fixed rate, and by many of the inhabitants of the neighbouring countries to be the original

with some exceptions, in which the usurper was opposed by minor usurpations; but even at this period lands were saleable at ten years purchase, and, in some instances, so high as twenty-five and thirty. The hereditary right to landed property in Canara and Malabar was, and continues to be, indefeasible, even by the longest prescriptive occupancy: the heir may at any distance of time reclaim his patrimony, on paying the expence of such permanent improvements as may have been made in the estate. It is unnecessary to go through the detail of the subsequent assessments on the revenue of this province up to the period of its conquest by Hyder in 1763: they were chiefly in the nature of temporary aids, which the exigencies of the times rendered it necessary to continue from year to year: the public contributions were still comparatively moderate, and the condition of the people comfortable and affluent. "The whole course of Hyder's administration was (in the forcible language of the report already alluded to) nothing but a series of experiments for the purpose of discovering the utmost extent to which the land-rent could be carried, or how much it was possible to extort from the farmer without diminishing cultivation. The increase of assessment of Hyder and Tippoo Sultaun has, in some places, annihilated the old proprietors, and it has everywhere diminished the quantity, but not altered the nature, of the property. If, after paying the Sircar rent, and what is due to himself for his labour, there remain the most trifling surplus, he will almost as soon part with his life as with his estate." A subsequent collector informs

tax. I was led into the latter error, and some others relative to Bednore (which I had not visited) in my report on Mysoor.

us, that under Tippoo's government the proprietors had actually begun to disavow their property; but in the very second year of English management, they claimed as their own, what the year before had been held in the names of their tenants. The demands of the government had, from their excessive amount, in some cases annihilated the property, in others it was on the very verge of extinction: and there can be no question that another century of similar exaction would have extinguished private property in land altogether: and, in conformity to the fact stated by the collector, by being constantly denied, it would soon have been forgotten. The whole system has been revised by the judicious and able hand which has described it: property has been restored by diminishing the exactions of the government, and *leaving a proprietor's share;* and the reporter observes, that "in reforming the revenue system of that province, government has no new rights to private property in land to create; they may augment the value of the property by diminishing the assessment, but the right itself is already as strong as purchase or prescription can make it, and is as well understood as it is in Great Britain." We pass to Malabar.

According to a tradition common to Canara and Malabar, but more anxiously preserved in the latter, the royalties of both countries were formerly vested in the priesthood; but I am disposed to consider the historical conqueror and the fabulous Parasa Rama, who created and gave them to the bramins, as one and the same person. If it might be permitted to risk a conjectural statement of the facts on which these extravagant fables are founded, I should consider Parasa Rama as a mighty conqueror, who, struck with remorse for the injuries which he had inflicted on mankind, endeavoured to expiate his offences by resigning the greater part of his revenues to the priesthood. The * insatiable Bramins thus become possessessed of all that he had the power to bestow, began artfully and incessantly to urge the best possible reasons for new conquests, in order that they might have new grants: and the sovereign, disgusted at their unfeeling rapacity, undertook the conquest of Kerala † and Concan for the express purpose of getting for ever rid of them, prohibiting any Bramin on pain of death from following him into those countries. His new dominions being provided with no separate order of priesthood, Parasa Rama founded the cast of the *Concan ‡ Bramins*, who are to this day disclaimed as such by those of the rest of India. They compose a large portion of the ruling characters in the Mahratta state; and in their various predatory incursions into other countries are stated to seek with avidity for the copies of a work containing § the history of their origin, for the purpose of destroying it: and the eastern Bramins affirm that

* This interpretation of the fable was chiefly suggested to me by the present minister of Mysoor.

† *Kerala*, as already explained, is the ancient name of the western tract below the ghauts, which comprises the modern countries of Travancore, Malabar, and Canara. Concan, the northern extension of the low country, is well known. The fable relates that, perched on the summit of the hills which were then washed by the sea, he begged a new country from the god of the ocean, who caused that element to recede from the breadth to be measured by the flight of the suppliant's arrow. The country, it seems, was not only created, but peopled with savages, whom Parasarama is made to hunt and domesticate for the service of his future priesthood.

‡ According to the fable, he created them by restoring to life the putrid bodies of some men drowned in a river; or, according to more general tradition, of shipwrecked mariners; indicating, apparently, the fact of foreign origin, which their appearance at this day does not much discredit.

§ Whether real or fabulous I do not know.

the orders for this purpose given to their illiterate troops have produced a large and indiscriminate destruction of manuscripts. In the decline of life Parasama was visited by renewed compunctions, and again sought for expiation in a complete surrender of his new kingdom to his new priesthood. Under this hierarchy *the prescribed portion of one-sixth of the produce was allotted for the support of the government. No distinct means appear at present to exist of tracing the †history of this country from this period until the year 970, when a sovereign of the country embraced the Mohammedan faith, and retiring to Mecca, divided his dominions among his officers or subordinate chiefs.

The whole country now distinguished in our maps by the names of Malabar and Travancore was thus subdivided into a number of petty clans, perpetually at war with each other, and paying little or no tax to their respective chieftains, but that of constant military service. The Raja of Travancore was one of these insignificant chiefs, and the ancestor of the Indian hero of Camoens then possessed no inheritance but his sword. With the variations arising from the increase of some little states by the subjugation of others, Malabar was found nearly in the state which has been lightly sketched, when subdued by Hyder. Under that dynasty the efforts of the government were constantly directed to the forcible reduction of these chiefs, and to the introduction of the same system of revenue which prevailed in the

* Asiatic Researches, Vol. V. p. 3.

† The Mackenzie collection is rapidly enlarging in materials for the history of the three ancient dynasties of Cherun, Cholun, and Pandian, which at different periods possessed the greater portion of these countries.

rest of the dominions of Hyder. The northern and more inaccessible parts of Malabar continued to oppose a successful resistance; but the more open southern districts, where armies could act with effect, would (in the opinion of a * member of the board of revenue, who has lately visited the province) "in a few years have paid the whole rent to the Circar; they would have lost their property in the land, and have virtually become farmers like the Rayets in the ceded districts; but Cotiote and the northern districts of Malabar were never thoroughly subdued by the Mysoor government, and it is only now that we are beginning to establish our authority there. The strength of the country has enabled the people to defend their rent and remain landlords. Perhaps the strength of the country along the ghauts is the true cause of the existence of private property in the soil, which the inhabitants of Bednore, Canara, Malabar, and Travancore, not only claim, but have been generally ready to support by force of arms. It would most likely have existed everywhere, but in other parts of India armies of horse could carry into execution the immediate orders of a despot, who never admitted of private property, because his wants incited, and his power enabled, him to draw the whole landlord's rent."

Private property in Malabar and Travancore is distinguished by the emphatical word *Junmum* †, "a term bearing the express signification of *birthright*." The various gradations of mortgage, temporary transfer, and conditional possession (as ‡ described in

* Mr. Thackray's report on a personal inspection of *Malabar*, *Canara*, and the *ceded districts* in 1806-7; a performance of great force, and full of clear views and just thinking.

† Colonel Macaulay's excellent report on the lands of Travancore.

‡ A very satisfactory and clear general account of *Juumum* may be found in

the several official reports from Malabar) which are all requisite before a deed of complete and final sale can be effected, mark a stronger reluctance to alienation, and a more anxious attachment to landed property than can be found in the institutions of any other people ancient or modern: and the high selling price of twenty* years purchase, reckoning on the clear rent or proprietor's share, in a country where the legal interest of money is more than double that of Britain, testifies the undiminished preservation of this sentiment to the present day.

The chief of a clan, whose military excursions seldom carry his followers above a day's march from their homes, has little need of revenue; and the landed property which, in arriving at power, by whatever means, he will not fail to have acquired, furnished in Malabar the principal fund for his requisite disbursements. The Raja of Travancore was one of the most successful of these chiefs in the subjugation of his neighbours. "†The forfeiture of the estates of fugitives from the country, and the assumption of the estates of Rajas or principal Nayrs, who were forcibly dispossessed, transferred into his possession extensive lands, of which he became the immediate proprietor." These circumstances, and the profitable law of confiscation for alleged crimes, have vested in this Raja a large extent of direct‡ landed

Mr. Strachey's report, I think in 1800 (for I state from memory), and in those of Major Walker, and the commissioners, a complete detail of the forms adhered to.

* Adverting to the respective rates of interest, it will be recollected that this is as high as forty years purchase in England.

† Colonel Macaulay's report on Travancore.

‡ The description which is given of private property, royal domains, predial slavery, and light taxes of Travancore applies, with not very important variations, to the principality of Coorg, where the land-tax is about ten per cent.

property or royal domain. From the previous state of anarchy and intestine war, his own old subjects, as well as those of his successive conquests, had paid but slender taxes beyond military service: serious difficulties would accordingly have arisen in levying any considerable tax on the land; and, without the tradition of an ancient institution of that nature, it would perhaps have been impracticable. It will be difficult to discover in the history of any nation, a more absolute and ample dominion than that which is left to the proprietor by the land tax of Travancore, which, in proportion to the fertility of the soil, amounts at the highest to five per cent. of the gross produce, and at the lowest to one half of that estimate; the proprietor's share of the crop, to a person who superintends his own estate, being estimated so high as forty or forty-five per cent. leaving fifty per cent. at the least for the expences of cultivation *, conformably to the estimate of similar husbandry in Canara.

The favourable condition of the landed proprietors is, however, lamentably contrasted, not only by the predial slavery of the lower orders, which is general in the whole of this western tract, and too common in all parts of India; but by the most impolitic † capitation taxes on inferior casts, by heavy duties on particular articles, and by engrossing the produce of the domain

* I omit the calculations on the produce of plantations. The most minute information may be found detailed with clearness and interest in the able report of Colonel Macaulay, from which these statements are derived.

† Anquetil du Perron (Preliminary Discourse to the Zend Avesta) exhibits a grant containing some curious details, *not exactly of capitation,* from *Perumal* to Thomas " Chretien *Paradeshi.*" It seems strange that his interpreters could not explain the latter term, which signifies *a person from a strange country*, and is familiarly and constantly so applied by travelling mendicants in every part of India.

lands, thus merging the features of sovereignty in the more profitable character of farmer, merchant, and monopolist.

In passing to the eastern coast we shall commence with the northern part of the tract which has been described; that being the point at which it first sustained the impure contact of the northern invaders. The territories of the three contemporary dynasties of the Chola, the Chara, and the Pandian, which contended with various success for the northern, the south western (including Malabar), and the south eastern portions of this extensive region, under its general name of Drauveda, met near to Caroor, a town situated about thirty miles west of Trichinopoly, which appears to have passed alternately into the possession of each of the opponents: they were all conquered by Narsing Raja and Crishna Raja of Vijeyanuggur* in the period between † 1490 and 1515. Over the whole extent of this country, as in every other in which the authority of the Shasters was acknowledged, one-sixth was the legitimate share of the crop payable to the sovereign. Before and after the period at which we are arrived, the evidence of private property in land is so abundant, that I will spare the reader the ample detail which might easily be presented to him of public recorded gifts of land from individuals to the temples, and of the constant transfer of lands by sale and mortgage, in spite of all the oppressions which the proprietors had sustained, even after that period when the pestilent doctrine of the sovereign being the actual, instead of the figurative, proprie-

* It was first called *Videya*, and afterwards *Vijeyanuggur*, the city of *science*, then of *victory*. This is ascertained by the grants.

† *Cherun* had long before been absorbed in the dominions of the other two, and chiefly of the Chola.

tor of the soil, began to be promulgated by the British government. The historical documents of the Mackenzie collection are not yet so numerous as to afford the means of following with precision the effect of successive revolutions on the state of property in this part of India. Nearly eighty years after the subversion of the Hindoo government at Vijeyanuggur, seven years after the grant of territory by the descendant of that house reigning at Chandergherry for the erection of the first English fort at Madras *, the dissentions of the Hindoos had brought down two distinct armies from the Mussulman states of Golconda and Vijeyapoor, which respectively possessed themselves of the strong posts of Chanderghery and Vellore in 1646. Having determined by an amicable convention the lines within which they should respectively limit their incursions, so as not to in-

* The English founded an establishment at Armagon, about thirty-six miles north of Puliacate, in 1626; and on receiving on the 1st March, 1639, the grant alluded to in the text, they commenced the fortress on the 1st March, 1640, finally removed to it *from Armagon* on the 24th September, 1641, and finished it in 1643, at the expence of nine thousand two hundred and fifty pagodas, or three thousand five hundred pounds sterling! abandoning altogether the old establishment at Armagon. The grant from Sree Rung Rayeel expressly enjoins, that the town and fort to be erected at Madras shall be called after his own name, *Sree-Runga-Raya-patam;* but the local governor or Naick, *Damerla Vencatadree,* who first invited Mr. Francis Day, the chief of Armagon, to remove to Madras, and engaged to procure the grant of his sovereign, had previously intimated that he would have the new English establishment founded in the name of his father *Chennapa,* and that name having probably been assigned to it before the execution of the royal grant, was not superseded by that superior authority. It is not even distinguished by the name enjoined by the sovereign in any of the public acts of the government; and the name of *Chennapatam* continues to this day to be universally applied to the town of Madras by the natives of *Drawveda:* while in Mysoor, and other countries, it is still distinguished by its ancient name. These incidents illustrate the facility with which places change their names, and the necessity of attending to this source of confusion in all local investigations.

terfere with each other. Meerjumla, the general of Golconda, invaded the lower country about ten years afterwards, and retained a precarious hold on some of the northern districts of Coromandel. In the next year an army from Vijeyapoor, a division of which was commanded by Shahjee, father to Sevajee the founder of the Mahratta empire, extended its conquests as far as Tanjore, and probably farther south, plundering or assessing these countries in several periodical visits, until 1669, when Ginjee fell into their hands, and gave them a more firm possession of the country. This fort was afterwards seized by the wonderful Sevajee, who, encouraged by the establishment of different branches of his own family at Bangalore, and recently at Tanjore, made in the year 1677 his astonishing irruption into the lower country; but the commencement of the first fixed Mohammedan government may be dated about the year 1691, when Zulfecar Khan, the imperial general, entered on a systematic plan for the conquest and fixed occupation of the country, and obtained possession of its last strong hold, Ginjee, in 1698. The whole financial plan of a Mohammedan government exercised over infidels is comprised in the following short extract from their most celebrated law tract *. "*The learned in the law* allege, that the utmost extent of tribute is one half of the actual product, nor is it allowable to exact more: but the taking of a half is no more than strict justice, and is not tyrannical, because

* Hedaya, book 9, chap. 7. I believe, however, that *the learned in the law* did not find their authority in the Koran. The ancient tribute from infidels is certainly one-fifth, or, according to one interpretation, three-tenths. This tract was written in the sixth century of the Hijera, and has undoubtedly been the chief rule of action since that period.

as it is lawful to take the whole of the persons * and property of infidels, and to distribute them among the Mussulmans, it follows that taking half their incomes is lawful *a fortiori*."

We are informed on the authority of the same tract, that one half was the share of the crop which the original Mohammedan *proprietors* received from Mohammedan farmers or tenants cultivating their lands, and defraying the expences of agriculture; and if this fifty per cent. remaining to the farmer or tenant for defraying the charges of agriculture and maintaining his family be taken, as I believe it may, as the most general average † in those parts of India which have been conquered by strangers, it is obvious, and the first Mussulman invaders must have known it, that the owner of land from whom the remaining fifty is exacted is at once reduced to the actual condition of a tenant; and that instead of one half, they were taking the whole income of the ancient *proprietors*. Those who contend for the proprietary right of the sovereign will, at this stage of oppression, certainly find him to possess one half of the produce, as a barbarous remuneration for not having murdered the original proprietor: but I will not insult my countrymen by supposing that an individual can be found among them, who, knowing the nature of the right (if right it may be called), would desire to succeed to it. These Mo-

* The same injunction which inculcates war against infidels as a religious duty, condemns the women and children to *slavery*, and the men to *death*. Sale, Prelim. Disc. p. 191.

† The amount varies according to climate, soil, and facility of irrigation, from about thirty-five per cent, which I believe is the lowest, to fifty-five, and perhaps in some few cases to sixty per cent. There are certain general charges, from ten to eighteen per cent, which are deducted previously to the division, excepting where lands have been allotted to defray them.

hammedan rulers combining, in a character full of extravagant contradiction, the worst extremes of the savage, with some prominent features of civilized man, did not effect at one blow the extinction of the ancient proprietors; these unfortunate persons resisted, in their way, the successive exactions which were imposed, by flying * to the woods, from whence they were recalled by persuasion, by false promises, by hunger, or by force, to renew the culture of their lands: but the plain and undeviating principle of the government was to extort the utmost sum that could be levied, without the certainty of thereby diminishing the revenue of the succeeding year. These polished barbarians, bringing along with them a compound of the system of revenue established by Tooril Mul † under the emperor Acber ‡, and of that introduced

* Some of these scenes have been acted within my own time, and under my personal observation.

† The introduction to the *Asophia Dufter*, or financial register of the Deckan and south, in the Mackenzie collection, which I translated at his request, shews that the system of *Tooril Mul* accompanied the southern conquests of the imperial forces.

‡ Ayeen è Acberi, translated by Mr. Gladwin. It is difficult to discover from this strange and desultory work of Abul Fuzzul the actual intentions of Acber with regard to the character of the government which he meant to establish. In his collection of letters is one of considerable merit and eloquence addressed to the viceroy of Goa, desiring to be furnished with a person capable of unfolding to him the principles of the Christian religion. His adoration of the sun is at direct variance with the fundamental dogmas of the Mohammedan religion; and it would seem, from many insinuations of Abul Fuzzul, and particularly by the sort of Masonic parole and countersign (Alla Acber; Jil e Jollâlehoo), of the *new light* (Jillal u Deen was his name before his accession), that he had determined to be not only the prophet but the *deity* of his new religion. Much has been written of the spirit of wisdom and moderation which breathes through these institutes. Acber certainly was not a Mussulman; but if general exhortations be the criterion of a protecting government, they may be found in the orders or regulations of all the Mohammedan tyrants down to Tippoo Sultaun. I cannot at present refer to the original of the Ayeen è Acberi. Judging from the translation, Abul Fuzzul obtained from the public offices all that was necessary for his purpose, but either had not a sufficient knowledge

by the independent Mohammedan princes of the Deckan, applied the technical language of these systems to the actual state of Arcot; but they found a sort of occupant who had either *been forgotten or purposely passed over* in those systems. *Cawney Atchey*, in Tamul, the vernacular language of the country, is a compound term, each member of which signifies "*independent hereditary property*," according to the genius of the language,

of his subject to compile a clear abstract of the system of Tooril Mul, or, as is more probable, thought proper to misrepresent the facts. In vol. i. p. 285, the third of the produce is clearly stated to be the proportion for which an equivalent is received by the state; and in p. 292, the husbandman has his choice to pay the revenue either in ready money (meaning I presume a fixed rent) or Kunkoot (an estimate of the produce), or Behawvely (the same as Buttai), an actual division of the produce, not in equal divisions, but *according to agreement*, as explained in 305. The increasing, incredible, and contradictory proportions payable from fallow land, amounting in the third and fourth years to four-fifths of the *produce*, in p. 290, may be an error of the press or of the translator's copyist. But it is difficult to comprehend what can be meant by affirming, p. 285, that "what was exacted by Shere Khan exceeded the present produce of the lands." Abul Fuzzul states in one place, that a third of the produce was the highest revenue taken by Acber in any case; and in another, that four-fifths was exacted: but the Edinburgh Review, No. 19, p. 38, cites two authorities, the *Muntükheb ul Bab* and *Shah Navaz Khan*, in his biography of Tooril Mul, to shew that the system of this minister was *an equal division* of the crop between the government and the husbandman, and that this division was called *Buttai*: the name and the thing in this precise sense are well known in the south of India at this day. Both these authorities add, that when the dues of government were taken in money, a fourth of the estimated produce was taken. We are not furnished with the technical term describing this money assessment, but the practice, as far as I can determine, has never travelled to the south in the company of *Buttai*; and I venture to add, that the two facts taken together are, prima facie, incompatible and incredible. It would therefore appear that we have still to learn the truth regarding the system of Tooril Mul. The reign of Acber comprises the period between 1555 and 1600. We know, on the authority of the accurate Ferishta (vol. i. p. 291), that in consequence of a reform of government suggested by a council of the nobles in 1300, the Zemindars were restricted from taking more than the regulated tax of *one half* the produce, and there is neither evidence nor probable ground of conjecture that this tax had been reduced in the intermediate time, between 1300 and the æra of the work of Abul Fuzzul, which is too much a panegyric to be received as an unsuspected authority on any subject.

CHAP. V.

which joins two words of similar import to render the meaning more positive and absolute; or *Cawney* may be taken in its other alleged signification of *land* *, and the compound word, according to that interpretation, will signify *independent hereditary landed property*: there is no third meaning of which the words are susceptible. This word even these unfeeling barbarians translated in their records of revenue by the Arabic word *Meerass, inheritance;* and its possessor by the Persian inflection *Meerassdar, hereditary proprietor* (or possessor of inheritance). The terms Meerass and Meerassdar have since been continued under the British administration, but for the purpose of assimilating every thing to the system of Bengal, where a proprietor, unknown to

* I give this etymology because it is stated on record; but I am assured on the first authority (Mr. Ellis), that Cawny never means *land*, although it often means a certain measure of land. The following is a short abstract of the etymology with which I am favoured by Mr. Ellis. The Tamul root à ì m̀ means to rule, to govern, to possess in permanent authority; whence, by the usual adjunct, is formed the abstract term, à ì c chì, Âtchi, dominion. Canì, in high Tamul, is property generally, but in low Tamul, is in this sense applied to landed property only: the compound therefore signifies literally, *absolute dominion in landed property. Vellalen* is the name of the cast which, throughout the Tamul principalities, were the aboriginal holders of Cániyatchì; and the word is compounded of the superlative or corroborative particle *Vell*, and *âlen* from the root abovementioned: *He who is fixed in dominion.*

I observe in a report from the collector of the Jaghire, dated in 1795, a russoom (custom. Pers.) of the Meerassdar; i. e. a certain share of the gross produce when cultivated by Pyacarees (tenants hereafter to be described) is termed *Càni Seema*, which signifies literally, "property of the country, land, soil, district;" and, by context, proprietor's share or due; which *Cani Mara*, another name for the same thing, literally signifies. But I do not claim a *critical* knowledge of the Tamul or Sanscrit languages, and write this note where I cannot refer to better authority (on the South Atlantic ocean). This share had been reduced by successive exactions so low as two and a half per cent; in some cases even to less than one per cent: among other remaining rights, they still possessed a small *manium* free from all taxes; *tunderwarum*, literally *a warum* (share), *composed of scraps* (Ellis) and other trifling dues. These were the sad remnants of proprietary right.

the history of India, had for some years been created under the modern name of Zemindar; these occupants of *absolute dominion in landed property* were declared to possess merely the "hereditary right of cultivation."

The first discussions of importance on this subject that I have been able to trace on the records of Madras, occurred in the year 1795-6*, when the inhabitants of Trimashy, a village in the district of Poonamalee, firmly refused to accede to the terms demanded by the collector; and that officer, considering the refusal to proceed from a refractory disposition incited by the intrigues of the *dubashes* of Madras (viz. native interpreters and agents to gentlemen in office who were not conversant with the languages of the country), proposed, that "the *Meerassy* inhabitants of that village should be deprived of their *Meerass*, and that it should be transferred to others who are willing to cultivate on the proposed terms." The Board of Revenue opposed, and the Governor in Council supported, the expediency of this measure, and the discussions on the subject were protracted to a voluminous length. The Board of Revenue defended the rights of the occupants under the varied designations of "Meerassy right," "which implies inheritance, property;" "proprietary right;" "Meerassy privileges;" "rights of inheritance in regard to the soil," &c.: but, misled by supposed historical facts, which had not then been sufficiently examined, they unadvisedly admitted a position which had been assumed "as a fundamental † axiom" by the government, viz.

* The Indian year of revenue, which begins in July and embraces portions of two of the Julian calendar, is here adverted to. The English have adopted from the Mohammedans the term *fussilee*, for this description of year, viz. the *year of the seasons*, to distinguish it from the lunar, which confounds all seasons.

† Minutes of Consultation, April 16, 1796.

"that the actual property in the soil is vested in government, who alone have the power of making an absolute sale* of the land;" and their defence of rights and privileges, incompatible with this admission, sunk before the superior talents of their opponent. It is certain, from the known characters of the men, that each party sincerely believed itself to be defending the cause of justice. Facts appear to have been on the side of the Board of Revenue; mental power and logical skill on the side of the government: and in commenting, among other expressions, on the phrase "certain defined rights and privileges of the Meerassdars," they arrive at the following conclusion. "This definition then of the *original* right of a Meerassdar, which has been adopted and defended by the Board of Revenue, involves a contradiction of terms; for it defines it to be an *indefeasible proprietary right* in the cultivation of the soil, the proprietary right of which soil is, a priori, vested in the Circar † alone: and it is further defined to be a definite right under an indefinite system of law, and an independent right dependent upon the will of an arbitrary sovereign." This (it is added) is the abstract state of the question: but if questions of this nature were to be determined by metaphysical abstraction, it might with equal justice be argued, that law is the child of property and not the parent: that property must exist before laws are invented to protect it: that absolute independence being a creature of the imagination, the words "dependent" and "inde-

* They admit, however, the fact of lands having been sold with and without the consent of government; and give to such sale the strange description of "gratuitous recompence for the alienation of arable lands."

† It is necessary to inform the English reader who does not possess any of the glossaries which have been published, that *Circar* here means the government.

pendent," when employed to describe the qualities of property, can in point of fact be considered no otherwise than merely relative terms: and that it is not the abstract right, but the practical protection, which is wanting under an arbitrary sovereign. We have however shewn the existence not only of a definite right, but of a definite law for its protection, which never had been repealed, excepting by the infamous Mohammedan precept of seizing property as a remuneration for sparing life. However this may be, the doctrine defended by the government was decided in the affirmative; viz. that the occupants of land in India "can* establish no more right of inheritance in respect to the soil, than tenantry upon an estate in England can establish a right to the land by hereditary residence;" and the *Meerass* of a villager was defined to be "a preference of cultivation derived from hereditary residence."

This decision necessarily became the rule of conduct to all subordinate boards and officers: and in 1799 we find the board of revenue in a report preparatory to the introduction of the system of Bengal, affirming for the government, and denying to the inhabitants, all property in the soil; and unfolding a slight glance at the difficulties with which they were surrounded in the remarkable phraseology of "proprietary † indefeasible fees of hereditary cultivators."

Early in 1800 orders were issued to the collectors to make the requisite preparatory arrangements for dividing the country into estates, for the purpose of being *sold* to persons to be denominated Zemindars: and some of these officers had the courage

* Consultation January 8th, 1796.

† September 3d, 1799.

CHAP. V.

to plead anew the cause of the actual proprietors. The collector of Dindegul * observes that the sale will be "generally impracticable from the poverty of the people, who were expected to become the purchasers, as well as from the objection these very people would have to purchase a proprietary right in what prescription had already made their own."

"The Nautumcars," a local name for the same description of persons, "certainly consider the farm they cultivate *as their own property*, and no government, save the Mussulman, appears to have considered the soil as its own. In forming the present benevolent system this solitary precedent surely will not operate as an example to act upon; but where no written document is found, what has been known as usage will be established as law; this would confirm the prescriptive right of many industrious natives to the lands they have long occupied, and be the certain means of making them comprehend whence their advantages are derived."

The collectors of Tinevelly †, and of Salem and Coimbetoor, suggested objections of a similar tendency; and the very collector ‡ of the jageer, who had formerly proposed the disfranchisement of the *Meerassdars* of Trimashy, appears to have been now satis-

* Mr. Hurdis, March 1, 1800.

† Mr. Lushington of the former; Major Macleod of the latter. I cannot recover the notes which I made from the able and intelligent report of the former, and I state the fact from memory. Salem was the portion of the latter collectorate to be prepared. It is known that the local institutions of that district and the Baramahal do not materially differ, and had been entirely assimilated by Colonel Read, who, in spite of a speculative tendency which is too often the associate of genius, and the acknowledged error of over-assessing the lands, may be considered as the *founder* of all correct knowledge of revenue in the south, and perhaps of a more correct and detailed knowledge than had previously existed in any part of India.

‡ Mr. Place.

fied "that the *Meerassdar is the actual proprietor*," and the tenant a very distinct person, the *Pyacaree*, who cultivates the land of another on condition of receiving a portion of the produce. "If" says the collector, "he *(the Meerassdar)* had only a right to cultivate, or only a preference in the cultivation, it would be equally to him as to the *Pyacaree* a thing of no real value; whereas the Meerassdar sells, mortgages, gives away, or leaves his lands to his posterity, which the other cannot." "Meerass then," he adds in another place, "is the ultimate and the largest interest that they can covet or have in their lands; and if it bears a construction different from that which I have always given it, and which it has in the *acceptation of the natives themselves*, I can only hope to be excused from having mistaken the rights of government by the beneficial effects of the illusion." Under a government certainly of as much purity as ever directed the affairs of any state, it is truly wonderful that no effect whatever should have been produced by these powerful and eloquent appeals. In this latter report, however, and in several others on the condition of the company's jageer, I recognize the state of things which has already been noticed in Canara: the occupants clung to the property as long as any proprietor's share was left; and at length, strange as it may appear, the *Pyacarees* are stated generally to have received a larger share of the crop in return for their labour than the proprietors who cultivated their own lands. The latter were probably capable of bearing large exactions, rather than desert their patrimony: they discovered the distinction, and began to disavow their *Meerass* or *Canyatchee*, and to enter themselves on the books as *Pyacarees*, who are free to labour where they please. Property, it would seem, had been absorbed in the exactions of the government; and under a continuance of the same order of things, there can be no doubt that the rights which were systematically denied would speedily have been forgotten.

The system however proceeded; the lands were sold* in several districts; and on the first January 1802, laws † and regulations were enacted for protecting the property thus created.

* "The Salem estates originally sold for 19 per cent. on the annual jumma. What kind of an estate is that which sells for 19 per cent. of the land-tax of one year? In England where the rental is 2,000*l.* the land-tax, at four shillings in the pound, is 400*l.* What would be said to a man who sold such an estate for 76*l.* which is 19 per cent. on 400*l.*?"—*Mr. Thackeray's report, already referred to.*

† In order that I may not inadvertently misrepresent this final and solemn decision, the words of the regulations shall be scrupulously quoted.

The proprietary right of the government is affirmed in the following terms.

REGULATION XXXI.

"Whereas the ruling power of the provinces now subject to the government of Fort St. George has, in conformity to the ancient usages of the country, reserved to itself and has exercised the *actual proprietary right of lands of every description,*" &c. &c.

The preamble of Reg. XXV. determines "*to grant to Zemindars* and other landholders, their heirs and successors, a permanent property in their land in all time to come," &c. &c.

And the II. (or first enacting) clause of the same regulation thus proceeds.

"In conformity to these principles an assessment shall be fixed on all lands liable to pay revenue to the government; and in consequence of such assessment the *proprietary right of the soil* shall become vested in the *Zemindars* or other proprietors of land, and in their heirs and lawful successors for ever."

The condition of the *Meerassdars* or *Canyatchikars* (under farmers or Ryots, as they are named) is determined in the following clauses.

REGULATION XXX.

IX. "Where disputes may arise respecting rates of assessment in money or of division in kind, the rates shall be determined according to the rates prevailing in the cultivated lands, in the year preceding the assessment of the permanent jumma on such lands; or where that may not be ascertainable, according to the

Suspicions however arose, and began to acquire strength, that there had been some error in these proceedings; and in 1805-6, Lord William Bentinck, then governor of Madras, on whose mind

rates established for lands of the same description and quality as those respecting which the dispute may arise.

X. Where under farmers or Ryots may refuse to exchange mutual engagements in writing with proprietors or farmers of land, defining the terms on which such under farmers or Ryots are to hold their lands, and may persist in such refusal for the space of one month after the prescribed pottahs may have been offered in presence of witnesses by the proprietors or farmers of land, or may refuse to fulfil those engagements when entered into; such proprietors or farmers of land shall have power to grant the lands of the under farmers or Ryots so refusing to other persons."

The few public officers on the establishment of Fort St. George, who, having the means of examining the question, continue to be the advocates of this system, give to these clauses the distinction of being the *bill of rights* of the Ryots. The modern Arabic term "Ryot," is in these regulations made to be synonimous with "under farmer" or "tenant;" and considering him in that capacity, his rights are respectably protected: but believing, and having, as I think, proved that the *Canyatchikars* are the proprietors of the soil, it is unnecessary to give a name to the act which vests "the proprietary right of that soil" in other persons, and only secures to them the rights incident to the condition of a tenant. An able and respectable member* of the board of revenue in a note on a report of inspection of the southern provinces observes, that "Zemindars, Rajas, Poligars, Jagiredars, are the representatives of the government to whom the collection of the government rent has been transferred, not the absolute property in the land, and right to demand any rent." If this definition be correct, and I object to no one word of it, *rent* alone excepted, it only shews that the government intended to create *hereditary proprietors of the soil,* and have only made *hereditary farmers of revenue:* that a great error has been committed; and that the attributes as well as the ideas of property have been so mistaken, confounded, and dispersed, that it will be a work of no ordinary difficulty to replace them where they ought to be found.

The same gentleman affirms that the *Meerassdars* or *Canyatchikars* have every where "the right to sell or transfer by deed, gift, or otherwise, the land they occupy, subject always to the condition of paying the *standard rent,*" viz. the payment named "assessment" and "revenue," in Reg. xxv. c. II. above quoted; and in other places "permanent assessment," "moderate assessment of public revenue." "That they exercise the right above stated wherever the standard rent (revenue)

* Mr. Hodgson, March 28, 1808.

these suspicions had made a deep impression, prepared and circulated a set of queries for the purpose of obtaining farther information for his guidance in the settlement of those districts not yet alienated; the result of this investigation, afterwards recorded on the proceedings of the government, strengthened the opinions which he had previously formed, and induced his lordship to make a journey to Calcutta for the express purpose of obtaining the sanction of the governor general for suspending the farther operation of the Zemindary system. The answers to these queries, and the spontaneous reports of collectors about this period of time, will enable us to discuss the condition of the remaining provinces which we had proposed to examine.

Passing south to regions somewhat more remote from the first impressions of the northern conquerors, we arrive at Trichinopoly and Tanjore, sometimes united and sometimes separate: the latter principality containing the town of Combaconum, the ancient capital of the *Chola* race, one of the oldest Hindoo dynasties of which any traces have hitherto been discovered in these lower regions, and from which the whole coast * in later times has taken its name. Tanjore in 1675 fell into the hands of Eccojee, the brother of the celebrated founder of the Mahratta

has not been encreased so as to absorb all the profit on cultivation, or arable land, is sufficiently scarce to be of value in the acquisition."

It is satisfactory to observe on the same authority, that evidence of private property "not absorbed" exists at the present time in the sale of land in the following districts besides *Canara* and *Malabar*; viz. *North Arcot, South Arcot, Jageer,* now *Zilla of Chinglepet, Tanjore, Trichinopoly, Dindigul, Madura, Ramnad, Tinnevelly.* Paddy lands and wells (he adds) are transferred by sale in *Coimbetoor,* and wells (i. e. lands in which wells have been sunk for the purposes of irrigation) in *Salem.* Such lands I believe to be saleable even in the Deckan.

* See the note on p. 7.

empire. Throughout all its revolutions this country had remained under a Hindoo* government, with the exception of the very short period that it was possessed by Mohammed Aly; and it is of no material importance to our present purpose to trace the ancient history of its private landed proprietors, since the whole province continues at this day to exhibit every character that constitutes a highly respectable proprietary right. I cannot describe the state of landed property in this part of India more forcibly than by adopting the very words of a late report†. "Without entering on the question of who is proprietor of the soil, I will content myself with stating that immemorial usage has established both in Tanjore and Trichinopoly, that the occupants, whether distinguished by the names of Meerassdar or Mahajanums‡, have the right of selling, bestowing, devising and bequeathing § their lands in the manner which to them is most agreeable. Whether this right was granted originally by

* It was tributary, or at least paid occasional contribution to the Mohammedan state of Vijeyapoor, and at an earlier period to the Hindoo Rajas of Vijeyanuggur.

† Report, 8th September 1805, by Mr. Wallace.

‡ Mahajenum—this is not the appellation usually given by the natives themselves, but a Sanscrit term (Maha *magnus*, Jenam *gens*, persons of consequence) introduced probably by the Mahratta Bramins. *Canyatchikar* is unquestionably the name universally known to the proprietors of Tanjore.—*Ellis.*

§ The bequest when a man dies or becomes an *anchoret* must of course be conformable to the restrictions of the Hindoo law, and can only be requisite in the latter case to announce the fact of devesting the property; in the former, the laws determine, and the testator cannot change the rule of succession. Since writing this note, I have observed in the public papers the report of a decision in the supreme court at Calcutta, which affirms the power of bequest by a Hindoo in unequal portions; I have also been assured on good authority, that this power had been denied in the decision of a learned judge of the supreme court at Madras, in conformity to the explanation of the Hindoo law stated in the first part of this note.

the ancient constitution of the country, appears to me not worth considering at the present day. I think it a fortunate circumstance that the right does at present exist, whether it originated in encroachment on the sovereign's right, in a wise and formal abrogation of those rights, or in institutions coeval with the remotest antiquity. It is fortunate that at a moment when we are consulting on the means of establishing the property and welfare of the numerous people of these provinces, we find the lands of the country in the hands of men who feel and understand the full rights and advantages of possession, who have enjoyed them in a degree more or less secure before the British name was known in India, and who, in consequence of them, have rendered populous and fertile the extensive provinces of Tanjore and Trichinopoly *.

The class of proprietors to whom I allude are not to be considered as the actual cultivators of the soil; the far greater mass of them till their lands by the means of hired labourers, or by a class of people termed *Pullers*, who are of the lowest cast, and who may be considered as the slaves of the soil. The landed property of these provinces is divided and subdivided in every possible degree; there are proprietors of four thousand † acres, of four hundred acres, of forty acres, and of one acre.

* I conclude that Trichinopoly is indebted for this advantage to its contiguity to Tanjore—the Mussulman rulers of the former could not, without a revolution involving the loss of the whole revenue, place their husbandmen on a footing materially differing from that of their immediate neighbours.

† The authors of the Zemindary system in Bengal rested much on the expediency of gradations in society. He must be a strenuous disciple of aristocracy who does not recognize in this and the subsequent passages an abundant gradation in property, distinction, privilege, and power.

The occupants and Meerassdars above described are far from being mere nominal proprietors; they have a clear, ample, and unquestioned proprietor's share, amounting, according to the same authority, to the respectable proportion of twenty-seven* per cent. of the gross produce, a larger rent than remained to an English proprietor of land who had tithes and land-tax to pay, even before the establishment of the income-tax. The report of a most respectable committee on the affairs of Tanjore in 1807, gives a very clear detail of the distribution of property over the whole province, which consists of five thousand eight hundred and seventy-three townships: of this number there are one thou-

* One hundred and fifty is the whole produce of a fixed portion of land on which the calculation is made; of which eighteen goes to general charges, and one hundred and thirty-two remains to be divided between the government and the proprietor. The government receives $59\frac{51}{128}$, or forty-five per cent. and the proprietor $72\frac{57}{127}$, or fifty-five per cent: this latter amount is again to be divided between the proprietor and his *Paragoodie*, the same person as the *Pyacaree* of the vicinity of Madras; an independent labourer, who receives a fixed share of the produce, and out of it defrays the expenses of cultivation his share of the above seventy-two is thirty-eight, and the proprietor's thirty-four, the former being twenty-eight per cent. and the latter twenty-seven per cent. upon the whole sum to be divided, viz. one hundred and thirty-two. The difference is remarkable (as it necessarily must from the facility of culture) between the expenses of cultivation and maintenance of the farmer's family in this province and in Canara, viz. twenty-eight per cent. and fifty per cent; but I am not certain of the exact nature of the eighteen for general charges excluded in the first instance in the above calculation. If the greater portion of this sum should be chargeable as expenses of husbandry, and consequently be added to the farmer's share, he would have near thirty-seven per cent. instead of twenty-eight, which is still a wonderfully small proportion. When Anquetil du Perron informs us that the government of Tanjore exacted from sixty to seventy per cent. the nature of this error is explained by supposing that he had conversed with Paragoodies, who informed him of the share, *which they did not receive*; and he, following the prevalent doctrine that no private property existed in the land, concluded that the whole share not received by the farmer must necessarily go to the government.

CHAP. V.

sand eight hundred and seven townships, in which one individual holds the whole undivided lands: there are two thousand two hundred and two, of which the property in each is held by several persons having their distinct and separate estates: and one thousand seven hundred and seventy-four, the landed property in which is held in common by all the *Meerassdars* or proprietors of the village, who contribute labour and receive a share of the crop in the proportion of their respective properties. The same report states that the number of Merassdars who are Bramins is

computed to be	17,149
Of Soodras, including native Christians,	42,442
Mohammedans,	1,457
	62,048

The fact of the existence of so considerable a number of Mohammedan* proprietors is a curious and conclusive proof of the unrestrained facility of alienating landed property in Tanjore; but I do not observe the rate or number of years purchase at which land is usually sold, to be stated in any of the reports which I have perused.

Passing south to the provinces of Madura and Tinnevelly, portions of the ancient Pandyan region; the collector of the former†, with an able and honest simplicity which is altogether admirable, enumerates among the impediments to the free sale

* They are all Lubbiès (Ellis): the descendants of Mohammedans who emigrated from Arabia during the tyrannical rule of Hijaj bèn Yusuf, in the early part of the eighth century.

† Mr. Parish.

of landed property "the regulations of government declaring the property of the soil to be vested solely in them:" previously to that regulation he intimates that "this was not the case, the inhabitants considering the ground attached to their villages, their own property, and the Circar entitled to receive the tax, should it be brought under cultivation." Land however continues to be sold and mortgaged* in that province, but I cannot extract the number of years purchase from the rates described by the collector, from not being sufficiently acquainted with the local coins and standards of measure which are peculiar to that province.

The report to which I have before adverted, of a respectable member of the Board of Revenue of Madras †, who made a personal inspection of Tinnevelly in 1807, informs us, that *Cawnee Autchee* or Meerass (the thing as well as the word), is familiarly known throughout the province: and discusses with great ability the question of the property in uncultivated land, which he determines to be the right of the Meerassdars of the village, or, in other words, the corporate property of the township, to the exclusion of the claim of the newly invented personage named Zemindar or Mootadar, already introduced into some provinces under the government of Fort St. George. With regard to the

* The same forms of sale, mortgage and redemption, and the very same technical terms, are in use in Tanjore and the southern provinces, as are employed in Malabar. The most important of these technical terms are common to Canara also, and to the rest of the eastern and western low country, over the greater part of the tract which I have proposed to examine. "The terms are all of Tamul origin; the few Sanscrit terms to be found in the reports probably have been adopted by the collectors from conversation with their official servants, many of whom are Mahratta Bramins.—*Ellis.*

† Mr. Hodgson.

CHAP. V.

actual limits of the individual Meerass, "each Meerassdar considers himself proprietor (I here, says the reporter, use the word proprietor in a limited * sense to describe the Meerassee property) of all the land of his Meerass, whether it be cultivated or not." If from misfortune or other circumstances another person cultivates any part of his land, he is entitled to receive a share of the gross produce, amounting to about $18\frac{1}{3}$ per cent. which in that province is called *Swamy bhogum* †, literally, lord's (landlord's) share. On the banks of the never failing Tumbrapurny river, a former Hindoo prince, in the excess of his piety, dispossessed and expatriated the former proprietors, to make way for a colony of northern Bramins, whose posterity, or that of subsequent purchasers, hold these lands on more favourable terms, but to what extent we are not exactly informed. These lands, as well as the others, are every where throughout the province a transferable and saleable property: the lowest commutation for a proprietor's share, as may be observed, being only about one half the value of similar property in Tanjore, and of course when managed by the proprietor himself it is considerably greater. But Madura and Tinnevelly, exclusively of numerous revolutions under the Hindoo government, had been subjected to a scourge which Tanjore had escaped during a tedious tyranny of upwards of sixty years of direct Mohammedan rule; in which it can only be

* Every where I trace the doubts, or reservations, regarding the existence of landed property in the lower countries, to the limitations on *absolute dominion*, although absolute and unlimited dominion over any kind of property is no where on earth to be found.

† This is the term throughout the whole of the lower country to the east. *Bhogum*, in its primitive signification, is *enjoyment*, and by an easy transition signifies right, share.—*Ellis.*

attributed to the plain fact of their never having been completely subdued, that the existence of a landlord's share has survived to the present time.

For the satisfaction of those who may desire to inspect the forms of alienation, an abstract is subjoined * (preserving the verbal translation of what may be considered as the enacting clauses) of two documents from the Mackenzie collection, one of them dated before, and the other after, the conquest of the lower countries by the Rajas of Vijeyanuggur, for the purpose of exhibiting the practice which prevailed in the sale of private landed property north of the Coleroon at those respective periods; and a translation is added of a bill of sale for the alienation of landed property, according to the forms of the present day, to the south of that river. Specimens are not offered of similar instruments in Canara and Malabar, because their existence is notorious and acknowledged.

We have now passed over the tract which I had proposed to trace, and, as I hope, have proved to the satisfaction of every impartial mind the positive and unquestionable existence of private landed property in India. After proving its distinct recognition in the ancient Sasters or sacred laws of the Hindoos, we have clearly deduced its † derivation from that source, and its

* See Appendix, No. 2.

† It may be convenient to recapitulate the grounds of this derivation in Canara. 1st. that such is the tradition; 2d. that the people are Hindoos, and such is the Hindoo law; 3d. that the conversion from a grain to a money rent by Hurryhur Ray is professedly founded on the Hindoo law; and continued until, first, indirectly, by the pressure of a Mohammedan attack, and afterwards, directly, from Mohammedan conquest, the property had nearly become extinguished. It is incumbent on those (if such there be) who may still question this derivation, to shew another, or to refute these facts.

present existence in a perfect form in the provinces of Canara and Malabar, and the principalities of Coorg and Travancore, which had longest evaded the sword of the northern barbarians: we have found it preserved in considerable purity under Hindoo dynasties, and comparatively few revolutions in Tanjore* until the present day: we have traced its existence entire, but its value diminished, in Madura and † Tinnevelly, which had experienced numerous revolutions, and had long groaned under the Mohammedan yoke. In the provinces adjacent and west of Madras, which had sustained the close and immediate gripe of these invaders, we have shewn by ancient documents its immemorial existence in former times, and even at the present day the right, in quality, clear and distinct, but in value approaching to extinction: and we have observed in the latter years of the dynasty of Hyder, the perfect landed property of Canara approaching the same unhappy state in which the proprietor from fear disowned

* Tanjore was under Mohammedan rule (Mohammed Ali) no longer than the period necessary for referring the question to England, and receiving an answer. Short, however, as it was, large strides were made towards the extinction of landed property by the removal of considerable numbers of the ancient proprietors. On the restoration of the country: the exigencies of government, and the distresses of the people, caused the introduction of a new order of persons named Puttuckdars, men of wealth, a sort of middle man or contractor between the proprietors and the government, who by authority, influence, and chicanery, contrived to get possession of a large share of the landed property in their respective Puttuckcams, or, as the Tanjoreans emphatically express it, they swallowed up their neighbours as the large fish swallow the lesser ones. The Puttuckdars were abolished in 1801-2; but the English government has introduced and *threatens* to extend a system essentially the same, substituting for the word *Puttuckdar* the word *Zemindar.—Chiefly from Mr. Ellis.*

† In the report of the Ceylon commissioners I trace a close resemblance to the Hindoo institutions of the continent at the traditionary period when the share of the sovereign was one-tenth of the produce, as it is (or was in 1795) in Ceylon; and private property (Sahaperveny) unquestioned and unquestionable.

his property, and a small interval remained before its very existence would be buried in oblivion. The enquiry has led us over a large portion of the provinces subject to the government of Fort St. George, and a necessity has occurred for touching lightly on its territorial policy. Before this branch of the subject be dismissed, it may be useful to take a rapid glance, imperfect from the nature of my materials, over the provinces subject to Bengal, whence this policy has been received.

It is to be regretted that the long and uninterrupted subjugation of Hindoostan by Mohammedan princes had so far obliterated the best characters of the ancient Hindoo constitution, as to present to the first English observers nothing but Mohammedan institutions and edicts, as the earliest documents which it was necessary to consider. Institutions derived from the best practices of a code which inculcates war against infidels as a religious duty, condemns the women and children of the vanquished to slavery, and the men * to death, and condescends to accept submission and the highest possible tribute as a merciful commutation † for liberty and life, do not seem to be very proper objects of imitation for an English government.

But the examples already presented to the reader, of the circumstances which have accelerated the decay of landed property in the south, afford sufficient ground to conjecture that the

* Sale Prel. Dis. p. 191.

† Tippoo broadly avows this principle in his account of the seizure of 60,000 Christians to be forcibly converted to the Mohammedan religion. Their lives were forfeited: to spare them was mercy, to honour them with Islam a favour. No fault is imputed, excepting their being Christians. *Sultaun u Towareekh.* See also Hedaya, book ix. chap. 7. as quoted in page 56.

same causes may have effected its entire extinction in many parts of Bengal. The political and official relations of the English government were long and generally confined to intercourse with Mohammedan authorities; the few Hindoos of consequence with whom they communicated were either usurpers or official servants, brought up in the trammels of Mohammedan principles and forms, which had long superseded the ancient constitution of the country. Our first impressions and prejudices were received from these impure sources, and the ancient Hindoo law was concealed by an impenetrable veil which has not yet been entirely removed.

The perplexity (and, without meaning disrespect, it is not of small amount) which pervades the official discussions of those great personages who established what is called the permanent settlement of Bengal, seems chiefly to have arisen from viewing the condition of the people through the medium of Mohammedan institutions. Although the royalties of the very ground on which these eminent men conducted this important controversy* were granted by a Mohammedan prince, on the express condition that the English company should purchase the thirty-eight villages of which the grant was composed, from the *owners* † (not the owner), neither of these personages could perceive any claim to the property of the soil, excepting in the sovereign or the Zemindar; and both were agreed in recognizing the rights of

* The object under discussion was whether the demand of government on the land should then be unalterably fixed; or whether government should postpone this measure until they should be better informed? Lord Cornwallis supported the first, and Sir John Shore the second of these propositions.

† I quote from "Patton's Principles of Asiatic Monarchies," p. 147. I have never seen a Persian copy of the grant.

the latter*. It is really curious to observe the inextricable puzzle in which they are reciprocally involved by this admission. Sir John Shore† observes that "it is equally a contradiction in terms to say thatth e property of the soil is vested in the Zemindar, and that we have a right to regulate the terms by which he is to let his lands to the Ryots, as it is to connect that avowal with discretionary and arbitrary claims‡." They had here discovered a proprietor, whom it was found necessary to deprive of the first characteristic of property, the right to manage it in his own way (a ward of chancery, or a proprietor under a statute of lunacy). §Lord Cornwallis had observed that "the numerous prohibitory orders against the levying new taxes, accompanied with threats of fine and imprisonment for the disobedience of them, have proved ineffectual," but nevertheless thinks that the Zemindars must and can in future be restrained. His lordship, however, comforts himself by reflecting, that if they do levy new impositions, the rents will, in the end, thereby be lowered; because, "when the rent becomes so high as to be oppressive and intolerable to the Ryot (what inference does the reader expect?) he must at length desert the land!" the very land, the rents,

* The fate of this opinion is singular. I imagine there is now not one man in England or in India, who conscientiously believes that the person designated by the modern term Zemindar ever was proprietor: I of course mean the Zemindar in the contemplation of these disputants, for, in the modern technical language of Bengal, the word means equally the descendant of the officer who collected the dues of government from the proprietors, and the proprietor himself where he has been permitted to exist.

† Now Lord Teignmouth. Minute, Dec. 21, 1789:

‡ What would the noble lord say to his English tenant who should stigmatize as an arbitrary claim, his lordship's right to get the best rent he can for his land?

§ Minute, February 3, 1790.

taxes, or impositions on which the Zemindar ought to be punished for attempting to raise; and yet in a document selected, strangely enough, as an Appendix to such a minute, *a collector, after giving an account of certain *Baboos* who had obtained by fraud and misrepresentation a grant of some villages, and now, in the expectation of the proprietary right in land being vested in Zemindars, claimed to be considered in that capacity, goes on to state that this property was in the same expectation claimed by the heads of villages as *Malicks*† or *proprietors.* These unfortunate men are described to have arrived at a state nearly resembling that which has already been noticed in Canara and Arcot; they had been compelled to disavow their property, and had placed their villages under the protection of a Zemindar, as being more able to skreen them from the vexatious interference of the provincial officer Hâkim. "These persons (continues the collector) have occasionally disposed of the whole or a part of such villages, and the *purchasers* claim to be *Mâlicks* or *proprietors.* Some of these purchasers of land have sold their land to others, and it is possible that such sales may have been variously multiplied. The *old proprietors* again represent, that the sale was made to answer oppressive exactions, and ought to be declared void." The collector concludes with the following remarkable words; "In truth, gentlemen, these old *Mâlicks* have urged their claims with much anxiety and importunity; they absolutely refused to enter into any engagements but as Mâlicks (proprietors), declaring they would rather lose their lives than ac-

* Of Shawabad, September 29, 1789.

† Arabic, and adopted in Persian. I find these modern terms exclusively used in the whole of these discussions.

quiesce in a relinquishment of their hereditary rights." I have said that the perplexity observable on this controversy is curious; and I will now add that it is astonishing, because the simple recognition of private* property in land, so broadly announced and so unquestionably proved by this contest of the new and the old proprietors, who reciprocally admitted the fact of repeated sale, would have solved every difficulty, and served as a guide through the mighty maze in which these noble personages continued to involve themselves and their readers to the end of the controversy.

In the appendix to a minute by Sir John Shore, the date of which I cannot recover, two very singular documents are exhibited: one, the extract of a report (apparently from the Board of Revenue), which, after conclusively proving that the Zemindar is a mere official servant, states that "the Utlumgha † Sunnud is all sufficient to establish, beyond controversy, that the property of land in these countries is exclusively vested in the crown:" and the other, a Mohammedan law authority which establishes, beyond controversy, that the fact is not so. The distinction has already been noticed between the practice of Mohammedan rulers towards conquered infidels, and a country inhabited by the faithful: and the document which I now sub-

* "I am fully persuaded that we had the same authority for considering many classes of the Ryots proprietors of the soil: and the benefits to be looked for from such a measure far exceed those we can derive from that of declaring the Zemindars and a few Talockdars, the only proprietors"—Grant, as quoted in "British India analyzed," vol. ii. p. 428. I regret that I could not procure a copy of the late Mr. Grant's work, which, as I understand, was printed, but not published; and I still more regret that circumstances have prevented my having access to the valuable collection of manuscripts in the possession of his heir, my friend Major A. Grant, as it is probable that they would have supported the opinion for which I contend.

† The name proving the thing to be of Mohammedan origin.

mit to the reader is a curious and important refutation of the doctrine of European travellers already alluded to, which denies the existence of private property in land, in the Mohammedan countries of the east. It is entitled, Extract from the Mohammedan Law on Landed Property. Verbal translation from the Arabic.

In the book *Khazanatul Rewayah* it is written, *" Tributary land is held in full property by its owner; and so is tithed (or decimated) land: a sale, a gift, or a charitable devise of it is lawful, and it will be inherited like other property. Thus *in the Book Mohodeyah*, in a passage quoted from *Almohit* (a work of the lawyer Mohammed), lands are held in full property by them, they shall inherit those lands, and shall pay the tribute out of

* The word translated *tribute* I suppose to be *Kheraj*, and the decimated land *Asheree*. Abul Fuzzul has an elaborate and, as I think, unsatisfactory discussion regarding the tribute and taxes of Mohammedans in vol. i. of the Ayeen e Acberie. I understand the *Asheree*, or tenth, to be the *Zecat* or *Alms* first levied by *Mohammed*, ostensibly for charitable purposes, and afterwards much modified for political objects by himself, and more by his successors; and *Kheraj* to have been originally the larger tribute, or fifth, exacted from a conquered country (the exaction of one-half being a more modern invention, see p. 164). The former was the distinction of the faithful, and the latter of the infidels, inhabiting one and the same country. Many of the countries now entirely inhabited by Mohammedans submitted on condition of paying the *Kheraj:* which imposition on the infidel has continued to be levied on his Mohammedan successor, although, on embracing the faith, he was strictly entitled to exemption on paying *Zecat;* but as this latter was properly an *apostolical*, and *Kheraj* a *royal* right, the conqueror, who had no claim to direct divine mission, found it more profitable to exercise the rights of royalty. Persia originally paid *Kheraj*, but there are some lands (perhaps occupied at first by the faithful) which continue to pay but a tenth of the produce. While on the subject of Persia I will add, that unless all the intelligent natives of that country with whom I have conversed have, without communication with each other, accidentally united to deceive me, private hereditary property in land now exists, and always has existed, in Persia. The *Asheree* I understand to be the fixed *land-tax* of the Ottoman government at this time.

them;" and in the book *Alkhanujah* it is written, "The sovereign has a right of property in the tribute or rent;" so in the book *Modena Sharhi Baaz* it is written, "A town and the district* annexed to it shall not be sold by the sovereign, if it pay tribute or rent to the crown, nor shall it be given nor inherited, nor shall it belong to the royal domains; for inheritance is annexed to property, and he who has the tribute from the land has no property in the land: hence it is known that *the king† has no right to grant the land which pays tribute, but that he may grant the tribute arising from it.*"

Under the only doctrine which was recognized in this discussion, the proof, and it is abundantly satisfactory, that the land is not the king's, leaves no alternative but to consign it to the Zemindar. The author of "The Principles of Asiatic Monarchies," argues with great force, that the claim of the Zemin-

* The township which we have so often had occasion to notice.

† Sir William Jones, in his preface to the Translation of *Alsirajeyyah*, has the following passages.—"Nothing can be more certain than that *land*, *rents*, and *goods* are, in the language of all Mohammedan lawyers, *property alike* alienable and inheritable;" and again, "The old Hindoos most assuredly were *absolute proprietors of their land*, although they called their sovereigns Lords of the Earth," &c.: the passage is quoted by the anonymous author of a work called *British India analyzed*, who proceeds to express his chagrin, "to find, on Sir W. Jones's authority, that reference to additional Mohammedan authority is yet necessary to decide whether any species of property was compatible with the Koran." Where has the author found the necessity on the authority of Sir William Jones, or on any other authority? And has the Koran in establishing minute and distinct rules for the descent and partition of estates, and the alienation by sale, mortgage, or gift, of moveable and immoveable property, only decided the incidents of a nonentity? The author of the present work may well despair of being heard where the authority of Sir William Jones has been condemned to neglect and oblivion. Sir William, however, had apparently gone no farther than to ascertain that there was a proprietor distinct from the sovereign, and *seems* to have taken the authority of the rulers of the day in supposing this proprietor to be the Zemindar.

dar being limited to one tenth of the sum collected for the king, it is absurd to distinguish as proprietor the person entitled to one tenth, * while the remaining nine tenths are called a duty, a tax, a quit rent. The argument is conclusive: but the ingenious author has not unfolded the whole of the absurdity. Under the utmost limit of exaction recorded in the modern history of India, the sovereign has received one half of the crop. The real share of the crop, which, even under such exaction, would go to this redoutable proprietor, would be one twentieth, or five per cent.; according to the laws of Menu and the other Sasters, his share would be one sixtieth, or one and two-thirds per cent.; and this is the thing which a British government has named *proprietor of the land.* In the controversy to determine whether the sovereign or the Zemindar were the proprietor, each party appears to me to have reciprocally refuted the proposition of his adversary, without establishing his own: they have severally proved that neither the king nor the Zemindar is the proprietor.

At a very early period of the company's government in Bengal, Mr. Verelst, when charged with the collections of the province of Chittagong, looking at the condition of the people, with that sound plain common sense which distinguished his character, and not through the medium of Mohammedan institutions, confirmed the rights which he found the people actually to possess, of transmitting and alienating their landed property by inhe-

* The technical name of this proportion in the Mohammedan Records is Nankar. I do not know the ancient Hindoo term in the north: this I suppose to be modern, and an irregular compound from the Persian word *Nan*, bread, and signifying subsistence, provision, or salary; but I have only seen the word in the *English* records of Bengal; it is not in use in the south.

ritance, mortgage, sale, or gift. *The recognition of that right (in the words of the judge and magistrate of that province in 1801) "has fixed a value on real property here which is not attached to it in other parts of Bengal, and has given existence to a numerous body of land-holders unknown elsewhere," who are afterwards stated to consider themselves, and to be recognized by the court, as "*the actual proprietors of the soil.*" In a subsequent passage we find these remarkable words: "If comfortable habitations and a numerous and healthy progeny be proofs of a happy condition, the Ryots in this province enjoy it in a high degree; and the small estates in this division have contributed to increase population, and to rear a temperate and robust species of man fit for every sort of labour." The opinions received on the same occasion from other provinces are uniform in stating that the condition of the cultivators has been meliorated (slender melioration if they ought to be the proprietors:) by the establishment of courts to which they can apply for redress against great oppressions: but I find nothing from the Zemindaries resembling or approaching the delightful picture which has been drawn of the condition of these *rightful proprietors* confirmed in the possession of their estates.

About the same time that Mr. Verelst confirmed in Chittagong the rights which he found established, Bulwunt Sing, the Zemindar of Benares, then subject to the Vizier of Oude, found the same rights in that province; but instead of confirming, he invaded and usurped them: forcibly subverting the rights of the landholders, he reduced them from the condition of proprietors to that of mere tenants. This usurpation continued until the

* Answers to questions circulated in 1801.

system of considering the Zemindar as the proprietor of the soil had been for some time established, and the courts of the English government had been erected at Benares. The usurpation had not been of sufficient standing to obliterate the knowledge and the remembrance of the ancient proprietary rights; and, after due investigation, the present Zemindar was prevailed on by the British government formally to recognize these rights, and they have accordingly been restored *.

* I am indebted for this fact to verbal information from a gentleman now holding a very high office in India, and officially conversant with the whole history of revenue in Bengal. The restoration occurred during the period that Mr. Duncan, now governor of Bombay, presided over the affairs of that province; and I have also the obliging permission of that gentleman to state that he considers the account here given to be generally correct: but I do not know the exact extent to which Bulwunt Sing had proceeded in his exactions. The present settlement is made with the actual occupants (whether individually or collectively by villages is virtually the same;) and according to the nomenclature of Bengal as applied to Chittagong; we have here the *great* Zemindar of Benares, and a multitude of *small* Zemindars paying ten or twenty rupees of revenue through the medium or on account of the *great* Zemindar, who retains one rupee in ten of the nett collections as his commission. It will scarcely be denied that the Zemindars of Benares and Burdwan, when we first became acquainted with them, were considered to be the same description of persons, and to bear the same relation to the inhabitants of their respective provinces. Yet in one the occupants of the lands have been made proprietors, in the other they are tenants.

I have observed in the Minutes of Sir John Shore an account of two descriptions of Ryots in Bengal, which seem to correspond with the *Canyatchikar* and *Payacaree* of the south; and, I have no doubt, were originally possessed of the same rights, namely, *Khodkasht* and *Paykasht*, modern Persian terms translated from Hindoo appellations, which it would be satisfactory to ascertain. In the copy which I first saw, the words were written without the letter *h* in the last syllable; and I had no conjecture what they were until a few days before I left Madras. I found them on looking over a Persian copy of the local regulation for Benares; which, however, savours more of the general system of Bengal than I had been induced to expect from what is above stated. It is not always safe to interpret technical terms according to their strict grammatical import; and these Persian compounds are too equivocally composed to have any positive import. The following is a verbal

I observe that a similar question was depending before the provincial court in 1801, between the Zemindars and Muckuddums (heads of villages), in * Bhaugulpore; but I am not informed whether any other attempts have been made by the inhabitants of Bengal for the recovery of their ancient rights. The reader will probably be of opinion that enough has been adduced to establish the existence in that country of the same rights, and the traces of a gradation similar to that of the south, by which they have been partially obliterated, or entirely destroyed. Happily, in a large portion of the territory subject to the government of Fort St. George, the question is still open to consideration: the rights which still exist are ripe for confirmation; and those which have been partially or wholly usurped or destroyed may yet be restored. Instead of creating, by the most absurd of all misnomers, a few nominal † proprietors, who, with-

translation of the written explanation procured for me by a judge of the Sudder Adaulet at Madras from one of the muftees of that court.

" *Paykâsht* is a compound word from *pai* and *kasht.* The meaning of *pai* (foot, or footstep) is obvious, and *kasht* is the preterite of the verb *kashten* (to cultivate), that is to say *he travels to another village and cultivates there. Khodkasht* is also a compound from *khod* (himself, his own, &c.), that is to say, *he himself cultivates his own land* :" and I am satisfied with this definition, for if any person should contend that *khodkasht* merely means a person who himself cultivates, *i. e.* with his own hands, he must give up all difference between him and the *Paykasht*, who certainly does the same, and deny the important distinction which is established in that regulation, namely, that the latter may, and the former cannot, be ejected at pleasure from his farm at the expiration of his potta or lease.

For reasons which it would be tedious to discuss, some of the details of management in this province appear to me to be still objectionable.

* It may not, perhaps, be altogether unconnected with the Zemindary system, that the revenues of this province should, in little more than thirty years, have dwindled from rupees 319,911 to rupees 141,255! Answers to Circular Questions in 1801.

† I had the satisfaction to learn, before my departure from Madras, that a disposition prevails in the government to suspend for the present the progress of this

out farther usurpation, can by no possible exertion of power be rendered either more or less than farmers or contractors of revenue*; the British government may still restore property and its concomitant blessings to the great mass of its subjects. In this portion of India its ancient constitution may yet be revived. A company of merchants may confer a more solid benefit than was announced in the splendid proclamation of the Roman consul to the cities of Greece: freedom, in its most rational, safe, and acceptable form, may be proclaimed to the little republics of India, by declaring the fixed and moderate revenue that each shall pay, and leaving the interior distribution to themselves, interfering only on appeal from their own little magistrate, either in matters of revenue, or of landed, or of personal property. Under such a system, varying only from their ancient constitution in substituting for the tax on industry, involved in the exaction of a proportion of the crop, a fixed money payment, which is also

system: and that a suggestion from the Board of Revenue for the formation of a village settlement has been approved and ordered to be carried into execution in the ensuing year in those districts which have escaped the Zemindary system. I had not the opportunity of perusing the details, but have reason to believe that they are well adapted to serve as a sound basis for a better order of things.

* At one time I was disposed to think that, besides the name of contractors of revenue, they might also claim the title of *Lords of the Waste*: but even this right is indisputably shewn by the able report above quoted to be the corporate property of the township. In other countries escheats in land fall to the king, according to the first principles of government, by which that which ceases to be individual property becomes the general property of the community of which it formed a part. According to the genuine principles of Hindoo law it appears to me that, although personal property may, landed property cannot, escheat to the king, but to the township; because all within its limits that is not individual property is the corporate property of the township: to this principle there is, however, an exception. When, as we have seen to be the case in Tanjore, a whole township belongs to an individual, the escheat will fall to the sovereign.

of great antiquity in India; the waste would quickly be covered with luxuriant crops, because every extension of culture would be a clear profit to the proprietor; and without running into the wild fancies of a golden age, the mass of the people would be interested in the permanency of a government which had essentially improved their condition, and, with the religion and laws * of their fathers, had revived their long forgotten proprietary rights. But the British government will only deceive itself, and harass the people, in the vain attempt to improve their condition by mere theories and innovations, while they continue to exact the whole landlord's rent, as is done in some districts, and the greater part of it as in others: they must not expect to create property in land by a certain number of magical words inscribed on paper or parchment: the only operation by which property in land can be restored is simply to leave to the farmer that which constitutes property, a rent, a proprietor's share; and this may be effected without any material diminution of that revenue which the exigencies of the time so imperiously demand, by conceding to the proprietor the abatement which has, in all cases, been made to the newly invented Zemindar.

In adverting, however, to a *fixed* revenue, I bend to received opinions, without absolutely acquiescing in them. With the most unfeigned deference for the superior talents and knowledge of some of those great men who applaud the *permanent* and *unalterable landed assessment* of Bengal, I must still be permitted to doubt the expediency of the irrevocable pledge which has been given. It is not intended here to examine whether those

* See Appendix, No. 3.

provinces have flourished in consequence of the present system, or in spite of it. I admit, without reserve, that almost any thing was better than the incessant fluctuation of our former plans; but there is an infinite distance between condemning capricious innovation, and approving that political nullity, an irrevocable law. To terminate abuses by shutting out improvement; to render it impossible for the land tax to increase, and probable, nay certain, that it will diminish; is the system of revenue which has succeeded to our former errors. An English chancellor of the exchequer who should propose to pledge the national faith to an unalterable tax, might captivate the multitude, but would be smiled at by the financiers of Europe: and yet principles do not alter in traversing the ocean. If the facility so confidently alleged by the authors of this plan, of raising in India the requisite revenue from other sources, had any real foundation, we should not now hear of the deficit of Indian revenue: and it may be permitted more than to doubt whether we should not at this day have witnessed lighter taxes and more ample revenue, if a less rash and ambitious haste for unattainable perfection had left improvement to be the offspring of knowledge, and the landlord's rent to have enriched the real proprietor of the soil, instead of pampering the hereditary farmer of revenue.

CHAPTER VI.

FROM 1672 TO 1704.

Changes introduced by Chick Deo Raj into the condition of the landholders—pliability of his religious principles—The land tax authorized by the Hindoo law not yet exceeded—comparison of past and present amount—Comparative value of the precious metals—curious facts shewing that the value has not changed—Vexatious taxes intended to be commuted for an increase of the land tax—consequent insurrection—treacherous murder of the Jungum priests—insurrection suppressed—Present state of property in Mysoor—Buttai—home fields exempted—average assessment—land not saleable—inference—exceptions—home fields descend as inheritance—in the later conquests and northern tracts property absolutely extinguished—Death of Chick Deo Raj—conquests—State of Deckan and the South—Siege and capture of Ginjee by Daood Khan, and its consequences—Aurungzebe's distribution of command—Kasim Khan—Foujidar—Dewan—Nabob—Revolution of words and things—Carnatic Hyderabad—Vijeyapoor—Balaghaut—Payeen Ghaut—their respective limits—necessity for explaining these technical divisions to render intelligible the future narrative—names of countries lost or changed—Pretensions of the natives absorbed in the contests of foreigners—Regularity and order confined to the pages of the imperial register—Anarchy of the country ably described by a cotemporary author.

WE return to the changes introduced by Chick Deo Raj Wadeyar into the condition of the landholders of Mysoor. The religious principles of the Raja seem to have been sufficiently flexible to adapt themselves without difficulty to the circumstances of the times. There is little doubt that he was educated in the principles of the Jungum*; but he openly conformed to the ceremonial of the Vishnoo, which was the ruling religion. His early and long intimacy with Visha Lacsha †, the Jain Pundit ‡, whom on his elevation he had appointed his first minister, created a general belief that he was secretly converted to that persuasion, and an expectation that he would openly profess it; and this circumstance was supposed chiefly to have influenced the Jungum to assassinate that minister. When Tremalayangar, a Vishnavite, became afterwards the confidential minister, the Raja evinced as strong an attachment to that persuasion: but political considerations alone would have rendered him the decided enemy of the religion in which he was supposed to have been educated. The contempt and abhorrence in which the Jungum hold the bramins (whom they stigmatize with the opprobrious appellation of *dogs*) is adverse to despotism in a country where any considerable portion of the people is subject to the braminical code, by its tendency to subvert the subordination which arises from the artificial distinction of casts or ranks in society, and to shake the obedience which the Raja usually secures, by enlisting the priesthood on the side of the throne; and the hostility and hatred of the Raja was farther increased by the opposition which the Jungum incited against his financial measures.

As far as the most scrupulous enquiry has enabled me to judge, there is no reason to think that any Raja of Mysoor had hitherto professedly deviated from the Hindoo laws on the assess-

* For the tenets of the Jungum, see Appendix, No. 4.

† He was usually called by no other name than the Yellandoor Pundit, from the place of his birth.

‡ Jain. See Appendix, No. 5.

ment of land, as taught in all the (Mula Smirtis) Sasters or text books, and particularly inculcated in the treatise* locally in use, which condemns the Raja who shall augment the assessment to "infamy in this world, and the pains of hell in the next." The ancient *Candaiam* or money rent of the land, probably established in this part of the country at a period antecedent to the government of Vijeyanuggur, is well known at this day, and in some of the districts continues to be distinguished in the village accounts; although, from the incessant convulsions of the country, the record of the details of the original settlement is perhaps irrecoverably lost. It is certain that the total amount of the *new* impositions is considered, at this time, generally to equal the ancient *Candaiam;* and although in all general imposts glaring irregularities will be found to prevail, the average assessment of lands paying a fixed money rent is now reckoned one-third † of the produce, and the ancient Candaiam one-sixth ‡.

Although general opinion may be considered, in this case, to constitute as good evidence as any that can be obtained from calculations depending on elements in their nature so fluctuating and uncertain as the money price of grain, the varying expences of agriculture, and the average increase on the seed, I am aware that political economists will expect some attempt to discover

* Parasara Madaveeum.

† Of the accuracy of this proposition the following fact appears to be conclusive The Dewan is at this time engaged in a survey of the lands, for the purpose of detecting frauds on the revenue by false entries of the quantity of land. To persons who may be dissatisfied with the *measurement of the land*, the option will be given of *measuring the crop* and paying one-third as the fixed assessment, at the liberal conversion of seventy-five seers of ragee for a rupee.

‡ I have in numerous instances calculated the proportion of the old Candaiam to the present value of the crop, and uniformly found it about a sixth.

what allowance should be made for the supposed decrease in the value of the precious metals. I have attempted to obtain from the records of temples (to which I had free access), and by every other research which has occurred to me, a table of the selling prices of grain for a long series of years; but I dare not place reliance on the few authentic facts which have been procured, because, in the place where I am now writing*, I know that within the last eight years the price of grain has fluctuated to the astonishing amount of two hundred per cent. between its extremes, and I should incur the same risk of error in arguing on the insulated facts to which I have adverted, as in taking one of these extremes as the money price of the nineteenth century. We have, however, within our reach two curious facts of unquestionable authenticity, namely, the rates at which grain was converted into money in the payment of revenue in Canara, before and after the year 1336. The rate of conversion which Hurryhur Roy found established at that period was thirty seers for a rupee; and there is no reason to suppose that this rate had been altered from its reputed establishment by Bootè Pandè Roy, in 1252, until 1336, at which latter period the existence of this rate is perfectly authenticated. We have before observed that Hurryhur called in the aid of the Sasters to increase his revenue; and, for the purpose of qualifying the increased demand by a rate of conversion more favourable to the husbandman, calculated its price at $33\frac{2}{3}$ for the rupee. The settlement of Hurryhur Roy provided for his being paid always in money, and never in grain. In the ancient settlement, the government reserved the option of

* The town of Mysoor.

being paid in money or in kind. The rate of conversion established by the government therefore could not have materially varied from the real average; but we may be tolerably certain that it was rather dearer; and this circumstance, joined to Hurryhur Roy's having adopted a more popular rate of conversion, affords evidence as convincing as can reasonably be required, that the average price of rice in 1336 was not far removed from thirty-five seers the rupee, which we know to be pretty nearly the average rate in those countries at the present time*: and, by analogy, we are justified in concluding that the difference of the money price in Mysoor at the present period, and about one century ago, could not be material. The sixth was accordingly the lawful share of the crop for which the Raja received his equivalent in money; and, from previous reasoning and subsequent fact, we have every cause to believe that he was unwilling to risk the odium of increasing this proportion in a direct manner. He therefore had recourse to the law of the Sasters, which authorized him, by no very forced construction, to attack the husbandman by a variety of vexatious taxes, which should compel him to

* I leave this fact to be accounted for by more skilful political economists, observing only, that the money price of grain may be permanently affected in two ways: 1st. It is supposed to be rendered really dearer, by the natural increase of population being very much greater than the natural increase of food; and 2d. it is rendered apparently dearer, by the increased amount of the precious metals in circulation. The quantities of the precious metals which in India are secreted under ground, and by unexpected deaths are for ever removed from circulation, may in some degree explain why the money prices of food do not increase so rapidly in India as in Europe; and a decrease of population may, plausibly enough, be added to this cause: but the proof of this decrease is far from satisfactory, or rather, there is strong reason to distrust the fact altogether; and the proportion which the increase of population really bears to the increase of food in India is a subject which well merits a separate and ample discussion.

CHAP. VI.

seek relief by desiring to compound for their abolition by a voluntary increase of the landed assessment: and this is the arrangement which generally ensued; although, from the great discontent excited by the taxes, the compromise was generally made on the condition of excepting some one or more of the most offensive, and proportionally increasing those which remained: but the Raja, with that profound knowledge of human nature which distinguished all his measures, exempted from these new imposts all the lands which were allotted to the provincial soldiery in lieu of pay, according to the ordinary practice of the smaller Hindoo states, and thus neutralised, in some degree, the opposition to the measure, and ensured the means of eventual compulsion. Those who may be desirous of comparing the ingenuity of an eastern and a western financier, may examine the subjoined detail of these taxes*. The whole system is stated to have been at once

* 1. *Menne Terege*, or house-tax. 2. *Hul Henna*, (Hanna, Fanam; Hul, grass), a tax upon the straw produced on the ground which already paid *Kundaia*, or the land tax, on the pretence that a share of the straw, as well as of the grain, belonged to government. 3. *Deo Rai Wutta*. *Wutta* is literally *loss*, the difference of exchange on a defective coin. Deo Raj, on the pretence of receiving many such defective coins, exacted this tax as a reimbursement: this was now permanently added to the Ryots payments. It was different according to the coins in use in the several districts, and averaged about two per cent. 4. *Beargee*. A potail (for example) farmed his village, or engaged for the payment of a fixed sum to the government; his actual receipts from the Ryots fell short of the amount, and he induced them to make it up by a proportional contribution. The name of such a contribution is *beargee*, and the largest that had ever been so collected was now added under the same name to the Kundaia of each Ryot. 5. *Yeare Soonca*. *Soonca* is properly a duty of transit on goods or grain. *Yeare*, a plough. The Ryot, instead of carrying his grain to where a transit duty is payable, sells it in his own village. The *Yeare Soonca* was a tax of one to two gold fanams on each plough, as an equivalent for the tax which would have been paid if the grain had been exported. 6. *Jatee Munnia*, a tax upon the heads of those casts (Jogee Jungum, &c.) who do not come within the general scope of Hindoo establishments, and form separate communities which occasionally oppose

unfolded, with intimation that it would be gradually introduced according to circumstances; but the commotions which it produced, by leading to measures of extreme severity, precipitated its total and abrupt introduction.

One of the earliest measures of this Raja's reign had been to compel the dependant Wadeyars and Poligars, who, like his own ancestors, had commenced the career of ambition by affecting in their respective districts to be addressed by the title of Raja, publicly to renounce that assumption of independence, to disclaim the local prerogatives of punishment and confiscation without previous authority from the Raja, and to revert to their original character of obedient officers of the government. This object was aided by first inviting, and then compelling them to

the braminical rule. On every occasion of marriage, birth, or law suit, or quarrel, a certain fine was levied on each house concerned as parties or judges, and a chief of each cast was made responsible for the collection. 7. *Mugga Candaia*, or loom tax. 8. *Cootki teregee*, a tax on fornication. 9. *Mudeve terege*, a tax upon marriage. 10. *Angudee Puttedè*, or shop tax. 11. *Angeree Pessera*, a tax upon the moveable booths which are set up daily in the middle of the Bazar streets. 12. *Cowdee Teergee* (Cowdee is the name of a bullock-saddle), or a tax upon bullocks kept for hire. 13. *Mareké* (selling), a tax upon the purchase and sale of cattle. 14. *Oopin Mulle*, a tax upon the manufacture of the inland salt, produced by lixiviating saline earths. 15. *Oobè Caunka.* Oobè is the kettle or vessel made use of by washermen to boil and bleach their cloths; this was a tax on each kettle. 16. *Cooree teergee*, a tax of a certain sum per cent. on flocks of sheep. 17. *Pashwara.* Pasha is a fisherman's net. This is a tax not on each net, but on the privilege of fishing with nets in certain lakes. 18. *Girgavul*, a tax upon wood for building, or fuel brought in from the forests. 19. *Gulven Pummoo.* Gulla is the name of a ploughshare. This is a separate tax on that instrument, exclusively of the plough tax, No. 5, which is professed to be a tax on the alienation of grain. 20. *Teared Baguloo* (opening a door). In a country and a state of society where window-glass is unknown, this is a most ingenious substitute for the window tax. The husbandman paid it, as expressed by the name, for the permission to open his door. It was, however, levied only on those made of planks, and not on the common bamboo door of the poorer villagers.

fix their residence at Seringapatam; by assigning to them offices of honour about the Raja's person, and gradually converting them from rebellious chieftains to obsequious courtiers. The insurgents in the districts were left, in consequence, destitute of the direction of their accustomed leaders, and the Jungum priests, deprived of their local importance, and much of their pecuniary receipts, by the removal of these mock courts from the provinces, were foremost in expressing their detestation of this new and unheard-of measure of finance, and in exhorting their disciples to resistance. Every where the inverted plough, suspended from the tree at the gate of the village, whose shade forms the coffee-house or the exchange of its inhabitants, announced a state of insurrection. Having determined not to till the land, the husbandmen deserted their villages, and assembled in some places like fugitives seeking a distant settlement; in others, as rebels breathing revenge. Chick Deo Raj, however, was too prompt in his measures to admit of any very formidable combination. Before proceeding to measures of open violence, he adopted a plan of perfidy and horror, yielding in infamy to nothing which we find recorded in the annals of the most sanguinary people. An invitation was sent to all the priests of the Jungum to meet the Raja at the great temple of Nunjendgode, about fourteen miles south of Mysoor, ostensibly to converse with him on the subject of the refractory conduct of their followers. Treachery was apprehended, and the number which assembled was estimated at about four hundred only. A large pit had been previously prepared in a walled inclosure, connected by a series of squares composed of tent walls, with the canopy of audience, at which they were successively received one at a time, and after making their obeisance were desired to retire to a place, where, according to custom, they expected to find refreshments prepared at the expence of the Raja. Expert executioners were in waiting in the square, and every individual in succession was so skilfully beheaded, and tumbled into the pit, as to give no alarm to those who followed, and the business of the public audience went on without interruption or suspicion. Circular orders had been sent for the destruction, on the same day, of all the Jungum *muts* (places of residence and worship) in his dominions; and the number reported to have been in consequence destroyed was upwards of seven hundred. The disappearance of the four hundred Jungum priests was the only intimation of their fate received by their mournful disciples; but the traditionary account which I have above delivered has been traced through several channels to sources of the most respectable information, and I profess my entire belief in the reality of the fact. This notable achievement was followed by the operations of the troops, which had also been previously combined. Wherever a mob had assembled, a detachment of troops, chiefly cavalry, was collected in the neighbourhood, and prepared to act on one and the same day. The orders were distinct and simple; to charge without parley into the midst of the mob; to cut down in the first selection every man wearing an orange-coloured robe (the peculiar garb of the Jungum priests); and not to cease acting until the crowds had every where dispersed. It may be concluded that the effects of this system of terror left no material difficulties to the final establishment of the new system of revenue; and there is a tradition which I have not been able to anthenticate, that the Raja exacted from every village a written renunciation, ostensibly voluntary, of private property in the land, and an acknowledgment that it was the right of the state. If such documents ever existed, they were probably destroyed in 1786, as noticed in the preface.

It remains to sketch the present state of property in Mysoor, connected with the view which has been taken of its condition in the surrounding countries. I cannot trace the period at which the system of *Buttai* *, or an equal division of the crop, was introduced into Mysoor. Its authors probably found it most expedient and profitable to leave untouched the ancient money-rent of what may be called the † home fields, and to levy the buttai on the rice irrigated from artificial reservoirs, and on the less expensive and more slovenly farming of the distant lands; compelling the possessor of the former to cultivate a fixed proportion of the two latter, and thereby raising the aggregate proportion of the crop paid to the government to about 40 per cent. as I have stated in another place ‡, but perhaps exceeding that average from one to three per cent. Following the prevalent doctrines, I at that time considered the husbandman of Mysoor simply as the tenant: and to that situation he has certainly been reduced, with the exception before explained, of Bednore, which follows the system of Canara; and of plantations of cocoa-nut, areca, and other perennial trees, which in every part of Mysoor are a transferable and saleable property. From 57 to 60

* For the uncertain history of this term the reader is referred to page 167.

† This is the *hulcandaya* (old assessment) land mentioned in Tippoo's regulations, Art. 4, and in other places *ijara* (rented). The English reader may consult Mr. Crisp's translation.

‡ *Report on Mysoor*, printed for official circulation in 1804 by order of the Governor-General in council, and published *(with whose permission the author does not know)* in the Asiatic Annual Register for 1805.

per cent. of the amount of the crop appears to be a large proportion in India for replacing the charges of agriculture and the maintenance and profit of the farmer: the proportions, however, will not seem so enormous on considering the details of culture sketched in the subjoined note*, and I rest the conclusion of these proportions being necessary on the broad fact of the land not being saleable. That a liberal tenant's share generally remains, is, however, rendered probable by the fact that the home fields have

* The whole world does not, perhaps, exhibit a cleaner system of husbandry than that of the cultivation of Ragee (Cynosurus Corocanus of Linnæus) in the home fields of Mysoor. On the first shower of rain after harvest the home fields are again turned up with the plough, and this operation, as showers occur, is repeated six successive times during the dry season, at once destroying the weeds and opening the ground to the influence of the sun, the decomposition of water and air, and the formation of new compounds. The manure of the village, which is carefully and skilfully prepared, is then spread out on the land, and incorporated with it by a seventh ploughing, and a harrowing with an instrument nearly resembling a large rake, drawn by oxen and guided by a boy: when the field is completely pulverized, a drill plough, of admirable and simple contrivance, performs the operation of sowing twelve rows at once by means of twelve hollow bamboos (reeds) at the lower end, piercing a transverse beam at equal intervals, and united at the top in a wooden bowl, which receives the seed and feeds the twelve drills: a pole at right angles with this beam (introduced between two oxen) is connected with the yoke; the bamboos project below about three inches beyond the transverse beam, being jointed at their insertion for the purpose of giving a true direction to the projecting parts, which being cut diagonally at the end, serve, when the machine is put in motion, at once to make the little furrow and introduce the seed: a flat board, placed edgewise and annexed to the machine, closes the process; levelling the furrows and covering the seed. If the crop threatens to be too early or too luxuriant, it is fed down with sheep. Two operations of a weeding plough of very simple construction, at proper intervals of time, loosens the earth about the roots and destroys the weeds; and afterwards, during the growth of the crop, at least three hand weedings are applied. This laborious process rewards the husbandman in good seasons with a crop of eighty fold from the best land. The period between seed-time and harvest is five months. There is another kind of ragee, which requires but three months. It is sown at a different season in worse ground, and requires different treatment.

continued to descend as heritage to all the sons equally, according to the Hindoo law. I have observed several gradations in the affection and attachment with which the husbandmen in different districts adhere to their patrimony; and in some few places they appear to consider it with an indifference which seems to indicate an unfavourable tenant's share. With sufficient leisure and health for the investigation, these variations might probably be traced to the state of the public assessments at the period of their conquest by the several Rajas of Mysoor. It is not intended here to advert to the later conquests, in which the Mussulman rule had long been established. They, with some gradations also, and several exceptions, arising from imperfect conquest, may be included in the general sketch of the condition of the countries north of the present territory of Mysoor, and chiefly those south of the Toombudra, now usually termed the Ceded Districts, long, very long, the seat of incessant revolutions. The condition of these countries with regard to proprietary or hereditary right in the land shall be given in the words of the final report on those provinces, delivered in August, 1807, by Lieutenant-Colonel Munro. "In the ceded districts, and throughout the Deckan, the Ryot has little or no property in land; he has no possessory right; he does not even claim it. He is so far from asserting either a proprietary or a possessory right, that he is always ready to relinquish his land, and take some other which he supposes is lighter assessed*." The connexion of this fact

* This enlightened and excellent public servant estimates the average assessment paid to government in that district at about 45 per cent. of the crop, and states an opinion in which I most cordially concur, that private property in land can never be established in those countries until it is reduced to one-third. I will not deny myself

with those which have been noticed in the preceding chapter, requires no farther comment. It is apparently the extreme limit of descent in a lapse from long-forgotten proprietary right, and completes the last step of the gradation which I had proposed to describe. CHAP. VI.

Chick Deo Raj died on the 12th December, 1704, after a reign of thirty-one years and twenty days, and his conquests conclude, in our accustomed order, the narrative of his reign. 1704.

Chickadavaroydroog from Narasapa Wadeyar. 1675.

Honovelly from Ismaul Cawn, an officer of Rand Dhoola Khan. 1676.

Bondasamoodrum, belonging to the Hobly of Chickadavaroydroog, from Hussein Khan.

Cadanaud, from Boojangia, son of the Wadeyar of Voomatoor.

Aundoor from Patadomodelare.

Mudgerry, Mergasee, and ten other forts and districts depending on them, captured from this year to 1678.

Toomcoor. 1687.

Chickanaikhully from the house of Eccojee.

Condecara from the same.

Tamagondala, by the treaty of Causim Khan, from Eccojee. 1687.

Bangalore was captured in the year Prabava on the 11th Au-

the pleasure of stating an incident related to me by a respectable public servant of the goverment of Mysoor, who was sent in 1807 to assist in the adjustment of a disputed boundary between that territory and the district in charge of this collector. A violent dispute occurred in his presence between some villagers, and the party aggrieved threatened to go to Anantpoor and complain to their *father*. He perceived that Colonel Munro was meant, and found upon inquiry that he was generally distinguished throughout the district by that appellation.

CHAP. VI. shadum, by Causim Khan from the house of Eccojee, and on the 15th of the same month it was occupied by the people of the Raja. (The original date is here inserted for the purpose of affording the means of examining the note to which it refers.)

1688. Auvamparoor, Auraseraumany, and Oscotta.

Darmapoory from the people of Aura.

Manoogonda from the same.

Ponara Goodai from Saulyada.

Waumaloor from the people of Aura.

1689. Parametty from the same.

Kauvarypatam, by treaty with Coyamatoor.

Coontoordroog.

Aununtagerry; these three by the treaty concluded by Lingurajayah with the Aurachee.

1690. Baugadee by capitulation.

Hauranhully by ditto.

Baunavaram by assault in the night.

Caaloor by capitulation.

Sakarapatam by ditto.

Baloor by ditto

Waustaura by assault.

Chicka Mogooloor by capitulation

Maharajdroog by ditto.

Ausana (Hassan) by ditto.

Grauma by ditto.

1694. Aurkalagodoo by siege.

Igoor by capitulation.

Salaswerpoora by ditto.

Codalepata.

Of fifteen districts conquered by the Mysoreans from the state of Ekaree or Bednore, two, namely Igoor and Wastara, were returned by treaty, and the remaining 13 districts were retained.

We have had occasion to trace in the progress of this reign some of the leading circumstances which enabled the Raja of Mysore not only to secure the calm and tranquil establishment of his little state, but to enlarge its boundaries in every direction, during political convulsions which shook the whole of Deckan in its largest acceptation, and exposed it to calamities which are felt at this day in their direct consequences. But before we proceed in our narrative, it may be useful once more to look around us, for the purpose of endeavouring to understand the actual situation of those unhappy countries at the period of the death of Chick Deo Raj.

The capture of Ginjee had been a special object of the emperor's vigilance and attention, from the expectation that in its fall the last hope of the Mahratta nation would be crushed, and an impregnable seat of provincial government be obtained, which should insure the future tranquillity of the most southern possessions of the empire. The tedious and ill-conducted siege of this eastern Troy was prolonged for many years, by the treachery, cabals, and intrigues of the chiefs, and by a secret struggle between a prince of the blood and Zulfecar-Khan, the commander in chief, for the independent sovereignty, which each of them had designed to establish in his own person in the future capital of Ginjee. The attack and defence were equally a theatrical exhibition, in which the chief actors performed their concerted parts; but the stage effect was occasionally marred by a drunken manager or ill-instructed performer. The prince, apprised of the secrets of the scene, wrote an explanatory letter to his father, the emperor Aurungzebe: Zulfecar Khan, duly informed by his spies, seized the prince before the letter was dispatched, and sent him in silver fetters to his father, with a letter full of regret at having discovered the base and undutiful design of the prince, to throw off his allegiance and to subvert the emperor's authority. It was the chief object of the general in protracting the siege to keep the army together, in order that he might profit by events on the death of Aurungzebe, which was daily expected. But to preserve appearances, it was necessary to report frequent attacks and repulses. Rama, the son of Sevajee, who commanded at Ginjee, was constantly intoxicated by the habitual use of ganja (hemp leaves) and opium; and his officers, finding his arrangements insufficient to guard against the danger even of a sham attack, held consultations to deliberate regarding his deposition; but on reflection, their perfect understanding with Zulfecar Khan, and a new distribution of the subordinate commands, seemed to afford an adequate security. On the other side, Daood Khan, second in command of the Mogul army, drank largely of the best European liquors, and when full of the god would perpetually volunteer the extirpation of the infidels. Zulfecar Khan necessarily assented to these enterprizes, but always gave secret intelligence to the enemy of the time and place of attack; and the troops of Daood Khan were as often repulsed with slaughter. The prince at length arrived at court: his tale, which unfolded the truth, but not the whole truth, was believed; and Zulfecar Khan received secret intimation from his friends, that nothing but the immediate capture of Ginjee could save him from disgrace and dishonour. Rama, apprized of this necessity, retired to Vellore, which was still in the possession of the Mahrattas, and Zulfecar was adjusting with him a double negociation for the capture of Ginjee, and the release of Rama's wives and family, who had been surprized at an early period of the siege, when one of Daood Khan's drunken frolics actually carried the place early in 1698, and Rama proceeded in haste to the western coast. But the capture of this post, which was of more reputation than real importance, disappointed the expectations of the Moguls; for the name of Sevajee, and the ties of common interest, rallied around Rama and his son the whole resources of the Mahratta people; and Ginjee was found to be so extremely unhealthy, that some years afterwards the Mogul armies were obliged to canton on the plains of Arcot, which led to the establishment of that capital of the lower province (in 1716).

One of the first measures of Aurungzebe, after the conquest of the Mohammedan states of Vijeyapoor and Golconda in 1690, was the appointment of Kasim Khan as Foujdar over the provinces of Carnatic, lately dependant upon those two kingdoms. We shall presently have occasion to describe the provinces into which this extensive command were afterwards divided; and, as they did not materially vary from those adopted in the first arrangement under Kasim Khan, it will only be necessary in this place to observe, that the province of Carnatic Vijeyapoor consisted chiefly of the settled districts of Sera and Bangalore; and the forced tribute exacted from the chiefs of Harponelly, Conderpee, Anagoondy*, Bednore, Chittleedroog, and Mysoor, and some others of smaller importance. The reader has had some

* A supposed descendant of the former Rayeels, who had now settled at this suburb of the former capital.

opportunity of understanding the nature and origin of these smaller powers; and he is requested to remember, as an illustration of the manner in which the term Zemindar was understood by the Moguls* themselves, that these chiefs (and all others of a similar description) are entered in the imperial records as the *Zemindars* of these respective places. In this, as in the subsequent arrangement, the administration of each of the divisions to which we have adverted was committed to an officer possessed of civil and military powers, under the designation of *Foujdar* and *Dewan*, offices which were sometimes divided, but more frequently united, in the south; sometimes subordinate to a provincial governor, and sometimes holding their appointments direct from the Soubadar of the Deckan; or the provincial government was exercised by the officer above adverted to, under the designation of *Nawaub*, or *Nabob*†, a term conveying the direct recognition of dependance, which, in the revolution of words and things, afterwards became the title under which these officers maintained their right to independent sovereign authority.

Kasim Khan was surprised in 1698 by the Mahrattas, aided by the chief of Chittledroog, at *Dodairee*, about thirty miles east of the latter place, where he either put an end to his own existence, or was secretly assassinated. He was succeeded by Zulfecar Khan, whose command in the Carnatic Payeen Ghaut, some years before the death of Kasim Khan, being ostensibly

* They are also uniformly so named by the Hindoo author of the transactions of Aurungzebe in the Deckan. See Scott's Deckan, passim; and particularly the journal of the Bondela officer.

† The plural of *Naib* (a deputy), to render the term more courteous.

directed by the presence of a prince of the blood (and the advice of his father Assud Khan), must be considered to have been then separated from the general command of the Carnatics. He was employed in a course of incessant and destructive warfare, for nearly nineteen years, until the death of the emperor in 1707. The express statement of nineteen actions fought, and three thousand coss marched, by this officer in the course of six months only, may afford some faint idea of the wretchedness in which the unfortunate inhabitants were involved during that period; and these miseries of war, in the ordinary course of human calamity, were necessarily followed by a long and destructive famine* and pestilence. Within the period which has been thus briefly discussed, Zoolfecar Khan appears to have made three different expeditions to the south of the Caveri, levying heavy contributions on Tanjore and Trichinopoly.

The subsequent division of the Deckan (now extended over the whole south) into six soubas or viceroyalties, is no farther connected with our purpose than as it relates to the two last in the official enumeration; viz.

1. Candeish (capital) Burhanpoor.

2. Aurungabad, lately the capital of the Nizam Shahee dynasty.

3. Beder, the ancient capital of the Bahmine Sultauns.

4. Berar.

5. Hyderabad, capital of the late Golconda, or Kootub Shahee dynasty.

* The horrors of a famine, which commenced in 1687, and its consequences for a long period of years, are affectingly described in many of the memoirs in the Mackenzie collection, and may be traced in several passages of Scott's Deckan.

6. Vijeyapoor, capital of the Adil Shahee dynasty.

Of the fifth and sixth in this enumeration, we shall only have occasion to advert to the portions designated in the public records as *Carnatic*, named from the capitals to which they formerly belonged, or were now assigned; viz. *Carnatic Hyderabad*, and *Carnatic Vijeyapoor;* subdivided again into *Balaghaut* and *Payeen Ghaut*, to distinguish the countries situated above and below the passes of the mountains. *The Carnatic Hyderabad Balaghaut* comprehended the provinces forming, under a later arrangement, the five circars of, 1. Sidhout. 2. Gunjeecota. 3. Gooty. 4. Goorumcunda. 5. Cummum. The first, second, fourth, and fifth, of these provinces, afterwards formed the petty state of the Patan Nabobs of Kurpa, who established themselves there about this period, and within a few years extended their possessions along the back of the eastern Ghauts, nearly to the Cavery, including most of the Baramahal, which now belonged to Mysoor. The third of these, namely Gooti, fell afterwards into the possession of the Mahratta house of Gorepora, which was distinguished in the wars of the south under Morari Row. *The Carnatic Hyderabad Payeen Ghaut* was composed of the whole country extending from Guntoor to the Coleroon, along the sea-coast of Coromandel; afterwards better known as the province of Arcot. *Carnatic Vijeyapoor* seems to have been all considered as Balaghaut; for its Payeen Ghaut, including Vellore, Ginjee, Tanjour, still held by the descendant of one of its officers, and Trichinopoly, so far as it might be deemed a dependency, seems to have been included in the Hyderabad Carnatic Payeen Ghaut. In other respects its Balaghaut did not materially differ from the former distribution, namely, the whole of the conquered provinces, and the forced tribute from the *Zemindars* of the Balaghaut south of the Toombuddra, and west of *Carnatic Hyderabad* as above described. The two circars of Adoni and Ghazipoor, or Nundial, situated south of the Toombuddra, were excluded from the Carnatics in this arrangement; the first certainly, and the second probably, because they had been so excluded by the Mussulman powers after the battle of Tellicota in 1564. They were now rated as distinct Circars in the Souba of Vijeyapoor (not Carnatic), and this separation continued seventy-three years afterwards, when the Carnatic Balaghaut fell under the dominion of Hyder. The important frontier province of Savanoor Buncapoor, which had been conquered by Vijeyapoor shortly after the battle of Tellicota, was also excluded from this arrangement, although distinctly a part of the ancient Carnatic. It was now possessed by one of the Patan officers of Vijeyapoor, who opportunely embracing the party of the conquerors, was continued in its command as a military dependant, defraying the expences of his quota of troops from the revenues of the province, and remitting a stipulated sum to the imperial treasury.

The two Patan families of Savanoor and Kurpa, and a third at Kurnool, began about this time to rally around them the remains of the genuine Patans, or ferocious bands of the same tribe, who were perpetually descending from the Indian Caucasus to improve their fortunes in the south. The power of these petty states was yet in embryo, but was destined to make a considerable figure in events connected with Mysoor.

These enumerations, however apparently tedious, will save to the reader the trouble of frequently returning to unravel the same dry intricacies, and were indispensable for enabling us to travel together, with any tolerable precision, over the narrative of future events. A general recollection of these territorial divisions will enable us to understand, without much farther reference, the subsequent political contests of the south, in which the Carnatic itself lost its original designation, and by a strange misnomer, that appellation was in European instruments of high importance applied exclusively to a portion of *Drauveda;* a name which is not to be found in the European geography of Asia. These recollections will also enable us to comprehend how the rights of the unhappy natives of those countries were consigned to the same general oblivion; absorbed in the conflicting pretensions of foreigners, regarding the respective ranges of military command of the deputies of a deputy; or of persons who, in the disturbed state of the times, had purchased or seized their titles and authorities.

The reader will scarcely have inferred, from the technical division and subdivision of these extensive territories, on which his patience has been exercised, that they were organized and governed with the same regularity and order which they exhibit on the pages of the imperial register: the state of this fact is so ably and faithfully described by a cotemporary author, that I shall anticipate the approbation of his learned translator, in transcribing, without alteration, the English translation of this very interesting sketch, as the most unaffected and intelligent picture of the times that can be offered to the public.

" The government of provinces was now held by new nobles of inferior rank, poor and rapacious, who neglected to maintain proper troops, and at the same time oppressed the people. The

Zemindars would not obey Foujedaurs without troops, and became rebellious and remiss in their payments. As the Foujedaurs could not force them, they were glad to content themselves with what they could get; and in order to lead a quiet life, entered into secret agreements with them, and winked at their disobedience, which made them still more insolent.

"In the countries dependant on Hyderabad and Beejapore, which, before their conquest, maintained above two hundred thousand horse, there were not now stationed above thirty-four thousand. The Jaghiredars could not get possession of their Jaghires for want of troops; and if they did, their holding them for any time was so uncertain, that they did not consider the ease of the farmers, but oppressed them for money by every mode avarice could devise; so that they entered into combinations with the enemy. While the newly conquered countries were thus unsettled, the ancient territories of Deckan were not less troubled by the tyranny of governors, and the frequent changes of them and the Jaghiredars; who were obliged not only to supply their own necessities, but furnish large bribes to the civil officers about the court. It was represented to the emperor, that the Zemindars were in confederacy with the enemy; upon which he ordered all their weapons of defence to be seized; and this left them an easy prey to invaders, whom at last they joined for self-security. Contributions were then collected in lieu of regular revenues, and the parties sent every where to collect supplies for the grand camp, were guilty of every sort of excess. Added to this, the collectors of the *odious religious capitation* forced millions from the farmers, and accounted but for small sums with the royal treasury. *Whenever the emperor appointed a Jaghiredar, the*

Mahrattas appointed another to the same district, and both collected as they found opportunity; so that, in fact, every place had two masters. The farmers, thus oppressed, left off cultivating more ground than would barely subsist them, and in their turns became plunderers for want of employment.

"The emperor having taken most of the Mahratta fortresses, they were left without any resource but plunder, out of which they paid a share to their chief, the son of Rama. Many of the powerful disaffected Zemindars joined them, so that they amounted to above one hundred thousand horse. The imperial amras, deprived of their revenues from the Jaghires, had recourse to false musters, and did not keep up above half their complements of men; so that detachments could not be sent every where to punish the invaders, and the grand army was always employed in sieges, which left the Mahrattas at liberty to plunder almost without molestation. But particularly during the siege of Khalneh their excesses were unbounded; they stopped every communication of supply to the imperial camp, where numbers perished by famine; and their insolence grew to such a pitch, that they once a week offered up mock prayers for the long life of Aurungzebe, whose mode of making war was so favourable to their invasions and depredations."

CHAPTER VII.

FROM 1704 TO 1751.

Canty Reva Raj son of the late Raja born deaf and dumb—succeeds to the throne—military operations—Daood Khan called from the two Carnatics—leaves Saadut Oolla Khan as his Foujedar and Dewan—his campaign in Mysoor—Death of the dumb Raja—and succession of his son Dud Kishen Raj—Saadut Oolla succeeds to the government of the two Carnatics, which he retains four years—division of this command—Sera—Arcot—Kurpa—Kurnool—Savanoor Gooti—Contest for the spoils of Mysoor—its result—Mahratta invasion of Mysoor—conquest of Maagree and Savendroog—extinction of a dynasty which had ruled two hundred years—character of this reign belongs to the ministers—contemptible conduct of the Raja—his death—state of the administration—conditional nomination of Cham Raj as pageant king—his emancipation—new ministry—their absurd conduct—concerted revolution—and murder of the Raja—departure from all pretext to hereditary succession in the choice of the next pageant, the infant Chick Kishen Raj—Ministry—singular preparation and death of the minister Nunjeraj—unfortunate choice of a successor of the same name—Doast Aly Khan Nabob of Arcot invades Mysoor—defeat of his army—Campaign of Nunjeraj in Coimbetoor—Nasir Jung sent by his father to levy a contribution on Mysoor—"Lake of pearls"—Marriage of the pageant Raja—suspicious motives—Siege of Deonhully—first scene of Hyder's achievements—history of his family—Mohammed Bhelole—his sons Mohammed Ali and Wellee—remove to Sera and thence to Colar—Futtè Mohammed, son of the former—left destitute and protected by a stranger—early distinction as a soldier—his first marriage and its issue—circumstances of his second marriage—he removes to Arcot—declines the service on a point of etiquette—goes to Chittoor—death of his second wife and marriage with her sister—returns to Sera—appointed Foujedar of Colar—birth of Shabaz and Hyder—their father slain at Sera—plunder and destitute condition of the family—seek the protection of their uncle Ibrahim at

Bangalore—Shabaz enters the service of the Raja of Mysoor, and is promoted—early habits of Hyder—performs his first service at Deonhully—is distinguished and promoted—Nasir Jung marches to Arcot accompanied by the troops of Mysoor—circumstances leading to this event—Saadut Oolla—Doast Aly—Sufder Ali—treacherous seizure of Trichinopoly—dangerous nomination of Chunda Saheb to be governor—desperate intrigue for his removal—Mahratta invasion—Doast Aly slain in battle—Farther intrigues of Sufder Ali—Conquest of Trichinopoly and capture of Chunda Saheb by the Mahrattas—Assassination of Sufder Ali—temporary appointment of Anwar u Deen—murder of his reputed successor the son of Sufder Ali—Release of Chunda Saheb—Remarkable battle of Myconda and its consequences—Chunda Saheb and Muzzuffer Jung with a French corps invade Arcot—battle of Amboor—death of Anwar u Deen, and escape of Mohammed Ali to Trichinopoly—approach of Nasir Jung—review of the pretensions of the four rival candidates—English and French support opposite parties—Nasir Jung arrives—dispersion of his opponents and surrender of Muzzuffer Jung—fresh exertions of the French—defeat of Mohammed Ali—conspiracy of the Patan Nabobs—attack and death of Nasir Jung—reflections on that event—Desperate fortunes of Mohammed Ali—relieved by another revolution—State of the English and French interests in India—character of their respective governors—Chunda Saheb besieges Trichinopoly—Extraordinary talents and achievements of Mr. Clive.

CANTY REVA RAJ.

CHAP. VII.

The son of the late Raja was born deaf and dumb (and thence called Mook Arsoo, the dumb sovereign) an incapacity which under a less settled government would have excluded him from the throne; but he succeeded without opposition through the influence of the minister Tremalayengar, who survived his old master no more than a year and a half. The vigour and regularity of the late long reign continued for several years to be perceptible in the administration. The Dulwoy (commander in chief), Canty Raj, attempted the reduction of little Balapoor, the possession of a warlike Poligar close to the hill of Nundydroog, and was killed before the place; but his son *Busoo Raj*, a man of talent and enterprize, continued the siege and reduced the Poligar to become a tributary of Mysoor: and the state of the Mohammedan government being favourable to his views, he still farther attempted to extend his exactions westward towards Mergazee and great Balipoor. During the short civil war between the competitors for the imperial crown after the death* of Aurungzebe, Daood Khan, the conqueror of Ginjee, already noticed, and now the successor of Zulfecar Khan in the government of the two Carnatics, was called to take the command of the army, which ultimately placed Shah Alum, or Behauder Shah, on the throne. He left Saadut † Oolla Khan (afterwards Nabob)

* Of Daood Khan I find the following brief, homely, and very intelligible account in the Records of Madras 1709. "Very precarious in his temper when sober, free and generous when supplied with the liquors he asks, which we always take care to supply him with;" "a great favourite with the late and present king as a soldier fit for rough work." In the Records of 1701 a curious account is inserted of a dinner given to this Nabob in the council chamber: the number of dishes is detailed, and the toasts drank accompanied by the discharge of cannon: the Nabob pledges the governor largely in cordial waters and French brandy, and afterwards mounts his horse very steadily and returns home. A few mornings afterwards a message is brought to the governor that the Nabob *at the head of his army, to enhance the compliment,* is on his way to pay him a visit at his country house. The best possible preparations are made with great bustle, as well for the reception of the great man, as to guard against treachery; but before they are concluded, intelligence is brought that the Nabob has reeled dead drunk into a Portuguese chapel, where he has fallen asleep. His own army on the spot, and the governor and council at the house of the former, continue to wait his pleasure until four o'clock, when he awakes; and without apology or explanation marches his army about eight miles in a westerly direction, and there encamps.

† His original name was Mohammed Saeed, and his subsequent title *Saadut Oolla Khan.*

CHAP. VII. as his Foujedar and Dewan to manage those possessions during his absence. Saadut Oolla having ascended to the upper country in the prosecution of what, in the English records of those days,
1712. was not improperly called a "contribution war," was opposed by the Mysoor army in a skirmishing campaign of various success in the tract of country between Bangalore and Sera, and the service terminated in the partial accomplishment of its object, namely, a very moderate contribution *.

DUD KISHEN RAJ

1714. succeeded on the death of his father the dumb Raja in 1714. We have formerly noticed in some detail the extent of the different commands in the Carnatics, above and below the Ghauts, in which, according to the last distribution which we discussed, Carnatic Vijeyapoor was all Balaghaut, and Carnatic Hyderabad both Balaghaut and Payeen Ghaut. At the period at which we are now arrived, only six years from the death of *Aurungzebe*, the whole of Carnatic Hyderabad Balaghaut enlarged to the south was possessed by the Patan chief of Kurpa, and by Siddojee Gorepora the Mahratta: the latter, from the convulsions which have been described, establishing a Mahratta power at Gooti, far beyond the bounds of Maharashtra. The command of he two Carnatics therefore now consisted of Vijeyapoor Bala-

* The amount is not mentioned. *The Saadut Nama*, a manuscript history of Saadut Oolla Khan, states that while encamped at Deonhully waiting for the payment of the contribution agreed upon, he received the appointment of Nabob of the two Carnatics from Nizam ul Mulk, immediately after the succession of Furrucksere, viz. 1713: the Records of Madras fix this event in the same year. Mr. Orme places it in 1710.

ghaut and Hyderabad Payeen Ghaut, together with the territory of the Patan of Kurpa, who was properly subject to the authority of the officer holding this joint command, but sometimes referred directly to Hyderabad, according as the interests or influence of the several parties determined the degrees of their connexion. The three Patans of Savanore, Kurnool and Kurpa, being about this time designated *Nabobs,** the latter might be considered as the subordinate Nabob (or deputy of a deputy's deputy) of the *Carnatic Hyderabad Balaghaut*, of which he possessed the whole excepting Gooti, and had acquired to the south more than an equivalent for that possession. Saadut Oolla Khan† retained for four years the united governments of the two Carnatics as thus described, when it was deemed expedient to appoint a separate officer, namely, *Ameen Khan*, to the government of Carnatic Vijeyapoor, and thenceforward it became more usual to designate those several officers as the Nabobs of Sera, Arcot, and Kurpa from the names of their capitals. Saadut Oolla, aware of the riches possessed by the Raja of Mysoor, and jealous of the dismemberment of his own command, entered into a secret com-

* In the *Saadut Nama*, a Persian history of the house of Saadut Oolla Khan, they are not so designated. In relating the confederacy against Mysoor (not exactly as stated in the text), they are called the *Foujedars and Dewans* of Kurpa Sera and Arcot.

† This part of the detail, and that which relates to the fraud in the division of the spoil, is given to me by Budder ù Zeman Khan, aged eighty-two, a connexion of the family. The appointment of Tahir Khan (a dependant of Saadut Oolla) many years afterwards, was the tardy result of his incessant endeavours directly or indirectly to recover the government of Sera. The march of the confederates, stated in the text, is related in the Saadut Nama, with no other reference to date than the third year of the king. The Mysoor manuscript of Poornia places an invasion of Saadut Oolla Khan in 1723-4, which being the third year of Behader Sha, fixes the date, and identifies the events.

bination with the Patan Nabobs of Curpa, Kurnool and Savanore, and Siddojee Gorepora the Mahratta chief of Gooti, to wrest this rich prey from Ameen Khan of Sera, to whom the tribute or plunder of Mysoor, according to the distribution of their respective commands, regularly belonged. Ameen Khan, being apprized of the design, resolved to anticipate their project; and marched with a small but select force, with which he had just attacked the army of Mysoor and sustained a slight check, when the forces of the confederates appeared. Ameen Khan, a
1724. rough and impetuous soldier, exasperated at this illiberal interference, drew out to offer them battle with about a tenth part of their numbers; but he was ultimately reconciled to the plan of a joint operation by the address of Saadut Oolla Khan, who was also nominated by the confederates to conduct the negociation, the forces of Mysoor not daring to move from the protection of the Fort of Seringapatam before so superior a force. The amount ostensibly levied was twelve lacs of rupees for each, amounting to seventy-two lacs; a crore was the sum secretly stipulated, and afterwards discovered by the confederates: the remaining twenty-eight lacs being a simple fraud of Saadut Oolla Khan, with the secret consent of the Patan Nabobs, in return for past and expected alienations of the imperial revenue. The other confederates being deterred from attempting forcible means to exact their just proportions, Saadut Oolla with his forty lacs, and his five associates with twelve each, returned to their respective homes.

The success of this predatory expedition was but an invitation
1726. to other freebooters; and the Peshwa (the designation of a Mahratta officer or minister, who in the reign of the second only in

lineal descent from Sevajee had already in a great degree usurped the powers of the government) in two years afterwards levied a contribution, the amount of which is not stated, at the gates of Seringapatam.

These drains on the treasury were in part replenished by the conquest of Maagree, under the conduct of Deo Raj, recently appointed Dulwoy*. Kempè Goud, the chief, having been so imprudent as to suffer himself to be surrounded in this weak fortress, 1723. the blockade and siege were pressed with such vigour as to compel him to surrender at discretion. The rock of Saven Droog, then justly deemed impregnable, containing the accumulated plunder of near two hundred years, fell also by this event into the hands of the victor; and the power of this formidable chief was finally extinguished in the state prison of Seringapatam.

Whatever portion of vigour or of wisdom appeared in the conduct of this reign, belonged exclusively to the ministers, who secured their own authority by appearing with affected humility to study in all things the inclinations and wishes of the Raja. Weak and capricious in his temper, he committed the most cruel excesses on the persons and property of those who approached him, and as quickly restored them to his favour. While no opposition was made to an establishment of almost incredible absurdity, amounting to a lac of rupees annually, for the maintenance of an alm's house to feed beasts of prey, reptiles, and insects, he believed himself to be an unlimited despot; and while amply supplied with the means of sensual pleasure, to which he devoted the largest portion of his time, he thought himself the

* For the origin of this family, see p. 57.

greatest and happiest of monarchs, without understanding, or caring to understand, during a reign of nineteen years, the troublesome details through which he was supplied with all that is necessary for animal gratification.

CHAM RAJ.

1731. It is scarcely necessary to repeat, that during the twenty-seven years which comprized the reigns of such persons as the two last Rajas, the whole power and influence of the state must necessarily have fallen into the hands of the ministers: and that they would be disposed to regulate the succession in such a manner as should secure to themselves the continuance of unlimited authority. The division of public business was distributed in the offices of Dulwoy, Serv Adikar, and Perdhan; the first of these, as the name imports, was commander in chief of the forces, and director of all departments connected with military operations; the second presided over revenue and finance; and the third was a sort of privy councillor placed near the person of the Raja for the general purposes of the government; but the two latter offices appear to have been frequently united, and at this period were possessed by Nunjeraj *, a man of vigour, superior talents, and experience. The Dulwoy, his cousin german, Deo Raj, was of a bold and ambitious, but cool and deliberate character. He had recently succeeded to his relation Cheleviea, of the house of the Wadeyar of Cullella, in which family the office of Dulvoy had become hereditary; by ancient compact, as is affirmed in the manuscripts

* The uncle of Nunjeraj who undertook the expedition to Trichinopoly in 1751.

of that house, but probably by the genius and tendency of all Hindoo institutions to render offices as well as property the objects of inheritance. In point of fact, however, the whole power of the state in all its departments was already possessed by the various branches of this family. It cannot be positively ascertained, although there is probable ground to conclude, that a nearer claimant to the throne than Cham Raj was then in existence; but it is perfectly certain that he* was nominated as a person supposed to be every way qualified for the office of pageant king, to which he was destined; and the usurpation of the ministers was farther secured by a previous compact, exacted before he was admitted to cross the bridge at Pechum† Wahinee, to undergo the requisite ceremony of adoption by the widow of the late Raja, binding himself to conform in all things to their counsel, and that of his adoptive mother.

The contempt of the ministers for the intellectual powers of their nominal master, who had scarcely attained his eighteenth year, rendered them careless and unsuspicious in the arrangements of the palace; and Cham Raj, little disposed to observe the compulsory conditions of his elevation, had, in three months, secretly completed all the arrangements for a new‡ administration, which were contrived with such skill and address, as sud-

* He was of the elder branch of Hemanhully, but, as far as I can judge from a comparison of authorities, which now become exceedingly defective, more direct lineal descendants must have existed: he lived at the time in Karoogully.

† The bridge over the little Caveri, now called the second Periapatam bridge: *Pèchum Wahinee* flowing to the west. The river at that place makes a sweep towards the west, and wherever a stream is found to run opposite to the general direction of the river, it is considered holy by the Hindoos.

‡ Devaia (a bramin) Dulwoy; *Veer Settee* Serv Adikaar; Gopeenaud, Perdhan.

CHAP. VII. denly to displace the former ministers without opposition or difficulty.

The new administration began the exercise of their authority with the unsettled mixture of rigour and moderation which usually marks a feeble character. While the former ministers were, after a short period, incautiously released, and imprudently left at large at the seat of government, the most rigid and ill-concerted economy in every department, from the measure of disbanding a large portion of the troops, and reducing the allowances of the remainder down to an inquisition into the kitchen of the dowager, created a gradual disgust, and a general disposition to regret the former liberal administration. The dowager and Deo Raj found means of communicating to each other their sentiments and views, and after the lapse of two years and a half, the plan of a counter revolution, more fatal in its consequences than that by which they had been displaced, was com-
1731. pletely organized.

The Jemmadars of two thousand horse, and the chiefs or *Naicks of six thousand peons, affecting to be disgusted with the service, demanded and received their discharge; and encamping at the distance of three miles from the fort, seemed to be making arrangements for their final departure to seek for service elsewhere; and passed without observation in small parties backwards and forwards from the camp to the town: the loose habits of the time not requiring that they should deposit their arms at the gates.

It was the custom of those days for the Dulwoy on every

* Among these I find the name of *Hyder Naik*; he was a distant relation of the celebrated person of the same name, afterwards so well known as Hyder Ally.

Friday to make a march of six or seven miles, accompanied by the forces which were present at the capital, as a sort of military exercise, but frequently as a mere ostentatious procession; and so complete was the extinction, not only of all suspicion, but of ordinary precaution and common prudence, that the personal guard of the Raja accompanied the Dulwoy on this occasion for the purpose of swelling a slender train reduced by the late improvident economy. Deo Raj had now obtained the long expected opportunity: the small parties which had passed as usual into the town, at an appointed signal reunited within the gate; while the main body from without, headed by Deo Raj, rushed through without opposition, disarming the guards, and proceeding direct to the palace. In the first impulse of astonishment and surprise, the unhappy Raja sent an humble message acknowledging his breach of compact, and promising a better observance if his servant and conqueror would forget the past, and accept the office of Dulwoy. Deo Raj was not to be ensnared a second time: but in the bitter remembrance of his former credulity,
passed to the opposite extreme; and, after securing the signet 1734.
and sword of state, seized the Raja and his wife, and despatched them to the well known hill of *Cabal Droog* (an imprisonment at all times equivalent to sentence of death), where the dreadful insalubrity of the climate was mercifully aided by unwholesome food to shorten the sufferings of the victims.

A younger * brother of the deposed Raja was passed over in the next succession, because possessed of promising talents; and

* His name was *Vencat Ers.* Dhermia the *old* Jain Pundit knew him well at Karoogully many years afterwards, when he was an old man, and Dhermia just rising to manhood.

CHAP. VII. the son of a younger and more distant branch, a child of five years old, was selected as a more safe and convenient instrument.

We may consider the lineal succession of the Rajas of Mysoor to have ceased at this period, if not in 1731; for whatever slender ground may be conjectured to exist for acceding to the regularity of the succession in the person of Cham Raj; the murder of that prince, the rejection of his lineal heir, and the election of an infant of a younger branch, extinguishes all imaginable pretext to hereditary claim in the person now elected to therank of pageant Raja, from which he never emerged: and from this period forward, the mock successions to a faulty title determined by Hindoo and Mohammedan usurpers, will not be entitled to occupy any considerable share of our attention. The name of the infant now elevated to this dangerous and humiliating station was

* CHICK KISHEN RAJ.

The administration was replaced on its former footing, with the addition of Vencataputty of Caniambaddy as nominal Perdhan, on condition of being in all things subservient to the will of the Serv Adikaar Nunjeraj. This intelligent minister conducted the civil departments of the government with his usual ability during the six years which succeeded this event. He was still in the vigour of middle life, but having been reduced by a fit of sickness, and being sensible of the approach of his

* *Chick, little,* junior; the former Raja of the same name being distinguished by the prefix, *Dud, great,* or senior.

dissolution, he determined to adjust his worldly affairs, and, as far as he was able, the concerns of his conscience, before his departure to render a final account. He deposited in the treasury the sum which he supposed himself to have improperly acquired in the public service, amounting to about eighty thousand pounds: he had no issue, and to his wife he presented twenty thousand, the remainder of his property being distributed in rewards to his domestics, and in charitable and religious donations, with the hope of expiating his former crimes, he quietly expired at the very moment that he had finished the adjustment of his temporal concerns; his last words conveying a testamentary warning against the employment of the person who became his actual successor.

This person was his cousin-german of the same name, the younger brother of Deo Raj, and surnamed * Kerachoory, a brave, but violent, presumptuous, and improvident man of about thirty years of age. His elder brother Deo Raj being upwards of fifty, vainly expected, that in conferring upon this person an equal share of the government, he should be able to regulate his public conduct with the same facility that, in the days of childhood, he had controuled his private education. The internal quarrels or external wars of all the neighbouring powers rendered this a period of comparative tranquillity to Mysoor: and the profligacy of Nunjeraj made a shameless job of the revenue; appointing his own menial servants to the nominal office of Aumildar, and still retaining them about his person; leaving to

* *Kera*, the *hand*, *Choory*, a *dagger*, or, according to the English proverbial idiom, a word and a blow.

themselves, or to the Perdhan, to provide deputies, but prodigal at once and rapacious, exacting a certain proportion of the public plunder as a joint fund for himself and his brother. The Perdhan appears to have been equally attentive to his own interests; for in ten years after the revolution we find him imprisoned in the fort of Ossoor, after refunding three lacs of pagodas of which he had defrauded the treasury, and succeeded by a superannuated and incompetent person named Chinnapeia. It was a few years before this change in the general administration that an attack of serious and threatening aspect was rendered abortive by the skill and energy of the elder brother.

The reputed riches of the treasury of Seringapatam continued to attract the attention of the Nabobs of Arcot; and the prodigal conduct of Tahir Khan, the Nabob of Sera, to whose government the tribute (when he could obtain it) of Mysoor was considered to belong, left the field open for this irregular object
1737. of ambition and cupidity. Doast Aly Khan prepared a powerful and well appointed army, and selected for the posts of first and second in command two brothers, officers of courage and experience, named Kasim Khan and * Morâd Khan, who marched with the confidence of certain victory to exact the largest contribution that had ever been received from this supposed deposit of inexhaustible wealth. Deo Raj, although no longer young, possessed a vigorous constitution, mental faculties in full energy, and the perfect attachment and confidence of his army. He advanced without dismay to meet this formidable host about forty miles to

* This was the father of Budder u Zemân Khan. The Madras Records mention this defeat, and say that the army was commanded by the Nabob's sons, which B. Z. Khan considers to be a mistake.

the N. E. of Seringapatam. At a village named Keilenchee near Chennapatam, the light troops of the Mussulman army reported the approach of a body of the enemy towards the encampment, and the two chiefs proceeded with the usual detail of troops on duty to reconnoitre. Deo Raj had come forward for a similar purpose with a select body of horse, leaving the rest of his army prepared to follow or to encamp. A small body only was shewn by Deo Raj of the strength of an ordinary reconnoitring party, and the Mussulman chiefs being induced to push forward for the purpose of examining the main body, were suddenly attacked by superior numbers, and, after a brave resistance, were both slain; the advanced troops of Deo Raj, supported by his whole army, followed up the blow; the Mussulman camp was completely surprised and overthrown; the remains of this mighty expedition fled in dismay and confusion to the lower country, and Deo Raj returned in triumph to Seringapatam.

The year 1746 was distinguished by the first military com- 1746.
mand of Nunjeraj in an expedition against the Poligars of Darapoor, in the tract now better known by the general name of the district of Coimbetore: the *Dulwoy*, his brother Deo Raj, being so far advanced in years as to yield without reluctance to his younger brother the fatigue and distinction of military operations, and to undertake, during his absence, the more sedentary occupation of the temporary direction of the revenue and finances; an arrangement which produced the confusion of authority during the quarrel and separation of these brothers, which we shall hereafter have occasion to observe. During the absence of the army in the district of Coimbetore, Nasir* Jung was

* *Serv è Azád*, a work composed by *Meu Gholam Ali Azád*, a philosopher, a

CHAP. VII. detached by his father Nizam ul Moolk, now Soubadar of the whole Deckan and the south, to levy a contribution on the Raja of Mysoor. He advanced to the vicinity of the capital without opposition, and was met by a deputation tendering allegiance and tribute, but to what amount I have not discovered. During the period which passed in the adjustment of payment, this military expedition was converted into a party of pleasure. Nasir Jung encamped in the vicinity of the lake of Tonoor, amused himself with sailing on that clear and beautiful water, and gave it the fanciful name of Motee Talab, the "lake of pearls," which it still retains.

The service under Nunjeraj was successfully conducted, and on his return, the brothers, with the view of more effectually securing in their own family the usurpation of the throne, married the nominal Raja, who had now attained his seventeenth year, to
1746. the daughter of Nunjeraj; a connection, according to Indian habits, not altogether usual; Nunjeraj being one of the most zealous sectaries of Siva, and the family of the Raja (ostensibly at least) of the most inveterate subdivision of the followers of Vishnoo: the marriage, besides, was so late* as in itself to furnish

fakir, and a poet, the confidential friend and companion of Nasir Jung, himself a poet. The work consists in historical and biographical sketches and anecdotes of kings or rulers who were also poets, with specimens of their performances. Nizam ul Moolk, the father of Nasir Jung, has also a niche in this elegant little temple of fame. The author relates that Nizam ul Moolk at an early period of his political life retired in disgust, and assumed the *khrka*, or habit of a derveish who has renounced the world; and that afterwards when he became reconciled to public station, he was constantly scoffed at by that fraternity, who ever afterwards continued to decline his bounty. The author may in this case be excused for a little exaggeration; he was himself a derveish, although not of the particular order which his hero had forsaken; for he acknowledges that he had personally benefited by the munificence of Nizam ul Moolk.

* According to Indian habits.

suspicion regarding the previous views of the brothers: and the eventual use to be made of this connection will be hereafter unfolded.

In the year 1749, the ardor of Nunjeraj in his new profession required fresh employment; and he undertook the siege of Deonhully, twenty-four miles north-east from Bangalore, then considered a place of some strength, and held by a Poligar, who, partly by vigorous resistance, and partly by address, had rendered himself for many years in a great degree independent of the powers around him, and had at no period been subordinate to the house of Mysoor. 1749.

An unknown volunteer in this obscure service was destined in after times to become the head of a mighty empire; to establish a reputation in arms, which, fairly viewing the scene on which he moved, and the instruments he was able to employ, has seldom been exceeded, and to threaten with no ideal terrors the extinction of the British power in India. As no statement of tolerable accuracy has yet been presented to the public of the origin and rise of this mighty adventurer, a short account may be acceptable of the genealogy and history of the house of Hyder*.

* This account is chiefly extracted from a written memoir, prepared by the religious officers at the mosque and tomb of Futti Mohammed, the father of Hyder, at Colar, and checked, by a variety of records and oral information. According to another statement, the father of Futtè Mohammed, here named Mohammed Ali, is called Sheickh Ali (names frequently used indifferently by the same person), and is said to have had four other sons, a descendant of one of whom was married to Tippoo Sultaun: this statement I believe to be correct; but the authors of the manuscript scrupulously confine themselves to the facts which are authenticated by the history of the mausoleum: and it is foreign to our purpose to trace the other branches.

The first of the family of whom any tradition is preserved was Mohammed Bhelole, a religious person, who came from the *Penjab* to the south, accompanied by two sons, Mohammed Ali, and Mohammed Wellee, and settled at the town of Alund in the district of Calburga, about one hundred and ten miles west, and by north, from Hydrabad. He is said to have founded a small mosque, and fakir's mokan*, by charitable contributions, and to have accumulated some property by this religious speculation. He married his son Mohammed Ali to the daughter of one of the servants of the celebrated mausoleum at Calburga, and Mohammed Wellee into another family in the same neighbourhood. After some time, the expences of this augmented family being greater than the saint was able to defray, the two sons proceeded to the south in search of any service by which they could procure a subsistence; and were engaged at Sera, in the capacity of revenue Peons, in the department of the collection of the town customs. Futtè Mohammed, the son of Mohammed Ali, and the father of Hyder, was born at Sera.

In the course of duty, or for some cause not explained, the two brothers came to Colar, where Mohammed Ali died†, and Mohammed Wellee, seizing on all the domestic property, turned Futtè Mohammed and his mother out of doors.

A Naick‡ of Peons in Colar, commiserating their destitute con-

* Mohammedan travellers, in moderate circumstances, generally put up at such places: the fakir and his family assist them in procuring what provisions they require, of which a portion is usually allotted to the fakir, together with a small present on the departure of his guest.

† His grave is shewn by the religious attendants, as the oldest of the family buried at the mausoleum.

‡ Naick, the former designation of a provincial governor, was now degraded to signify the commander of from twenty to two hundred or more Peons, or irregular

dition, received them into his house, brought up Futtè Mohammed, and at a proper age enrolled him as a Peon in his own command.

1720. While Derga* Kooli Khan was Soubadar† of Sera, or affected to be so named, Futtè Mohammed had an opportunity of attracting his attention. The service was the siege of Ganjecottah, near to Balipoor, then the strong hold of a refractory Poligar. The troops were repulsed in a general assault, when Futtè Mohammed seized a standard, and planted it once more on the breach: the assailants rallied, and the place was taken; and the young man, who had so gallantly restored the fortune of the day, was brought before the Soubadar, and rewarded with the command of twenty Peons as a Naick.

Futtè Mohammed, now Futtè Naick, continued to distinguish himself in the service of the Soubadar, and was gradually advanced in rank and consequence. His first wife was Seydanee Saheba, the daughter of Burra Saheb, a religious person at Colar, who bore him three sons, Wellee Saheb, Ali Saheb, and Behelole Saheb. It was on the death of this lady at an early age that he began the mausoleum, mosque, tank, and gardens, at which the authors of the manuscript, which is chiefly followed in this statement, now officiate: the buildings are said to have been finished several years afterwards, when he was appointed Foujedar of the

soldiers, armed with matchlocks, pikes, or swords and targets; such infantry are by the Mohammedans usually named Carnatics. I have not been able to recover the name of this Naick, or the extent of his command.

* He was appointed in 1729.

† We have formerly seen the designation of Souba to be an officer of extensive command, having Nabobs under him. Now that every deputy was meditating independence, every Nabob became Soubadar as the next step in the scale of usurpation.

CHAP. VII. 1749. district; but in whatever manner these dates may be arranged, the buildings themselves, although far removed from architectural grandeur, exhibit unquestionable evidence, that the founder, at the time of their erection, had attained a very respectable degree of rank, property, and consideration. Of the second marriage of Futtè Naick the following account has been communicated to me by several authorities, and confirmed by the written narrative of Budr ù Zeman Khan, for one of whose relations the lady was intended. A Nevayet* of respectable family, from the

* *Nevayet*, generally supposed to be a corruption of the Hindoostanee and Mahratta terms for *new comer*. The following account of their origin is taken from the *Saadut Nama*, and from conversations with many intelligent individuals of the two classes into which they are now found to be divided.

About the end of the first century of the Hejira, or the early part of the eighth century of the Christian æra, *Hejaj Bin Yusuf*, governor of *Irak* on the part of the Khalif *Abd, al, Melik bin Merwan*, a monster abhorred for his cruelties even among Mussulmans, drove some respectable and opulent persons of the house of Hâshem to the desperate resolution of abandoning for ever their native country. Aided by the good offices of the inhabitants of Kufa, a town of celebrity in those days, situated near to the tomb of Ali, west of the Euphrates, they departed with their families, dependants, and effects, and embarked on ships prepared for their reception in the Persian Gulph. Some of these landed on that part of the western coast of India called the Concan; the others to the eastward of Cape Comorin: the descendants of the former are the Nevayets; of the latter the *Lubbè;* a name probably given to them by the natives, from that Arabic particle (a modification of Lubbeik) corresponding with the English *here I am*, indicating attention on being spoken to. The *Lubbè* pretend to one common origin with the Nevayets, and attribute their black complexion to intermarriage with the natives; but the Nevayets affirm that the Lubbè are the descendants of their domestic slaves; and there is certainly, in the physiognomy of this very numerous class, and in their stature and form, a strong resemblance to the natives of Abyssinia. The Nevayets of the western coast preserved the purity of their original blood by systematically avoiding intermarriage with the Indians, and even with the highest Mohammedan families, for many centuries after the establishment of the Mussulman dynasties of the Deckan. Even at this time there are some Nevayets whose complexions approach the European freshness. Their adherence to each other as members of the same family preserved their respectability; and they were famed at the Mohammedan courts of the

Concan, was travelling across the peninsula with his wife, one son (Ibrahim Saheb), and two daughters, to Arcot. At Tarrikera, near the borders of Bednore, he was robbed and murdered; and his family, in the greatest misery, begged their way to the eastward, until their arrival at Colar, where their distresses induced the widow to listen to the proposal of Futtè Naick to be united to one of her daughters. After this marriage, the rest of the family, relieved from their difficulties, proceeded to Arcot.

Derga Kooli Khan of Sera soon afterwards died, and was succeeded by his son Abdul Russool Khan. The new Soubadar or Nabob, and Futtè Naick, for some reason not mentioned, were unfavourably disposed to each other; and the Naick accordingly prepared to seek another master, the Nabob Saadut Oolla Khan, at Arcot. The terms of his service, with fifty horse and fourteen hundred Peons, by whom he was accompanied, were nearly adjusted, when a difficulty arose with regard to his being received with the *tazeem*, or the compliment of other officers rising to salute him when he approached them in the Durbar: a mark of deference which is usual towards persons of rank, but at that period was reserved for officers of horse, who, like the ancient cavaliers of Europe, looked down on the pretensions of an officer of infantry. The Naick could not procure the tazeem, and being

1721.

Deckan for uniting the rare qualities of the soldier, the scholar, and the gentleman. I have seen nothing in India to approach the dignified manners, the graceful, and almost affectionate politeness, of an old gentleman of this family, who resided at Avilcunda, about thirty miles north of Arcot. I became accidentally known to him at an early period of my residence in India, from having lost my way in a dark night, and wandered into a village about a mile from his habitation, whence I received an immediate invitation, conveyed by two of his sons, and a reception which might grace a castle of romance.

CHAP. VII.

1749. resolved not to serve without it, departed to Chittoor, where he was better received by the Foujedar, or provincial commander, Tahir Khan.

The mother-in-law of Futtè Naick had been ill received at Arcot, on account of her connection with the Naick; and the family into which she expected to marry her other daughter declined the alliance for the same cause. She therefore joined her son-in-law at Chittoor, and he having in the mean time lost his second wife without issue, took to himself* her younger sister as a third.

Tahir Mohammed Khan was soon afterwards recalled to court at Arcot; but the Naick, still remembering the tazeem, declined to accompany him. He negociated for the service which he had formerly rejected, and was received by Abdul Russool Khan of Sera as Foujedar or provincial commandant of Colar, with Boo-
1721. dicota as his Jageer, and the title of Futtè Mohammed *Khan*.

His two sons by the Nevayet lady, the younger of the sisters, were both born at Boodicota; viz. 1. Shabaz Saheb†; 2. Hyder Saheb.

When Nizam ul Moolk formed the design of establishing a separate and independent empire in the south, the removal from subordinate commands of all persons who either retained any principle of fidelity to the house of Timour, or had indulged in views of independent authority for themselves, was essential to his success. The money and influence of Saadut Oolla Khan

* This is not contrary to the Mohammedan law, and many similar examples have fallen under my own observation.

† It may be proper to state for the information of the English reader, that *Saheb* annexed to a Mohammedan name has nearly the same meaning as *Mr.* prefixed to an English one.

had long been employed to obtain the office of Soubadar of Sera for a dependant of his own; and it was chiefly through his interest that Tahir Khan was appointed to that office, and aided by Saadut Oolla to fight for its possession. He found the standard of his former Naick marshalled on the side of his opponent Abdul Russool, who was slain in a well contested battle, with 1728. most of his officers of rank. Futtè Mohammed, and his son Wellee* Saheb, fell on this sanguinary field; and the bodies being removed by the pious care of their attendants, their tombs are now shewn in the mausoleum of the family at Colar.

Great Balipoor was the Jageer of the deceased Abdul Russool, and previously to the battle, the families of all his principal officers, and among the rest that of Futtè Mohammed, were, according to the routine of suspicion customary in similar cases, thrown into that fort.

Abbas Kooli Khan, the son of the deceased, was not disturbed in the personal Jageer of his father: maternal feeling, combined with good sense, suggested to his mother, who in a few short years had seen the mangled corpses of her husband and father-in-law, the expedient of securing the Jageer on the condition of a formal renunciation of the office of Soubadar or Nabob, and a solemn promise to exert the influence of the family at court for the confirmation of Tahir Mohammed: and Saadut Oolla Khan, who directed in all things the proceedings of Sera, readily perceived the policy of acceding to this moderate proposition.

Abbas Kooli Khan, however, did not neglect to avail himself of the circumstances in which he was placed, to plunder to the

* He died without issue, as did his brothers Ali and Bhelole.

CHAP. VII. 1749. extent that he durst the families deposited in the fort; and that of Futtè Mohammed was not among those which escaped. The pretext was a balance due from the deceased while Foujedar of Colar. The sons, Shabaz Saheb, and Hyder Saheb, the former about nine, the latter seven years of age, were called upon for payment. The usual methods were resorted to and succeeded; but not before the torture, in its most cruel and ignominious forms, had been applied to both the boys, and probably to their mother. This inhuman conduct was not forgotten; and it will be seen in the sequel that Hyder, in his prosperous fortune, sought his revenge after the lapse of thirty-two years, with all the virulence belonging to the memory of a recent injury.

1729. The family, plundered of its property, was permitted to depart, and *the mother**, *after the loss of every thing but her children and her honour*, proceeded to Bangalore to seek the protection of her brother Ibrahim Saheb †, who was in the service of the Killadar of that place, with a small command of Peons. When the elder brother Shabaz Saheb had attained a sufficient age, his uncle procured for him a recommendation to a Hindoo officer of rank at Seringapatam, and he was received into the service as a subordinate officer of Peons, in which situation he distinguished himself, and gradually rose to the command of two hundred horse and one thousand Peons, which he now held in the army before Deonhully. Hyder, although twenty-seven years of age, was not in the service; and as he remained through life unacquainted with the first elements of reading or writing, it may be

* The exact phrase of the original *Suttaun ù Towareekh* by Tippoo Sultaun.

† The youth formerly mentioned, who was the companion of her unfortunate journey across the peninsula.

inferred that the misfortunes of his family prevented an attention to this object during his early age, and that his subsequent temper was not found fitted to bear the controul of a pedagogue. When approaching maturity of age, he had shewn a greater disposition to the pursuit of pleasure and the sports of the chace than to the restraints of a military life; and would frequently absent himself for weeks together, secretly immersed in voluptuous riot, or passing with facility, as was the habit of his whole life, to the opposite extreme of abstinence and excessive exertion; wandering in the woods while pursuing, not without danger, his favourite amusements. In the siege of Deonhully he began to pay attention to the profession of arms, first appearing as a volunteer horseman in his brother's corps, and afterwards occasionally entrusted with the command of parties of infantry in the trenches. He was observed on every service of danger to lead the way, and to conduct himself with a coolness and self-possession seldom found in a young soldier. This bungling and unskilful siege, directed by a man who had neither seen nor studied the profession of arms, and possessed no quality of a soldier but headlong courage, was protracted for nine months, when the Poligar consented to evacuate the place on the condition of being permitted to retire unmolested with his family to his relation the Poligar of little Balipoor. In the course of this service Hyder was distinguished by the particular favour of Nunjeraj; and, at its close, was raised at once to the command of fifty horse and two hundred infantry, with orders to recruit and augment his corps, and to the charge of one of the gates of this frontier fortress.

The army had scarcely returned from this siege to the capital, when a mandate was received from Nasir Jung, as Soubadar of

CHAP. VII. 1749. the Deckan, demanding the attendance of the troops of Mysoor. The arrangements for this purpose were quickly adjusted, and a body of the forces of Mysoor, consisting of five thousand horse and ten thousand Peons, in which were included the commands of Shabaz and Hyder, under the command of Berki Vencat Row, joining the army at Mudgery, accompanied the numerous host of Nasir Jung for the prosecution of his designs in the province of Arcot. For some years after the period at which we are now arrived, the transactions of the government of Mysoor are so much interwoven with the important operations of the war of Coromandel, that the narrative can scarcely be rendered intelligible without attempting a short retrospect of the circumstances which led to those events.

Saadut Oolla Khan, of the respectable race of the Nevayets, who has already been introduced to the passing notice of the reader as the Foujidar and Dewan of Daood Khan, and the suc-
1732. cessor of that officer as Nabob of Arcot, died in 1732, and was succeeded by his nephew Doast Ali Khan, according to the previous dispositions of his uncle, but without the sanction of Nizam ul Moolk, who was then the nominal Soubadar or viceroy of the south, but actually independent of the throne of Delhi, from which he affected to derive his authority.

Doast Ali had given one of his daughters in marriage to a distant relation, named Hussein Doast Khan, better known by the name of Chunda Saheb, a man of talents and military ardour, whose daughter, by a former marriage, was the wife of Gholam Hussein, the Dewan or minister assigned to Doast Ali by the dispositions of his uncle. This double connection offered to the enterprizing spirit of Chunda Saheb all the opportunities and allurements that can be presented to an ambitious mind. Under the cloak of aiding his son-in-law in the duties of a laborious office, he gradually obtained the chief direction of the civil affairs of the government, and at length the formal appointment of Dewan; and by mixing in every military expedition with the spirit of a volunteer, and the liberality of a prince, the hearts of the soldiers were entirely his own.

The Naick, or Raja, of Trichinopoly and Madura died without issue in 1732; his second and third wives burned with the body, but in conformity to the alleged desire of the deceased, communicated to his confidential minister, his first wife succeeded to the government. Vencatraya Acharee, the commander-in-chief of the forces, supported the pretensions of a collateral male heir: he succeeded in forcibly entering the fortress, and was near destroying the Ranee (queen), when the opposite party collected their forces and expelled him. The death of Saadut Oolla Khan, and the arrangements of the succession which happened in the same year with this event, prevented the Mussulman power from taking advantage of these confusions. The seeming submission of the late commander-in-chief produced a reconciliation, and the authority of the Ranee appeared to be fully established; but this officer, with the concealed aid of the Mahratta Raja of Tanjore, had gradually organized so powerful a party, that this unhappy lady was driven to the desperate resource of soliciting the aid of the Nabob of Arcot. An army under the command of *Sufder Ali*, the eldest son and heir apparent of the Nabob, with Chunda Saheb as his civil Dewan and military second in command, moved over the province, ostensibly for the ordinary purpose of enforcing the collections of the revenue, and approached Trichi-

1732.

1736.

CHAP. VII. 1749.

nopoly to afford the promised aid. The negociations were of course conducted by Chunda Saheb; and the daring preparations of the opposite party within the fort of Trichinopoly rendering the secret introduction of a body of auxiliary troops a measure of seeming urgency, the Ranee was induced to give her consent to this fatal proceeding, on receiving the solemn assurance of Chunda Saheb, confirmed by a false oath on a false Koran *, that the troops should be employed for no other purpose than the confirmation of her authority, after which they should be faithfully withdrawn. The arrangements thus rendered necessary for the establishment of the Ranee's authority placed the actual power in the hands of the Mohammedan troops, not only at Trichinopoly, but at the principal provincial stations; and these measures being effected, Chunda Saheb threw off the mask, imprisoned the Ranee, and hoisted in the fortress the flag of Islam.

Sufder Ali soon afterwards returned to the capital, leaving under the government of Chunda Saheb this important conquest, which extended, with the single exception of Tanjore, over all the provinces south of the river Cavery and east of Caroor. The office of Dewan was in consequence of this arrangement conferred on Meer Assud, the preceptor of the heir apparent, who quickly perceived the error which had been committed by his pupil, and represented to the Nabob the certain dismemberment of provinces formerly tributary, as the least dangerous consequence which could ensue from leaving a man of Chunda Saheb's principles and talents in the possession of such resources.

The Nabob, however, who at this period is represented by the

* It was actually a *brick* wrapped round with the same splendid covering in which a Koran is usually enveloped.

government of Madras as " negligent of affairs, despised by his subjects, and suffering robbery, exaction, and oppression on the part of his officers in all quarters," could not be prevailed upon to risk the consequences of recalling Chunda Saheb, or to believe in the reality of his treasonable views. The new Dewan and 1737. heir apparent, who clearly perceived their danger, and the impossibility of moving the Nabob to vigorous measures, determined on averting the impending peril by a measure of dangerous policy; namely, a negociation, to be concealed from the Nabob, for the purpose of introducing a body of Mahratta* troops, ostensibly to invade the province, but actually to unite with Sufder Ali in destroying Chunda Saheb, who was of course expected to take the field in the general cause of Islam. The great body of the army under Sufder Ali was placed with this view to the southward, in the expectation that the aged Nabob would, on the approach of the Mahrattas, finding himself without sufficient force to oppose them in the field, shut himself up in Arcot or Vellore, when the Mahrattas would pass, according to previous compact, to the pretended attack of Sufder Ali and Chunda Saheb, and leave the former free to regulate his concerted plan. But the old man, roused by this imminent danger from the lethargy in which he had long reposed, resolved not to

* This invasion is stated by Mr. Orme to have been incited by Nizam ul Moolk. I have given the relation of facts as they are stated to me by the Nevayets, and as seems consistent with probability. Nizam ul Moolk was at this time at Delhi, too deeply engaged in the intrigues which led to the invasion of Nadir Shah to be able to give attention to those affairs, if the fact were otherwise probable. But wherever I dissent, with or without a specific notice of this nature, from the statements of Mr. Orme, I desire to be understood as doing so with the utmost deference for his authority.

CHAP. VII. 1749. survive the disgrace of suffering the infidels to ravage without resistance the very precincts of his capital; and took the field with the handful of men which he could collect, sending orders to Chunda Saheb, and to his son, to join him without delay. Chunda Saheb obeyed the order with alacrity; and Sufder Ali, finding one part of his project defeated, had no alternative but to proceed by forced marches to join his father. Before the arrival of either, Doast Ali, who had taken a position in the gorge of the pass of Damalcherri, expecting, in the prevalent but erroneous opinion that this was the only pass through that part of the range of mountains, that he should be enabled there
1740. to arrest the progress of the Mahrattas, was surrounded and defeated, himself being slain in the action, and the Dewan, Meer Assud, being made prisoner. Sufder Ali, who had advanced as far as Arcot, when he heard this intelligence, fearing with reason that the change of circumstances might alter the measures of the Mahrattas, placed his army under the protection of the fort of Vellore, negociating with them through the medium of their prisoner Meer Assud; and Chunda Saheb returned to the care of his own interests at Trichinopoly.

The Mahrattas, as Sufder Ali foresaw, had completely changed their tone, and converted a mock invasion into that system of desolation which every where marks the course of these cool and insatiable robbers*. They perceived that any price might be

* They are well characterized by the Persian compound *Muft-Khoor*, eating at other people's expence. A modern Mahratta is utterly destitute of the generosity and point of honour which belongs to a bold robber. If we should attempt to describe him by English terms, we must draw a character combined of the plausible and gentle manners of a swindler, the dexterity of a pickpocket, and the meanness of a pedlar: equally destitute of mercy and of shame, he will higgle in selling the rags

exacted from Sufder Ali by the simple threat of selling themselves to Chunda Saheb; and the treaty was soon concluded by which they evacuated the province, on the secret condition of hereafter receiving a large portion of the provinces in the possession of Chunda Saheb as the price of his effectual removal. The Mahrattas quitted the province, the rivals were apparently reconciled, and Chunda Saheb, completely deceived by these demonstrations, sold off the provisions with which he had stored his fortress on the alarm of invasion. In December the Mahratta army, which on various pretences had proceeded no farther than Sevagunga, about 250 miles N.W. from Trichinopoly, suddenly returned and invested the place. After a gallant resistance of three months, Chunda Saheb, reduced by famine alone, surrendered at discretion; and, with his eldest son, was sent a prisoner to *Sittara*, now the declared capital of the Mahratta empire, and the prison of its prince, whose authority his minister had usurped. Morari Row was left as the Mahratta governor of the conquered province; the whole of the lower countries south of the Coleroon being thus placed under the dominion of that people.

1740.

1741.

Sufder Ali was soon after assassinated by his relation Murteza Khan*, who was compelled to fly from an insurrection of the

of a beggar whom he has plundered or overreached: and is versatile, as occasion offers, to swagger as a bully, or to cringe as a mendicant when he dares not rob. Of his acknowledged and unblushing treachery, the reader may take the following anecdote. A Vakeel of the Mahratta chief Gockla, conversing with me on the events of the late war, stated among other topics, as an example at once of Lord Wellington's contempt of danger and confidence in his master, "that he had driven Gockla in an open carriage from his own to the Mahratta camp without a single attendant." I affected not entirely to comprehend him, and asked what the general had to fear on that occasion. "*You know* what he had to fear," replied the Vakeel, "*for after all we are but Mahrattas.*"

* Written Mortiz Ali in most English prints. The Nevayets palliate this crime

CHAP. VII. 1749. army; and * Mohammed Saeed, the infant son of Sufder Ali, was announced as successor to the office of his father by Nizam ul Moolk, who, about this period, found leisure to march to Arcot. He found the province in that state which illustrates the series of Indian revolutions to which we have so often referred: the Mohammedan deputies, of every deputy's deputy, and the officer of every mud fort, or town, affected the fashionable designation of Nabob as the first step towards independence; and so many of those important personages were announced at his first public levee, that he is said to have threatened with personal flagellation his *Chobdars* (or gold sticks in waiting) if they should dare thenceforth to announce any person by the title of *Nabob*. In appointing Khajah Abdulla to be a temporary deputy, and de-
1743. claring his intention of conferring the office on Mohammed Saeed when he should attain a proper age, Nizam ul Moolk recognised the principle of hereditary descent, which, however dangerous in his own subordinate officers, he was desirous of recommending to public estimation, for the purpose of strengthening and perpetuating in his own family the mighty empire which he had usurped; and having recovered Trichinopoly and its dependencies from the Mahrattas, he returned to Golconda, accompanied by Khajah Abdulla, who did not live to return to the possession of his government.

by asserting, what I believe to be true without adopting a favourable opinion of his general character, namely, that he had been made to believe that Sufder Ali had applied to Nizam ul Moolk to reverse his appointment of Killedar. When after the murder his writing desk was examined, the draft was found of a letter from Sufder Ali to the Nizam soliciting his confirmation. Murteza was overwhelmed with sorrow and remorse, from which he never effectually recovered. Sufder Ali had gone to Vellore, not from any apprehension, but to pass the festival at the house of his sister, his own family being at Madras.

* *Mohammed Saeed*, in Orme *Seid Mohammed:* the former word *Seyed*, prefixed

Anwar u Deen arrived at Arcot in April 1744, tainted with the suspicion of having poisoned his predecessor; and as he was the guardian of Mohammed Saeed, his reputed successor, his character did not exempt him from the imputation of being* secretly concerned in the murder of that unfortunate youth. In the same year he was confirmed as Nabob by Nizam ul Moolk, and continued for a few years to exercise the government without any material interruption from foreign or domestic hostility. 1744.

So long as Sufder Ali lived, his knowledge of the danger to be apprehended from the release of Chunda Saheb rendered him punctual in the regular discharge of the sum exacted by the Mahrattas, as the price of his perpetual imprisonment: but Anwar u Deen, from avarice, from confidence, or perhaps from want of means, declined to continue the accustomed payment.

to a name, always indicates the person to be a descendant of the prophet, which the Nevayets are not. I observe the same error in the Records of Madras with regard to the former name of Saadut Oolla Khan, who is sometimes called *Seid Mohammed*, his real name being *Mohammed Saeed*. The words Seyed and Saeed are from different roots.

* The adherents of the family of Anwar u Deen acquit him of the murder; the Nevayets acquit both him and *Murteza Khan*, and transfer the suspicion to Mohammed Hussein Khan Tahir, and Gholam Imaum Hussein Khan. On the murder of Sufder Ali these persons are stated to have appropriated the treasure of the state at Arcot. The young man had heard this, and had been so imprudent as to hint that he would hereafter look to it. The partizans of each may be expected in all such cases to give to the transaction the colours most favourable to their own cause; but I incline to the statement of a sensible old man, with whom I lately conversed, who was present at the murder, as a personal attendant of the young prince: "People of different parties (said he) invented different tales; but according to the general opinion, those persons were engaged in the murder who were most interested in effecting it; namely, Murteza Khan, who knew that Mohammed Saeed would retaliate for the murder of his father, and Anwar u Deen, who wanted to be Nabob without a future rival."

CHAP. VII. 1749. The celebrated Mons. Dupleix had arrived at Pondicherry soon after the capture of Chunda Saheb, and found in that fortress his wife and younger son, Reza Saheb, who had been sent thither for security on the first alarm of the Mahratta invasion. The sagacious and penetrating mind of this statesman was not slow in perceiving the advantages which he might procure for his country by the liberation of Chunda Saheb, whose relations and connexions had held under the former rule the government of most of the strong places in the province of Arcot; and were not yet dispossessed by Anwar u Deen, only because the enterprize was too dangerous to be yet undertaken. A communication was accordingly opened with the prisoner at Settara, through the medium of his family at Pondicherry, and a negotiation with the Mahrattas ensued, which terminated in the release of Chunda Saheb.

Attended by his eldest son, Aabid Saheb, and eight or ten faithful friends, who had followed his desperate fortunes, with a decent but not numerous train, he departed from Settara early
1748. in the year 1748, and proceeded slowly to the south, waiting the communications of his friends. On his arrival at the river Kistna he was met by the Vakeels of the Poligar of Chittledroog, and the Ranee of Bednore, then engaged in open war, who severally solicited the advantage of his great name at the head of their respective troops. A Nevayet named Mohee u Deen, who commanded the forces of Bednore, was considered the most proper person to direct the negociation and dictate the letter to a personage of his own tribe. The difference between "your humble" and "your most humble" servant would sound to an English ear as a most ridiculous object of political discussion: but the Ne-

vayet knew the momentous consequences of distinctions equally futile; and fearing that the presence of Chunda Saheb would interfere with his own views, dictated the formalities of the address in a manner which he knew would give offence; and did actually determine the question in favour of the Raja of Chittledroog. A few days after the junction of Chunda Saheb, the rival armies met at Myconda, south of the Toombuddra. The contest was obstinate and sanguinary; and the troops of Bednore, being superior in numbers, were gaining some ground, when the Poligar of Chittledroog ordered his elephant to be picketed on the spot, thereby indicating to his troops his fixed determination not to retreat. Chunda Saheb directed the operations in another part of the line, having his son on the same elephant; and attempting to restore the fortune of the day by a forward movement, he encountered the elephant of the Bednore general, who did not shun the distinction of meeting him. They discharged at the same instant their respective pistols. Mohy ù Deen was killed, and Chunda Saheb, in the fall of his son Aabid by his side, felt for a moment a pang more grievous than the loss of victory; his exertions were enfeebled, and the day was lost. The Poligar was slain, surrounded by a heap of his faithful adherents, the bravest troops of the south; and Chunda Saheb was taken and conducted in triumph to Bednore. The Ranee was desirous of detaining him as a prisoner, but he was still in the custody of the Mussulman troops, to whom he had surrendered; and having opened his views to their Jemadars*, they not only resisted the orders of the

* Meer Shereef u Deen, and Nebbee Yar Khan: their whole command did not exceed one thousand five hundred horse. This transaction is differently related by Mr. Orme. The narrative stated in the text is taken from the local memoirs of

CHAP. VII. 1749.

Ranee, but marched off under the command of their prisoner, to whom a recent event had opened new and unexpected means of pursuing his objects at Arcot.

The death of Nizam ul Moolk *, and the battle of Myconda, happened on one and the same day; and the news of the former event was accompanied with intelligence that Hedayet Mohy ù Deen Khan, the son of his favourite daughter, strong in the possession of the celebrated fortress of Adwanee† (Adoni) claimed the succession to the prejudice of six legitimate sons‡. Whatever hereditary pretensions Chunda Saheb might offer were also derived from the female line, and this similarity in their fortunes determined him to seek the court of this young adventurer; to whom he explained the means of acquiring the services of a French corps, and the strength and resources which, by fixing at Arcot a Nabob entirely devoted to his service, he would acquire, in the arduous enterprize of establishing his own paramount authority in the Deckan.

The negociations with Mr. Dupleix were conducted without interruption, and a body of French troops, consisting of four hundred European and two thousand disciplined native infantry, under the command of Mons. D'Auteuil, and accompanied by Reza Saheb, the son of Chunda Saheb, were permitted, by the

Chittledroog and Bednore, from a comparison of different authorities, Hindoo and Mohammedan, and from the information of Budr u Zeman Khan, who has frequently heard Chunda Saheb relate the circumstances.

* Nizam ul Moolk died 24th March 1748: the battle of Myconda was fought on the very same day. Local memoir in the Mackenzie collection.

† Adoni and Rachore were his personal Jaghire.

‡ First, Ghazee u Deen, who held an office at Delhi. Second, Nasir Jung, the next in succession, who obtained the treasures and commanded the army. Third, Salabut Jung. Fourth, Nizam Ali Khan. Fifth, Basalut Jung. Sixth, Moghul Ali Khan.

ignorant and unmilitary combinations of Anwar u Deen, to CHAP. VII.
traverse the lower country without molestation, and join his ad- 1479.
versary as he approached. Thus strengthened, Hedayet Mohy ù Deen Khan, who had received or assumed the title of Muzuffer Jung (victorious in war), descended at the head of forty thousand men into the province of Arcot. Anwar u Deen with twenty thousand men had fortified a position with one flank resting on the hill fort of Amboor, and the other extending towards a hill which bounds one of the valleys or passes leading into the lower Carnatic. If this position (as is generally said) was taken up with the view of preventing the entrance of the enemy into the province, it is a strange example of military incapacity, as the position may be either turned or altogether passed to the north or the south over a country sufficiently practicable for every description of troops. It cannot be supposed that a soldier of Chunda Saheb's reputation was ignorant of this fact; but the cause in which he was engaged required a brilliant opening. The entrenchments were accordingly stormed and carried after a respectable resistance, chiefly through the aid of the French troops. Although this achievement evidently decided the fortune of the day, Anwar u Deen continued with great personal bravery to animate his troops, and was at length slain, in pushing forward his elephant to close with the standards of his rival, on the twenty-third July, 1749. Of the two sons of Anwar u Deen who were in the action, the eldest, Maphuz Khan, was taken prisoner, the youngest, Mohammed Ali, saved himself by timely flight, and reached in safety the fort of Trichinopoly, of which he had been governor under his father, distant near two hundred and fifty miles from the field of battle. There he proclaimed himself the lawful

Nabob, and for a time solicited in vain the assistance of the English.

1749. Muzuffer Jung and Chunda Saheb marched without farther opposition to Arcot; where, in assuming the state, and receiving the obeisance due to their new dignities, they seem to have wasted in puerile ceremonials the precious time, which ought to have conveyed them without a halt to the gates of Trichinopoly. This childish vanity was still farther evinced in a pompous procession to Pondicherry, where Monsieur Dupleix, naturally disposed to magnificence and splendour, gratified his guests with a most ostentatious reception; but urged them to permit no object longer to delay their immediate march to Trichinopoly. The splendid ceremonials of Arcot and Pondicherry had not much replenished the military chest, and the necessity of their situation obliged them to deviate to Tanjore with the hope of levying a large contribution. Chunda Saheb pursued the means which in ordinary circumstances would have effected his purpose; but seemed from the first to have utterly forgotten the value of time, and suffered himself to be amused before Tanjore by absurd and inefficient military measures and negociations, which the Mahratta, who knew that Nazir Jung was approaching from Golconda, and had already arrived in the territories of Mysoor, broke off, renewed, and skilfully protracted till that chief had actually entered
1750. the province of Arcot. Such was the security and improvidence of Muzuffer Jung and Chunda Saheb, that this intelligence was first conveyed to them by Monsieur Dupleix, and the contemptible proceedings before Tanjore ended in a still more disgraceful retreat towards Pondicherry.

Before we proceed to sketch the conduct of these mighty

opponents, it may be useful to review the actual pretensions of the four rival candidates. The authority of the Mogul, although nominally resorted to when convenient, had positively no existence in the south. Nizam ul Moolk had been avowedly independent of the court of Delhi; neither tribute, nor obedience, were rendered by him, nor by any of the officers really or nominally dependent on him; and it was puerile to claim the exercise of power under an authority with which none of the parties had any other relation but that of rebellion. With regard to hereditary right, or a modification of that right, by the dispositions of the former possessor; where the whole was usurpation, and the line of hereditary descent had not yet begun, the pretensions on this head seemed to have as weak a foundation as the mock mandates of the Mogul. On grounds, however, such as these, Nasir Jung claimed to succeed to the general government of the Deckan, on the false pretence that his elder brother had resigned his right. Muzuffer Jung claimed the same authority on the pretended will of his rebel grandfather. Mohammed Ali claimed to the prejudice of his elder brother Maphuz Khan (the only legitimate son of Anwar u Deen), a patrimony which had been in his family *just five years*, because Nizam ul Moolk had promised, and Nasir Jung would confirm to him, the succession. Chunda Saheb did not put hereditary right into the front of his pretensions, but rested his claims and fortunes on the authority of Muzuffer Jung. On pretensions futile and absurd as these, two enlightened European nations wasted their ingenuity in volumes of political controversy; rendering homage to virtue and justice, in respectively claiming the reputation of supporting the rightful cause; but adding to the numerous examples of

1750.

CHAP. VII. 1750. failure in attempting to reconcile the discordant elements of politics and morals; without daring to avow the plain and barbarous truth, that the whole was a trial of strength among bands of foreign usurpers, in which the English and French had as much right to be principals as any one of the pageants whom they supported: but these nations were at peace, and they could only appear in the contest as the mercenary troops of these polished barbarians.

Nasir Jung having been present and without a rival when his
1748. father died at Boorhampoor in 1748, was acknowledged by the army without any opposition; obtained possession of the public treasures; and employed himself for some time in adjusting the business of revenue in these northern parts of his dominions; when a mandate from the emperor Ahmed Shaw announced the approach of the Abdalees, and summoned him to join the imperial army with his forces. He obeyed with alacrity, not for the purpose of fighting the Abdalees, but because the removal of his elder brother could only be accomplished by such an opportunity as had now presented itself. He had reached the river Nerbudda, when hearing that Hedayet Mohy u Deen Khan, whom he had hitherto treated as a childish pretender, had ac-
1749. tually gained the battle of Amboor; he retraced his steps with speed, and descended into the plains of Arcot, attended by the forces of all the Mussulman and Hindoo officers and chiefs whose possessions were adjacent to his route. Among these were the Patan Nabobs of Savanore, Kurnoul, and Curpa, Morari Row the Mahratta chief of Gooti, and the troops of Mysoor under one of the best officers of that state, Berki Vencat Row; the whole comprising an army rated at three hundred thousand

fighting men, and which might possibly have mustered near one third of that number. On entering the province of Arcot, he summoned Mohammed Ali to join his standard, and requested the English to send him a body of Europeans. Mohammed Ali joined with a nominal six thousand horse; and six hundred English under the command of Major Laurence repaired to his standard. The French had marshalled their own forces, and those of their allies, in an excellent position; in which there was little doubt of their repelling with heavy loss the attack which Nasir Jung had determined to risque; but a discontent among the French officers, which induced thirteen of the number to adopt the unworthy expedient of resigning their commissions in the face of an enemy, ruined for the time the cause in which their nation was engaged. Mons. D'Auteuil, justly alarmed at the consequences of a general action while his men were in the state of insubordination produced by that event, determined to march by night to Pondicherry. Muzuffer Jung, who had for some days been engaged in a secret negotiation with his uncle, with a view of preparing for the worst, distinctly saw that there was not a moment to be lost; and having received the most solemn assurances of personal security, threw himself on the mercy of Nasir Jung. Chunda Saheb accompanied the French battalion to Pondicherry, and behaved with distinguished gallantry during a difficult retreat. The camp of Muzuffer Jung, deserted by its chief, was surprized, plundered, and destroyed; and on the evening of the ensuing day not a man remained in the field, of the formidable confederacy which had contended for the empire of the Deckan.

The character of Mons. Dupleix was of that elastic frame

which disaster only stimulates to increased exertion; and firm in the resources of his own mind, he immediately entered on the course of measures necessary to retrieve his affairs. An attempt at negotiation, through the medium of a mission to the camp of Nasir Jung, was intended for the sole purpose of gaining intelligence, and opening a communication with the disaffected. It failed of course in its ostensible object; and Nasir Jung, impatient at being detained from the sensual delights which awaited him at Arcot, broke up his camp about the end of April, highly incensed by the conduct of Major Laurence, who, fatigued with the duplicity which he experienced in his negotiations, retired to Fort Saint David in complete disgust.

About the beginning of July, Mohammed Ali obtained the permission of Nasir Jung, and the aid of some of his troops, to take the field for the purpose of defending the territories of which he was declared to be Nabob; and he received from the English the aid of a body of four hundred Europeans and one thousand five hundred Sepoys, on the express condition of punctually defraying their expenses. The experience of a single month was sufficient to shew the military pretensions, as well as the punctuality, of their new ally; who, disheartened by a trifling loss, had no money to pay the English troops, unless they should consent to degrade their reputation, and sacrifice their own possessions, by marching away from the enemy to a distant part of the province: and Major Laurence, provoked by this absurd and prevaricating conduct, ordered the troops to return to Fort St. David about the middle of August.

Mohammed Ali, with the same military inconsistency, maintained, after the departure of his allies, the ground which he had considered it necessary to desert while he possessed their aid. His forces were still four times the number of the French and their allies; and although the conduct of the latter in the attack which they made was perfectly steady and spirited, it was scarcely possible to have failed in overcoming the unsoldierlike disposition and feeble resistance of Mohammed Ali, who fled almost alone to Arcot.

Mons. Dupleix followed up the blow with his usual spirit and decision, and by a daring enterprize led by Mr. Bussy obtained possession of the stupendous rock of Ginjee, a fortress literally impregnable by the ordinary modes of attack, which is situated about forty miles N. W. from Pondicherry. This fortress was either built or improved on an old foundation of the Chola kings by the son of Vijeya Runga Naick, governor of Tanjore, an officer of the government of Vijeyanuggur in A. D. 1442; it was successively strengthened by the Mussulmans of Vijeyapoor, who possessed it from 1669 until 1677; by the Mahrattas, who held it from 1677 to 1698; by the imperial general Zulfecar Khan, and the dynasty of his Rajpoot Killedars become Rajas; and lastly, by Saadut Oolla Khan, who, on the conquest of the place from the second Rajpoot Raja in 1715, had contributed more than any of his predecessors to render it unassailable.

Nasir Jung, roused by this event from his voluptuous slumbers at Arcot, marched exactly at the season of the year which he ought to have devoted to preparation, and was subjected to the greatest distress by the storms and floods of the monsoon, which burst upon his army before he approached Ginjee.

The brilliant exploit at Ginjee had lowered the tone of this presumptuous and incompetent chief, and he had condescended,

CHAP. VII. 1750. before he left Arcot, to send deputies to Mr. Dupleix, whose intuitive knowledge of eastern character was aided by the experience and penetration of Chunda Saheb in the arduous circumstances which called for his decision. He had for about seven months carried on a secret correspondence with the Patan Nabobs of Kurpa, Kurnool, and Savanore, who had obtained from former Nizams or Soubas successive grants from the imperial possessions; and who, perceiving in Nasir Jung a disposition rather to scrutinize these alienations than to comply with new and insolent demands, were consequently ready to indulge the characteristic treachery of their race in the means of effecting a revolution more favourable to their views. A select body of three thousand eight hundred men and ten field pieces, under M. de la Touche, was kept ready at Ginjee to obey at a moment's warning the summons of the insurgents; and M. Dupleix continued, without abstaining from hostilities, to negotiate the terms of accommodation: leaving the ultimate question of peace or war to be determined by the conduct of his adversary, in concluding or postponing the treaty before or after the measures of the insurgents were matured. The ratification of the treaty by Nasir Jung, and the summons of the insurgents, were determined on one and the same day; but the latter arriving at Ginjee before the former had reached Pondicherry, M. de la Touche instantly marched, and before day-light the next morning, namely the fifth of December, entered the straggling encampment of Nasir Jung, which he penetrated in firm and compact order, surrounded by hosts of enemies, advancing slowly through the reiterated but unskilful opposition which he sustained. Among the troops who remained faithful to Nasir Jung were those of

Mysoor*; and Hyder was forward in an unsuccessful attempt on the flank of the French column; but the director of the elephant of Berki Vencat Row having been killed by a cannon shot, the temporary appearance of flight caused the troops to give way; and although this accident was quickly repaired, and the elephant resumed his proper place, the charge was not renewed. The insurgents drew up in order of battle; and although, according to the practice of undisciplined troops, they were not sufficiently alert in moving to the support of their friends, and thereby exposed the whole enterprize to the imminent risque of failure, there is no positive evidence that any other plan had been concerted than that of open attack, until Nasir Jung, unsuspicious of treason, directed his elephant to that part of his army with the intention of giving orders. Approaching the elephant of the Nabob of Curpa, he anticipated his salutation b y first raising his hand; it was not yet clear day-light, and thinking the Nabob did not recognize him, he raised himself up in the houda and repeated the salutation, when two carbine shots from the opposite elephant pierced his body, and he instantly expired †.

* They are stated by Mr. Orme to have joined the insurgents.

† I take this part of the narrative almost verbally from the *Serve è Azâd* (see p. 237). The author was in the tent of Nasir Jung when the alarm was given, and assisted him to dress for the field. He relates with simplicity and truth the irregular life of Nasir Jung at Arcot, his own respectful and repeated admonitions, and the vow which his patron made after his departure from that city, and kept, until the day of his death, to renounce all practices that were inconsistent with the sacred law; that fortified with these fruits of repentance, and confident in the protection of heaven, he prepared with cheerfulness for the combat, and as he approached the mirror to adjust his dress, and perceived the reflection of his own figure, he addressed it in the following words,—" O *Meer Mohammed*," (his origiual name; *Nasir Jung*, *victorious in war*, being a title), " the Almighty is thy protector;" and proceeded to mount his elephant without being induced by the hurry

CHAP. VII. 1750. The Patans cutting off the head, and fixing it on the end of a spear, exhibited to their associates in the conspiracy this ultimate and direct evidence of complete success; and it is only useful to add, as a feature of the manners of the people, that after the confusion of the day, the troops reunited* the head and the trunk of the corpse, and preserving them with pious care in a chest or spacious coffin filled with *Abeer*, a powder formed of various per-

of the moment to omit any one of the religious observances prescribed by the sacred law: that it was his general practice on the day of battle to be clothed in armour from head to foot, but, on this occasion, he put on a simple muslin robe; and in this state fulfilled his destiny, and attained the crown of martyrdom. This narrative discredits the published reports of Nasir Jung having deceived his nephew, who was allowed a degree of liberty, and treated with a consideration, against which the best friends of Nasir Jung strongly remonstrated, and advised his being put to death. The reason for dissenting from this advice is not stated in the Serv è Azâd, but is very generally known. When Nasir Jung several years before rebelled against his father and attempted to cut him off near Aurungzabad, the father of *Hedayet Mohy u Deen* (Muzuffer Jung) was ordered to meet the elephant of Nasir Jung, who, after the battle was lost, rushed on in a fit of desperation against the standard of his father. Nasir Jung was wounded, and his opponent was about to transfix him with a spear, when Hedayet Mohy u Deen, then a boy, who was on the elephant with his father, seized his arm, crying "Spare my uncle!" and he was accordingly saved. When Nasir Jung was afterwards pressed to put him to death, on suspicion of the intrigue with M. Dupleix, he answered, "I will never take the life of the man who saved mine." The character given of him in the Serv è Azâd would justify the opinion of his being capable of such a sentiment. I add an incident relative to the battle between Nasir Jung and his father Nizam ul Mulk, as highly characteristic of the bright side of the Mussulman portrait. The latter, sitting as usual in state after the battle, announced that he would receive three successive *nezers* of congratulation, which were accordingly presented without enquiry; and at the conclusion of the ceremony he thus explained them: of these three *nezers* of congratulation, the first was intended to announce victory: the second that my son is safe: the third that he did not fly.

* The ferocious custom of exhibiting or insulting the heads of the slain seems to have been universal in all parts of the world. An epitaph on the last of the Seljuck dynasty slain by the king of Kharizm is nearly thus: "Yesterday his head (in imagination) touching the skies, to-day distant a league from its trunk." This, if I recollect aright, is the same king of Kharizm whose history contains internal evi-

fumes, and the filings of odoriferous woods, dispatched these remains of their late chief to be deposited in the tomb of his ancestors. The intelligence of the death of Nasir Jung was quickly conveyed to the French column; the insurgents had taken their measures for the preservation of Muzuffer Jung, during this confusion, by confiding his guard to one of their accomplices; and by nine o'clock in the morning he was quietly acknowledged by the whole army as Soubadar of the Deckan, although four brothers of the deceased were present in the camp. Mohammed Ali, now for the third time flying singly from a field of action, reached the fort of Trichinopoly. Scenes of this nature are particularly favourable to private plunder. Hyder had already prepared the means of availing himself of such opportunities, by keeping in pay a body of three hundred select *Beder Peons,* who may well be characterized as brave and faithful thieves. In the ordinary circumstances of a campaign they more than realized the charges of their establishment by a variety of plunder and simple theft, from friends when the enemy did not offer convenient means. During the confusion of this day they mixed with the crowd near the treasure of Nasir Jung, which, as usual, the treasurer had begun to load at the first alarm; and these expert marauders, exclusively of minor thefts, separated from the crowd two camels laden with gold coins, and before the confusion had ceased, were clear of all the outposts, and well advanced on their route towards Deonhully (Hyder's fixed home

dence of his having extended his conquests beyond the arctic circle. To the astonishment of the true believers, the sun performed his course above the horizon: an assembly of the learned was convened to advise the king regarding the prescribed hours of prayer; and this conclave very gravely decided, that as the sun neither rose nor set, the king could perform neither morning nor evening prayer.

CHAP. VII. 1750. and station), whither, during this service, about three hundred horses and five hundred musquets occasionally picked up upon the field, or stolen in the quiet of night, had also been conveyed. The troops of Mysoor obtained permission to return to their own country immediately after this eventful day, and a large portion of the remainder of the army moved towards Pondicherry. In the conduct of this complicated scene of diplomatic dexterity and military boldness, M. Dupleix had certainly merited every mark of gratitude that could possibly be conferred by Muzuffer Jung; and he was declared governor, on the part of the Mogul, of all the provinces south of the Kistna. His address in compromising the extravagant pretensions of the insurgents entitled him to a liberal consideration in the distribution of the treasure which was saved; and the new Soubadar of the Deckan, accompanied by a select body of three hundred French and two thousand
1751. sepoys under Mr. Bussy, proceeded early in January 1751 towards Golconda by a north-western route. A great degree of obloquy has been attached to the conduct of M. Dupleix in this transaction, and much demerit may justly be imputed to this and to many other political transactions, if we examine them by the laws of private morals exclusively: nothing, however, is proved but that he had negotiated for dividing his enemy's force, and attacking him by surprise; means of hostility which are at least sanctioned by universal practice: and whatever may be the state of the other facts, it is certain that the forces under Mr. de la Touche performed a service of noble daring, and amply merited their success.

During the period that the fortunes of the French and their allies seemed to be placed above the reach of any interruption from Mohammed Ali, and he had reason to tremble for his existence in the fort of Trichinopoly, he is said, with a strong degree of probability, to have finally concluded with Mr. Dupleix the terms of an agreement by which he was to renounce his claims on Arcot, and to be provided for by an inferior appointment; and it is affirmed that nothing remained to be adjusted but the minor arrangements for the evacuation of the fort of Trichinopoly. It is not probable that M. Dupleix would have permitted the army of Muzuffer Jung to leave the province without deciding this question by the sword, if he had not confided in the completion of the arrangement settled with Mohammed Ali. The strange error of reposing this confidence is only to be accounted for from the contempt in which Chunda Saheb held the prowess and military skill of his rival, without sufficiently appreciating his talents for dissimulation and intrigue. During the whole period of these minor discussions, Mohammed Ali was actively engaged in negotiations with the English, with Morari Row the Mahratta chief of Gooti, and with the government of Mysoor, for aid, not only to defend Trichinopoly, but to engage in offensive operations whenever the aspect of affairs should admit of his breaking off the treaty of capitulation with M. Dupleix: and with the semblance of sincerity which he could at all times assume, he had the address to protract the negotiation, feeding his own expiring hopes with the phantoms of unknown and half-imagined events, according to the practice of fatalists*, until one of these events did actually occur.

* This seems to be universal in the east: the first and fundamental maxim in the *Pancha tantra*, probably the oldest book of apologues in the world, inculcates the sound wisdom of procrastination, whether with or without a reasonable hope, in all cases of difficulty; because by gaining time we gain the chance of success.

1751. Muzuffer Jung had only reached *Raichoutee*, or about half his journey to Golconda, when a conspiracy of the same Patan Nabobs who had effected his elevation by the death of Nasir Jung, accomplished his destruction; two of this number, the Nabobs of Carnool and Savanore, being also slain in the contest. This new scene of confusion and blood was composed by the address of M. Bussy, whom M. Dupleix had judiciously selected for the command of the troops, and the charge of the political interests of his nation at the court of the Soubadar. Salabut Jung, the eldest of the imprisoned brothers of Nasir Jung, then in the camp, was proclaimed Soubadar by general consent, and the army continued its march.

This new revolution revived the fainting hopes of Mohammed Ali. The branch of the family by which he had been appointed Nabob of Arcot was now elevated to the Soubadaree of the Deckan, and there was reason to hope that Salabut Jung would be favourably disposed to the adherents of his deceased brother. His army was at all events far removed from the provinces, and was pursuing its march to the northward, where its presence was demanded. Mohammed Ali possessed a place of some strength, and its dependencies, if well managed, afforded considerable resources; and the local alliances in the negotiation of which he was engaged were such as, if successfully effected, would enable him to contend with Chunda Saheb, at least on equal terms, for the Nabobship of Arcot.

The English interests on the coast of Coromandel had suffered material depression from the capture of Madras in 1746, when the seat of the government was removed to Fort St. David; and although its restoration in 1749, in consequence of the peace with France, had enabled the English nation to repair in a considerable degree the financial injuries which it had sustained, the affairs of the Company continued to be regulated on the principles of a commercial monopoly, while their servants viewed, with a mixture of apathy and astonishment, the mighty machinery of political intrigue and military conquest by which M. Dupleix was preparing for his nation the subjugation of all India, and the consequent expulsion of every European rival. These views were so obvious and prominent as to have excited on the part of the English some desultory attempts, which were abandoned almost as soon as undertaken; but no person seemed to have viewed the state of public affairs with a sufficient grasp of mind until the arrival of Mr. Thomas Saunders, a man inferior perhaps to M. Dupleix in splendour of talents, and in all that constitutes the decoration of character, but not yielding to that distinguished statesman in the possession of a sound and vigorous judgment, a clear and quick perception, a constancy of mind not to be disturbed by danger, and a devotion to the cause of his country no less ardent and sincere than that of M. Dupleix.

Mr. Saunders was altogether without instructions for the regulation of his conduct in so difficult an emergency, but the resources of his own judgment supplied what was defective in the views of his employers. The first object was to enable Mohammed Ali to defend Trichinopoly against any sudden attack; and the next, to prepare the means of meeting his enemies in the field. The former was effected by sending a detachment of about six hundred men to his aid early in February. Mohammed Ali possessed not a single post north of the Coleroon; and Chunda Saheb's acquisition of Madura by a dexterous intrigue, deprived him not only of the resources of that district,

CHAP. VII.

1751.

but, by its intermediate position between Trichinopoly and Tinnevelly, rendered the revenues of the latter unproductive, and its possession precarious. The officer commanding the English reinforcement failed in an attempt to retake Madura; and the cause of Mohammed Ali became still more desperate from the defection of a considerable proportion of his troops in consequence of that repulse.

Chunda Saheb, after going through the usual formalities of receiving the homage of his subjects at Arcot, had prepared for the siege of Trichinopoly: his force, besides the French battalion, consisting of twelve thousand horse and five thousand sepoys. The exertions of Mr. Saunders had not been able to oppose him to the north of the Coleroon with a larger force than six hundred Europeans and one thousand sepoys; which, added to two thousand six hundred horse, and three thousand regular and irregular foot, of Mohammed Ali, did not equal one-half of the enemy's force: and this actual inferiority was farther increased by a panic in the English ranks in one of their earliest encounters; which, although afterwards relieved by one or two examples of steady conduct, prevented their attempting any thing of importance in a series of indecisive operations, which terminated in their retreating under the walls of Trichinopoly in the month of July.

Mr. Clive, born, if ever human being was born, a soldier and a statesman, had already assumed alternately the civil and military character as the interests of his country seemed to require. In the former capacity he had witnessed the discreditable retreat to Trichinopoly; in the latter, promoted to the rank of captain, he had afterwards successfully aided in conducting a reinforcement to that place from Fort St. David; and now offered with a handful of men (two hundred Europeans and three hundred native infantry) to make a diversion in favour of Trichinopoly by a direct attempt on the capital. In this he succeeded, without the necessity of executing the daring enterprize in his contemplation, by one of those accidents, which, outstripping the ordinary routine of Indian superstition, induced eleven hundred men to evacuate the fort of Arcot without firing a shot; because, while consulting the astrologers regarding the aspect of the celestial bodies, a report was brought that the enemy, careless of the thunder of heaven and the rage of the elements, was marching through a dreadful storm direct to his object. This diversion was attended with all the advantage which Captain Clive had foreseen, and afforded considerable relief to Trichinopoly, by compelling the enemy to detach upwards of eight thousand men to the northward for the purpose of attempting to recover the fort of Arcot. In a siege of fifty days, which terminated on the 14th November, Captain Clive, infusing his own spirit into the remnant of his little party, displayed in the defence of this place that ready perception of the best possible resources, under every varied emergency, which men of ordinary talents are contented to acquire as the result of study, long experience, and attentive observation. The aid of one thousand of the Mahrattas of Morari Row, detached from the main body which was on its march to join the army of Mysoor, and of a small detachment sent from Madras, had contributed to compel the enemy abruptly to raise the siege; and Captain Clive, thus reinforced, in a short and active course of operation, completely cleared the province of Arcot of all that had opposed him in the field, the places of strength being, however, still in the possession or in the interests of Chunda Saheb.

CHAPTER VIII.

FROM 1751 TO 1754.

Mohammed Ali sends an embassador to the Raja of Mysoor—nature and result of the negotiation—Army of Mysoor marches to Trichinopoly under Nunjeraj—Major Lawrence assumes the command of the British troops—relieves Trichinopoly—Talents and conduct of the opponents in this contest—Detachment under Captain Clive—its objects and consequences—Distress of the French and Chunda Saheb at Seringham—treacherous capture and murder of Chunda Saheb—Reflexions—Surrender of the French—The English discover for the first time the fraud intended by Mohammed Ali regarding Trichinopoly—subsequent negotiation—English and Mohammed Ali proceed towards Arcot—Nunjeraj remains—his absurd plots for seizing Trichinopoly—French Nabobs—Military successes of Lawrence and Clive—Morari Row—Wavering conduct of Nunjeraj—The English after long indecision treat him as an enemy—disastrous commencement—Distress of Trichinopoly from a corrupt sale of its provisions—French operations in the Deckan—Coromandel—new Nabob—Ineffectual efforts of Major Lawrence—marches for the relief of Trichinopoly—unsuccessful attack on the troops in Seringham—the French largely reinforced—fearful inferiority and extraordinary victory of Major Lawrence—he moves towards Tanjore—returns with a large convoy—another victory—strange deception regarding the convoy—exertions to obtain supplies—the French powerfully reinforced—the English partially—another singular victory—Trichinopoly well stored with provisions—Major Lawrence moves into winter quarters—Attempt to carry Trichinopoly by surprise, and remarkable circumstances in its failure—Defection of the Raja of Tanjore—Total loss of a large English convoy—Incident of Heri Sing and Hyder—Maphuz Khan's appearance and views—procrastinates and deceives—Dangerous treachery of Major Lawrence's interpreter—its circumstances and result—the interpreter executed—Morari Row detached from the confederacy prepares to depart—Major

Lawrence's illness—Critical action under Polier and Calliaud—The French and their allies invade Tondiman's woods—destroy the dyke of the Caveri for the purpose of ruining Tanjore—Major Lawrence moves to that country—Morari Row's conduct—Major Lawrence joined by the Raja's troops and a respectable English reinforcement is in a condition for offensive operations—returns to Trichinopoly—successful action in depositing his convoy—The French assume the defensive—Suspension of arms and conditional treaty—causes to be explained in the ensuing chapter.

CHAP. VIII.

1751.

SHESGEER PUNDIT, the embassador of Mohammed Ali to Mysoor, on his arrival at the capital towards the close of 1750 or early in 1751, found the Raja a pageant, the Dulwoy Deo Raj advanced in years and interfering but little in the active administration of public affairs, and the conduct of the government directed chiefly by Nunjeraj, the young Dulwoy, as he was usually called. Deo Raj was at first decidedly adverse to engaging in a field of action, to which they could not even bring the requisite previous information; but the Vakeel addressed himself with so much success to the inconsiderate ambition of Nunjeraj, that he was soon made to consider as already accomplished, engagements which, from their very absurdity, a man of sober thinking would have rejected without discussion. The cession of Trichinopoly and of all its dependencies, down to Cape Comorin, constituting a dominion little inferior to that which he already possessed, was the stipulated price of his successful assistance; and as a refuge against ultimate failure, and an intermediate security for the family of Mohammed Ali, the fort and district of Ardenhully, half way between the head of the pass leading from Trichinopoly to Seringapatam, were to be assigned to him in personal Jageer. It would seem to have been the intention of Mohammed Ali to

CHAP. VIII. 1751. deposit his family in this place, in the desperate state of his affairs, which immediately followed the death of Nasir Jung: but this project was relinquished when the English discovered a disposition to aid in the defence of Trichinopoly. Mohammed Ali had also the address to render the important aid of Morari Row, and of course the payment of his subsidy, the immediate act of Nunjeraj. Morari Row had been practised in an extensive school of warfare; his troops were the most select, the most faithful, and the best organized of any in the south, being composed of a judicious mixture of Mohammedans, Mahrattas, and Rajpoots, with an ample accompaniment of Beder Peons already mentioned. Although expert in the national tactics of plunder, Morari Row was also a genuine soldier where the occasion demanded; and he engaged with more facility in this cause, from the hope of being able, in the course of events, to seize the place for himself and reassert his former pretensions.

About the same time that Mr. Clive undertook the romantic enterprize against Arcot, Morari Row began his march from Gooti, and Nunjeraj from Seringapatam: the force of the former was estimated at six thousand men, and of the latter, five thousand horse and ten thousand infantry, of which the only regular troops were a small body in the corps of Hyder Naick; who, with the five hundred stand of arms acquired in the manner already noticed, and a few French sepoy deserters to drill his recruits, had assiduously attended to this object, and was much advanced in the favour of Nunjeraj by exhibiting* to him these invincibles who

* Matchlock muskets were before this period the only fire-arms used in Mysoor, and it is related, perhaps with some exaggeration, that the first exhibition was spoken of, and particularly in the Raja's palace, as a wonderful "hocus pocus," by

were to conquer Trichinopoly. The troops arrived in the district of Caroor towards the latter end of the year, and early in the next moved to form the junction. The second in command to Nunjeraj was Veerana, a man resembling himself in arrogance and military incapacity, but suspected of being destitute, in those situations which most demanded it, of the steadiness and presence of mind which Nunjeraj was generally allowed to possess. But there were not wanting in the army other officers capable of directing its operations, with the degree of knowledge and skill then possessed by the native chiefs of India. The English had sent a detachment to join this chieftain, for the express purpose of quieting his alarms in passing a French post established to interrupt his progress; and Nunjeraj, too arrogant to be guided, and too ignorant to direct, presented the singularly ludicrous spectacle of a night march intended to be secret, guided by the lights of innumerable torches. We have formerly * adverted to an ancient practice of this nature in the armies of Mysoor; and the present exhibition may either be ascribed to that abundant source of wisdom, and equal sanction for absurdity, *the custom of his forefathers*, or to the desire of impressing his new allies with an exalted opinion of his splendour and magnificence. Fortunately, this invitation to attack was not accepted, and he arrived in safety at Trichinopoly early in February. In conformity to the uniform principle of Indian policy, as the affairs of Mohammed Ali appeared to improve, he

which five hundred musquets were discharged at once by repeating certain magical words: it being ascertained by previous inspection that not one of the five hundred men was provided with a match.

* Page 98.

acquired more friends. Monajee, the general of the Raja of Tanjore, with three thousand horse and two thousand foot, and the Poligar Tondiman with four hundred horse and three thousand irregular foot, soon afterwards joined him. The forces marshalled on his side became accordingly more numerous than those by which he had been for some months blockaded; but Chunda Saheb and the French, who had established themselves in several strong posts near to the fortress, were still decidedly superior in regular troops: Captain Gingen, therefore, the officer commanding, very properly resisted the repeated applications of his allies, convinced that in such a service they would unquestionably have left the English troops without support, to be crippled in the desperate attempt of forcing strong posts with inferior numbers: and knowing that a reinforcement might soon be expected from Fort St. David, he reserved his men for better purposes.

The enemy had again appeared in some force in the province of Arcot; and Captain Clive, with a body of one thousand seven hundred men against five thousand, after completely dispersing his opponents, and capturing the whole of their ordnance, consisting of twelve pieces, had now returned to Fort St. David for the purpose of taking the command of the reinforcement for Trichinopoly, which was to consist of such of the troops then under his orders as could be spared for that service. Major Lawrence, however, arrived from England on the fifteenth of March, and assumed the command of this detachment, consisting of four hundred Europeans, one thousand one hundred sepoys, and eight guns; and Captain Clive marched under his orders towards Trichinopoly by the route of Tanjore. The fate of this reinforcement was of the utmost importance, and M. Dupleix had given the most peremptory orders that it should be intercepted at all risks; but Mr. Law, the officer who commanded the troops before Trichinopoly, had not discovered much enterprize in the operations which he had hitherto conducted at that place; and he was now to be opposed by military talents of the highest order. He committed the great error of leaving this contest to be decided within sight, and almost within shot, of Trichinopoly; which enabled Major Lawrence to obtain reinforcements of regular troops from that place, and to arrive in safety with the valuable convoy of military stores which had accompanied him, marching clear of the injudicious position which Mr. Law had assumed, and foiling his subsequent movements and ineffectual cannonade. The troops of Mysoor and Morari Row performed no other part than that of spectators of the operations of this day, and their inaction was supposed to proceed from Morari Row's being in treaty to change sides; a fact, which, if founded, rendered the error which has been noticed still more unpardonable.

Mr. Law, after remaining for a few days in his former position south of the river, adopted the sudden and precipitate determination of abandoning his posts, and assuming a defensive position on the island of Seringham, which is formed by two branches of the Caveri opposite to Trichinopoly; leaving behind him on the south side the single untenable post of Elemiserum, which fell of course on the second day. Chunda Saheb is said to have remonstrated in the strongest terms against this feeble and most unaccountable measure; and the whole of the subsequent operations evinced a distraction of councils approaching

CHAP. VIII.

1752.

to absolute infatuation. The magazines which they had collected to the south of the river were lost or destroyed in the disorderly retreat of the army, which now became dependant for subsistence and stores on the country to the northward. The position which Mr. Law had assumed on the island was too strong to be attempted by main force, without battering cannon, with which Major Lawrence was not provided; while the obvious measure of acting on the enemy's communications with Pondicherry, and the country in their rear, must, if judiciously conducted, necessarily either dislodge or starve them. Captain Clive, although the junior of all the captains, was selected by the general voice of the allies to conduct this difficult service. A small but select detachment of regular troops, added to one half of the corps of Morari Row under his best general Yoonas Khan, together with one thousand Tanjore horse, were placed under his orders; and the village of Samiaveram, a forced march from the head quarters of the army, was formed into a post of support for his operations, and rendered capable of sustaining a sudden attack from the whole force of Mr. Law, if such a measure should be attempted. M. Dupleix saw, when it was too late, that he had made an unfortunate selection of an officer to co-operate with Chunda Saheb; and M. D'Auteuil was detached from Pondicherry with six hundred and twenty men, the largest reinforcement which could be spared, with directions to throw himself into the island of Seringham, and supersede Mr. Law in the command. Considerable activity and military enterprize were displayed by M. D'Auteuil in his repeated attempts to accomplish his object; and in one of these the post of Captain Clive was completely surprised, in consequence of a mistake of one of the outposts, but instantly recovered by an exertion of that admirable spirit and presence of mind which distinguished this officer on every occasion. The efforts of the enemy were effectually foiled by the able combinations of the two English divisions, and M. D'Auteuil was at length compelled to surrender to Captain Clive.

The effects of these judicious operations soon began to unfold themselves on the island of Seringham: the scarcity of food, added to the constant annoyance sustained from the posts which the English had gradually established in all directions around, induced the greater part of the chiefs commanding the troops of Chunda Saheb to demand their dismission from his service. Despondency had succeeded to chagrin in the mind of this chief, on finding his repeated exhortations to vigorous action treated with neglect; he no longer confided in his allies or in himself; his health declined; and his bodily strength became unequal to the only determination worthy of his former character, that of cutting his way with a select body to the numerous places of safety which still remained to him: he mildly acquiesced in the demands of his officers, and apparently resigned himself to his fate. These chiefs, on receiving assurances of safe conduct, passed with facility into the service of their late enemies; and in a few days, not more than two thousand horse and three thousand foot remained to Chunda Saheb, of the mighty host with which but a few months before he threatened the extinction of his rival. In the choice of difficulties which opposed themselves to a selection of the person among his enemies to whose faith he should confide, the national prejudice which has been ascribed to Mr. Law, in distrusting the protection of Major Lawrence, does not appear to be a liberal construction of his conduct. It is incredible that Mr.

Law should have thought a British officer of high honour and established reputation capable, under any circumstances, of permitting the murder of a prisoner who should throw himself on his special mercy; but it is obvious that by surrendering his person to the English, the cause of Chunda Saheb would be more permanently and irretrievably ruined, than by an imprisonment under the capricious counsels of any other of the confederates who should consent to spare his life. Mr. Law was accordingly justified by the fairest considerations of the national interests committed to his charge, in recommending to Chunda Saheb to incur any risk rather than surrender to the English; and he unhappily trusted to the desperate faith of a Mahratta. Monajee, the Tanjorean general, plighted the most solemn oaths to convey him in safety to one of the French settlements; but he had not reached the place appointed for his reception, when he was seized and put in irons. It is impossible, at this distance of time, to unravel the secret history of the mock conference regarding the disposal of this unhappy prisoner, held on the ensuing day, in the presence of Major Lawrence. Judging from the ordinary routine of deception in similar cases, there is reason to conclude that the native chiefs were secretly agreed; and that Major Lawrence was to be deterred from interfering, by shewing that he would thereby incur the resentment of all the confederates: but it is above all other conjectures most improbable, that Monajee murdered his prisoner simply for the purpose of preventing farther disputes. That he should incur the disgrace of open perfidy without an object is not very probable, even in a Mahratta: but that, certain of a large reward for facilitating his escape, he should thus dispose of a valuable prisoner without securing his price, is absolutely incredible. I copy literally from my manuscript in stating that Chunda Saheb "was murdered at the instigation of Mohammed Ali." It is a fact of public notoriety, that his head was immediately sent to that personage, and after being subjected to unmanly insult, was delivered to Nunjeraj, and by him sent to Seringapatam; where it was suspended in a cheenka* over the southern or Mysoor gate, to be gazed at by the multitude during three days, as a public trophy of the victories in which the troops of Mysoor had certainly as yet borne no very distinguished part. The death of Chunda Saheb is hardly ever mentioned by a Mussulman, without noticing, as a visible manifestation of Almighty vengeance, that he was treacherously murdered in the same choultry, in which, sixteen years before, he had profaned the holy Koran by a false and treacherous oath to the Ranee† of Trichinopoly. The fondness for recognizing in remarkable events the immediate interposition of the Deity, appears to arise more from a taste for the marvellous than from any particular dogma of the Mohammedan faith: fatalism implies a fixed order of events, and the doctrine of particular judgments, a deviation from the ordinary course of things: and a sensible Mussulman observed to me, that this doctrine has a tendency unfavourable to the cause of morals, by pointing to temporal expectations, and unsettling the steady hope of future retribution.

The surrender of the French troops with fifty-two pieces of

* A sort of open net of small rope, in which natives usually suspend food to preserve it from the rats. Mr. Orme had been informed that the head of Chunda Saheb had never been carried out of the Carnatic (Drauveda).

† Page 250.

1752. ordnance was the immediate consequence of these events, and the war seemed to be concluded. But the English, in discovering for the first time the state of the discussion between Nunjeraj and Mohammed Ali regarding the possession of Trichinopoly, had the mortification to learn that the splendour of their military achievements was associated with the cause of fraud and dishonour. The treaty, attested with all the accustomed formalities, precluded a recourse to the usual arts of prevarication; and Mohammed Ali, when pressed by Major Lawrence, plainly avowed, that he executed that solemn instrument, and confirmed it with the sanction of a religious oath, without any intention of observing its engagements. The stale pretext of the authority of the Mogul being necessary, was too ludicrous for serious discussion; but the assertion, certainly most true, that the Mysorean *ought to have known* that Mohammed Ali could not, or would not, perform the stipulations, was the lowest point of moral degradation, and a formal avowal that he had been enabled to defraud his friend, because that friend was so weak and absurd as to trust to his honour. Such was the cause in support of which the British arms were now to be engaged; and such the disgraceful consequence of the alternative imposed by the necessity of their affairs, when they followed the example of their European opponents, and engaged as mercenaries in the service of barbarians, rather than acquiesce at once in the ruin of the national interests committed to their charge. The spirit of the negotiations which ensued may be described in a few words. Mohammed Ali endeavoured to deceive Nunjeraj with new promises: and this personage, who, in addition to his other follies, had at different periods lent to his dear ally a sum now amounting to ten lacs of Pagodas, was completely undeceived; and sought, with his inferior powers of simulation, to retort the deception of a master in the art. Morari Row, as an impartial umpire, meditated to seize the object of discussion for himself. Mohammed Ali engaged anew to cede the fort and dependencies of Trichinopoly at the expiration of two months, when he should have acquired another place of safe deposit for his family; and in the mean time relinquished to Nunjeraj the revenues of the island of Seringham and of the adjacent districts, and admitted into the fort, as an acknowledgement of his right of possession, a body of seven hundred Mysoreans under Gopaul* Rauze. Each party was now perfectly aware of the insincerity of the other; and although Nunjeraj, in consequence of these concessions, engaged to march with his ally to the northward, it was perfectly understood that he had no such intention. An English garrison of two hundred Europeans, and one thousand five hundred sepoys under Captain Dalton, with a numerous rabble in the pay of Mohammed Ali, was left to guard against surprise; and the whole force which really marched to the northward was an English corps of five hundred Europeans and two thousand five hundred native infantry, and a nominal two thousand horse with Mohammed Ali.

The Mysoreans and Mahrattas remained with great composure under the walls of Trichinopoly, and Nunjeraj was not slow in unfolding his clumsy designs. He expended large sums in gaining over one of Mohammed Ali's corps; which Captain Dalton

* The father of Letchmè Ammab, the venerable dowager still alive of the then nominal Raja of Mysoor.

CHAP. VIII. 1752.

in consequence detached to join its master to the northward. He also employed assassins to shoot Captain Dalton, and Kheir u Deen, the brother in law of Mohammed Ali, who was left to represent him at Trichinopoly: they were discovered, and condemned to be blown away from a gun, but very unaccountably pardoned at the intercession of Morari Row. His next exploit was to send secret emissaries to corrupt the troops, openly furnished with written engagements: they addressed themselves to a faithful Jemadar, were seized, and publicly executed; and Nunjeraj could procure no more *secret emissaries.* He had been so impatient for the possession of Trichinopoly, that all these attempts followed each other with the intermission of only a few days. The next pause was not of much longer duration. A Neapolitan named Poveiro, an ensign in the service of Mohammed Ali, who occasionally traded in the Mysorean camp, was next addressed, with promises of immense reward. He listened with complacency to the proposals, and the whole plan was soon fixed, by which the French prisoners were to be liberated and armed, the western gate seized, and the Mysorean army admitted into the city. Poverio, however, had arranged all these projects in secret communication with Captain Dalton; and the garrison was perfectly prepared to inflict an easy and memorable punishment on this military pretender, when the unmanly apprehensions of Mohammed Ali's vicegerent foiled the well concerted plan. He feared the consequences of so close a struggle; and sent to reproach Nunjeraj with his treachery, and to inform him that the garrison was ready to receive him. Nunjeraj did not think proper, after this disclosure, to remain under the guns of the garrison, but moved three miles to the westward, with the intention of seizing a weak post established at Warriore: this post, however, he found reinforced, and moved from thence to Seringham. During all this time, he was Captain Dalton's very sincere friend; he sent daily messages of compliment, with the view of discovering some opportunity of surprising him; and at the stipulated expiration of two months, sent a deputation in form to demand the surrender of the city. The English, in their character of mere subsidiary allies, referred him to Mohammed Ali's representative Khier u Deen, who haughtily produced the treacherous agreement of Nunjeraj with Poverio as a forfeiture of all claims which he might otherwise advance.

In the mean while M. Dupleix, roused to fresh exertion by the disaster at Seringham, produced abundance of viceroyal mandates, which Mr. Bussy's influence with Salabut Jung had obtained, first appointing himself Nabob, and afterwards conferring the office on Reza Saheb, the son of the deceased Chunda Saheb; and these pretensions he prepared to sustain with fresh levies of troops, and new negotiations with the Mysoreans and Mahrattas. His first attempts against some English detachments in the central parts of the province were successful; but being too much elated by these advantages, and deceived by a retrograde movement of Major Lawrence for the express purpose of drawing the troops to a distance from Pondicherry, the French detachment was completely defeated at Bahoor, with the loss of all its artillery and stores, at the very moment that his negotiations had succeeded in detaching from the confederacy the corps of Morari Row. A detachment of that force under the command of Yoonas Khan was actually on the march to join the French; and in consequence of their defeat very gravely directed their

CHAP. VIII. 1752.

route to the camp of Mohammed Ali; lamenting that they had not come up in time to share with him in the glories of the day! During the subsequent operations of Major Lawrence for the purpose of establishing the authority of Mohammed Ali in the centre of the province, Captain Clive reduced the posts of Covelong, and Chengliput, between thirty and forty miles south and south-west of Madras, regularly garrisoned by French troops, European and native. For the performance of this service he marched with the only troops which could be spared, consisting of two hundred raw European recruits just landed, and five hundred newly raised sepoys, with a few heavy guns; evincing, in the promptitude with which he reclaimed this disorderly rabble from a state of panic and insubordination to the character of steady and forward troops, that distinguished mental ascendancy which placed him so much above the level of ordinary men. His health, however, had been so much impaired in the course of the late services, that he was compelled to return to England for its re-establishment; and Major Lawrence, a chief worthy of such a second, had the mortification to lose his aid at the period when new and increasing perils were gathering around him.

The success of Major Lawrence at Bahoor, in the reduced state of the resources of M. Dupleix, ought to have been productive of the most extensive advantages; but the total absence of military talents or resource in Mohammed Ali, who was permitted to arrange the whole plan of the subsequent campaign, rendered all its operations spiritless, inefficient, and undecisive. Nunjeraj, on the first intelligence of the defeat at Bahoor, which occurred in August, gave up the design of executing his engagements with

M. Dupleix, regarding the connexion as desperate. But the feeble conduct of Mohammed Ali in failing to derive any material advantage from the events of the campaign, excepting those achieved at the point of the English bayonets, naturally raised the spirits of his adversaries; and on the return to monsoon quarters of the English troops in November, Nunjeraj, at the request of M. Dupleix, detached from Seringham the remainder of the Mahrattas, to be joined near Pondicherry by those under Yoonas Khan, who had obtained from Mohammed Ali permission to seek convenient cover for his own winter quarters. The Mysorean expected a body of Europeans from Pondicherry to join him at Seringham; and until their arrival he thought it expedient to veil his hostility in exaggerated professions of friendship, ascribing the march of Morari Row to a dispute which had arisen in the settlement of their accounts.

The English government had endeavoured to evade the ignominy of being associated in the fraud of Trichinopoly, by representing themselves as mere auxiliaries*, who took no part in the political direction of the war. The disgrace of acting in such a cause while the impressions were fresh, had probably restrained them from an earlier determination: but the conduct of the Mysorean had changed the object of decision, and furnished them with arguments to obscure, or elude, the original question, by retorting the complaint of greater and more recent injuries. In fact, the repeated machinations of Nunjeraj, and the indirect hostility of intercepting at a distance all provisions passing towards Trichinopoly, by which that garrison was now considerably

* November 3d, 1752. "We wrote to the king of Mysoor that we were merchants, allies to the circar, not principals."

CHAP. VIII. 1752. distressed, reduced the question to the simple alternative of treating him as an enemy, or of placing before Mohammed Ali the option of performing his engagements, or forfeiting the English alliance; leaving, as the result of either choice, an open field for the designs of M. Dupleix, which were by no means doubtful. They determined in December to treat him as an enemy.

The camp of Nunjeraj was pitched to the northward of the great Pagoda of Seringham, and his own quarters were within the lofty outer wall of the temple, which was furnished with stages for musquetry; the gates being covered by temporary outworks. Captain Dalton, who commanded the garrison of Trichinopoly, on receiving the determination of his government regarding Nunjeraj, commenced his operations on the night of the 23d of December by an attack on his camp, which, like that of most Indian armies, exhibited a motley collection of cover from the scorching sun and the dews of night; variegated according to the taste or the means of each individual, by extensive inclosures of coloured calico surrounding superb suites of tents; by ragged cloths or blankets stretched over sticks or branches; palm leaves hastily spread over similar supports; handsome tents and splendid canopies; horses, oxen, elephants and camels; all intermixed without any exterior mark of order or design, except the flags of the chiefs which usually mark the centers of a congeries of these masses; the only regular part of the encampment being the streets of shops, each of which is constructed nearly in the manner of a booth at an English fair. He reached it undiscovered by a circuitous route; and, after striking the panic, and doing the degree of mischief which such attacks, without a farther object, are intended to accomplish, returned to the fort without attempting the Pagoda, or sustaining any material loss. The distress of the garrison for provisions could not, however, be effectually relieved while Nunjeraj maintained a position so near to the fort, with others at greater distances in different directions intercepting the supplies; and on the following night, Captain Dalton established a post on the island, a few paces beyond the northern bank of the Caveri, or southern branch of the river, and within thirteen hundred yards of the Pagoda, which it was intended to bombard. A second post on the southern bank commanded the passage of the river to the first; and was itself protected by the cannon of the fort. In a consultation of the officers of Nunjeraj it was determined that they must either dislodge the enemy from this post, or evacuate their own; and on the following day about noon they began to marshal their troops in their irregular way for carrying it by assault. This attempt must have been repulsed, with a severe chastisement for its rashness, if the English troops had behaved with common steadiness; for the post was nearly finished, had two field pieces mounted in a commanding situation, and was occupied by about four hundred men, of whom near one hundred were Europeans; a force abundantly sufficient for its dimensions: but one of those unaccountable panics to which the best troops are sometimes liable, said to have been occasioned by mistaking the intention of an officer who, after the repulse of one attack, was crossing the river with a message to Captain Dalton, induced the whole party suddenly to evacuate the place in the utmost confusion; and Heri Sing, a Rajepoot Jamedar of cavalry in the service of Mysoor, and the rival of Hyder for military distinction,

CHAP. VIII. 1752. seizing the moment of action, charged, without hesitation, among the fugitives, who were nearly all cut to pieces before they could cross the river to the intermediate post. This misfortune compelled Captain Dalton in his turn to act on the defensive. As a measure of necessary precaution, the seven hundred Mysoreans under Gopaul Rauze were turned out of the fort; but this chief was detained as a prisoner of state, under the erroneous supposition that he was the brother* of Nunjeraj. A more successful night-attack on a smaller post at Veloor merely tended to relieve the depression of the garrison. The Mysoreans in the mean while directed their whole efforts to the interception of supplies, terrifying the people of the country by cutting off the noses of all who were detected in the attempt to introduce them; in conformity to the ancient and barbarous practice of Mysoor. Nunjeraj with the same view divided his forces; assigning to Veerana the command of a large detachment, which established a fortified camp on the opposite side of Trichinopoly. The blockade might
1753. be considered as complete about March 1753, and provisions of every description began to sell at an enormous price: Captain Dalton had frequently communicated with Kheir u Deen on the subject of the quantities in store, and was always assured that they were abundant; but now that these stores were to be his only resource, he prudently insisted on examining them himself, and establishing such arrangements for their issue and expendi-

* The natives of India employ the term "brother of attachment," where in the west we should say "particular friend," and this term probably led to the mistake. There was certainly no brotherhood nor relationship, nor connection of family of any kind at this time; some years afterwards, on the death of the Raja's first wife, the daughter of Nunjeraj, he married the daughter of Gopaul Rauze.

ture as should satisfy his mind with regard to his actual situation, and means of sustaining the blockade. Kheir u Deen, as corrupt as he was incompetent in every part of his character, had absolutely sold the greater part of the provisions; and the examination ended in ascertaining that the remnant in store was sufficient for the consumption of fifteen days only! Regret at having too long postponed this essential enquiry was now unavailing; and Captain Dalton had no other resource but to communicate his actual condition by express to Major Lawrence, to whose situation in the province of Arcot it will now be necessary to revert.

The falsehood of the former pretensions of Nasir Jung, and the subsequent assertion of Salabut Jung, with regard to the resignation of the claims of Ghazee u Deen, their eldest brother, was established in October 1752 by the appearance of that person, with the sanction of the Mogul, at the head of a mighty army, near to Aurungabad, which he entered in great state, and proclaimed himself Soubadar of the Deckan. The two competitors at this time were the sons of Nizam ul Mulk by different mothers; and Salabut Jung employed a more certain agency than military force by prevailing on his mother, then at Aurungabad, to poison Ghazee u Deen, who received, without suspicion, the compliment usual between such relatives, of a dinner prepared under her own inspection. The death of Ghazee u Deen was followed, as usual, by the dispersion of his army. Salabut Jung had frequently before this event exhibited the mandates of the Mogul, appointing him Soubadar of the Deckan; and although the public opinion of these forgeries was sufficiently established by the late events, and the son of his murdered

1753. brother was supported at court by a powerful party, mock missions and mandates from Delhi were again exhibited with that unblushing falsehood which is indifferent to the expectation of belief.

M. Dupleix, who, on the murder of Chunda Saheb, had first proclaimed himself, and afterwards the son of the deceased, as
1752. Nabob of Arcot, found that neither of these arrangements had supplied his most urgent political want by filling his military chest; and he had now recourse to the farther experiment of conferring the appointment on Murteza Khan of Velloor, who was supposed to possess considerable treasures. After some hesitation this new Nabob marched, under the protection of the
1753. corps of Morari Row, to Pondicherry, where he was proclaimed with the usual formalities; but, on discussing with M. Dupleix the slender resources of the province, and the means which he was expected to supply from his own treasures, together with his personal efforts in the field, he discovered, after his first advance of a lac of pagodas, that he had made a very improvident bargain; and that his most prudent course was to secure his own person, and preserve the remainder of his wealth in his strong fortress of Velloor. The pretence of his departure was the necessity of his presence in the neighbourhood of that fortress, for the purpose of protecting and endeavouring to extend the revenue which he already possessed; and the European and Indian Nabobs parted apparently on excellent terms, but mutually dissatisfied, and perfectly understanding each other.

These unsuccessful political manœuvres did not, however, prevent M. Dupleix from directing in the mean time, with his usual energy, the resources which he actually possessed, to the extent of disbursing on the public account nearly the whole of his private fortune.

Early in January 1753 he was enabled to equip for the field a body of five hundred European infantry, and a troop of sixty horse, two thousand sepoys, and the excellent corps of four thousand horse under Morari Row. The English force under Major Lawrence consisted of seven hundred European infantry, two thousand sepoys, and fifteen hundred wretched horse belonging to Mohammed Ali. The French force was obviously superior for the general purposes of a campaign; and the troops of Morari Row distinguished themselves in a variety of small affairs. Major Lawrence felt the confidence of superiority in a close conflict, but the French were prudently directed to avoid affording him the opportunity of decisive action; because, by protracting the campaign in that part of the province, they prevented the relief of Trichinopoly, and hoped that Nunjeraj might succeed in starving it into surrender. The caution of the French was so decided as to induce them to fortify their position on the bank of the Pennar, while Major Lawrence, harassed by the Mahratta cavalry, failing in all his attempts to draw the French from their works, and finding them too strong to be forced, was satisfied of the necessity of changing his plan of operations, and embarrassed in the selection of a better; when, on the 20th of April, the express from Captain Dalton reporting the state of Trichinopoly determined his choice. He arrived at that place on the 6th of May, and found that Captain Dalton, by constantly disturbing the camp of Veerana during the night, and annoying it from an advanced post during the day, had been enabled to operate so effectually on the nerves of that chief, that

CHAP. VIII. 1753. he had suddenly evacuated his position on the 15th of April, and on the intelligence of Major Lawrence's approach, rejoined Nunjeraj at Seringham, leaving the access open to supplies from the south.

M. Dupleix, on learning the route of Major Lawrence, detached two hundred Europeans and five hundred sepoys to support Nunjeraj; and this force, commanded by M. Astruc, an officer of experience and talents, arrived by a different route at Seringham the day after Major Lawrence entered Trichinopoly.

The English force had suffered materially on the march from the desertion of foreigners, but still more from the deaths and sickness occasioned by the heat of the season; and Major Lawrence, on adding to his own corps the proportion which could be spared from the duties of the garrison, found that the whole effective force which he could muster for a general action amounted only to five hundred Europeans and two thousand sepoys: for three thousand horse in the service of Mohammed Ali, always ill paid, ill commanded, spiritless and mutinous, refused to move when they found there was to be an action. Major Lawrence determined, on the 10th of May, without their aid to cross into the island of Seringham by the south-western ford, four miles above the town, and offer the enemy battle. He commenced his march early in the morning, and at day-light crossed the river, now nearly dry, dispersed the usual guard of the ford, and began to form in order of battle on the opposite side. The firing at the ford gave the first notice to Nunjeraj of the approach of the enemy, and he had, on this occasion at least, the prudence to be guided by better talents than his own. The confusion of an Indian army hastening on an alarm through an irregular encampment to their stations, furnishes the most favourable moment for attack; and in order that Major Lawrence might not avail himself of this opportunity, M. Astruc advised that his left, not yet completely formed, should be instantly charged by whatever cavalry was ready. Herri Sing and his Rajpoots were first abroad, and made a vigorous charge fairly through the first line, but were checked by a reserve of Europeans and by the sepoys, who rallied with spirit, and compelled the Rajpoots to retire with great loss, sustaining in their precipitate retreat the fire of ten pieces of cannon. The object, however, was gained, for time was afforded to M. Astruc to make his dispositions; his own troops were advanced to a water-course within musquet-shot of the English line, which served every purpose of a regular work, by enabling him to annoy the enemy while his own troops were under cover; and his field pieces (four only in number) were placed in an elevated and commanding situation, while those of Nunjeraj kept up a distant and ill-directed fire. The cavalry hovered on each flank, with directions to charge the instant that the English should make a forward movement; and Major Lawrence, finding such a movement to be too hazardous, placed his troops under the cover of a bank, until he should examine the means of forcing the excellent position assumed by the enemy. M. Astruc meanwhile occupied with native infantry a building which imperfectly enfiladed the left flank of the English, and compelled Major Lawrence to risk a detachment of Europeans for dislodging them: the service was performed with celerity and spirit, and the pursuit led the detachment so near to the right flank of M. Astruc, that, supposing it to be supported, and his position to be turned, he commenced his retreat to the protection of his second line, which was formed of the infantry of Mysoor. The return of the detachment undeceived him; he re-occupied the water-course, and made the requisite arrangements for the safety of his flank, which was not again attempted. The cannonade continued throughout the day; and in the evening Major Lawrence recrossed the river, disappointed, but maintaining a countenance and order which deterred the enemy from molesting his march. All the dispositions of M. Astruc throughout the day were made with a degree of promptitude and military skill which commanded the respect of the English; and Major Lawrence, finding the attempt to force the position on the island beyond the strength which he possessed, directed his whole attention to replacing the provisions of the garrison, for which purpose he moved into the former camp of Veerana, as the most favourable position for covering supplies from the S.E., chiefly from Tanjore, and from the woods of Tondiman to the westward of that country, and south of Trichinopoly.

The Raja of Tanjore, who, in a contest which appeared so precarious, very naturally wished to avoid the resentment of the eventual conqueror, gave no public support to either party, except when induced by money or compelled by fear; but was generally disposed from national considerations to sustain the cause supported by Morari Row, with whom he always preserved a secret communication, although his territory was not always respected by his brother Mahrattas. Tondiman, from the beginning, had evinced a partiality to the English; but the unfavourable aspect of their affairs, and the threats of future vengeance from Nunjeraj, restrained him at this time from any active assistance. Hence Major Lawrence, so far from being able to deposit a proper supply in the stores of Trichinopoly, obtained with the greatest difficulty provisions for the current use of the day, during about five weeks that he was occupied by this sole object, without attempting any thing against the enemy; who, on their part, remained also on the defensive, M. Astruc having seen enough of his allies to decline offensive operations until supported by better troops.

The French troops in the province of Arcot were left, by the departure of Major Lawrence, without an opponent in that quarter, and were enabled to carry several English posts of minor importance. Morari Row on such occasions was always forward and enterprizing, and at other times roamed at large over the province. Every chief at the head of a few men began, as usual in similar scenes of confusion, to strengthen himself and plunder on his own account; and even Murteza Khan of Vellore ventured abroad, and seemed to think again of his office of Nabob. M. Dupleix, however, justly considering the defeat of Major Lawrence as the primary object of the war, detached three thousand of the corps of Morari Row under Yoonas Khan, three hundred Europeans and one thousand regular sepoys, to reinforce the army at Seringham.

The decided superiority acquired by this reinforcement seemed to leave but little doubt of an early decision of the contest. For the French had now in the field, besides four hundred Europeans and one thousand five hundred sepoys of their own, eight thousand Mysoor horse, three thousand five hundred Mahrattas, one thousand two hundred Mysoor sepoys under the command of Hyder, and fifteen thousand irregular infantry: while Major Lawrence, having detached seven hundred sepoys for provisions,

CHAP. VIII. 1753. had no more than five hundred Europeans, one thousand three hundred sepoys, and one hundred horse, the only individuals who, of all the rabble of Mohammed Ali, consented even to encamp beyond the cover of the walls of Trichinopoly. With this immense disproportion of force the French and Nunjeraj moved to the southward of the rivers, and in a few days compelled Major Lawrence to withdraw his camp to a position rather nearer to the fortress, extending themselves precisely between him and the route of his supplies, so as to form an effectual blockade. Nothing now seemed to remain but to consider the terms of capitulation, and the general despondency was increased by the severe illness of Major Lawrence. He would not, however, until the last extremity, quit the ground he at present occupied with his handful of men; and in order to afford some chance of obtaining supplies by night, or the opportunity for striking some unexpected blow by day, he maintained a post of two hundred sepoys on a rock nearly a mile and a half to the south-west of his camp. This, in less desperate circumstances, might be censured as an improper disposition, the post being considerably farther from his own camp than from the superior force of his enemy: but their possession of the rock would have compelled him to retire under the walls of Trichinopoly. Without great risk, and the opportunity for some extraordinary effort, he knew that he must in a few days surrender at discretion for want of food; and the wonderful achievement which followed this dangerous disposition deserves a more detailed narrative than we are accustomed to give. M. Astruc was not slow in perceiving the advantage and the necessity of forcing this post, and he attacked it on the morning of the 26th of June with a select body, supported at a distance by the whole of his force. A portion of the English sepoys had just gone into the fort to receive their rations; and when Major Lawrence perceived the attack, which he did not so soon expect, he found that leaving the requisite guard for his camp, he could muster for the support of his advanced post no more than three hundred and forty Europeans, five hundred sepoys, and eight field pieces with their complement of artillery-men; and with these he hastened at a quick pace to reach the rock before the main body of the enemy. The post made a respectable resistance; but M. Astruc perceiving this movement, made a vigorous effort, and carried it just as Major Lawrence had reached half way, and was thus in a position in which the attempt to advance or retreat was equally desperate. He instantly made the decision which was worthy of himself, and the soldiers received his orders with three cheers. The grenadiers, supported by an equal number of select sepoys, were directed to carry the rock at the point of the bayonet; and literally obeyed their orders, not firing a shot till they had reached its summit and driven its recent captors down the opposite side. Major Lawrence with the remainder of his force moved at the same time round the foot of the rock, where the main body of the French had just arrived, in the hope of being sufficiently rapid in his movement to fall upon the flank which it seemed to present to his attack. M. Astruc, however, placed the right flank of the French battalion against the rock, and quickly formed with his front towards the British column, which, equally rapid and precise in its evolution, formed in line at the same moment within twenty yards of the enemy. M. Astruc had reckoned with confidence on the support which he had chosen for his right, and the rest of his troops were

CHAP. VIII. 1753.

moving up to deploy and encompass this handful of men, when at the instant that the English battalion gave its first discharge in front, a heavy fire on his right flank from the troops which had carried the hill, caused his men to waver, and the instantaneous charge of the English bayonets threw them into inextricable confusion; the most gallant efforts to restore order were of no avail, and the whole hurried off in complete dismay, leaving three field pieces in the hands of the English. The cavalry of Morari Row, with their usual gallantry, interposed to cover the retreat of the French infantry, and even made an effort to recover the field pieces, but were repulsed with severe loss; Balagi, the adopted son of Morari Row, a man of distinguished courage, being among the slain. Major Lawrence, who was determined not to relinquish the trophies of his victory, after remaining for some hours at the foot of the rock, had still the arduous service to perform of returning with them over the plain in the face of the whole body of the enemy's cavalry, which was drawn up just beyond the range of his shot, ready to charge in every direction the instant he should attempt the movement. The dispositions were made with corresponding care: his little square halted and formed; and the skill and coolness of the artillery, which commenced its fire at the proper moment, and continued it with judgment and vivacity, made such havoc in this disorderly crowd, that after the apparent stupefaction of a few moments, they broke and fled in all directions, and left this little band of heroes to pursue their march without farther molestation.

The disgrace of near thirty thousand men being defeated and foiled by one thousand and forty (including two hundred who had been destroyed in the early part of the day), produced the usual effects of mutual reproach and disagreement; and in this temper the whole body was so inactive as to permit the seven hundred men on detachment to join in a few nights afterwards with a convoy of provisions sufficient for fifty days consumption for the camp and garrison. This, however, was only a temporary relief; but it was expected that the reputation acquired by the late success, if supported by the presence of the troops, might determine the choice of the Raja of Tanjore, who had throughout this campaign been equally lavish of his promises to join each party; and this movement, which would also facilitate the junction of a small reinforcement expected from the sea coast, was resolved on. The presence of Mohammed Ali was considered to be useful for the purpose of negotiation, and he prepared to move into camp from his palace in the town: but the moment this intention was made known to his troops, they assembled in arms in the outer court, announcing their determination not to permit him to depart until he had paid their arrears; and it became necessary to send a body of Europeans to protect him from their threatened violence and escort him to camp. If, in the midst of more grave considerations, some ridicule has been provoked by the quick succession and unroyal deportment of the French Nabobs of M. Dupleix, we cannot impartially refuse a smile to the contemplation of the English Nabob escaping to the field from his own troops, under the protection of English bayonets, followed by exactly *fifty* horse, the rest going off in a few days afterwards to the service of the Mysorean.

To avoid the enemy's cavalry, Major Lawrence directed his march through the woods which approach within a few miles of Trichinopoly on the S.E., and encamped about half way between that town and Tanjore (distant thirty-two miles from each other), a position in which he was conveniently situated for all the objects of his attention. At the expiration of a month he was actually joined by the army of Tanjore, under the command of Monajee, consisting of three thousand horse and two thousand irregular infantry; and by the expected reinforcement of one hundred and seventy English, and three hundred native infantry. On his approaching Trichinopoly from the southward early in August, accompanied by a cumbrous convoy, he perceived the whole of the enemy's force drawn up on the plain to intercept him: and when arrived within a proper distance, he halted to examine their position. Weyconda, a tolerably defensible post on a rock, about two miles and a half to the west of Trichinopoly, had formerly been occupied by a detachment from the garrison; but Captain Dalton had, in the state of his force, found it prudent to withdraw this detachment and destroy the post. His mines having failed in their object, the post was now occupied and strengthened by the enemy. Two rocky eminences, each of them about the same distance as Weyconda, south of the fort, distant from each other about a mile, and the nearest of them not three miles S.E. of Weyconda, were the chief supporting points to the position of the French, now commanded by M. Brennier: a strong corps was on the westernmost of these rocks, and the main body occupied a position on and near the eastern rock; their allies to the left and N.E. of the latter formed a sweep which approached the river, and extended also to the right along the rear of the whole position. The first object of Major Lawrence was to deposit his convoy in safety; and he determined to seize the strong rocky eminence on the enemy's right, as a point which would enable him to pass round that flank without approaching too near to Weyconda. For this purpose he made a demonstration of attacking the main body near the rock on their left, while a select detachment, making a concealed and circuitous route, should carry his real object. This disposition had the intended effect of inducing M. Brennier to strengthen the point which seemed to be threatened, by withdrawing a part of the troops from his right: the rock was carried, and the army and convoy moved on. M. Brennier perceived his error when too late, and sent a detachment to preserve or recover the rock, which halted when they perceived it was lost, but being reinforced, seized an advantageous ground, and commenced a cannonade which severely annoyed the English troops, and compelled them to return it with disadvantage. The main body being still stationary, Major Lawrence conceived the idea of cutting off this detachment by the rapid movement of a body of five hundred infantry, European and native, without guns. The officer commanding this detachment hesitated as he approached the enemy, and Major Lawrence, galloping up and dismounting, placed himself at the head of the grenadiers, and pushed under a severe fire round their left. They did not stand the charge of the bayonet; but, cut off from their main body, ran with precipitation for their post of Weyconda, leaving three field pieces behind them. Captain Dalton, who had now sallied from the fort with a small body and two field pieces, annoyed them in their retreat, and then directed his fire against the enemy's rear, particularly the cavalry of Mysoor, which was sheltering itself in large groups from the fire of the English artillery, and was driven by this fire in reverse entirely off the plain. M. Brennier moved when it

CHAP. VIII. 1753.

was too late to sustain his party; but on seeing their precipitate flight, and the body of the English moving to support their detachment, his troops gave way before the main bodies had exchanged a shot, and retired in confusion, undisturbed by the Tanjorean horse, who had an open field in consequence of the dispersion of the enemy's cavalry. On the same night the enemy took up a position which was too strong to be attempted, under their fortified rock of Weyconda. The Tanjorean undertook and soon accomplished the reduction of Elemisuram, a post about four miles to the S.E. of Trichinopoly, which covered the communication with Tanjore; and Major Lawrence prepared to deposit in store the four thousand bullock loads provided by Mohammed Ali for the garrison of Trichinopoly, which composed this valuable convoy: but the example of Kheir u Deen had not yet taught the English the proper limits of belief. The delicacy or the credulity of Major Lawrence had restrained him from any express check over the mass of loaded cattle, public and private, which this ally was pleased to denominate the department of provisions; and he had now the mortification to learn that he had forfeited the opportunity of following up his victory, for the preservation of a convoy which, on examination, deposited in his stores just *three hundred* bullock load of grain, not ten days food!

During the absence of Major Lawrence from Trichinopoly, the town had been completely depopulated by the removal of the whole Wulsa * to seek for food elsewhere; and the enemy

* Illustrations of the manners and immemorial habits of a people are sometimes unexpectedly derived from a careful attention to the elements or the structure of their language. On the approach of an hostile army, the unfortunate inhabitants

had been earnestly occupied in designs for surprising the garrison. An officer, named De Cattans, had been engaged by M. Dupleix to desert to the English at Trichinopoly, and from thence to indicate to M. Brennier the proper time and place for an escalade; while the French prisoners within were to be liberated, and armed to attack the defenders in the rear. This person was suspected, but the suspicion was concealed; he was permitted to examine every thing, and prepare his report and project; which was seized on the person of his messenger. On this discovery Captain Dalton promised to intercede for his life, provided he would write in his presence another report and project for an attack on a part which he, Captain Dalton, should describe. A letter so prepared was accordingly dispatched by a native messenger; M. Brennier's answer acquiesced in the plan, and the garrison was prepared for his reception for several successive nights, but no

of India bury under ground their most cumbrous effects, and each individual man, woman, and child above six years of age (the infant children being carried by their mothers), with a load of grain proportioned to their strength, issue from their beloved homes, and take the direction of a country (if such can be found) exempted from the miseries of war; sometimes of a strong fortress, but more generally of the most unfrequented hills and woods, where they prolong a miserable existence until the departure of the enemy; and if this should be protracted beyond the time for which they have provided food, a large portion necessarily dies of hunger.

The people of a district thus deserting their homes are called the *Wulsa* of the district. A state of habitual misery, involving precautions against incessant war, and unpitying depredations of so peculiar a description as to require in any of the languages of Europe a long circumlocution, is expressed in *all the languages of Deckan and the south of India* by a *single word*.

No proofs can be accumulated from the most profound research, which shall describe the immemorial condition of the people of India with more authentic precision than this single word.

It is a proud distinction that the *Wulsa* never departs on the approach of a British army when unaccompanied by Indian allies.

CHAP. VIII. 1753.

attempt was made: Major Lawrence concluding from that circumstance that De Cattans had virtually broken the conditions on which Captain Dalton had promised his intercession, ordered him to be hanged in sight of the enemy's position.

A fortnight was employed in making arrangements to remedy the serious disappointment in the amount of expected supply, by means of a succession of smaller convoys. The enemy still remained under cover of their strong position of Weyconda, and Major Lawrence on the 23d of August moved towards them for the purpose of examining it more closely. The object of this movement was misapprehended; a large reinforcement dispatched by M. Dupleix was expected on the next morning, and the French, supposing the dispositions of the English to be directed to intercept this body, of whose march they were really ignorant, moved off with precipitation from Weyconda, and took a strong position on the southern bank of the river. The appearance of this reinforcement on the following morning on the northern bank explained the mutual error, and increased the spirits of the allies; while it gave to the English the mortification of knowing that their inferiority of numbers was again as decided as it had been at any period of the war: for the reinforcement consisted of three thousand Mahratta horse and some infantry under Morari Row, with four hundred Europeans and two thousand native infantry with six guns under M. Astruc, who was reinstated in his former command; while Nunjeraj was also reinforced from Mysoor by a large rabble of all descriptions. Major Lawrence, who also expected a small reinforcement, now moved to the south-eastward of the town to facilitate its junction and cover his supplies, determining to remain on the defensive until its arrival. The same reasons which induced this determination on his part, ought to have decided his opponents in making a vigorous effort against him, or his detachment, previously to the junction; but there was little harmony in their councils: and Major Lawrence, by making demonstrations which ought not to have deceived them, remained undisturbed; and on the sixteenth September the expected reinforcement, consisting of two hundred and thirty-seven Europeans and three hundred sepoys, marched without molestation into his encampment.

The disproportion was still enormous; but Major Lawrence had no further expectations, and his situation required the most daring efforts. The military dispositions of the parties were made in the converse order of their strength; the English encamped on the open field; while the French and their host of allies fortified their camp. Their position was exactly on the ground of the former action; the front only being reversed. The French troops had their right on the eastern rock; regular works for the protection of the front extended about five hundred yards in the direction of the western rock; and another line pointing southward to cover their left flank was begun at its southern extremity, but not yet connected with the western angle of the front line. To the right of the same rock the Mysorean and Mahratta infantry had extended a line of works to the east and then to the south, for the protection of their front and right. The western rock was occupied by a corps of one hundred French infantry, one hundred and fifty topasses, and six hundred sepoys, with two pieces of cannon: the space of about one thousand two hundred yards between this rock and the left of the French intrenchment, and the whole of the rear, from the Mahratta works on the right

CHAP. VIII. 1753. to this western rock on the left, was covered with the cavalry and irregulars in their usual disorderly mass. Colonel Lawrence drew out on the open plain on the twentieth of September to offer battle to this numerous host: but the invitation was declined, and he continued during the day to insult the encampment by a random cannonade, with the view of concealing his more serious intentions. His plan was to carry the western rock before day-light, and from thence to fall upon the unfinished left flank of the French position. The grenadiers were so fortunate as to reach the foot of the western rock before they were perceived: the surprise was perfect; and the post was carried before its defenders had time to discharge their cannon. The fugitives, while they gave the alarm, indicated also the point of attack, and compelled the French to change the disposition of their main body, and draw up fronting the west; the finished works now serving no other purpose but that of a support to their right. Their Europeans occupied the ground from the south-west angle to the end of the unfinished work; and their left, consisting of sepoys, extended farther south. After carrying the western rock, the disposition of Major Lawrence placed his Europeans in the centre, and his sepoys on each flank; and the day began to dawn when they received the orders for the attack of the main body with a general shout, and moved on to the sound of the military music of the parade. The sepoys of the English right first reached their destination, and had caused those of the French line to waver and retreat, at the instant that the European part of the attack in three divisions approached the French infantry, whose left was thus uncovered. The officer commanding the right division of English Europeans seized the opportunity with promptitude; and by a rapid evolution turned the French left, and charging it with the bayonet drove it in confusion on their centre and right, which was at the same moment sustaining a heavy fire in front. The sepoys of the English left meantime pushed on the outside of the works, and carried the eastern rock. The disorder and panic were irretrievable; and the result was an indiscriminate flight, of which the English could not avail themselves: for although the Mahrattas of Tanjore had moved on the left of the whole attack for the express purpose of seizing such an occasion, they were deaf to all the exhortations of Major Lawrence, and could not be restrained from the national tactic of plundering the enemy's camp; while the English were collecting and arranging the trophies of their victory, consisting of eleven pieces of cannon, one hundred French prisoners, with eleven officers, among whom was M. Astruc *, with the whole of their tents and stores of every description. The killed, wounded, and stragglers afterwards taken amounted to two hundred more: while the English killed, wounded, and missing, amounted to forty only. The fugitives covering the whole plain took the route of the south-western ford to the island of Seringham; and on the same evening Major Lawrence moved to dislodge the enemy from Weyconda, which was effected in the course of a few days, although the post had been considerably strengthened.

* The opinion of this officer's talents among the English was not uniform. Mr. Saunders and the government of Madras held them in the highest estimation. Major Lawrence gave the most decided proof of a different judgment. On the occasion of an exchange of prisoners, it happened to be optional with the English to retain or exchange M. Astruc. The government considered it an object of importance to avoid his exchange: Major Lawrence thought it deserving of no consideration; and distinctly states that he considered M. Pasco (whom I can no where else trace) as the most intelligent of the French officers then in Coromandel.

From Weyconda Major Lawrence moved for the conveniency of supply to the south-east of the fort; and after the expiration of a few days, provisions of every description were brought in without interruption, and in such abundance as enabled him to lay in a six months' store for the garrison.

This object being provided for, it became necessary to think of quarters for the troops during the heavy rains of the approaching monsoon, where they could be supplied without the harassing duty of constant convoys in that inclement season: and the place selected was Coilady on the frontier of Tanjore, about fifteen miles to the eastward of Trichinopoly, whither he moved, accompanied by Mohammed Ali, on the twenty-third of October; the Tanjoreans having proceeded to their capital some days before, for the purpose of celebrating the feast of the Dessera, or Maha Noumi.

In the beginning of November the French at Seringham received a farther reinforcement of three hundred Europeans, two hundred topasses, and one thousand sepoys; but continued in their quarters without even interrupting the access of supplies, in order that the garrison might be lulled into a negligence and security, favourable to their intended project, of carrying the place by a coup de main. This operation was attempted on the night of the twenty-seventh of November. The place selected for the main attack was one of those weak and awkward projecting works which cover the gateway of all Indian fortifications, and are by them considered to be strong in proportion to the number of traverses to be passed from the outer to the inner gate. Of these there were two; one, projecting considerably beyond the exterior line of defence, was intended to cover the gate of a sort of fausse-braye; and the other, retired from it, covered the gate of the body of the place. The outer projection of this work had, without much alteration of extent or form, been converted by the English into a tolerably strong outwork; and cut off, somewhat imperfectly, from the inner work of the same kind, which still retained its former traverses, for the purpose of communicating with the outwork. The excavation of the ditch of this outwork was imperfect in one part, where a smooth rock interposed, and now served the French to place their ladders on. The height to be ascended at this place was eighteen feet; that of the interior works was somewhat greater; but exclusively of the chance of succeeding by escalade, they expected, on carrying the first, to be able to pass through the traverses of the second, and apply a petard to the gate. Six hundred Frenchmen were appointed for the assault; the remainder, with the sepoys, were kept in reserve on the glacis, and the allies were to make false attacks in a variety of places. The long inaction of the enemy had certainly produced its effect on the garrison; for the outwork was carried by complete surprise; and if the orders prohibiting firing had been obeyed, the place must in a few minutes more have been in possession of the French. The first musquet shot, however, brought the whole garrison to their appointed posts, and a reserve was instantly moved to sustain the point of real attack. Captain Dalton had resigned the command, and was succeeded by Captain Kilpatrick, who had been severely wounded in the late action, and was now unable to leave his bed; he, however, gave his orders to the second in command with coolness and precision; but with the requisite discretionary power to act for himself. It was now between three and four o'clock of a very dark morning; and while the French had descended from the outwork, and parties were pressing forward to escalade the inner wall, and to apply the petard to the gate, the garrison commenced a vigorous fire of musquetry on the outwork, and on every return of the traverses leading to the gate, while the cannon opened on the points of approach which they respectively flanked, and were answered by the French from the English cannon on the outwork, which they turned against the body of the place. Although nothing was seen in the traverses, the fire of the small detachments stationed for that purpose was ordered to be kept up without the least intermission, and destroyed two parties who successively attempted to apply the petard. The escalade was not more successful. An officer and one man had ascended before the point was discovered; but they were quickly disposed of, and the ladders overset; more were called for, but none could be found. In fact, they had all been broken, some in the act of being overset by the garrison, and others by the flanking fire of the cannon. The most obvious of all precautions had been omitted; that of providing the requisite means of forming a lodgment, or effecting a retreat in the event of discomfiture; for not only had the ladders with which they ascended the outwork been drawn up and sent forward, but not even a rope had been provided or reserved, nor the turban of a native, by which they might have been let down one after another to the rock in the ditch. The assailants accordingly found themselves in the singular predicament of possessing an exposed work from which they could neither advance nor retreat, nor form a lodgment. To call for quarter was unavailing amidst the roar of musquetry and cannon: and the French, as their only resource, began to conceal themselves within the embrasures of the outwork, at the foot of the inner wall, and behind every object that offered cover. Day-light, long and anxiously expected by both parties, but with feelings very dissimilar, enabled the English to comprehend that quarter was demanded; the firing of course ceased, and the prisoners were collected and secured. On the first conviction that the enterprize had failed, about one hundred men had attempted the desperate resource of leaping down to the rock in the ditch; few of them escaped without fractures or severe wounds, but they were carried off by their associates from without; and the intimations from below discouraged the rest from repeating the experiment. The number actually found within the works was three hundred and ninety-seven Europeans, of whom one hundred and four were killed and wounded; and the whole casualties of the night may fairly be stated at five hundred Europeans; a severe loss, considering its proportion to their total strength. Nunjeraj, disappointed in all his hopes, now conceived the idea of achieving with his dismounted cavalry what the French infantry had been unable to accomplish; and on making the proposition, eight thousand volunteers were profuse in their assurances of determination to carry the place at all events. They moved across the river for that purpose on the third night after the former attempt; but finding the garrison alert, they quietly returned, without remembering the blusterings of the morning.

The firing of the first assault was heard at Coilady, and a detachment was sent to reinforce the garrison; while Major Lawrence, informed of the second project, and uneasy from his knowledge of the real weakness of the place against a judicious and determined attack, followed in a few days, and arrived at Trichinopoly on the third of December.

On the separation of the troops of Tanjore from the English for the purpose of returning into winter quarters, every engine of threats and promises, bribes and intrigues, was employed by Nunjeraj and M. Dupleix, effectually to detach the Raja from that alliance. Monajee was considered to be partial to the English, and the removal of this officer from the command of the troops was a necessary preliminary to their success. Succojee was the Raja's minister of finance; and Nunjeraj applied his gold with such effect, as to induce this person to excite the fears and suspicions of the Raja by tales of alleged intrigues and conspiracies of Monajee, to the extent of determining to remove him from the command. This was accordingly accomplished; and the Tanjoreans, under a new general named Gauderow, were preparing to change sides, and join the allies at Seringham, when the intelligence of the failure and serious loss of the French in the attempt on Trichinopoly induced the Raja to pause in his determination. After a fruitless negociation, the French found it necessary to inforce their arguments by the presence of a body of one thousand two hundred Mahrattas in Tanjore: who evaded the unskilful dispositions of Gauderow, and passed to his rear, down to the very sea coast, exercising their usual system of depredation on all that was moveable, and devoting the rest to fire and sword, with merciless indiscrimination. Instead of producing the intended effect, this outrage seemed for the moment to determine the Raja in favour of the opposite party: and he begged of the English to march to his assistance, which Major Lawrence assured him he should do as soon as the state of the roads should permit; for at this moment the whole country was inundated by the rains of the monsoon. In the mean while, he ventured to impute the success of the Mahrattas to the incapacity of Gauderow, and to suggest that Monajee might be restored to the command; but this suggestion only increased the Raja's suspicions; and it was not until the whole of the eastern tract was converted into a waste, that he saw the necessity of again employing that general, who gave early and decided proofs of his capacity, when seriously determined to exert himself. One of those sudden floods which sometimes fill the Caveri and Coleroon for a few days, in the north-east monsoon, had occurred, when he moved against the Mahrattas with three thousand horse. His intimate knowledge of the country enabled him to pass over to an island, between the branches of the rivers on which the Mahrattas were encamped, where their retreat was cut off by the rise of the waters; and after a gallant and obstinate defence, to destroy them to a man. His rancour was the more excited from the consideration that these cruel ravages had been committed by his countrymen, and he disgraced his victory by empaling or hanging all his prisoners.

The suspicions of the Raja, and the jealousy of his minister, had however been too deeply rooted; and it was determined to revert to the former policy of joining neither party, and giving assurances to both. On the return of Monajee, therefore, he was complimented and dismissed, and the army for the present was disbanded.

The number of French prisoners in Trichinopoly had obliged Major Lawrence to augment the garrison; and the amount of his sick was considerable. His disposable force was accordingly

CHAP. VIII. 1753. reduced to six hundred Europeans, including artillerymen, and one thousand eight hundred sepoys. The French, again reinforced, were exactly equal in Europeans; but they had four hundred topasses and six thousand sepoys: while the Mysorean and Mahratta force remained unimpaired, with the exception of the late loss in Tanjore; for although Nunjeraj had, on the requisition of his brother Deo Raj, made a detachment to reinforce Seringapatam against an expected attack of the Poona Mahrattas, this decrease had been more than compensated by a reinforcement received by Morari Row. The defection of the late allies of Major Lawrence had increased all his difficulties with regard to provisions; and he was once more left to the efforts of his little corps, and the resources of his own great mind. The possession of Trichinopoly was considered by both parties as the chief object of the war; and in order to be able to maintain his position in its vicinity, he was obliged to have recourse for supplies

1754. to large and frequent convoys; some from Tanjore, but generally from Tondiman's woods, which extended to within seven miles of the camp. Several of these had arrived in safety, and one still larger was prepared to march from the country of Tanjore in the middle of February. The long inactivity of the enemy had lulled even Major Lawrence into security; and instead of moving his whole force to cover the approach of this important supply, he made a large detachment, amounting to more than one third of his force, consisting of one hundred and eighty-eight Europeans, eight hundred sepoys, and four pieces of cannon. The approach of the convoy was from the east, and along the river: and at the distance of from eight to eleven miles to the eastward of Trichinopoly its route passed through the skirt of Tondiman's woods, where they were sufficiently open to admit the movement of troops. The allies, apprized of these circumstances, moved in the night of the fourteenth of February a corps consisting of twelve thousand horse, Mahratta, and Mysorean, six thousand sepoys, four hundred Europeans, and seven pieces of cannon. The infantry and guns took post in an advantageous and concealed position just to the westward of the wood: the cavalry was placed within it, in equal numbers on each side of the road; and it was concerted that they were to charge both flanks of the column of march, if a favourable opportunity should occur in the wood; and if not, that they should seize the moment of confusion on its being afterwards attacked by the infantry. In this order they waited the approach of the convoy, which appeared about an hour after day light; but the officer commanding, considering the cavalry which he perceived in the woods to be nothing more than a party of plunderers, was negligent in his dispositions; and an accident determined that destruction in the wood, which would probably have been only protracted for a short time by passing to the plain. Herri Sing was not only the rival, but the personal enemy of Hyder; whom he considered as an upstart, indebted for his success in life more to fawning and flattery than to military merit; and would never condescend to address him, or speak of him, by any other designation than the *Naick*. The horse of Meer Aly Reza, the brother-in-law of Hyder, happened to be restive, and on being corrected, became unmanageable, and ran off at speed towards the enemy's ranks. Herri Sing, seeing through the openings of the wood the brother-in-law of Hyder precipitate himself towards the enemy, concluded that he was followed by his troops; and calling out that the

CHAP. VIII. 1754. Naick would have the credit of the day, gave the word and the example to charge. A shot had not yet been fired, when the shout of the Rajpoots was heard; and the troops on both sides of the road, depending on the judgment of Herri Sing, who was deemed their best officer, charged at the same instant in all directions; and the English troops marching in platoons, without any expectation of such an attack, were cut down before they could make a second discharge. When the hurry of the action was over, Hyder, always attended by his Beder peons, was found to be in possession of all the guns and tumbrils: and Herri Sing, who now understood the nature of his first error, claimed them as his own right from having actually carried them; and such was the state of the fact. The honour of the day properly belonged to Herri Sing, but the guns were in possession of his rival; and after a long discussion, he was obliged to compound for one, and to leave the remaining three to Hyder, as the substantial trophies of a victory which he had not gained. The French troops came up in time to save the lives of a few of the English. Of a hundred and eighty-eight, thirty-eight were without wounds, fifty were killed, and one hundred desperately wounded. The whole of those invaluable grenadiers who had on all occasions led the way in the extraordinary victories which had been achieved, were unfortunately included in this disaster, the most serious which the English had sustained in the whole course of the war.

Mr. Saunders made the best efforts in his power to remedy this misfortune, by sending from Madras all the Europeans he could possibly spare, amounting to a hundred and eighty men, by sea to Devicota, there to wait for an opportunity to join: but Major Lawrence, convinced that the French were now commanded by a man (M. Maissin) who would lose no favourable opportunity of attacking his detachments, or attempting the garrison in his absence, was particularly anxious that a body of horse should, if possible, be obtained to accompany this small reinforcement in its approach; and some hope seemed to present itself by the appearance of Mahphuz Khan at the head of two thousand horse, and the same number of irregular infantry, in the north-western frontier of the province of Arcot; ostensibly to support his brother. This man, the eldest and only legitimate son of Anwar u Deen, had been taken prisoner at the battle of Amboor in 1749, and carried to Pondicherry: and Mohammed Ali, alarmed lest the French in the course of events might select him as their Nabob, had prevailed on Nasir Jung, when negotiating with M. Dupleix in 1750, to request the release of Mahphuz Khan, which was granted as a matter of courtesy. He remained with that army throughout the revolutions which caused the successive deaths of Nasir Jung and Muzuffer Jung, and the accession of Salabut Jung, until its arrival at Hyderabad, where he lived for some time, supported by a pension from that prince; but was unable, from the ascendancy of M. Bussy, to disturb the arrangement then established in favour of Chunda Saheb. Tired of a fruitless attendance at Hyderabad, he went to reside with the Nabob of Kurpa, with whom he had made acquaintance; and was now privately encouraged by him, and furnished with the means of trying his fortune among the rival Nabob-makers. Mohammed Ali, who did not misapprehend the views of Mahphuz Khan, made great efforts to embark him in hostility with the French, and thus increase the difficulties of a communication which he dreaded. Mahphuz Khan had reasons

CHAP. VIII. 1754. equally strong for procrastination; and at every successive march was unable to move without fresh pecuniary supplies; giving little hope that he should ever be moved so far south as the Coleroon. Major Lawrence, though almost despairing, as his letters evince, of the cause of his country, and oppressed with serious illness, which compelled him to make frequent applications to be relieved by an officer capable of assuming the command, was induced, by the urgent solicitations of his government, to continue his valuable services with the fearfully-insufficient means which he possessed.

It was now impracticable to risque distant convoys, and the woods of Tondiman were his only resource. His small convoys were generally commanded by Mohammed Issoof; a man who had entered the English service as a Soubadar under Mr. Clive, and was a worthy disciple of the school in which he was reared. His perfect fidelity, intelligence, and military talents, had deservedly obtained the confidence of Major Lawrence, and he was promoted to the rank of Commandant of all the English sepoys, and continued to perform the service of the convoys with admirable vigilance and address. Major Lawrence had no European officer capable of filling the office of interpreter in his communications with the natives; and this duty was performed by a bramin named Poniapa, who was necessarily admitted to a large portion of his confidence in all that related to those communications. This wretch, tired of the dangers of a military life, despairing of the English cause, and desirous of partaking of the inexhaustible treasures of Nunjeraj, suggested to him, by a secret message, to demand of Major Lawrence that Poniapa should be sent to Seringham, to hear some proposals which he had to make for the termination of the war. This was accordingly done; and, on his return, he made to Major Lawrence a plausible report of the substance of the conference; which had actually terminated in his engaging, on the promise of a large reward, to betray the cause of the English. He accordingly revealed to Nunjeraj the actual state of their provisions, and the whole detail of their arrangements for procuring supplies. The accidental confinement of the secret messenger of Poniapa caused some delay in their subsequent communications; but his next message suggested, that nothing could be done towards starving Trichinopoly without the removal of Mohammed Issoof, who was the only person in the army capable of conducting the convoys; that his vigilance might render it difficult to cut him off; but that the same end might be accomplished by means of a letter (to be intercepted) addressed by Nunjeraj to Mohammed Issoof. Poniapa had in this plot a double object: if the English should be betrayed, he secured his reward from Nunjeraj: if they should ultimately surmount the difficulties with which they were surrounded, he would have removed a rival, of whose influence he was jealous, and whose extensive trust in the department of supply interfered with his own plans of embezzlement. The letter was written in conformity to his own advice; and being purposely dropped by the messenger, on his return, was watched by him until he saw it taken up; when he disappeared, and gave indirect intelligence, in consequence of which it was brought to Major Lawrence, and opened* and interpreted by Poniapa.

* It is stated by Mr. Orme, (vol. i. p. 348) besides the usual seal, to have been stamped on the back with "*the print of a hand, a form equivalent with the Mysoreans to an oath.*" I have endeavoured, without success, to trace the existence of any *emblem* or *practice* of this nature.

CHAP. VIII. 1754.

It desired Mohammed Issoof, and another officer, to meet, according to promise, the deputies of Nunjeraj for the purpose of adjusting the terms and manner of betraying the garrison of Trichinopoly; and conveyed a formal obligation to pay Mohammed Issoof four lacs of pagodas on receiving possession of the place. Major Lawrence was completely deceived by this artifice. Mohammed Issoof was instantly imprisoned; and this diabolical plot, for the murder of a brave and innocent man, was on the point of succeeding, when the officers appointed to conduct the investigation were fortunately enabled to trace the person who had dropped the letter. A scene of impudent and villainous address on the part of Poniapa, and of complicated prevarication on the part of his messenger, terminated in an open confession by the latter of the whole truth; and Poniapa was publicly blown away from the mouth of a cannon as soon as Major Lawrence could obtain the sanction of the government of Madras, which he deemed it prudent to require. The transaction, however, revealed to Mohammed Issoof the danger of a connection with strangers, who were at the mercy of their interpreters: and his confinement made on his mind an impression of disgust which was never afterwards entirely effaced.

While Nunjeraj was occupied with these projects, Mohammed Ali, and the Raja of Tanjore, equally interested in detaching Morari Row from the confederacy, had prevailed on him by some payments, and larger promises, to consent to their proposals: and that chief, finding that the pecuniary supplies of Nunjeraj were not so liberal as formerly, and that his brother Deo Raj, who had uniformly disapproved the war, now threatened to withhold them altogether if he did not immediately make peace, demanded of him a settlement of his accounts; the stated balance of which, as usual, trebled the true amount. Altercations ensued; and Morari Row, in order to extort before his departure as much as possible from all parties, separated from the confederates on the 11th of May, and encamped on the northern bank of the Coleroon; offering, however, to return, provided his whole balance were immediately paid.

This appearance augured favourably for the English cause; but no intermission could be made in the business of convoys, and Major Lawrence was dangerously ill, and confined to his bed. A detachment marched under Captain Calliaud, accompanied by Mohammed Issoof, on the morning of the 12th, consisting of a hundred and twenty Europeans, five hundred sepoys, and two field pieces, with the intention of proceeding about two miles to the southward of the rocks, which were the scene of the late actions, to a post affording some cover, consisting of the excavation and bank of an old reservoir, where the convoy was appointed to meet him. Nunjeraj obtained intelligence of this design, and of the illness of Major Lawrence; and, on communicating with M. Maissin, the opportunity was judged to be favourable for striking a decisive blow. A detachment was accordingly made, consisting of two hundred and fifty Europeans, one thousand sepoys, four thousand select horse of Mysoor, and four field pieces; who moved by a circuitous route at an earlier hour, and occupied the post to which Captain Calliaud was marching. Mohammed Issoof reconnoitring in front ascertained the fact; and it was determined that it was most safe, whatever was their force, instantly to attack them before the day should dawn and discover their own. The alarm was taken on both sides; a mere demonstration was made of a scattered fire in

CHAP. VIII. 1754. front, while the English party in separate divisions fell on both flanks with perfect spirit, and fairly dislodged them with considerable loss: but they quickly rallied, and when the day appeared, commenced a cannonade, which was answered with the disparity of two to four. Captain Polier, who commanded in camp, no sooner heard the firing than he marched with his remaining force to their support. The remainder of the confederates had also crossed the river ready to act as circumstances should require; and, on perceiving this movement, marched to intercept it: but no time had been lost, and the junction was formed. The united force of the English now consisted of three hundred and sixty Europeans, and fifteen hundred sepoys, eleven troopers, and three field pieces: but the confederates drew up determined to intercept their return to the garrison, with seven hundred Europeans, fifty dragoons, five thousand sepoys, ten thousand Mysorean horse, and seven guns. The English corps moved for about a mile with great steadiness, but considerable loss, under a heavy fire of cannon and musketry, and took post at another bank and excavation of the same kind. Captain Polier had received two wounds, and the command devolved on Captain Calliaud, who now perceived the enemy making a disposition for a general and close assault. He judiciously turned his whole attention to the French battalion, which, in advancing, received a quick and well-directed fire of grape from the three field pieces on the flanks of the English, which materially thinned their ranks: he perceived them to waver, rushed forward, and, when close to their bayonets, poured in a volley of musketry, which threw them into a disorder that all the efforts of their officers could not remedy. The sepoys and Mysoreans followed the example; and Captain Calliaud was happy to pursue his march without farther molestation, with the loss of six officers out of nine, fifty-five soldiers, and a hundred and fifty sepoys killed and wounded: the enemy's casualties amounting to about double that number. The convoy, which, on the first alarm, had retreated into the woods, on receiving information of this event, proceeded on the same night, and arrived without interruption.

Nunjeraj and M. Maissin, irritated by this fresh disgrace, resolved to pursue another plan of operations, and destroy the country from which the supplies were received: for which purpose they moved with the whole of the Europeans and the greater part of the French sepoys and Mysorean horse. Tondiman had made his previous dispositions for such a visit; and on the approach of the confederates, three nights afterwards, his cordon of matchlocks gave the alarm: the inhabitants quitting their villages, and driving off their cattle to the depth of the woods, left the roofs of their houses, composed of bamboo and dry grass, to be burned by the enemy: the only injury (easily replaced in a single day) which they effected in this expedition, besides the destruction of a few bags of rice in the English depot. Before their return, however, they determined to wreak their vengeance on the Raja of Tanjore.

The river Caveri is separated into two branches by what is usually named the Island of Seringham, opposite to Trichinopoly. About thirteen miles to the eastward of the point of separation the branches again approach; but the northern branch has at this place obtained a level about twenty feet lower than the southern. The northern branch, named the Coleroon, is

CHAP. LVII. 1754.

permitted to run waste and unproductive to the sea; but the southern, which retains the name of the Caveri, has been led in a variety of channels by the skill and industry of the early Hindoos to irrigate the whole province of Tanjore, and is the cause of its extraordinary fertility. At the point of approach of the two branches, which has been described, the floods had, at some remote period, burst through the narrow intervening neck; and it had become necessary to construct a mound of masonry, of considerable dimensions, to prevent the Caveri, during the annual floods, from descending into the Coleroon, and to preserve it in its higher level to fertilize the province of Tanjore. The exploit of the confederates was the destruction of this mound; an operation which could, by no construction, be considered to have a military object, and must therefore be exclusively referred to political views. But if the destruction of a whole unarmed and unoffending people for the purpose of changing the political conduct of its prince be really authorized by the rules of war, it is time for every soldier to be heartily ashamed of his trade; and we should be disposed to hope, for the honour of civilized nations, that M. Maissin was not implicated in this act of his ally, if the supposition could be reconciled with the fact of the workmen subsequently employed in the repair of the dyke having been cannonaded by the French troops.

Major Lawrence prepared to avail himself of the impression which would probably be made on the Raja's mind by this disgraceful outrage: and marched on the 23d in the direction of Tanjore, having previously withdrawn all the distant outposts for the reinforcement of the garrison of Trichinopoly. He was met on the second day by the faithful Tondiman, who was received with suitable demonstrations of respect: and on the same day by letters from the Raja, full of gratitude for his prompt assistance. Meanwhile Gauderow had been dispatched with fifteen hundred horse to prevent, as far as possible, the extension of the enemy's ravages. The French and Mysoreans had returned to Seringham; but Morari Row, meditating the means of getting money from all parties before his departure, saw, in the approach of this corps, the prospect of at once promoting that object, and revenging the late destruction of his detachment in Tanjore. He accordingly crossed the rivers by night, with double the number of Gauderow's troops; and at day-light destroyed his whole detachment, with the exception of three hundred, who, with their general, saved themselves by a timely flight. Two days after this defeat Major Lawrence arrived at Tanjore, and was joined by the expected reinforcement from the coast, consisting of a hundred and fifty Europeans and five hundred sepoys. Major Lawrence was too much indisposed to attend personally the negotiation with the Raja; but it terminated favourably in the appointment of Monajee to the double post of commander in chief and minister of finance, with authority to prepare the troops for immediate service. Mr. Saunders had equipped a separate corps to accompany Mahphuz Khan, who after some timid skirmishing with the French parties about Ginjee, and abundant prevarication, had actually been moved by the force of money and reinforcements as far south as Fort St. David, where he made a stand for more money. The levy of the Tanjoreans proceeded but slowly; the conduct of Mahphuz Khan had shewn that he was entitled to little respect as a friend or as an enemy, and that it was a hopeless waste of time to wait his arrival. Major Lawrence accordingly ordered the English detachment to move without him, and they joined him on the 14th of August. Thus reinforced, he found himself at the head of twelve hundred English and topasses; three thousand English sepoys, and fourteen field pieces; two thousand five hundred Tanjorean cavalry, and three thousand infantry; and the fifty horse of Mohammed Ali. The confederates at Seringham now consisted of the French reinforced by two hundred Europeans, and the Mysoreans at their former strength; for they had finally lost the services of Morari Row, who (allowing for the exhausted finances of the contending parties) had levied a tolerably successful contribution previously to his departure. After the affair of Gauderow he wrote to Mohammed Ali, that on receiving good security for three lacs of rupees, he was willing to depart, never again to return to the Payeen ghaut. Mohammed Ali had neither money nor credit; but the Raja of Tanjore had both: and was finally prevailed on to furnish the sum by instalments; viz. half a lac on the arrival of Morari Row two marches north of Trichinopoly; a lac on his ascending the ghauts; and the remaining lac and a half on his arrival at Gooti. As soon as he found that this project would succeed, he unfolded the state of the negotiation, with an air of entire frankness, but suitable exaggeration, to Nunjeraj; professing his regret that the necessity of his affairs required that he should raise money by whatever means; and offering to break off the negotiation, and return to Nunjeraj, on a fair adjustment of his balance by instalments. The terms were soon concluded; and the first instalment of Nunjeraj, consisting of half a lac, had no sooner reached his camp, than he marched to receive the first instalment of the other party; and moving at his ease over the province, levying contributions without the appearance of direct hostility, he finally ascended the ghauts about the beginning of July.

Major Lawrence entered the plains of Trichinopoly on the 17th of August, accompanied by a considerable convoy; and found the confederates in motion to interrupt his approach. Observing that the French had neglected to occupy a water-course and bank in the direct route, which would have compelled him to engage at a disadvantage, or make a considerable detour, he moved directly to his object, securing the bank as he approached. The enemy formed in order of battle to the left of his principal column of march; and as he did not think proper to refuse the invitation, he wheeled into line and made his dispositions for their reception. They advanced deliberately, and at first with a good countenance; but the number of the English artillery was now superior, and before they had arrived at the proper distance for musketry, the French went suddenly about, with the appearance at first of some confusion, but afterwards retreated in good order towards their camp. This retrograde movement was in reality a feint. Hyder, at the head of a select body of Mysoreans, had engaged to fall upon the baggage and provisions, protected by the Tanjoreans and the usual English guard, as soon as he should perceive Major Lawrence to advance in pursuit of the French infantry. This attack of the convoy it was expected would either be completely successful, or if Major Lawrence should return for its support, the French were prepared to fall on his rear; while a reserve from the island was to cross and cover Hyder's retreat with his booty. But Hyder moved too soon; Major Lawrence was actually preparing

1754. for the pursuit, when he received the report of an attack on the baggage and convoy, which the English detachment, forming the usual guard, had very improperly left, without orders, for the purpose of partaking in the business of the advance. The best dispositions were immediately ordered by Major Lawrence: a sally from the garrison compelled the reserve from the island to return; and Hyder had only time to secure about thirty-five carts laden, some with public, and some with private stores, which he carried off to the island. The English casualties on this day were trifling: but M. Maissin had lost one hundred Europeans in performing a feint which failed in its object.

After depositing his provisions in the stores of the garrison, Major Lawrence prepared to force the enemy to a decisive action; but their movements being entirely defensive, nothing serious occurred: and he placed his army in cantonments, preparatory to the rains, on the 23d of September; detaching, according to his promise, the troops of Tanjore, accompanied by a small English corps, to protect the workmen employed in the repairs of the embankment. The English and French had at this time respectively received large reinforcements from Europe; and the former would have taken the field in the ensuing campaign with equal numbers and more sanguine hopes, but on the 11th of October a suspension of arms for three months terminated in a conditional treaty.

The extraordinary character of the war of Coromandel, in which the operations of a handful of troops assumed the political importance, and outstripped the military glory, of the mightiest armies, has imperceptibly led to a more detached* description

* The reader who desires to examine them in greater detail may consult with

than belongs to the general purpose of this work; and it appeared to be most convenient to continue until this period, without interruption from other matter, the narrative of military operations in which the troops of Mysoor were engaged. But it will now be necessary to revert to the circumstances which led to the cessation of arms between the European nations who have necessarily occupied the fore ground* in that narrative, and which occasioned the return of Nunjeraj to Mysoor. CHAP. VIII. 1754.

advantage the justly esteemed work of Mr. Orme. Having diligently examined the records of Fort St. George for the purpose of verifying facts and dates, I am enabled to add my humble testimony to the extreme accuracy of that author in describing the events recorded in this chapter: and from his authority, where it applies, I have seldom ventured to dissent, except on the ground of information to which he had no access.

* A general letter from Madras, dated the 29th October 1753, discusses the merits of the native allies. The troops of Morari Row are placed first, next to them the Tanjoreans. The letter thus proceeds, "Those of the Nabob (Mohammed Ali) and the king of Mysoor, fill a large space of ground, but it must be to their future courage that they will owe any thing that can be said in their favour."

CHAPTER IX.

FROM 1754 TO 1758.

Military operations in the province of Arcot—in Deckan—Distinguished talents of M. Bussy—Character of Salabut Jung—Cession to the French of the northern Circars—Views of M. Dupleix—Negotiation with the English—broken off—Nunjeraj also negotiates with the English—examination of the terms which they propose—Of the nature of Indian tribute—unjustifiable concealment of the terms from Mohammed Ali—M. Dupleix superseded by M. Godeheu in consequence of negotiations in Europe—Cessation of arms—Conditional treaty—its nugatory conditions—Nunjeraj offended—but recalled by Deo Raj on the invasion of Mysoor by Salabut Jung, accompanied by M. Bussy—embarrassment of that officer in discriminating friends and enemies—besieges Seringapatam—tribute exacted—hostages—application of these facts to the previous description of tribute—Nunjeraj arrives too late—reduction of his army—acquisition of Dindigul—Hyder appointed Foujedar—his proceedings become more interesting from this period—his system of warfare and plunder—Kundè Row—Hyder's conduct in his new government—ludicrous deceptions—address and talents—affairs at the capital—abortive designs of the pageant Raja—plan for removing him by poison—Dissention of the usurpers Deo Raj and Nunjeraj—outrageous conduct of the latter—secession and departure of Deo Raj—his appropriation of the revenues allotted to Hyder—Balajee Row besieges Seringapatam—compromise by the pledge of territory—evaded by the advice of Hyder—his negotiation with Deo Raj—facilitated by the result of a late invasion of Malabar—Hyder returns to Dindigul—invades the province of Madura—is defeated and retires—intention of returning to Madura prevented by the necessity of proceeding to the capital.

CHAP. IX. 1754. THE military efforts of the French and English and their respective allies in the province of Arcot had produced no decided advantage to either party; and the surplus revenues received by Mohammed Ali, after the defalcations and prodigal incapacity of his brother Abd-ul-Wahab at Arcot, and his other representatives, were stated to be little more than sufficient to defray his personal expences. But during four campaigns, in which the superior numbers of the French and Mysoreans to the south of the Coleroon so little corresponded with the energy of their cabinet, the operations of the French in the Deckan were directed by a man whose military talents and political address were fitted to execute, and even to outmarch, the gigantic schemes of M. Dupleix.

Salabut Jung, the Soubadar of the Deckan created by M. Bussy on the fall of Muzzuffer Jung in 1751, would, in common 1751.
life, have been reckoned a man of moderate talents; but he wanted the firmness, as well as the grasp of mind, which were necessary in the situation to which he was elevated: sometimes treating M. Bussy with the gratitude and consideration due to the author of his political existence, at others, suspecting him of direct intentions to usurp his authority. The latter sentiment was inflamed by a numerous party at his court, whose views were obstructed by the personal influence of M. Bussy, and by the essential services successively performed by the corps under his command. In the various political machinations which ensued, that officer evinced a sagacity and address which foiled the most experienced adepts in oriental intrigue, and a boldness which commanded their respect. The existence of the French corps was, however, held by a precarious tenure, so long as its resources of every description depended on the punctuality of an Indian court; and M. Bussy had found it necessary to insist on a permanent appropriation of territorial revenue, by the absolute

CHAP. IX. 1754. cession of the whole of those provinces now denominated the northern Circars: which not only afforded the requisite pecuniary resources, but furnished the convenient means of receiving reinforcements of men and military stores from Pondicherry and Mauritius; and thus enabled him to extend his political views to the indirect or absolute empire of all Deckan and the south. The
1753. cession of these provinces was concluded in November, 1753; and M. Dupleix, who was probably aware that the tendency of opinion in France was unfavourable, not to the extent, but to the practicability of his plans, was desirous of trying the effect of negotiation with these powerful means of deterring Mr. Saunders from a continuation of the war. In January, 1754, the deputies appointed by both parties met at the intermediate and neutral Dutch settlement of Sadras. The discussions commenced with unfolding their mutual projects: the English contending for the acknowledgment of Mohammed Ali as Nabob of Arcot, and the guarantee of the Raja of Tanjore: and the French, for the acknowledgment of Salabut Jung as Soubadar of the Deckan, and the rejection of Mohammed Ali as Nabob of Arcot. It was plain from this commencement, that the views of the parties could never be brought to coincide; but they began most gravely to discuss the legal titles of their several Soubadars and Nabobs on which these respective projects were founded, and to produce the authenticated instruments of investiture; all of them supported, as usual, by the mandates of the Mogul. Public discussion could scarcely have assumed more ludicrous shapes than arose from the scrutiny of seals, official forms, signatures and dates, and reciprocal accusations of forgery: and the conferences

broke up in eleven days from their commencement, after the expenditure of much paper, infinite rancour, and very distinguished ingenuity on both sides.

During these discussions between the English and French, Nunjeraj thought proper to open a separate negotiation with the English, for the purpose of inducing them to withdraw their sanction from the fraudulent detention of Trichinopoly. Vencat Row Berkie, the officer who had formerly commanded the troops of Mysoor in the campaign of Nasir Jung, was selected for this purpose, from his having formed, during the service against Chunda Saheb, a particular intimacy with an English officer*, whose introduction and aid at Madras were expected to be useful.

The Company's commercial concerns had been thrown into the greatest embarrassment by a war, supported almost exclusively from their own treasury, which had already cost them thirty-five lacs of pagodas for Trichinopoly only: and in whatever manner the political questions might be disposed of, the relief from this embarrassment appeared to Mr. Saunders to be of paramount consideration. After a variety of discussions, the propositions stated in the following abstract appeared to approach

* The Hindoos distort our names as much as we do theirs, and I cannot conjecture that which is intended by *Klees* (it cannot be Clive, for he was in England), as it is written in Poornia's MSS. from domestic memoranda in the family of Vencat Row. I cannot ascertain the date of his arrival at Madras. In the discussions between the French and English deputies, the former accuse Mr. Saunders of forcibly detaining Vencat Row, and Nunjeraj makes the same representation to Major Lawrence, who repeats it to the governor. The fact, as will be supposed, was absolutely unfounded, and was a simple *invention* of Nunjeraj to justify his disavowing the acts of his agent.

CHAP. IX. 1754.

sufficiently near to the views of both parties, to be submitted to Nunjeraj as the basis of adjustment.

1. The Raja of Mysoor shall renounce the French connexion, and aid in the establishment of Mohammed Ali. 2. He shall induce Morari Row to do the same. 3. Until Mohammed Ali be established, Nunjeraj shall defray the expences of his own army, and that of Morari Row. 4. He shall give soucar security for the whole amount expended by the Company in the war of Trichinopoly, to be paid on the actual delivery of that place; which, however, shall pay the *usual tribute* to the Carnatic. 5. He shall pay ten lacs to Mohammed Ali, and shall cede to him a district and fort in Mysoor equal to two lacs a year. It does not appear whether these ten lacs were intended for the extinction of the debt due by Mohammed Ali to Nunjeraj, or as a farther payment. The other articles relate to exclusive trade with Mysoor; the time of delivering the fort of Trichinopoly*; the arrangements regarding stores, &c.; an eventual invitation to the Raja of Tanjore to accede; and a reciprocal guarantee of the two Rajas, the English, and Mohammed Ali. It also appears in the course of the discussion, that Nunjeraj expected the English to assist him in the *conquest* of Madura, Tinevelly, and the southern dependencies; an obligation which would have involved them in a long, unprofitable, and sanguinary warfare. But the article which would seem to have been least considered,

* It was to remain in possession of the English until all the other articles should be fulfilled: and for the purpose of qualifying this detention to Nunjeraj, the government suggested to Major Lawrence to admit a certain proportion of Mysorean troops. His answer to this unmilitary proposition is somewhat abrupt. "Give me leave to tell you the proposal is absurd and impracticable." Letter, May 15, 1754.

was the payment of the *usual* tribute, without fixing a specific sum.

When an Indian conqueror leaves to a chief of any considerable power the interior management of his country on the condition of paying an annual sum as tribute, it is tolerably well understood by the parties that it will not be paid without, at least, the presence of an army to demand it; which usually occurs after an interval of some years. Exclusively of the habit and the views to farther power and independence which such a dependant generally entertains as a point of honour, and in some degree as a religious injunction *, he would be unwise to make regular payments, because they would be considered as evidence of treasures worth plundering. The army accordingly arrives. It is perhaps repelled; or a stout resistance is made; or efforts more feeble; and the operation terminates either in receiving nothing, or a sum as arrears of tribute calculated at an annual value, greater or less than the last amount paid, to which the expenses of the expedition real or pretended are or are not added, according to the degrees of success or of failure. In all questions of tribute, therefore, the party of whom it is demanded, if he acknowledge the claim at all, rates it at the lowest, and the party demanding, at the highest sum, which has ever been paid. This claim the parties in this case (as in all Indian negociations without exception) would for these very reasons severally desire to leave as indefinite as possible, or exactly in the manner stated in these propositions; which would have been to the English, as guarantees, a source of endless embarrassment.

* See note to p. 25.

CHAP. IX. 1754. It was supposed that the negotiation could best be conducted by Major Lawrence; but he excused himself on the plea of ill health: in some of his letters appearing to hesitate in his opinion, and in others to disapprove the proposed conditions, but uniformly expressing his regret "that the attempt had been made to keep Trichinopoly after promising to cede it." My materials do not enable me to trace with precision the future progress of this negotiation. Nunjeraj and Vencat Row Berki both returned to Mysoor, without any thing having been accomplished; and I can only find that in February 1756 the directors of the Company in England ordered the government of Madras to renew the agitation of a treaty on the basis above explained; and farther directed that Mr. Orme (the historian), then a member of council, should be employed to conduct the negotiation. The proposals had been communicated to Mohammed Ali in 1754, and the belief that this communication had occasioned their failure, had probably suggested to the directors in England an injunction of secrecy on the present occasion; for the government of Madras in replying to the letter from England observe, that they deem it imprudent to make any *public* advances to the Raja of Mysoor, because of the alarm it might unavoidably give to Mohammed Ali and the Raja of Tanjore; but they invested Mr. Orme with the prescribed authority. A correspondence ensued between that gentleman and Vencat Row; and the negociation* appears to

* Notices of these negociations are to be found in the general letters from Madras, 20th November, 1756; 28th February and 10th November, 1757; and 13th March and 10th October, 1758. References are made in these letters to the proceedings of what are named "private committees," not one of which has been preserved either at Madras or the India house in London, although the other re-

have been secretly continued by him, and successively reported by the government at different periods, until October 1758, after which time I find on the records no farther mention of these transactions.

Viewing the general objects of these propositions, if they had been made and enforced at the period when the shameful fraud practised on Nunjeraj was first discovered, the act would have claimed our admiration, as the indignant resolve of a generous people, who acknowledged "justice" alone "as the standing policy of nations," and spurned at association with dishonour. But after carrying on a long and sanguinary war ostensibly as auxiliaries in defence of that breach of treaty, to make these propositions as principals without the concurrence or the knowledge of Mohammed Ali, materially changes the colour of the transaction; the slender praise of tardy conviction is not even claimed upon the record, and the whole is referred to that commanding plea of necessity and self preservation, which so often overrules whatever of morals is mixed with political discussion.

The apprehensions of a change of politics in Europe, which had induced M. Dupleix to try the effect of negotiation in January, were verified on the second of August by the arrival of M. Godeheu to supersede his authority. 1754.

The directors of the English East India Company had in the preceding year made urgent representations to their ministry, regarding the ruinous war in which, during a period of profound tranquillity in Europe, they were involved with the French in

cords of the same period are tolerably complete, particularly at Madras. I can trace no notice direct or indirect of these transactions in the work of Mr. Orme, which is brought down three years later than the date of these records.

India, as ostensible auxiliaries to native chiefs; and demanded either that national support, which they represented the French company to receive; or the interposition of their government with that of France, to put an end to the war. The British ministry accordingly began a negotiation on that subject, and supported their arguments by dispatching the reinforcements of troops, whose arrival we have noticed, and preparing farther succours. The discussion terminated in Europe in the appointment of commissioners, empowered to investigate in India the state of public affairs; and to adjust a conditional treaty to be ratified in Europe, on grounds of perfect equality, without reference to the advantages which either party might have acquired. The French were aware that M. Dupleix, the author of the policy which had produced these hostilities, would be objected to as their commissioner; and considering his schemes to be more visionary and impracticable than perhaps they really were, spontaneously superseded him by the appointment of M. Godehue, with absolute powers over all their possessions in India. Mr. Saunders (aided by certain members of his council) was named on the part of the English: and they entered on the duties of their appointment with mutual demonstrations of good will, without relaxing in their efforts for the prosecution of the war while the negotiations were pending. But after the arrival of the reinforcements, Mr. Godehue pressed the necessity of suspending farther hostility, and Mr. Saunders consented to the cessation of arms for three months, from the eleventh of October, which has already been mentioned.

The object of the conditional treaty appears to have been the conclusion of hostilities in the Carnatic (Drauveda) alone;

for in no other respect was the basis of *perfect equality* at all perceptible. It stipulated that the two companies should for ever renounce all Moorish government and dignity, and should never interfere in any differences that might arise between the princes of the country, while M. Bussy continued to fight the battles of Salabut Jung against the powers of the country of every description; and to possess the substantial Moorish government and dignity of the extensive and valuable provinces of the northern Circars, not noticed in the treaty. The possessions to be held in the Carnatic (Drauveda) by the parties, during the reference to Europe, and the establishment of their several factories, were equitably fixed as far as regarded those exclusive objects. During the interval, neither party was to procure new cessions, and in all other respects the principle of uti possidetis was recognized until a definitive treaty should be adjusted in Europe. A cartel was established, which left a balance of six hundred and fifty French prisoners in the English prisons: and finally, the allies of each were included in a truce corresponding with the conditions of the provisional treaty, and if they should attempt to break it, were to be coerced by both parties.

1754.

The terms of this truce were published on the eleventh of January 1755; but Nunjeraj did not recognize the right of the French to make a treaty for him, or to prevent his committing hostilities against the English and their allies. He requested that the French might be pleased to retire with their troops to Pondicherry, if they, like Mohammed Ali, and the English, thought proper to recede from the obligations of their alliance. He pompously declared, that whether with them or without them he was determined never to leave the lower country until he

1755.

should take Trichinopoly; and accordingly recommenced his blundering operations for endeavouring to obtain possession of it by treachery, which were continued until the fourteenth of April; when the positive injunctions of his brother Deo Raj, founded on the most imminent domestic danger, induced him to depart, probably without much regret, at the necessity of relinquishing a service which had become absolutely hopeless; since, according to his own statements, he had long since discovered the determination of the French to keep the place for themselves if they should succeed in its conquest.

On the departure of Nunjeraj from a scene in which he had only covered himself with ridicule and disgrace, the French detachment was left in possession of the island of Seringham, the revenues of which, it will be recollected, had been formally given up by Mohammed Ali to Nunjeraj.

The danger which called for the return of the troops under Nunjeraj was the approach of Salabut Jung with a large army, accompanied by the efficient corps of M. Bussy, to exact, as Soubadar of the Deckan, the arrears of tribute due by Mysoor; a demand which Deo Raj had absolutely no means of paying, and therefore determined to resist. The French were by treaty in strict alliance with Mysoor; but they were also bound by treaty to fight all the battles of Salabut Jung, and consequently to treat as enemies their allies of Mysoor. The embarrassment was felt by M. Bussy, and he used all his influence to prevent hostility; but finding his efforts unavailing, he determined to execute the treaty which he himself had concluded. Few of the fortresses of Mysoor which they passed in their approach attempted to resist; among those which were so imprudent was the weak fort of Koongul, fifty-four miles north by east from Seringapatam, which stood the assault of the French troops, and suffered severely for its rashness. On their arrival before Seringapatam, Deo Raj quickly found that he had miscalculated in supposing that he could hold out until the arrival of his brother. The operations were carried on with a rapidity of which he had formed no previous conception, by regular approaches against the north-eastern angle, which would in a few days have brought the contest to the issue of an assault. M. Bussy repeated his admonitions and entreaties that this crisis should be averted; and, among other arguments, represented the approach of the Poona Mahrattas under Balajee Row, who would plunder the open country if Deo Raj should continue to occupy the army of Salabut Jung before Seringapatam; whereas if he would submit to the terms prescribed, M. Bussy engaged by negotiation, or force, to avert the Mahratta invasion. The sum finally adjusted was fifty-six lacks of rupees; but the treasury was entirely exhausted by the enormous expenses of the long service at Trichinopoly, aggravated by the subsidy paid during most of that period to Morari Row, and by the loss of ten lacs of pagodas lent to Mohammed Ali. The revenues had also been diminished in the preceding year by the contributions levied by Balajee Row in his route from a campaign in the Deckan along the northern borders of Mysoor: and it was necessary to devise some extraordinary means of paying, or satisfying, Salabut Jung and M. Bussy. In this extremity the whole of the plate and jewels belonging to the Hindoo temples in the town were put in requisition, together with the jewels and precious metals, constituting the immediate property or personal ornaments of the Raja and his family: but the total sum which could thus be realized

1755.

amounted to no more than one-third of what was stipulated. For the remainder Deo Raj prevailed on the Soucars, or bankers, of the capital to give security, and to deliver as hostages their principal Gomashtas, or confidential agents: but as he was never afterwards enabled to satisfy the Soucars, they left the Gomashtas to their fate: and of the two-thirds for which security was given, not one rupee was ever realized. Of the unhappy hostages some died in prison, others escaped, and after a period the remainder were released.

Before dismissing this transaction, it may gratify the curiosity of some of my readers to examine it in reference to the practical description of Indian tribute which has already been offered. We have the authority of a formal public instrument *, to which the court of Hyderabad was a party, for stating, that the annual sum received, or estimated to be received, as revenue, or tribute, or both, from *Carnatic Balaghaut Vijeyapoor*, was, "seven lacs of rupees, including durbar charges." Estimating Mysoor in 1755 at one half of Carnatic Balaghaut Vijeyapoor, which is considerably more than its actual value, its annual payment would be three lacs and a half. The last tribute formally exacted was by Nasir Jung in 1746: but on settling for the services of the corps which attended that prince in the expedition which terminated his life, the Mysoreans would claim to have liquidated the demand up to the year 1750 inclusive. If this claim were admitted, the whole demand would be fourteen lacs; if it were even totally rejected, the whole of the arrears would be twenty-eight lacs; the sum adjusted was fifty-six lacs.

Nunjeraj, proceeding by forced marches for the relief of the

* Tenth article of the treaty of 1768.

capital, received intelligence of this arrangement while he was ascending the ghaut; and halted at the distance of twenty-five miles to the south of Seringapatam, for the purpose of reducing the disposable army to the scale of the actual finances of the state by discharging one third of its number: an operation which was accomplished with the utmost difficulty from the necessity of paying their arrears.

The course of our narrative has not rendered it necessary, until now, to advert to an acquisition which had been made by the state of Mysoor, ten years before the period at which we are now arrived. The fort of Dindegul, about sixty-five miles south-east of Trichinopoly, and forty-seven miles north by west of Madura, is situated on a strong rock in the midst of a plain, or rather valley, which forms its district, bounded to the west by the great range of mountains which separates it from the coast of Malabar, and on the east by a lower range which runs between it and the province of Madura. During the period that Chunda Saheb possessed Trichinopoly and its dependencies, he had placed his brother Sadick Saheb in Dindegul, as one of the most important of his possessions. Nizam ul Moolk obtained Trichinopoly and its dependencies from Morari Row in August 1744, and shortly afterwards left the lower countries. The revolutions which succeeded have been already explained; and during the confusion and interregnum which ensued before the arrival of Anwar u Deen in April, 1745, Ram Naick, the insignificant Poligar of Ootem Palliam, had found means to surprise the fort of Dindegul; and the ministry of Mysoor seeing no symptoms of a regular government, sent a respectable force under Vencat Row Berki, which added this fort and district to their former

CHAP. IX. 1755. possessions in that quarter. During the short government of Anwar u Deen, he had never found himself sufficiently unoccupied to attend to this object: and when Mohammed Ali, in 1751, applied to Mysoor for aid, there was no question made regarding the possession of Dindegul, since Trichinopoly and all its dependencies were to be ceded to that power: and Mohammed Ali did not think proper, in the course of subsequent discussions, to agitate a question of right, which would retort so severely on himself. But at this time the presence of an English force of some magnitude in that vicinity, for the purpose of establishing the authority of Mohammed Ali in the districts of Madura and Tinnevelly, rendered it necessary to look with a jealous eye towards Dindegul. The Poligars, also, of that neighbourhood, headed by those of Pylny and Veerapatchy, situated on the skirts of the western hills between Dindegul and the former possessions of Mysoor, had formed a confederacy to resist the payment of tribute. These united considerations rendered it necessary to appoint a respectable force for the service of that quarter; and Hyder, who had continued to recommend himself to the increasing favour of Nunjeraj, was selected for the command. This may, perhaps, be considered as the epoch at which the germ of that ambition began to unfold which terminated in Hyder's usurpation of the government of Mysoor; and it will accordingly be necessary that we should henceforth trace with more attention the proceedings of this extraordinary man.

In the course of the operations before Trichinopoly, the Beder peons, in the service of Hyder, were gradually augmented, and exercised their usual industry; and a body of select Pindaries, or Beid, was also gradually raised for similar purposes. This description of horse receive no pay in the service of many of the states of India, but live on the devastation of the enemy's country. Hyder, on his first nomination to a command, had engaged in his service a bramin mutteseddy named Kundè Row, who will occupy a prominent place in our future narrative. To the cool and calculating mind of a bramin accountant, this man added great sagacity and original thinking; a boldness which did not hesitate regarding means; and a combination of ideas which enabled him to convert the unprofitable business of war into a regular system of finance. Hyder, who could neither read nor write, remedied this defect of education by trusting to a most extraordinary memory; and valued himself, at this early period of his political life, on going through arithmetical calculations of some length, with equal accuracy, and more quickness, than the most expert accountant. The consultations of these two persons produced a system, regularly organized, by which the plunderers received, besides their direct pay, one half of the booty which was realized: the other half was appropriated by Hyder, under a combination of checks which rendered it nearly impossible to secrete any portion of the plunder. Moveable property of every description was their object; and, as already noticed, they did not hesitate to acquire it by simple theft from friends, when that could be done without suspicion, and with more convenience than from enemies. Nothing was unseasonable or unacceptable; from convoys of grain, down to the clothes, turbans, and ear-rings, of travellers, or villagers, whether men, women, or children. Cattle and sheep were among the most profitable heads of plunder: muskets and horses were sometimes obtained in booty, sometimes by purchase. The numbers under his command increased with

CHAP. IX.

1755.

his resources; and before he left Trichinopoly, besides the usual appendages of a chief of rank, in elephants, camels, tents, and magnificent appointments, he was rated on the returns and received pay for one thousand five hundred horse, three thousand regular infantry, two thousand peons, and four guns, with their equipments. Of the horses, five hundred were his own property; and the difference between the sum allowed by government, and that disbursed in the pay of the man, and the provender of the horse, was Hyder's profit. In consideration of his furnishing the cannon and their draught, the muskets and accoutrements of regular infantry, he was allowed a certain sum for each gun with its equipments, and for every hundred men; and was permitted to make his own agreements with the individuals at inferior rates; they also, as well as the rest of his troops, regularly accounting for one half of the plunder they acquired. Some portion of this description belongs to the system of most native armies, and would enter into the history of most successful Indian chiefs; but none ever combined with so much skill the perfect attachment of his men, with the conversion to his own use of so large a portion of what was issued for their payment: and Sevagi alone could be brought into competition with Hyder for the regular organization of a system of plunder,

The designation of Hyder's new appointment was that of Foujedar of Dindegul; and having recruited his corps with the most select of the men discharged by Nunjeraj, he marched at the head of five thousand regular infantry, two thousand five hundred horse, two thousand peons, and six guns. The department of accounts under Kundè Row had necessarily been augmented, and furnished employment for several clerks, who were well versed in his system; and on the departure of Hyder to a distant station, it was considered expedient that his confidential friend and servant Kundè Row should remain at court, to watch over his interests. On approaching Pylney and Veerapatchey, he lulled those Poligars * into security by offering to exert his influence at court to obtain a remission of their tribute, on condition of their consenting to serve with his army; and was thus permitted to pursue his route as a friend until he had reached the proper position; when, the distribution of troops being previously made, he swept off the whole of the cattle of the open country, and drove them rapidly to Darapoor; where they were divided according to compact, and sold at high prices, generally to their former proprietors. He now commenced his operations against the Poligars, in which, after an obstinate and protracted contest, he was ultimately successful. Among the deceptions which he practised on the government in the course of this service, some were so ludicrously gross that I should hesitate to state them, if they had not been related to me by more than one eye-witness. Nunjeraj on the receipt of Hyder's dispatches with a long list of killed and wounded, sent a special commissioner with rich presents for Hyder and the officers who were represented to have distinguished themselves, and Zuckhum puttee for the wounded. This officer was soon made to understand his business. Zuckhum puttee is an allowance to wounded men, as some compensation for their sufferings, and for the purpose of enabling them to defray the expenses of their cure; for an Indian army

* These are among the *Telinga* Poligars formerly noticed, as I know from personal communication.

CHAP. IX. 1755. has neither hospitals, nor surgeons, provided by the state. The allowance on this occasion was fourteen rupees a month, until the cure should be completed. Hyder marshalled his wounded men, to be inspected by the commissioner: sixty-seven was the true number; but about seven hundred had their legs or arms bound up with yellow * bandages, and acted their parts with entire success. The money was paid to Hyder according to the muster, and to the probable time of cure reported by the attending surgeons, at the rate of fourteen rupees per man per month. To the really wounded he gave seven: and of the presents brought for the officers of the army he made a distribution equally skilful, while each officer was made to believe that he was the person most particularly favoured by Hyder. During these operations Kundè Row was perpetually sounding the exploits of his master to Nunjeraj; exaggerating the disturbed state of the country, and the necessity of augmenting the forces; which was accordingly authorized from time to time, and assignments on the revenues of other districts were added for that purpose to his other resources. Special commissioners were always deputed to muster the new levies; and on one occasion, Jehan Khan saw exhibited the manœuvre which he calls a *circular muster*, by which ten thousand men were counted and passed as eighteen thousand.

In the interior management of the district committed to his charge, Hyder evinced the same penetration and skill which distinguished him on all occasions; and, in a short time, could vie with the most experienced Aumildar in valuing the resources of a village, in detecting the mistatements of a fraudulent ac-

* Turmeric is an invariable ingredient in all their surgical applications.

count, from merely hearing it read; and in devising the best means of increasing the revenue. It was at Dindegul that he also first obtained from Seringham, Trichinopoly, and Pondicherry, skilful artificers, directed by French masters, and began to organize a regular artillery, arsenal, and laboratory. Meanwhile the care of Kundè Row preserved the ascendancy which Hyder had gained over the mind of Nunjeraj; and while claiming merit for public economy in being able to defray the expence of the augmented forces from the allotted funds, he was, in fact, accumulating an immense treasure. 1755.

The operations necessary for the complete establishment of Hyder's authority in the province of Dindegul occupied the greatest portion of the years 1755 and 1756: and, in the mean while, the affairs of the general government were conducted as usual by the brothers Deo Raj and Nunjeraj: whose usurpation, although complete in every thing essential, left to the pageant Raja a considerable share of the exterior appendages of royalty. This young man had now attained the age of twenty-seven years; and had manifested on some occasions symptoms of impatience at the ignominious thraldom in which he was kept: but he had been too much secluded from the world to be capable of forming a skilful plan for his emancipation; and some of his attendants, who were equally incapable of giving proper counsel, had suggested to him the project of seizing and confining the usurpers. The conferences on this subject were regularly reported to the brothers; and at the suggestion of Deo Raj a mild message was sent, remonstrating against these designs, and requesting that the evil counsellors might be dismissed from his presence. The 1756.

CHAP. IX. 1756.

Raja, instead of dissembling his intentions, indulged in a burst of resentment and indignation, and returned a harsh and contemptuous answer. He had already gained the ordinary guard of the palace; and his adherents gradually obtained and introduced additional numbers of troops.

It will be recollected that the daughter of Nunjeraj had been given in marriage to the pageant Raja. This lady had been brought up in the house of her uncle Deo Raj: she was pregnant of her first child at this period; and the usual Hindoo ceremonials required that she should, on her pregnancy being ascertained, pass a certain time under the paternal roof. Deo Raj continued to send conciliatory messages to the Raja, which were answered by outrages and puerile threats: and it was proposed in consultation, that instead of open violence, this lady should be induced to remove him by poison, on the condition that the throne should descend to her future offspring, his posthumous issue, under her own guardianship. The particulars of this negotiation cannot be positively ascertained: some accounts state that Deo Raj united with his brother in making this proposition, but the progress of these transactions seems to disprove that opinion: the fate of the last Raja hung heavy on his mind, and his subsequent conduct seems to evince that he had determined not to incur the guilt of a second murder. It is also stated in some accounts, that the proposition extended only to making the Raja a close prisoner; but this statement refutes itself, because it was obviously unnecessary to consult the lady on a plan which in no respect required her concurrence. Whatever the propositions were, it is universally admitted that she received them with abhorrence; and that, during her subsequent detention, she refused to partake of food until restored to the dwelling of her husband.

The brothers were entirely disagreed in the measures to be pursued regarding the Raja. Deo Raj argued, that his whole project and the councils by which it was guided were puerile, and the means which he could possibly command undeserving of serious alarm; that on proper precautions being adopted, a few days must convince the projectors themselves of their inability even to obtain the requisite provisions for the palace; and that measures of violence were equally unnecessary and disreputable. Nunjeraj was of a different opinion; and having arranged his plan, moved a column of troops, attended by four guns, to the exterior gate of the palace, accompanied by Veerana, his second in command, who had the reputation of instigating upon all occasions the violent proceedings of his principal. All the avenues were barricadoed, and the walls lined with troops; and Nunjeraj wished, before proceeding farther, to commence a parley. This, however, was rejected; and on a declaration of his intention to employ force, a heavy fire was opened from the palace which did considerable execution: but the guns having by this time been brought up near to the gate, it was quickly blown open; and the defenders, on finding that the column was rushing in, at once abandoned the walls, and fled for concealment to the courts of the women's apartments. Nunjeraj, leaving Veerana with a portion of the troops in charge of the gate, proceeded with the requisite attendants into the interior of the palace. The Raja was requested to seat himself in the usual hall of audience, while all the apartments were searched, and every

CHAP. IX. 1756. male produced. A certain number, on whose disposal he had not determined, were put in irons; and all the remainder had their noses and ears cut off in the Raja's presence, and in this state were turned out into the street. The creatures in his own pay, destined to replace the former attendants of the Raja, were then presented to him with an insulting mockery of respect: and after placing guards of his most confidential troops in the usual stations, he departed from the hall of audience, making the customary obeisance to the Raja, who had witnessed this extraordinary scene in an agony of silent terror and astonishment.

Deo Raj, who had protested in the most solemn and impressive manner against this outrageous proceeding, was so deeply offended at this open contempt of his admonitions, that he determined to renounce all future intercourse with his brother. It is difficult to ascertain the precise motives or ultimate object of his present conduct: but apparently not choosing to enter into a direct contest, and desirous of retiring from so disgusting a scene, he actually departed from Seringapatam in February
1757. 1757, accompanied by his whole family and personal adherents, with one thousand horse, and two thousand peons; and descending the pass of Gujjelhutty, fixed his residence at Sattimungul, on the bank of the river Bhavany. For his support, however, and that of his military escort, he had need of funds, and sent orders to the Aumils of several districts on which Hyder had assignments, revoking that appropriation of the revenues, and ordering them to be paid to himself. Kundè Row could readily have procured from Nunjeraj a repetition of the assignments; but in the distraction of authority caused by the separation of the brothers, the Aumils, on receiving contradictory

orders, would of course have refused to pay to either: or if a preference should be given, it would certainly be in favour of Deo Raj. Under these circumstances, he recommended to Hyder to try the effect of his personal appearance at Seringapatam, for which he accordingly prepared, attended merely by his ordinary retinue; but before his arrival, a new danger had threatened the capital, and had been averted by fresh sacrifices.

Balajee Row unexpectedly entered Mysoor in March 1757; and appeared in the neighbourhood of Seringapatam demanding a contribution. Nunjeraj in vain represented his absolute inability: the demand was peremptory, and the place was besieged. Nunjeraj made a spirited defence, and led in person several sallies upon the enemy's trenches; but their artillery being respectable, and the operations of the siege directed by Europeans, the place was reduced to extremity; and Nunjeraj was compelled to make a hasty compromise for thirty-two lacs of rupees. The cash and jewels which could be produced amounted to no more than five lacs: and for the liquidation of the remainder, he was compelled to surrender in pledge a large and valuable extent of territory*.

These transactions had been completed, and the Mahrattas had departed, after leaving their agents for the collection of revenue, and a body of six thousand horse in the pledged districts, before Hyder's arrival at Seringapatam: when, on inspecting, in company with Nunjeraj, the approaches and batteries of the Mahrattas, he ventured to remonstrate against the

* The districts pledged were Nagamungul, Beloor, Kickery, Chenroypatam, Cudoor, Banaver, Harunhully, Honavelly, Toorikera, Kundikera, Chickanaickunhully, Kurb, Culloor, and Hoolioordroog.

CHAP. IX.

1757.

omission of not ordering up the troops of Dindegul on so great an emergency: intimating, perhaps truly, that if they had been present, the service would have terminated in a very different manner. He strongly recommended to Nunjeraj to cause the revenues to be withheld from the Mahratta agents, and to expel their troops on the approach of the rains; at which period the swell of the rivers would secure the country against Mahratta invasion for another season, when he hoped his services would be called for: and this advice was accordingly followed.

Hyder's consultations with Nunjeraj regarding the resumed revenues ended in his determining to wait on Deo Raj at Sattimungul; but as he had no personal influence over the elder brother, Kundè Row accompanied him for the purpose of aiding in the negotiation. Before Hyder's departure from Dindegul, he had received a deputation from the Nair Raja of Palghaut, situated on the eastern frontier of Malabar, opposite to the great chasm in the range of western mountains, which leaves a communication between the two coasts of the peninsula, covered only with forests of the stately teak, without the intervention of a hill. This chief was at war with the Rajas of Cochin and Calicut; and being hard pressed by his enemies, the object of his deputation was to desire succour from Hyder, who, at the time of his journey to the capital, had detached his brother-in-law Muckhdoom Saheb with two thousand horse, five thousand infantry, and five guns (the first Mohammedan corps that had ever entered Malabar) to his assistance. This chief, in conjunction with the Nairs of Palghaut, carried his arms to the sea coast; and the enemy finding resistance to be unavailing, had compromised for the restitution of their conquests from Palghaut, and a military contribution of twelve lacs of rupees to be paid by instalments: but finding the presence of the strangers while waiting for the money to be burdensome, and meditating to evade the payment altogether, they had now sent secret agents to Deo Raj, offering to pay the money to him, provided he would rid them of the Mussulman troops of Hyder, and send Hindoos to receive it. This transaction furnished the means of arranging the negotiation between Deo Raj and Hyder. The resumed revenues were restored to him, together with soucar security for three lacs as a reimbursement of extraordinary expences incurred in the expedition to Malabar; and on these conditions Mukhdoom was recalled. Hyder relinquished his claim to the military contribution of twelve lacs; and the Rajpoot corps of Herri Sing, the most zealous adherent of Deo Raj, was sent to receive it.

These arrangements being completed, Hyder returned to Dindegul, and his troops being now unoccupied, an opportunity seemed to present itself of employing them to advantage. Mahphuz Khan, whom we left at Fort St. David in August 1754, had, on the cessation of hostilities between the French and English in the following October, compromised with his younger brother Mohammed Ali for the government of the southern provinces of Madura and Tinnevelly, with the view of there establishing for himself an independent kingdom. The English and French were now at open war; their troops were abundantly occupied in all directions: Hyder had received repeated invitations from the French and Mahphuz Khan to aid in expelling the English altogether from these provinces; and the distractions occasioned by Mahphuz Khan's incapacity seemed to afford a

CHAP. IX. 1757. favourable opportunity of seizing the fort and district of Madura for himself.

He commenced his operations by seizing the post of Sholavanden, situated in the pass between Dindegul and Madura; and marched without opposition to the vicinity of the latter place, which, on examining, he did not think proper to attempt by a coup de main, but confined himself for the present to sweeping off the whole of the cattle and moveables of the country, and despatching them to Dindegul. He was farther induced to suspend any serious operations against the fort of Madura, from knowing that Mohammed Issoof, the commandant of English sepoys, was on his march towards that place from Trichinopoly with a small but veteran corps. This body was very much inferior in numbers to that of Hyder, who, on its approach, was guilty of the mistake of taking post in the mouth of the narrow pass of Natam, and thus rendering his superior numbers of no avail against Mohammed Issoof. That excellent officer was not slow in perceiving the advantage thus offered to him, and made a vigorous and determined attack with the whole of his little corps, by which Hyder was completely routed. He retired without farther effort to Dindegul in November: meditating, however, to return, reinforced by a body of French troops. The corps at Seringham, which was most conveniently placed for the purpose, could not be diminished without danger from the garrison of Trichinopoly: and the difficulty of finding troops for a great variety of services prevented M. Soupire, who now directed the French operations, from sending from Pondicherry more than three hundred sepoys and seventy-five Europeans; who arrived at Dindegul in January 1758, under the command of M. Astruc. The smallness of this force would alone have determined Hyder to evade the proposed service, but other considerations of real moment demanded his presence at the capital. He accordingly made the requisite explanations of the necessity for his immediate departure, and excused himself to M. Astruc, who shortly afterwards returned to Seringham.

CHAPTER X.

FROM 1758 TO 1760.

Mutiny of the army at the capital—Hyder proceeds thither accompanied by Deo Raj—Reconciliation of the brothers and the Raja—Hyder's address and popularity—pays the arrears—Massacre of Herri Sing—Hyder receives a Jageer and assignment of territory—Mahratta invasion—capture of Cenapatam—Hyder appointed to command the field army—recapture of Cenapatam—Military operations—Terms of adjustment give the pledged districts to Hyder—Title of Behauder—Plot for compelling the retirement of Nunjeraj—its singular progress and result—Farther assignments to Hyder—Situation of Kundè Row—Nunjeraj departs to Mysoor—is besieged there—result—Raja's second marriage—Still farther assignments to Hyder—A French agent obtains the aid of troops—Retrospect—M. Bussy with Salabut Jung besieges Savanore—adjustment through Morari Row—made the pretext for supplanting him—Views of the different powers of the south—M. Bussy departs—pursued by Salabut Jung—takes post at Hyderabad—is reinforced—and restored to favour—Situation of Nizam Alee—and Basalut Jung—Dangerous intrigues—suppressed by M. Bussy—who seizes the fort of Dowlutabad—Murder of Hyder Jung, M. Bussy's Dewan, by Nizam Alee—Shah-Nawaz-Khan slain—order restored by M. Bussy—whose situation becomes perfectly secure and formidable—this prosperity subverted by the arrogance of M. Lally—who orders M. Bussy to march to Pondicherry—Evacuation of Dowlutabad—Departure of M. Bussy—astonishment and grief of Salabut Jung—Minor operations in Coromandel—Mohammed Ali's three brothers in open or concealed hostility—French interests improve—Character of M. Lally—creates universal disgust—Siege and capture of Fort St. David—of Tanjore—effects of petulance and mismanagement—the siege raised—M. Bussy precedes his troops—who also arrive—Nijèeb Oolla—Tripetty—Abd-ul-Wahab—Siege of Madras—raised—Important consequences of M. Bussy's recal from the Deckan—Capture of Masulipatam by Colonel

Forde—his treaty with Salabut Jung—Nizam Alee supplants Basalut Jung, who moves to the south, accompanied by a French corps—his views and connexions—with Sunput Row—Mahphuz Khan—Poligars of Calastri and Vencatigherry—Negotiations with Nizam Ali—and M. Bussy.

CHAP. X. 1758.

In consequence of the public misfortunes and errors which have been related, the troops at Seringapatam had fallen into a long arrear of pay, and they had now mutinied to obtain it; proceeding, according to the custom of India, not only to the ceremony of interdicting their chief by religious execrations from meat and drink until the arrear should be paid; a process which is usually called sitting in *Dherna;* but to the secular operation of preventing any water or provisions being carried into his house. In this extremity Nunjeraj was under the necessity of selling the provision stores of the capital, for the purpose of appeasing, not satisfying, the demands of the mutineers.

Hyder, on receiving this information, desired Kundè Row again to meet him at Sattimungul, and proceeded with the whole of his disposable troops in the same direction. He had written to Deo Raj before his departure from Dindegul, and went forward unattended to represent to him personally the evils arising from the disunion of the brothers, and the absolute necessity of a reconciliation to prevent the entire dissolution of the government. The personal influence of Kundè Row, added to the arguments of Hyder, prevailed on Deo Raj, although much indisposed, to accompany them; and they ascended the pass of Gujjelhutty in the month of March. On their arrival at Hurdanhully, the increased indisposition of Deo Raj compelled them to halt for fifteen days, after which they proceeded to Mysoor;

CHAP. X. 1758. where Deo Raj remained, while Hyder and Kundè Row proceeded to Seringapatam. Deo Raj insisted, as a preliminary to all terms of reconciliation with his brother, that he should make atonement for the violation of public decorum in his conduct at the palace; and the terms being easily adjusted by Kundè Row, Nunjeraj, on the 23d of April, made his humiliations to the Raja, whom he had not visited since the former outrage; and a salute was fired from all the guns of the garrison to announce the Raja's forgiveness and favour.

The next object was the public reconciliation of the brothers. Nunjeraj and Hyder, accompanied by all the chiefs, public officers, and principal inhabitants of the capital, went in procession to conduct Deo Raj from Mysoor. On the meeting of the brothers, Nunjeraj made the most abject apologies, and Deo Raj consented to be conducted to Seringapatam; where he died on the 19th of June, six days after his arrival. His death was, as usual, ascribed by the vulgar to poison, and the crime was attributed to his brother; but, exclusively of the absence of any adequate motive, I am satisfied, from the examination of persons who saw him about this period, that fatal symptoms of dropsy had appeared before his departure from Sattimungul.

The army was still clamorous for the remaining arrears; and Nunjeraj, who had been disgusted with the difficulties and insults which he had experienced in the adjustment of their former claims, and was now unaffectedly depressed in spirits by the death of his brother, requested of Kundè Row and Hyder to take the troublesome charge of making the best arrangement in their power.

Hyder throughout all these transactions had been enabled

to assume the character of a general benefactor. The gratitude of Nunjeraj was due for his conduct in effecting the reconciliation, and for the zeal and exertion which relieved him from much embarrassment: the troops considered him as their only hope for a liquidation of arrears; the Raja beheld as yet only his preserver and protector from the violence of Nunjeraj; and all orders of men began to look up to Hyder for the restoration of public prosperity. He proceeded, with constant demonstrations of deference to the Raja's orders, to distribute, in lieu of money, all public property that could be so applied, down to the elephants and horses of the Raja's retinue; and knowing from his own experience the probable amount of imposition in the charges of arrears, seized on all the accountants, and by threats and torture compelled them to produce the true accounts. By these means he was enabled in the course of a few days to discharge four thousand horse, and a large amount of other rabble.

The confusion, clamour, and irregularity which such a process necessarily created in a populous town, rendered it expedient that the well paid and obedient troops of Hyder should take all the guards of the gates and interior of the fort; an arrangement involving the possession of actual power, which might have suggested ambitious views to a mind less aspiring; but the present moment was obviously premature, and the opportunity was not embraced. The operation respecting the mutineers was not yet finished; for as the details of the adjustment, added to Hyder's previous acquaintance, enabled him to judge who were the most wealthy among the chiefs, he caused all but the most extravagant and indigent to be seized after their departure as the ringleaders

CHAP. X. 1758. of the late mutiny, and plundered of all their property as a forfeiture to the state.

Herri Sing, who had been sent to receive the military contribution of Malabar, found himself unable to realize any part of it; and on hearing of the death of his patron Deo Raj, marched, during the torrents of the S.W. monsoon, to the province of Coimbettore; where a distance of scarcely thirty miles from the periodical rains of Malabar always presents fair weather and the most striking change of climate. In this province he encamped at the village of Aounassee, ostensibly to refresh his troops, but in reality negotiating for the service of the Raja of Tanjore.

Herri Sing, whose personal enmity to Hyder we have already had occasion to notice, had been particularly protected by Deo Raj, as Hyder had been by Nunjeraj; and was, next to Hyder, the most opulent partizan in the service of the state of Mysoor. Deo Raj had always opposed his brother's rapid advancement of Hyder, adopting the opinion of Herri Sing and all the old chiefs, who attributed that advancement more to his intrigues as a courtier, than his merit as a soldier. Herri Sing, in particular, made no scruple of avowing on all occasions his contempt for the Naick. Their hatred, in short, was mutual and open, and the time had now arrived when Hyder was enabled to take a complete revenge.

On the pretence of returning a portion of his troops to Dindegul, he detached Mukhdoom Saheb with one thousand horse, and two thousand infantry, by whom Herri Sing, carelessly encamped at Aounassee giving repose to his men, naturally unsus-

picious as he was brave, and ignorant even of the movement of CHAP. X.
this detachment, was surprized and massacred in the dead of the 1758.
night, together with a large portion of his troops.

Among the plunder acquired by this infamous exploit were three hundred horses, one thousand muskets, and three guns, which were brought in triumph to the capital. To the Raja Hyder presented in form the three guns for the service of the state, and fifteen beautiful horses for the royal stables: the remainder of the horses and military stores, together with the money and property, found their accustomed appropriation.

During the absence of the force under Mukhdoom Saheb, Hyder revived the subject of the Soucar security for three lacs, which had been given by the late Deo Raj. The claim was recognized without difficulty by Nunjeraj, and approved by the Raja; and an assignment on the revenues of Coimbetoor was appropriated for its liquidation. It was also proper and decorous to reward by some public mark of confidence and distinction the fidelity and zeal of so excellent a servant; and the fort and district of Bangalore were conferred on him as a personal jageer.

The Mahrattas, as had been foreseen, did not tamely accede
to the expulsion of their troops and agents from the pledged 1759.
districts; and early in 1759 a large force under Gopaul Heri and Anund Row Rastea invaded Mysoor. They began with resuming the possession of all the pledged districts, and then passed to the northward of Savendy Droog, as if they had some farther object in view to the N.E. of Mysoor: but on arriving near to Bangalore they invested that place, and sent back a detachment, consisting of their best infantry, who, by a concealed march through

the thick intervening woods to the westward, surprized and took the fort of Cenapatam, situated thirty-five miles from Bangalore and forty from Seringapatam, where the woods cease and an open plain commences.

The arrangements which had lately been made for paying and dismissing the most mutinous of the troops had left some arrears still due to those who remained in the service; which had generally been adjusted by prevailing on the chiefs to make advances from their own funds: and on orders of march being issued for the purpose of opposing this danger, most of the chiefs of rank made excuses of inability without a previous liquidation of arrears. Hyder volunteered the service, and offered his personal responsibility for any arrears due to the *men*, of which he knew there was little; but the offer increased his popularity, and he was appointed to the chief command of the field army; on which occasion many of the most antient military servants of the state resigned, rather than serve under the Naick. Hyder's first care was to place respectable detachments at the intermediate forts of Madoor and Malavilly; places situated on the two principal approaches to the capital, at the distance of twenty-seven and twenty-two miles, and distant from each other about seventeen. That at Malavilly was under his maternal uncle Meer Ibrahim. Madoor was committed to Lutf Aly Beg, who had orders, if he should find the project feasible, to attempt the recovery of Cenapatam by surprise, the distance being only thirteen miles. That officer, a gallant and hardy Mogul, prepared for the enterprize by shutting up his troops in the fort of Madoor, with every demonstration of being himself in expectation of attack, and suffering the Mahratta horse even to insult his outguards with impunity. His spies having brought him satisfactory intelligence of the dispositions of the enemy, he moved by a circuitous route, and carried the place by escalade just before daylight, without any heavy loss on either side. CHAP. X. 1759.

Hyder, on receiving this intelligence, marched without a moment's delay, and concentrated his force near to Cenapatam: and Gopaul Heri, on his part, raised the blockade of Bangalore, and marched with a very superior force to oppose him.

All eyes were fixed on the conduct of Hyder in his present important charge: his friends anticipating complete success from his eminent talents, and his rivals predicting that he would now evince the military incapacity which they had always ascribed to him. He commenced with frequently practising on Gopaul Heri the lessons which he had learned at Trichinopoly, of the advantages of a well-ordered night attack against an irregular enemy. His own camp was generally fortified; and as he hardly ever made a movement by day, his intentions could seldom be conjectured. At the expiration of a various warfare of three months, in which his incessant activity and unexpected attacks foiled and embarrassed all the projects of the Mahratta, straitened his supplies, and, what was more important, intercepted his plunder; Gopaul Heri, wearied with an unprofitable contest, in which he was generally worsted, proposed a negotiation, which terminated in the following arrangement.—1. That the Mahrattas should relinquish their claim on the districts formerly ceded in pledge to Balagee Row; and 2. That in full of all demands, past and present, thirty-two lacs should now be paid. Hyder, in communicating the substance of this agreement, urged the necessity of making every possible exertion to

CHAP. X. 1759. raise the money: and the exhausted public treasury was recruited on this occasion by a nezerana (a forced payment under the name of a free gift) on all the principal public servants and monied inhabitants. Kundè Row, who was charged with the whole of these arrangements, realized the sum of sixteen lacs, with which he proceeded to camp, authorized to approve, in the name of the Raja and Nunjeraj, the means of liquidating the balance, which had previously been concerted between him and his principal. Such was Hyder's influence and credit, that he was enabled to make an arrangement with the Soucars (or bankers) of the enemy's camp; by which, on taking his personal security, they rendered themselves responsible for the remainder, on an understanding between all the parties interested in the transaction that Hyder was to have the direct management of the pledged districts, as the fund from which that remainder was to be liquidated. He accordingly despatched without delay his own agents and aumildars to these restored districts: and after concluding the requisite arrangements for their future management, and seeing the Mahrattas in full march for their own country, he returned in triumph to Seringapatam, where the Raja received him in the most splendid Durbar which had been held since the days of Chick Deo Raj; and on his approach welcomed him by the name of *Futtè Hyder Behauder* *, a title

* Nunjeraj and Deo Raj had been in the habit of addressing Hyder in public Durbar, by the name of *Naick*. *Bennee Naick rè; come hither Naick.* As Hyder's fortunes began to unfold, he thought this appellation not sufficiently respectful; and by means of a third person, prevailed on *Nunjeraj* to address him by the name of *Bahauder: Bennee Bahauder; come hither Hero.* For many years afterwards *Deo Raj* continued the appellation of Naick: and Hyder, when accompanying him from Sattimungul, remonstrated in a friendly manner. *Deo Raj* excused himself by

which Hyder had long affected, and henceforth received from all descriptions of persons. Nunjeraj, who was of course present on the occasion, paid him the novel compliment of rising on his approach, and embracing him; apparently proud of this public justification of his own discernment in the elevation of Hyder.

The large appropriation of revenue for liquidating the Mahratta debt, added to the previous assignments in the hands of Hyder for the payment of his own corps, and the discharge of the bonds of Deo Raj, left but slender means for the other expenses of the state; and in a few months considerable arrears were again due to the army. Hyder, from the course of events which has been described, had become commander in chief. Nunjeraj exercised the whole power of the state, without any farther control than the mere shew of royalty, which it had been concerted to allow to the Raja. He had hitherto seen in Hyder an obedient and zealous adherent; and in his rise, the acquisition of a powerful instrument, of which he held in his own hand the exclusive direction. He was now to view him in another character.

It will readily be imagined that the remembrance of the injuries and personal insults which the Raja had suffered from Nunjeraj, was too deeply impressed to admit of sincere reconciliation. Late events had given to Kundè Row a more frequent access to the palace; where the old dowager of the late Dud Deo Raj seems to have been the only person of sufficient capacity

pretending that the mistake was of habit and not of intention; and gave orders in *Hyder's* presence that all letters to him should be in future addressed Bahauder. Hyder was always more gratified by the single appellation of Bahauder than by any other title. His original signet was *Futtè Hyder*, the former being the name of his father; and this he never changed, except on those extraordinary occasions which required the great official seal.

CHAP. X. 1759.

and knowledge to communicate with him on so delicate a subject as the feelings and wishes of the family: and by her means it was soon concerted that the liquidation of the arrears of the troops was to be made the means of compelling Nunjeraj to retire from public life. Some confidential chiefs of the troops were accordingly instructed by Kundè Row in the part which they were to perform, without being aware of its ultimate object. They came to the quarters of Hyder, demanding, in a moderate tone, the payment of their arrears. He represented, in terms equally mild, that his own corps, for the payment of which he possessed fixed resources, was regularly paid, but that funds for the payment of the rest of the army were not under his direction. The troops then demanded that he should obtain payment from the person who had their direction, namely Nunjeraj; and he promised to use his best offices. These visits were daily repeated, and with additional urgency; until the troops at length positively insisted on Hyder's going at their head to sit in *Dherna* at the gate of Nunjeraj; and this was done, with every demonstration on the part of Hyder of compulsion and repugnance. Nunjeraj had received some oblique intimations of the subject of the dowager's private conversations with Kundè Row; the terrors of the former *Dherna* were still fresh in his recollection; and perceiving by Hyder's presence the full extent of the plot, he made his decision, and prepared to put the best face he could on his retirement from public life. After a separate interview with Hyder, in which the preliminaries were adjusted, he came out to the gate, and represented to the troops that the misfortunes of his administration had determined him to bow to the decrees of fate; and that the Raja had accordingly assumed the principal direction of his own affairs, with the express view of permitting him to retire; that all his arrangements were made for rendering his accounts and resigning his office; and that under these circumstances, it was unjust to hold him responsible for their arrears. This contingency had also been provided for; a few soldiers called out to remove the *Dherna* to the gate of the Raja; the measure was approved by general acclamation, and Hyder was again compelled to lead them to the palace.

As this measure had been expressly preconcerted, it occasioned no alarm; and a messenger came out to desire that Kundè Row might be sent to communicate with the Raja. Kundè Row returned, after a short interval, with a demand from the Raja that Hyder should take a solemn oath in the presence of the troops to obey his orders, and renounce his connexion with the usurper Nunjeraj, for whose retirement a munificent provision should be made; and on these conditions the Raja intimated that he would find means of satisfying the demand of the troops. Hyder took the oath, with suitable demonstrations of reluctance; was summoned to the palace, and returned to inform the troops that the arrangements ordered by the Raja would require a few days to be completed; and that in the mean time he rendered himself personally responsible for the liquidation of their arrears: an assurance which was received with confidence and satisfaction.

For the purpose of enabling Hyder to discharge the arrears, and provide in future for the regular pay of the troops, an addition was made to his assignments of revenue, which caused the districts in his direct possession to exceed one half of the Raja's whole territory. Kundè Row received from the Raja the formal appointment of *Predaun*, or *Dewan*, as he was more

CHAP. X. 1759. generally called (for the nominal title of Serv Adikar was reserved to Nunjeraj); and in his double capacity of Dewan to the Raja and to Hyder he exercised the revenue administration of the whole country; with the single exception of the provision settled for Nunjeraj, which was a jageer producing three lacs of pagodas. From this sum Nunjeraj was to maintain for the service of the state one thousand horse, and three thousand infantry, regular, and irregular, but was exempted from personal service, and permitted to retire altogether to his jageer; an arrangement which, according to the pay of those times, and supposing the troops to be actually maintained, would leave a surplus of about one lac of pagodas for his personal expenses. He accordingly departed from the capital in June 1759, with the whole of his family, adherents, and troops, with the professed intention of first paying his devotions at the great temple of Nunjendgode, twenty-five miles south of Seringapatam; but on the first day affected to be taken ill at Mysoor. It is not quite certain whether a residence at this place had been stipulated in the terms; but at the expiration of a few months, it was discovered to be extremely indecorous that a servant of the state should fix his abode at the seat of the ancient government, from which the whole country took its name; and unsafe to permit such a person as Nunjeraj to be strengthening himself, as he really was, at the distance of only nine miles from the capital. It was accordingly resolved, in conformity to the calculation above adverted to, that districts to the amount of two lacs should be resumed from his jageer and added to the assignments of Hyder, which were still found to be too small; that he should be absolved from the maintenance of the troops, and be compelled to depart from Mysoor. The districts were accordingly resumed; and a letter was written intimating the pleasure of the Raja, that he should fix his residence at some other place. The answer of Nunjeraj to Hyder was in the following terms. "I have made you what you are, and now you refuse me a place in which to hide my head. Do what you please; or what you can. I move not from Mysoor." Hyder was accordingly *ordered* in due form to enforce the Raja's commands, and sat down to the regular siege of Mysoor. The troops which had accompanied Nunjeraj to that place were some of the best in the service; but Hyder commanded the whole resources of the capital. Few of the natives of India sufficiently understand the principles on which the operations of a siege are conducted to be able to relate them intelligibly; but if I have comprehended aright the description which has been given to me on the spot of the operations of Hyder, they do little credit to the benefit which at that time he had derived from experience in that particular branch of the military profession; and may perhaps be attributed to an under-plot, of protracting the siege, with the view of rendering it, as he afterwards did, the ground of farther encroachment. However this may be, at the expiration of three months a negotiation was opened, and Nunjeraj capitulated on the conditions originally prescribed. He was permitted to select the districts composing his personal Jageer which were situated near the western frontier, and his residence was fixed at Cunnoor, about twenty-five miles west from Mysoor.

1759.

1760.

For the purpose of deluding the Raja and the public with the short-lived stage-trick of a happy change in his situation, he was invited by Hyder to visit, for the first time in his life, the

CHAP. X. 1760. residence of the ancient Rajas; and he inspected the approaches and batteries, which were reserved intire for that purpose, in order that he might be suitably impressed with the skill and prowess of his nominal servant, and real master.

Shortly before this period, namely, February 1760, the Raja's wife, the daughter of Nunjeraj, died, having borne him two sons, named Nunjeraj and Cham Raj: and he now espoused two wives at once; one of whom, Lechmee (the daughter of Gopaul Raj, formerly nominated Killedar of Trichinopoly), has survived the whole of the subsequent revolutions, and in August 1808 was in the perfect possession of her faculties; a sensible and amiable old lady, whose observations on the incidents of her eventful life are highly interesting and intelligent.

Hyder, not satisfied with actually possessing considerably more than one half of the dominions of the state, took advantage of the expenses incurred in the siege of Mysoor, and in the augmentation of the troops for the purpose of being prepared for external enemies, to represent the necessity of a farther assignment of revenue. Kundè Row strenuously opposed this indecent demand, which ultimately, however, he found himself unable to resist, and four districts selected by Hyder were added to his former possessions. But the discussions which preceded this arrangement produced a considerable degree of irritation between Hyder and Kundè Row, and left on the mind of the latter an impression of permanent disgust.

A French emissary arrived about this period at Seringapatam, with proposals which induced Hyder to detach a respectable corps for the purpose of co-operating with that nation against the English in the province of Arcot: these proposals arose from events which had occurred since the conclusion of the convention of Januury 1755; and although it does not enter into the design of this work to relate those operations in detail, a brief retrospect will enable us better to comprehend the general state of Deckan and the south, and to proceed with greater clearness in the more immediate purpose of our narrative.

Both parties seem to have distinctly understood that the convention of January 1755 was a mere truce, and both proposed 1755. to themselves separate advantages from acceding to it. The French expected the consolidation of the power which they had acquired in the Deckan, exclusively of the alleged equality in the province of Arcot. The English hoped, without a rupture of the truce, to confirm the power of their Nabob in the province of Arcot, and to extend it over Tinnevelly and Madura.

The course of our narrative has enabled the reader to perceive that whatever of military operations should be required to establish the nominal power of Mohammed Ali, must be performed by English troops, or not performed at all; for although a large rabble was maintained for the purpose of enforcing the collection of revenue, and aiding, as far as such troops could aid, in the general scope of military operation; the whole circle of his family and adherents during the fourteen years of revolutionary war which terminated in 1763 had not produced a single man fit to command an army or govern a province. The auxiliary operations of the English troops were accordingly complained of, and retaliated by the French, who put their troops in motion to prevent the important measure of the reduction of Vellore. The correspondence on these subjects unfolded to both parties what it would have been more convenient to discover at an earlier

CHAP. X. 1760.

period; namely, that the conditions of the armistice and conditional treaty were absolutely nugatory. The governor of Madras, in defending the aid afforded to Mohammed Ali, reproached the French for the expedition of M. Bussy to Mysoor, and distinguished the cases by affirming that "he had never opposed the French in collecting tribute from Poligars, Killedars, and others of their dependance." M. Deleyrit the French governor seized on the contradiction, by referring to the acknowledged dependance of Mysoor on Salabut Jung, and affirmed, "that it was not stipulated by treaty that the troops of M. Bussy should be withdrawn;" but in the triumph of superiority incautiously ran on to observe that the "principal view of the treaty was to re-establish a state of tranquillity in the province of Arcot." This concession was assumed by the government of Madras as a plain avowal that the convention was not considered to apply to the operations of M. Bussy in the Deckan, and justified the project of counteracting them from the side of Bombay; and the indirect warfare of Coromandel would necessarily have terminated in more open measures, if the parties had not been relieved from all doubt regarding their future proceedings by the direct declaration of national war in 1756.

The successors of M. Dupleix continued to M. Bussy the same large powers and unlimited confidence which his conduct had so amply deserved. Early in 1756 he marched with Salabut Jung to enforce the tribute due from the Patan Nabob of Savanore; a country situated between the rivers Toombuddra and Malpurba, in the direct route of all Mahratta armies proceeding to the countries of Mysoor or Arcot. Too weak to resist the Mahrattas, the local position of this chief led him to adopt the

policy of aiding them, on the condition of being supported against the Soubadar of the Deckan, who claimed his submission as an officer of the former state of Vijeyapoor. Morari Row, when negotiating with Nizam ul Moolk previously to the evacuation of Trichinopoly in 1744, had obtained his recognition of the state of Gooti as a dependency of the Soubadars of the Deckan; and when called on for tribute from Poona, evaded the demand under that pretext: the Mussulman thus sheltered himself behind the Hindoo, and the Hindoo behind the Mussulman. But Salabut Jung and Balajee Row had now severally agreed to withhold their support from the dependants of the other, and to unite in enforcing their obedience: and for this purpose moved from their respective capitals to commence with the siege of Savanore. The pressure of a common danger united the councils of the two chiefs to be attacked, and Morari Row, with a select body of his own troops, had thrown himself into Savanore. But he was quickly convinced of his error in supposing the place to be tenable against the skill and science of M. Bussy. During the war of Coromandel, when detached from Nunjeraj to Pondicherry, a debt of some magnitude had been contracted for the payment of his troops, which M. Dupleix, unable to discharge in money, had acknowledged in a public bond of the government of Pondicherry; Morari Row availed himself of this instrument in opening a negotiation with M. Bussy, and offered to cancel the bond on condition that his good offices should be successful in the adjustment of the double demand which has been explained. M. Bussy, who, exclusively of the liquidation of the debt, 1756.
attached some importance to the future enmity or friendship of this enterprizing chief, undertook the office of mediator: a recon-

CHAP. X. 1760. ciliation was effected on moderate terms, and the respective armies prepared to depart. But the party in the court of Salabut Jung which systematically opposed the introduction of foreign influence into his councils, did not pass over so fair an opportunity of exciting his jealousy. Shahnowaz Khan, who had been removed from the office of Dewan by the influence of M. Bussy, and had been restored on the promise of co-operating in his views, was secretly the chief of this party, and communicated his projects to Balajee Row; who, from different motives, was equally anxious for the expulsion of M. Bussy. Deprived of the aid of his regular troops, Salabut Jung could oppose but a feeble resistance to the designs of Balajee Row, who meditated the entire conquest of the Deckan, and was making advances to M. Bussy, with promises of a magnificent establishment, if he would leave Salabut Jung and enter the Mahratta service: and was negotiating also with the English for a corps to aid in the expulsion of the French from the Deckan. The suggestions of Shahnowaz Khan appeared to open a less expensive project for obtaining their services or their removal; and the discovery of M. Bussy's motives for mediation was easily converted into a charge of treachery to the interests of his principal, Salabut Jung. It does not appear whether M. Bussy was charged with concealing from Salabut Jung the transaction of cancelling the French bond; but it was sufficient for all the purposes of the party to prove, or attempt to prove, that the exertion of his usual
1756. skill and energy would have carried the fort of Savanore in half the time that the united armies had been before it if his own national objects had not interposed. Salabut Jung was accordingly induced to issue explicit orders, dismissing M. Bussy and

his corps from the service of the state, and directing them to retire from his territory without delay; but adding a condition which was not intended to be kept, that he should receive no molestation if he refrained from hostility in his retreat. The party was well aware that such a man as M. Bussy, at the head of two hundred European cavalry, six hundred European infantry, five thousand regular sepoys, and an excellent train of artillery, must be expelled by other instruments than the broad seal of the Soubadar of the Deekan: and an embassy, preceded by urgent letters, was immediately despatched to Madras, demanding the services of an English corps to aid in the expulsion of the French.

M. Bussy, at a distance from all his fixed resources, perceived that the confederacy was too strong to be openly resisted; and determined to move in the direction of the ceded provinces, and be governed by events; despatching at the same time to Pondicherry urgent demands for every possible reinforcement to be sent to Masulipatam. He quitted the army of Salabut Jung late in the month of May, without any demonstrations of resentment, and with the appearance of being disgusted with a scene, from which he was finally to retire, and to embark at Masulipatam.

Balajee Row, aware of the demand for English troops, perceived that all his objects would be equally thwarted by their presence as by the continuance of the French; and on the day of M. Bussy's separation sent an ambassador to renew his proposals for the service of that corps; or if that object could not be effected, the ambassador was followed by a body of select cavalry, who were directed to accompany and protect M. Bussy so long

CHAP. X. 1760. as he should deem their services to be necessary: for if an English corps should engage in the service of Salabut Jung, Balajee Row's negotiation for a similar purpose must necessarily fail, and he would in that case have need of M. Bussy, whose efforts from the ceded provinces he knew that a sense of common interest would ensure, whenever he might find it convenient to attack Salabut Jung and his English auxiliaries. M. Bussy, perceiving no symptoms of hostility, dismissed his Mahratta friends at an earlier period than might have been expected from his accustomed penetration; and immediately after their departure found the whole country instructed to treat him as an enemy, and the advanced guard of Salabut Jung's army in full pursuit. Sickness among the Europeans, desertion of the sepoys, and a scarcity of food and stores, compelled M. Bussy to halt at Hyderabad, where his influence still enabled him to command resources; and although the annual swell of the waters had fortunately interposed for a time the river Kistna between him and the great body of his enemies, the arrangements for placing his corps in a condition to pursue its march were not completed before he found himself encompassed by the whole army of Salabut Jung. To retreat under such circumstances a distance of two hundred miles to Masulipatam, presented, as its most favourable consequences, the desertion of a large portion of the sepoys, the loss of his sick, and the escape of a shattered remnant of his corps within the walls of Masulipatam; while a pursuing enemy would be destroying all his resources. He determined to take post where he was, and to abide the result of his military efforts, his intrigues among the chiefs, and the reinforcements expected from Pondicherry. These reinforcements enabled

M. Moracin, the French chief at Masulipatam, to equip a force of nearly five hundred Europeans, eleven hundred sepoys, and eleven field pieces, which marched for Hyderabad under the orders of Mr. Law. Great efforts were made to cut off this detachment: and although M. Bussy had purchased the inaction of some of the chiefs sent against it, the difficulties which opposed its progress were such as could only have been surmounted by the utmost coolness, determination, and military skill; and if this be the same Mr. Law who commanded the French troops at Seringham in 1753, it is just to his character to conclude, that his conduct on that service must have been governed by circumstances which he had not the power to controul. The able dispositions of M. Bussy kept the great body of Salabut Jung's army in his own presence, while he made a small but efficient detachment to aid this reinforcement on its near approach, when the enemy's efforts became most serious; so that Mr. Law formed the junction, with considerable loss it is true, but much less than might have been expected from the service performed, and with all his equipments in a perfect state of efficiency. The party at court was appalled by this unexpected success; and the junction was scarcely formed, when a messenger arrived from Salabut Jung proposing a reconciliation. M. Bussy was too prudent to be difficult in his terms, and on the 20th of August, not three months after his expulsion, he was received by Salabut Jung in public Durbar with all the marks of distinction and confidence that he had formerly enjoyed.

1756.

In the mean while, the troops which had been sent from England for the purpose of uniting with Balajee Row in the expulsion of the French from the Deckan had arrived at Bombay;

CHAP. X. 1760. 1756. and while waiting the result of his double negotiations, that chief had the address to procure their employment in the destruction of the piratical state of Angria, on the coast of Malabar; a service certainly of some utility to both parties, but altogether foreign to the great national object for which these troops had been sent to India; of which, from the loss of some despatches, the Indian governments seem not to have been apprized in sufficient time; and afterwards they disagreed in their opinion of the expediency and justice of the measure*. The operations against Angria employed the troops until the approach of the south-west monsoon, when the expulsion of M. Bussy and Salabut Jung's embassy to Madras left Balajee Row still more undecided in his views†.

The propositions of Salabut Jung opened to the government of Madras the most favourable prospect of accomplishing all their objects in Deckan and the south; and, as Balajee Row had foreseen, completely changed their policy with regard to a connection with the Mahrattas. The relative force of the French

* The plan of sending out these troops was formed in England while the Directors were still ignorant of the truce and conditional treaty. On their arrival, the governments of Madras and Bombay discussed the possibility of employing them consistently with the terms of those public instruments. On the avowal of Mr. Deleyrit, mentioned in p. 380, the government of Madras decided that they ought, and that of Bombay that they ought not, to be employed. It does not appear that the specific plan of employing them in the Deckan was ever proposed to Balajee Row: but the general object of obtaining the aid of an English corps was in his direct contemplation, and he made an earnest request to that effect when approaching Savanore, before it was certain that he would be joined by Salabut Jung and Bussy.

† His real views in the late service had, however, been entirely frustrated. He expected the whole of Angria's wealth, the accumulated plunder of a length of years; and, in a letter to Madras, complains grievously that his good friends had taken the prize to themselves as the real captors.

and English in Coromandel was so nearly equal as to justify their making a detachment, which was accordingly prepared, when misfortunes of the greatest urgency required the service of every disposable soldier in a distant quarter. The loss of Calcutta, aggravated by the horrible massacre of the black hole, demanded every effort that national indignation could suggest; and it was accordingly determined to apply to that purpose the troops which had been destined for the Deckan. M. Bussy's reconciliation with Salabut Jung had been entirely matured before these reinforcements could be ready for their new destination; and he considered his interests at court to be sufficiently confirmed to admit of his proceeding with the greater part of his force to regulate the ceded districts; leaving with Salabut Jung, who proceeded to Aurungabad, a guard of no more than two hundred select Europeans and five hundred sepoys.

Nizam Alee Khan, and Basalut Jung, the younger brothers of Salabut, were thought to possess some talents, and abundant ambition. According to the usual policy of eastern courts, they had been kept about the person of their elder brother without any employment, until the departure of the French troops at Savanore, at which period they had respectively attained the ages of twenty-two and twenty-three years. Where the sword is not only in practice, but in grave theory, the arbiter of political right, persons so circumstanced always find a party attached to their fortunes; and on this occasion, Shahnowaz Khan had found it expedient to secure these parties by yielding to the solicitations of the young men for a suitable establishment. Nizam Alee Khan was accordingly intrusted with the government of Berar; and Basalut Jung with that of Adwanee (Ado-

CHAP. X. 1760. ni) and Rachore, with suitable personal jageers; and the old statesman was supposed to have the farther view of affording an opportunity for the display of their respective talents, for the
1756. purpose of enabling him to make a proper selection of a successor to Salabut Jung, who had too much and too little capacity to be a vigorous master, or a pageant entirely passive.

. It is difficult to trace, and for our immediate purpose it is not of much importance to ascertain, the secret history of the combination between this minister and the younger brothers, by
1757. which a mutiny of the troops at Aurungabad in 1757 was rendered the pretext of confiding the seal of state to Basalut Jung; according to some accounts, before the arrival of Nizam Alee, who afterwards obtained it; and according to other statements, first to Nizam Alee, who resigned it under a secret compact to his brother: and it is equally difficult to extract any thing distinct or intelligible from the history of mock or real hostility and pacification with Balajee Row, about the same time. The confusion seemed to be distinctly aimed at the life of Salabut Jung, which was probably saved by the presence of the French guard alone: and M. Bussy, on receiving the intelligence, marched with the
1758. whole of his troops for Aurungabad, where he arrived early in February 1758, and found the armies encamped without any symptoms of actual or recent hostility: Balajee Row at the head of the Mahrattas, Nizam Alee commanding not only the troops of Berar but the army of the Soubadar; and Basalut Jung the troops of Adwanee. The presence of M. Bussy's army, and his personal influence and address, fixed his wavering friends, and deterred his enemies from executing the plan of revolution which had unquestionably been formed; but the danger to which his

interests had now for a second time been exposed from the defective arrangement of hazarding a corps in the midst of open or concealed enemies, without a depot or point of support within the distance of four hundred miles, suggested to him the necessity of possessing some place of strength in the neighbourhood of Aurungabad, which Salabut Jung seems at this time to have intended as his principal residence. He fixed on the impregnable rock of Dowlutabad; and having bought the place from the governor, it was concerted that it should appear to be taken by surprise, while M. Bussy, attended by a strong guard of Europeans (which the known projects of treachery had rendered not unusual at that period), should be on a visit to the governor at the summit of the rock; and the object was accomplished with little bloodshed, and without the loss of a single Frenchman. The Killedar or governor was a dependant of Shahnowaz Khan; the garrison was in his immediate pay; and according to the usual custom, the fortress was considered to belong more to the chief whose troops possessed it, than to the state of which he was the servant. This was consequently an unpardonable insult to Shahnowaz Khan; and as his removal from office was indispensable to the plan of administration in M. Bussy's contemplation, he was arrested* in camp by the troops of Salabut Jung, who was privy to the whole transaction, at the same time that M. Bussy seized the fortress. Until this period Nizam Alee continued to be refractory, and to express his open discontent at the arrangement suggested by M. Bussy, and announced by Salabut Jung, of removing him from Berar to the less extensive government of Hyderabad; but these decisive measures, of which he

CHAP. X. 1760. 1758. 1759.

* These arrests, usually named *nezerbundee*, do not in common remove the ordinary guards by which a chief is surrounded.

CHAP. X. 1760. 1758. did not clearly perceive the ultimate object, induced him to dissemble compliance, and he prepared to depart with apparent good will to his new government.

M. Bussy had selected for his Dewan a person named Hyder Jung, who had first recommended himself to notice by his zeal and intelligence as an officer of sepoys. Being a man of education and good connections, of great sagacity and excellent address, and possessing a subtlety of character which naturally fitted him for intrigues, he became the confidential agent of M. Bussy in all the secret machinations which he was obliged to adopt, and was in consequence elevated to high dignities and suitable jageers by M. Bussy's influence, for the purpose of facilitating his access in every direction. Shahnowaz Khan and Nizam Alee, whose interests the course of events had entirely united, determined that his removal was an essential preliminary to the accomplishment of their own views. The day on which Salabut Jung was to pay his devotions at the tomb of his father, some miles from Aurungabad, was fixed on by Nizam Alee for holding a public levee, to receive the compliments of the principal officers of the government, previously to his departure: and Hyder Jung, who was invited to a private audience in a separate tent, on the pretext of soliciting his protection for the friends of Nizam Alee at court, was there murdered by his direction. M. Bussy saw at once the probable extent of the plot; and on the first alarm, sent a strong detachment to secure the return of Salabut Jung, and another to remove Shahnowaz Khan to the fort of Dowlutabad. This prisoner, supposing his death to be intended, made a desperate resistance, and was killed with most of his adherents; and Nizam Alee, who expected a different result from the confusion of the day, fled on the same night, attended by a small escort, and did not stop till he arrived at Burhanpoor, on the Tapti, a distance of about one hundred and sixty miles, about the middle of May. CHAP. X. 1760. 1758.

Salabut Jung prepared to pursue, and made a few marches for that purpose to the northward; but as Nizam Alee would necessarily retire as he should advance, the pursuit of an unincumbered fugitive was given up from a conviction of its inutility; and the army returned by easy stages and a winding route to the eastward of Aurungabad, for the purpose of establishing the authority of the government. M. Bussy's endeavours to attach Basalut Jung to the interests of his elder brother seemed to be successful, and a degree of order and satisfaction began to appear in every department of the state.

The ceded provinces yielded abundant resources for the payment of M. Bussy's troops. He had acquired, by the possession of Dowlutabad, a place of security for the prince whom he supported, and an impregnable post to sustain his own future operations to any extent that ambition might dictate. He had fixed the interests of his nation in the Deckan on a foundation not to be shaken by any ordinary contingency: when the vanity, ignorance, and arrogance of one man, destroyed by a single dash of the pen, all that the vast conceptions of M. Dupleix, and the consummate genius of M. Bussy, had laboured for many years to advance to this state of prosperity.

M. Lally had arrived to command the French armies in India; and his orders, directing M. Bussy, with all the troops that could be spared from the defence of the ceded provinces, to proceed without delay to Pondicherry, were received in the true spirit of a soldier, who considers obedience as his first duty. The expecta-

CHAP. X. 1760. 1758. tion of these orders had induced M. Bussy to lead Salabut Jung towards Golconda: the garrison of Dowlutabad was withdrawn; and on the 18th of July, Salabut Jung, who was unable to comprehend these strange orders, took his last leave of M. Bussy in an agony of the deepest grief, astonishment, and despair. With the departure of M. Bussy our retrospect must return to Coromandel.

The year 1757, although full of minor incidents, produced no event in Coromandel that had any decisive influence on the fate of the war. In the center of the province the chief strength of the French and English troops manœuvred in each other's presence, without coming to serious action; and M. D'Autueil, by a well concerted movement to the south, attempted to acquire Trichinopoly, which was weakly garrisoned, while the English troops were engaged in distant operations in Tinnevelly. In this he was foiled by the superior address of Captain Calliaud, who, with a small corps, of whose approach M. D'Autueil was perfectly apprized, threw himself into the place, in the face of numbers which he was unable to meet in action, and compelled the French force to retire to Pondicherry without a farther effort.

In the northern and southern extremities of the province, two brothers of Mohammed Ali, Nejeeb Oolla at Vellore, and Mahphuz Khan in Tinnevelly, were in open hostility. Nejeeb Oolla, in close alliance with the French at Masulipatam, kept a respectful distance from Nellore, his own capital, when an armament sent under Colonel Ford besieged the place, and was repulsed by the officer left in command. Mahphuz Khan, sometimes affecting obedience, at others avowing hostility, was alternately a puppet in the hands of his own officers, or of the Poligars, who

sheltered their own views of independence under the pretext of adherence to his cause; and this capricious and incompetent man was one day elated with dreams of sovereignty, and on the next reduced to the want of the common necessaries of life. In the centre, in the meantime, the improvidence and profligacy of another brother, Abdul Wahab Khan, when a friend, was equivalent in its consequences to the presence of another enemy; a character which for some time he also assumed. The English officer commanding the garrison of Arcot had imprudently manifested some suspicions, which his government seems to have considered groundless: but they had induced Abdul Wahab to fly in the night to Chittore, from whence he seized and improved 1758.
Chanderagherry, the ancient capital of the fugitive kings of Carnatic, a citadel built on the summit of a stupendous rock, with a fortified town at its foot, which he intended to render the seat of a separate government. The French had acquired Chittapet and other less important places, and on the whole their interests in the centre of the province had been materially improved.

On the 28th of April, 1758, M. Lally arrived with a powerful 1758.
armament, which rendered the French force so decidedly superior to that of the English, as to leave little doubt of the success of their future operations; and the instructions from France prescribed their commencing with the siege of Fort St. David. M. Lally was an officer of some experience and ardent courage, and perfectly versed in all that may be considered as the mechanical part of the military profession. He had lived much in courts, and to the exterior manners of the best society added a quickness, point, and facility of expression; and when offended, a vi-

CHAP. X. 1760. rulence and asperity of remark which amounted to wit, or was mistaken for it. But defective in temper and good disposition, these superficial accomplishments rendered him insolent and vain; and while arrogating, from his experience and knowledge
1758. of the world, a superiority over all mankind, he was absolutely destitute of the reach of mind necessary for comprehending or directing great affairs. The practice of European warfare was with him the bed of Procustes, to which all Indian habits and prejudices must be forcibly accommodated; and the connexions with Indian states, and that of M. Bussy in particular, he treated as visionary jobs, puffed into importance by the interests of those who framed them. On the very evening of the day on which M. Lally arrived at Pondicherry, one thousand Europeans and as many sepoys marched for Fort St. David. Preparation was a mere pretext of Indian apathy, and he would teach another tactic. They marched without proper guides, and after wandering in the dark, arrived before Fort St. David soon after daylight, hungry and without provisions, which did not leave Pondicherry until the following day: and the men starving and wandering in quest of food, might have been cut off in detail if the English garrison had been directed by a proper degree of intelligence and vigour. No useful energy was omitted in seconding the impracticable orders of M. Lally; but the government of Pondicherry did not possess a train of ordnance cattle; the stores and equipments for the siege could not be moved by preternatural means; and the whole of the native inhabitants of Pondicherry must march with loads on their heads or shoulders. It was of no avail for the experienced and respectable members of his civil council and military staff to represent, that this unmanly outrage was a

violation of all that was sacred in immemorial habit and religious prejudice; and an offence more gross against the feelings of a whole people, than harnessing a mareschal of France to the shafts of a dung cart: these were the crude fancies of men who had never seen the world, and who yielded from motives of interest, or apathy, to the senseless habits and feminine indolence of the Indian blacks. The siege of Fort St. David was nevertheless conducted with skill and effect, and the defence being far from respectable, the place fell on the 1st of June. 1758.

For the purpose of collecting the French army for the siege, M. Lally had, among other detachments, drawn in that at Seringham, which place was delivered to a detachment of Hyder's troops sent from Dindegul in May, 1758. But the vigour and decision of Captain Calliaud's operations, the instant that the French troops had departed, induced the Mysoreans to abandon it precipitately on the same night; leaving behind some valuable military stores, and eight pieces of French artillery.

The English, concluding from the superior force of M. Lally, that his next operation would be the siege of Madras, which had lately undergone some reforms, and was in a weak and unfinished state, had been early in their arrangements for withdrawing all their stores and troops from the central stations of Carangooly, Chinglapet, Conjeveram, and Arcot, which were consigned to the charge of a provincial rabble, for the purpose of strengthening the garrison of Madras: adverting to the condition of that place, it might be doubted whether M. Lally ought not to have attacked it in its dismantled state with his actual force, rather than wait for reinforcements, and thus give time for completing the unfinished works and augmenting the garrison: but the opposite opinion prevailed: the troops of M. Bussy had not

CHAP. X. 1760. yet arrived, and M. Lally had the choice of two intermediate operations until he should be in strength to undertake the siege of Madras. The whole centre and west of the province was at his mercy, and its conquest would enlarge his fixed resources:
1758. but he was in want of large and immediate supplies of money. The general detestation which his conduct had excited in all descriptions of men, European and native, deprived him of the resources of public or personal credit, which better measures would have insured; and in concurrence with the advice of his council he marched against Tanjore. When the Raja of that place was besieged in 1750 by Muzzuffer Jung and Chunda Saheb, he amused them by various pretences for the purpose of protracting their operations, in the expectation of the arrival of Nasir Jung; and, among other means, had executed a bond to Chunda Saheb for fifty-six lacs of rupees, which remained in the possession of the government of Pondicherry. A competitor for the Raj of Tanjore, who had been supported by the English in 1749, had also been found at Fort St. David, and the apprehension of being supplanted by this person might add to the other fears of the Raja.

About the middle of June the army marched towards Tanjore; but such was the abhorrence of the natives for M. Lally, that few could be induced to engage with draught or carriage cattle for the service of the army. The only routine of supply which experience had shewn to be practicable was still held in contempt; and the soldiers, hungry, indignant, and scrambling for a precarious supply in the villages, marched one hundred miles to Karical, whither supplies and stores had been sent by sea, before they obtained a regular meal; and the number of sick was proportionably increased by these wanton and unnecessary privations. On advancing from hence, M. Lally found at Trivaloor abundance of paddy, or rice in the husk; but from the total want of followers it could not be deprived of its husks, by which operation alone it can be rendered fit for human food. Contracts for the plunder and ransom of towns, and sweeping off the cattle to be sold on the sea-coast, caused his march to resemble an Indian predatory expedition rather than the warfare of a civilized people. The pagodas were violated to search for imaginary idols of gold; and six unfortunate bramins, who returned to linger about the temples of their religion, were blown away as spies from the muzzles of his cannon. On his arrival before Tanjore, with a train and equipment insufficient from the want of conveyance, the Raja negotiated, and seemed disposed at one time to compromise with M. Lally; but on the mean threat, if he did not immediately comply, of being carried with his family as slaves to the island of Mauritius, he determined to defend himself to the last extremity. Captain Calliaud at Trichinopoly, who, on the movement of M. Lally to the south, had been joined by the corps of Mohammed Issoof from Tinnevelly, was cautious in his aid to the Raja of Tanjore so long as any probability appeared of his uniting with the French, to proceed, according to M. Lally's plan, to the siege of Trichinopoly; but as soon as he was satisfied, from his intelligence, that the Raja's indignation would hold him steady to his resolve, he was more liberal and efficient in his reinforcements. In the mean while the French and English squadrons had fought two naval actions, indecisive with regard to captures, but honourable, if not advantageous, to the latter; and M. Lally, when the operations of the siege were drawing to a crisis, and his ammunition to a close, received in-

1758.

CHAP. X. 1760. telligence that the English squadron, after the second action, had appeared before Karical and threatened a descent.

The plunder of the country, instead of ensuring plenty, had produced its inevitable effect of averting every description of
1758. supply; scarcity and distress prevailed in the camp; a council of war determined that the army must relieve itself and Karical by an immediate retreat from Tanjore: and the expedition terminated in raising the siege, spiking and abandoning the battering cannon, and retreating without any other food than a few cocoa-nuts, gathered on the road, with which the soldiers, exhausted, famished, and disgusted, sustained life until relieved by the supplies of Karical.

Captain Calliaud, on the approach of M. Lally, had concentrated his force by withdrawing the garrison of Seringham. The troops of Hyder from Dindegul returned a second time to occupy that place, and were a second time dislodged with equal facility, as soon as the retreat of the French army was ascertained.

M. Lally on his return to Pondicherry directed his attention to the central and western posts evacuated by the English; and in September was joined at Wandewash by M. Bussy, who had left the command of the troops to M. Moracin, and proceeded without an escort under the safeguard of a passport, which, in respect for his personal character, had been readily granted by the government of Madras. On the 4th of October, M. Lally's public entry into Arcot, the capital of the province, was announced by salutes from all the French garrisons, and he now only waited the arrival of the northern troops; but neglecting the capture of Chinglapet, reinforcements from England enabled the government of Madras to reoccupy that important post, in such a manner as to place it beyond his reach without the delays of a regular siege.

M. Moracin on passing Vellore was joined by Nejeeb Oolla and his troops; and leaving on his left the eastern range of hills which approach the sea near to Paliacate, proceeded through the valley of Calastri and Tripeti, and was met at the latter place, 1758.
which is only ten miles from Chandergherry, by Abdul Wahab. The pagoda of Tripeti, the resort of pilgrims from the farthest limits of the Hindoo religion, is situated in an elevated bason surrounded by a circular crest of hills; and during the successive revolutions of the country, these sacred precincts, guarded by four Poligars, or Cawilkars, who are its hereditary watchmen, had not only never been profaned by Mohammedan or Christian feet, but even the exterior of the temple has never been seen * by any but a genuine Hindoo. The reciprocal interests of the bramins and the successive governments had compromised this forbearance by the payment of a large revenue, which the bramins exacted from the pilgrims; and at this time the stipulated annual sum paid to the government was thirty thousand pounds. As this was a certain source of revenue, generally collected without trouble, and conveniently situated for the purposes of Abdul Wahab, he strenuously urged its being ceded to him as the price of uniting permanently with the French, against the English and his brother: but M. Moracin, who was instructed to realize as much money as possible, rented out the collections of the pagoda for the current year on receiving a considerable portion in advance; and Abdul Wahab, disappointed in this object,

* The author was formerly on duty for eighteen months in the woods of that neighbourhood, and frequently climbed to the summits of the neighbouring hills without being able to get even a distant glimpse of the pagoda.

 left the French on the next day's march, and made a merit of this defection in negotiating a reconciliation with Mohammed Ali.

1758. M. Lally, on receiving all the reinforcements that he expected, moved against Madras, where he arrived on the 14th of December, and broke ground against the place on the 17th. The relative numbers of the besiegers and besieged were pretty nearly proportioned to their respective situations; but M. Lally's means of conveyance for the immense quantity of stores required for a regular siege continued to be defective. The English garrison was composed of select officers and excellent troops. The forms of the company's government at that time required that the civil governor should exercise the chief command; but fortunately, Mr. Pigot possessed all the zeal, and much of the knowledge, required in that arduous situation: and all the operations were in effect conducted by his second, Colonel Lawrence, one of the best soldiers of his age. The precaution had been taken of ordering Mohammed Issoof with the regular troops of his command, and as many more as he could raise, to move from the southward; and he was joined by a small detachment from Chinglapet under Captain Preston, by a body of horse procured by Captain Calliaud in Tanjore, and by Abdul Wahab with one thousand horse. This corps acted with some success on the line of the enemy's com-
1759. munications with Pondicherry and the countries from which they obtained their supplies, and materially increased the difficulties of the siege; which, after the most vigorous and skilful efforts on both sides, was raised on the 17th of February, 1759, exactly two months from the day of breaking ground; M. Lally leaving behind him thirty-three pieces of battering cannon, and nineteen of smaller calibres. Mohammed Ali had taken up his residence

in the fort on the approach of the besiegers; but being of no use, and much embarrassment, was sent off by sea to the southern coast, from whence he proceeded to Trichinopoly. The slender services of Abd-ul-Waheb were rewarded by a confirmation of his possessions at Chandergherry and Chittore. Nejeeb Oolla had accompanied the French army to Madras; but the operations of a siege were not suited to his taste; and as soon as he began to suspect that Madras might not be taken, he departed with the entire concurrence of M. Lally, who found him and his troops to be an useless incumbrance. The intelligence of the siege being raised, indicating that the English might in their turn be superior, determined him to change sides; and as a preliminary to negotiation, this infamous wretch perpetrated the foul murder of every Frenchman in his service, one officer alone excepted. 1759.

The English army took the field from Madras as soon after the siege as their defective means would permit; but the operations in the province of Arcot were not productive of any very decisive event. In the mean while, the consequences of withdrawing M. Bussy from the Deckan were truly important. The English government of Bengal, after the re-establishment of their affairs, and the conquest of all the French stations in that province, had sent into the northern Circars an armament under Colonel Forde, who, after an active campaign against the French forces left in those provinces under M. Conflans, sat down before Masulipatam. Salabut Jung had been induced by various considerations to march to the relief of the French; and on his approach Colonel Forde achieved, on the seventh of April, the capture of Masulipatam by the daring enterprize of storming in the night a breach scarcely practicable, and across a ditch

CHAP. X. 1760. fordable with difficulty at ebb tide, defended by a garrison more numerous than the assailants, and possessing one hundred and twenty pieces of cannon. This brilliant exploit, and the advance towards Hyderabad of Nizam Alee, who had collected an army to supplant his brother, or, in the Indian phrase, "to regulate
1759. the affairs of the state," induced Salabut Jung to negotiate with Colonel Forde. The treaty executed in consequence was entirely in favour of the English, without any reciprocal obligation. A territory was ceded of the annual value of four lacs of rupees. The French were to be entirely expelled from the Deckan*, and each party was merely not to support the enemies or refractory subjects of the other.

This instrument was scarcely executed, when Salabut Jung was urgent for the aid of Colonel Forde against Nizam Alee: an object which might probably have been secured, if he had rendered it a condition of the treaty. But Colonel Forde was still more anxious for the destruction of a French corps of observation which had kept the field, and was now under the declared protection of Basalut Jung. Each considered his own object to be of primary importance; neither would yield; and Salabut Jung, accompanied by the French corps which he had agreed to expel, marched towards Hyderabad. When arrived near to that city, a negotiation ensued, which replaced Nizam Alee in the exact position from which he had been removed in the preceding year by the address of M. Bussy; and Basalut Jung, who in his office of Dewan had really exercised the chief power of the state, finding himself thus supplanted in the Deckan, marched for the establishment of an empire of his own in the south, accompanied

* This treaty defines the Deckan to be bounded on the south by the Kistna, according to the popular acceptation which has been noticed.

by the French corps of observation, in which were two hundred Europeans only, and which, added to his own troops, formed a body of about two thousand horse, and eight thousand infantry, with a tolerably good train of artillery. He gave out that he was merely proceeding to his government at Adwanee, but soon directed his march to the south-east, levying contributions as he proceeded; and in the month of July approached Nellore, from whence Nejeeb Oolla, full of terror and conscious guilt, sent incessant dispatches to Madras supplicating assistance: but Basalut Jung was satisfied with a contribution, and crossed the river Pennar to the westward of that town. He now publicly gave out that he was on his march to join the French in the province of Arcot; but in the uncertainty of the times he did not neglect to provide himself with eventual resources, if their cause should become desperate.

1759.

A Hindoo named Sunput Row had been the Dewan or minister of finance of Anwar u Deen; and as, during his life-time, he had shewn a disposition to support the views of the elder and only legitimate son, Mahphuz Khan, he had been discarded by Mohammed Ali, and continued to preserve a secret correspondence with Mahphuz Khan; but had not yet considered the prospects of that chief sufficiently promising, to justify the risk of the great wealth which he possessed by openly espousing his cause. He was now, for the purpose of escaping observation, residing at Kalastri; and opened a negotiation with Basalut Jung, who saw in Mahphuz Khan a pageant sufficiently apt to be employed under any circumstances which might occur, as a French or an English Nabob: for the last of the French Nabobs, Murteza Khan, seemed to have tacitly relinquished his appointment.

CHAP. X. 1760. The letters of Basalut Jung to Mahphuz Khan, assenting to the plans communicated through Sunput Row, found him in his accustomed state of sordid splendour, but under difficulty to obtain the ordinary meal of the day; and the hopes which had so often been crushed were once more revived, previously to 1759. their entire extinction. Sunput Row opened his own treasures, and prevailed on the Poligars of Calastri and Vencatigerri to assist with money and troops; and Basalut Jung was equally, but with different views, solicited by the French, and by the party of Mahphuz Khan, to advance into the center of the province: while Nizam Alee, who dreaded in his connexion with the French the return of M. Bussy to the Deckan, and was desirous of inducing him to relinquish every plan of ambition, and return to a private station at his jageer, had sent an agent to his camp, who was profuse in his offers of additional grants of territory to obtain a reconciliation. Basalut Jung was thus equally ready to side with either of the parties in the province of Arcot, against that which should prove to be the weakest: or to return to his jageer, if the course of events should render that the most prudent measure. An English corps of observation which had been sent to act upon his rear if he should determine to advance was now in the neighbourhood of Calastri: and M. Bussy was in motion with a French corps, which, according to calculation, and repeated assurances, ought long since to have joined him. But an alarming mutiny of the French troops for want of pay had delayed M. Bussy's advance; and Basalut Jung, who had now obtained from Sunput Row and the Poligars all the money that he expected, and did not like the vicinity of the English troops, on receiving accounts of the disorderly state of the French army, struck off to the west on the nineteenth of October, and crossing the hills, entered the county of Kurpa, still accompanied by the French corps and by Sunput Row. CHAP. X. 1760.

As soon as the agitation of the French troops had subsided, M. Bussy pursued his march by a different route, and arrived at Kurpa on the tenth of November. Basalut Jung, who foresaw 1759.
the fate that awaited his elder brother, in all his negotiations with M. Bussy stipulated for the aid of French troops against Nizam Ali; and distinctly unfolded the extent of his own views, and of those which Sunput Row continued to indulge. He demanded "that he should be recognized by the French as sovereign of the whole Carnatic, meaning thereby all the countries south of the Kistna: that the government of the province of Arcot should be regulated in whatever manner he should hereafter determine, without any interference of the French, who should give up whatever territory they possessed, and receive from him a pecuniary remuneration equal to one-third of the revenues; and that their auxiliary troops, which he might require in offensive or defensive war with Nizam Ali, should be entirely paid by himself: on the adjustment of which conditions, and the advance of four lacs of rupees for his troops, he would instantly accompany M. Bussy to Arcot." These were rather the terms of an established sovereign, than of a person subsisting from day to day: but in the judgment of Sunput Row, they were the only conditions on which he could safely break altogether with Nizam Alee, or form a reasonable hope of establishing a real sovereignty independant of European control. The negotiation accordingly broke off; but he gratified M. Bussy with an instrument which it seemed of little utility to solicit, namely, a sunnud, enjoining all officers in the province of Arcot to pay obedience to M. Lally,

1760. who had lately, of his own authority, made a fifth change since the beginning of the war, in the office of French Nabob, by the reappointment of Reza Saheb. M. Bussy found the French corps with Salabut Jung in distress, even for their daily food; but his personal credit every where commanded money, of which he
1759. raised at Kurpa enough, not only to satisfy the immediate want of these troops, whom he now incorporated with his own, but to engage a body of four hundred good horse, with which on the tenth of December he returned to Arcot.

CHAPTER XI.

Retrospect continued—Appointment and character of Colonel Coote—his capture of Wandiwash—Adverse opinions of M. Lally and M. Bussy regarding the plan of the campaign—Siege of Wandiwash—raised by a splendid victory—M. Lally, pressed by the vigorous operations of Colonel Coote, applies to Mysoor, as has been related—A detachment of Hyder under Mukhdoom was in the intermediate and recently conquered country of Baramahal—and is ordered to Pondicherry—terms of his service—occupation of Thiagar—he defeats an English detachment—Hyder elated with this success re-enforces Mukhdoom—Plan of the Dowager, the Raja, and Kundè Row, for Hyder's destruction—singular result—flies in the night and deserts his family—arrives at Bangalore—recals Mukhdoom—Accession of Fuzzul Oolla—who is defeated in attempting to join Mukhdoom—Desperate state of Hyder's affairs—relieved by an event which he could not comprehend—its explanation—once more takes the field—is defeated by Kundè Row—Effrontery of Hyder's application to Nunjeraj—who is deceived, and unites with him—Stratagem practised on Kundè Row—and consequent dispersion of his army—Hyder descends to Coimbetoor—and after recovering that province returns to Seringapatam—another stratagem completely decisive—Despair of Kundè Row and the Raja—Negotiation—terminates in Hyder's final usurpation of the government—Deception regarding the fate of Kundè Row—Hyder proceeds to Bangalore.

THE French and English governments had, after the truce of 1755, been competitors for the fame of impolicy and injustice, in superseding two such men as M. Bussy and Colonel Lawrence. Five French officers of superior rank had done still greater honour to themselves than to M. Bussy, in signing a request to M. Lally that he might be placed above them. Colonel Lawrence had in 1757 given his services as a volunteer to the second

CHAP. XI.

1760.

1759.

CHAP. XI. 1760. officer by whom he had been superseded, but the recal of Colonel Adlercorn left him in command of the troops which defended Madras. The fatigues of that trying service had again impaired his health, and he had lately carried with him to England the affectionate regret of all his countrymen, and the general respect
1759. of the natives of India. Colonel Brereton, on whom the command devolved, conducted the operations of the campaign of 1759, in the center of the province, with intelligence and vigour; but naturally wishing to achieve some distinguished exploit before the arrival of his successor, had in September failed with great loss in an attempt on Wandiwash; and the English government had now redeemed all their errors, by the appointment of Colonel Coote to the command of the army of Madras. He arrived on the twenty-seventh of October: and joined the head quarters of the troops cantoned for the rains at Conjeveram on the twenty-first of November, 1759.

The earliest measures of this officer seemed to infuse new intelligence and decision into all the operations of the troops. Nature had given to Colonel Coote all that nature can confer in the formation of a soldier; and the regular study of every branch of his profession, and experience in most of them, had formed an accomplished officer. A bodily frame of unusual vigour and activity, and mental energy always awake, were restrained from excessive action by a patience and temper which never allowed the spirit of enterprize to outmarch the dictates of prudence. Daring valour and cool reflexion strove for the mastery in the composition of this great man. The conception and execution of his designs equally commanded the confidence of his officers; and a master at once of human nature, and of the science of

war, his rigid discipline was tempered with an unaffected kind- CHAP. XI. 1760.
ness, and consideration for the wants and even the prejudices of those whom he commanded, which won the affections of the European soldiers, and rendered him the idol * of the native troops.

His first act was to assemble a council of war, for the purpose of hearing and discussing the opinions of his principal officers regarding the operations of the ensuing campaign. A detachment of the French army had re-occupied Seringham, and other divisions were employed in distant parts of the province: it was accordingly resolved to open the campaign by attacking Wandewash. The first movements were ostensibly directed against Arcot; but the preparations were so skilfully combined, that Wandewash was carried on the twenty-ninth of November before
it was possible for the French to move a sufficient body of troops 1759.
for its relief: and Carangooly was reduced in a few days afterwards. The distant detachments made by M. Lally were partly occasioned by the urgency of his affairs; but the loss of these two places shewed him the necessity of concentrating his force. The two armies arrived in each other's presence in the neighbour-
hood of Arcot early in January 1760. Colonel Coote's inferiority 1760.
in cavalry determined him to avoid a general action under any circumstances of disadvantage. M. Bussy's conception of the campaign was to make use of this superiority, to act on the communications of the English army, and thus compel it to fight at a disadvantage, or retire to Madras for supplies; and in

* His portrait is hung up in the exchange at Madras; and no sepoy who has served under him ever enters the room without making his obeisance to *Coote Bahauder*.

1760.

either case the recovery of Wandewash and Carangooly would be easy and certain. M. Lally was of a different opinion, and expected to be able, under circumstances entirely dissimilar, to retake Wandewash, with a select corps, while the rest of his army should occupy the attention of the English. Colonel Coote was not to be so amused, but approached within two easy marches of Wandewash: and M. Lally, finding his original intention frustrated, was also obliged to concentrate his force. Colonel Coote had entire confidence in the garrison; they reciprocally trusted to the wisdom and energy of his measures, and prepared to sustain the attack with perfect coolness and decision; he therefore determined to leave M. Lally to waste his strength in an unprofitable siege, until the breach should be practicable, when he hoped to relieve the place by striking a decisive blow either at the trenches and batteries, or the army which protected them, according to the opportunity which might be afforded by the manœuvres of the enemy. On the twentieth of January the report of the officer commanding in Wandewash determined him to move: and on the twenty-second he obtained a decisive victory over M. Lally's army, which retreated with the loss of upwards of one-fourth of his European troops, twenty-four pieces of cannon, and all its equipments and military stores. M. Lally had committed great errors in the plan of his campaign; and in the early operations of the twenty-second had been completely out-manœuvred by Colonel Coote; who, by a most judicious movement, had placed his little army in a position where he had a free communication with the fort, and a flank protected by its fire; with the advantageous choice of attacking the batteries and trenches, or the French camp. Although M. Lally did not penetrate in sufficient time to prevent it, the intention of this able movement, it must be admitted that he exerted himself with judgment and skill to remedy the oversight: but the superior mind of Colonel Coote, who provided with caution against every contingency, restrained his troops until he saw the opportunity of turning a flank, and deciding by corresponding efforts the fortune of the day. M. Bussy was among the prisoners; and Colonel Coote did homage to his character, by immediately complying with his request for a passport to Pondicherry. The judgment of Colonel Coote, in availing himself of the consequences of this brilliant victory, was, if possible, more conspicuous than the skill by which he had achieved it. M. Lally in his retreat committed the farther error of not re-enforcing Chittapet, which was taken on the twenty-ninth; on the tenth of February the capital was once more in possession of the English: and the indefatigable activity of Colonel Coote left scarcely a day of the ensuing campaign without some acquisition. A body of three thousand horse of Morari Row, who had served with M. Lally, left him on the reverse of his fortunes; the consequent superiority of the English cavalry enabled them to improve every advantage; and by daily circumscribing more and more the resources of the French, to look with some distant hope to the capture of Pondicherry. Under these circumstances, M. Lally was induced to turn his attention towards Mysoor, with a view of obtaining the co-operation of that power. The negotiation was opened by a church militant prelate of doubtful history, who called himself the bishop of Halicarnassus; and on his report, two officers of rank were sent to settle the terms with Hyder, who protracted the final adjustment; and detached his brother-in-law Mukhdoom Ali, with powers to conclude the treaty.

CHAP. XI. 1760. Mukhdoom Ali was already in the field, for the conquest of the Baramahal; a province situated on an intermediate level, between the first and second ranges of hills which separate the higher from the lower countries, and taking its name from the twelve fortresses built chiefly on rocky summits, which protected an equal number of subordinate divisions. This province, formerly part of the domain of the celebrated Jug Deo, had been conquered from Mysoor by the Patan Nabob of Kurpa; but in the year 1758 Kurpa was invaded by the Mahrattas, and reduced to the necessity of ceding one-half of its possessions. Assud Khan Mehteree, governor of the Baramahal on the part of Kurpa, a brave but improvident man, was superseded about this time by another officer; and came over to Hyder, representing the facility of seizing the province, and offering the aid of his own local information. This advantage, and the reduced strength of Kurpa, induced Hyder to undertake the conquest of Baramahal; but it was first expedient to reduce the intermediate fort and country of the Poligar of Anicul, situated on the eastern verge of the tract of woody hills extending from Savendy Droog to the Caveri, twenty-three miles south of Bangalore, and in the most direct road from Seringapatam to Baramahal; through which province also runs the best and most direct road to Pondicherry. Hyder had received a mission of similar import from Pondicherry in March 1759: and he availed himself of the first convenient opportunity to occupy those intermediate territories; and thus obtain a safe and uninterrupted communication with the center of the province of Arcot.

As soon as Mukhdoom had accomplished these two objects, he proceeded, in conformity to Hyder's orders, to Pondicherry. The following were the general objects of the treaty which Mukhdoom was impowered to ratify. "That a corps of three thousand select horse and five thousand sepoys, with a due proportion of artillery, should be furnished by Hyder to serve with the French, and to be paid by them in the war of Coromandel: and that the fort of Thiagar, which had been taken by the French in September, should be permanently ceded to Mysoor, as a post of deposit and communication." This place is most commodiously situated for the purposes which have been stated; being about twenty miles from Ahtoor, which commands the pass leading from the districts of Salem and Shenkerrydroog, long in the possession of Mysoor; thirty-five miles from the gorge of the pass of Tingrecota, or Changama *; an easy and convenient access from the recent acquisition of Baramahal, and about fifty miles E. S. E. from Pondicherry. "On the favourable conclusion of the war of Arcot, Trichinopoly †, Madura, and Tinnevelly, were to be ceded to Mysoor; and the French agreed to assist in their reduction. In the mean while the Mysoreans were to retain whatever they should themselves conquer in Arcot, but return these conquests, on the possession of equivalent territory in Madura or Tinnevelly."

Mukhdoom arrived at Thiagar with the first division of his troops on the 4th of June 1760; and soon after at Pondicherry, 1760.
where he ratified the treaty on the 27th; and evading the English troops, returned on the following day to bring up the re-

* Towns situated at the western and eastern extremities of the pass, which in Baramahal is named the pass of Tingrecota, and in Arcot the pass of Changama. Most passes in India take their names from the towns at their entrance, and are thus differently called by the people at their different extremities.

† Mr. Orme, who seems to have had access to French official documents, states Madura and Tinnevelly only, and is perhaps correct. But all my manuscripts add Trichinopoly.

mainder of his corps, and a convoy of provisions, for the supply of which he made a most profitable contract.

Colonel Coote had by this time captured every French post of importance in the province, Thiagar and Ginjee excepted; and had circumscribed their force within the limits of a few miles round Pondicherry. For the purpose of confronting this new danger, he detached a corps under Major Moore, to which, holding too cheaply the military prowess of the Mysoreans, he appointed no more than one hundred and eighty European infantry, thirty Abyssinians, fifty hussars, eleven hundred sepoys, and sixteen hundred irregular horse. This corps was met on the 17th of July near to Trivadi by the whole body of Mysoreans proceeding to Pondicherry, and completely routed: the native horse and foot were entirely dispersed; the European troops escaped into Trivadi; the infantry, with the loss of one third, and the cavalry, of one half of their numbers. Hyder was much elated with the intelligence of this success; and sent reinforcements considerably exceeding the stipulated number, who were to act according to circumstances, and at all events to be employed in securing territory, which should be the pledge of his future conquests to the south of the Caveri. He prepared to augment still farther the troops in Arcot, by directing several detachments from different stations to assemble in Baramahal: and these increasing efforts might have given a different aspect to the war, which was terminated by the capture of Pondicherry in January 1761, if the greatest danger to which Hyder was ever exposed had not compelled him to look exclusively to his own preservation.

The old dowager, perceiving by the late indecent encroachments of Hyder, that the removal of Nunjeraj had only substituted another more dangerous usurper, who was gradually preparing the complete subversion of the government, opened her views to Kundè Row, under a previous oath of inviolable secrecy. She observed to him, and to the Raja, that a large portion of Hyder's troops was absent in the province of Arcot, in the reinforcements moving to the Baramahal, and in the detachments serving in the assigned districts; that he was himself cantoned under the fire of the garrison, with one hundred horse and fifteen hundred infantry only. The remainder of the disposable troops, and the greater part of his artillery, being cantoned to the northward of the river, which was now full, the possession of the fort, which commanded the bridges over both its branches, cut him off from all reinforcement, and made him a prisoner in the island. Beenee * Visagee Pundit, with an army of twenty thousand Mahratta horse, was ravaging the country between Balipoor and Deonelly, to the north-east of the territory of Mysoor, and looking out for some power to whom he might sell his services; and the aid of a body of his troops might be secretly obtained: and if this opportunity were lost, the Hindoo house of Mysoor might be considered as extinct.

Kundè Row had been from his earliest youth the personal servant of Hyder, and entered with reluctance on a project involving the destruction of a person whose success in life he had so long considered as inseparable from his own: but the impression left on his mind by the late discussions, the more pow-

* The "Beenee Walla" in the Mahratta armies is a sort of quarter-master general, commanding the advanced guard, and a person who has filled that office generally retains *Beenee* as an epithet prefixed to his name.

erful consideration of religious attachment, and probably the view of placing himself in the exact position from which Hyder was to be removed, at length determined him; and with the dowager and the Raja he united in an oath of mutual fidelity, at the feet of the holy idol of the great temple of the capital.

There was at this time in Seringapatam a Soucar named Boucerjee, who had formerly resided at Poona, and had still commercial transactions in that city and country. He was the person selected to conduct, by means of his connections in the Mahratta camp, the negotiation with Visajee Pundit; and six thousand horse were engaged, and approached Seringapatam. On the morning of the 12th of August, the day on which they were expected to arrive, the gates of the fort were not opened at the accustomed hour; and with the first of clear day-light, a tremendous cannonade opened on Hyder and his troops from all the works which bore on the position; which was the Maha* Noumi Muntup, situated on the ground now occupied by a part of the Deria† Dowlut Baug. Hyder, surprised at this unexpected salutation, gave immediate orders to call for Kundè Row; but was still more astonished to hear that Kundè Row was distinctly perceived on the works, directing the fire of the artillery. He saw at once the extent of the treachery, and prepared to meet it with his accustomed presence of mind. The troops soon found cover in the ravines and hollows, without sustaining much loss;

* "The pavilion of the great ninth," viz. the last day of the festival commonly called the Dessara: on which day the Raja performed at this pavilion the ceremony of preparing his arms and pitching his tent and standard.

† "The garden of the wealth of the sea" with a palace erected and so named by Tippoo. The walls are covered with rude paintings of his military exploits, and particularly the defeat of Colonel Baillie in 1780.

and his family in a miserable hut sheltered by its situation from the fire of the fort. At the same moment that the cannonade commenced, a detachment from the fort, which had passed the bridge before day, fell by surprise upon the infantry and artillery on the northern bank, and completely succeeded. Exclusively of the bridge over the northern branch, which was then situated opposite the western extremity of the fort, the convenience of the inhabitants who lived in the center and eastern parts of the island required an establishment of ferry boats*, which are of a simple but excellent construction for military purposes; made of bamboo wicker work, constructed exactly in the manner of a common circular clothes-basket, covered, and rendered water tight by green hides; and from eight to twelve feet diameter. Hyder's first care, after making a disposition of his small body of troops, was to secure all the boats and boatmen, in a situation concealed from the view of the fort, and see that they were all put in a state of perfect repair. The Mahrattas, according to custom, did not arrive at the appointed time; and Kundè Row postponed until their arrival his final attack upon Hyder; and

* Herodotus, chap. i. sect. 94. notices as one of the most remarkable things he had seen at Babylon boats of a construction so exactly similar, that the description of one would precisely answer for the other with the single difference of substituting willow for bamboo. These boats carried the produce of Armenia, and "the parts above Assyria" down the Euphrates to Babylon: and each boat along with its cargo carried a few asses for the purpose of conveying the returns by a shorter overland route; a process not altogether unlike the trade on a larger scale of the Ohio and Missisippi at this day. Boats of the description noticed by Herodotus, although apparently unknown in Greece at that period, were in after ages commonly used in Italy on the Po; and in Britain in the time of Cæsar. Boats of the same materials but of different shape are used at this time in South Wales, and the north-west of Ireland: in the former country they are named *corracle*, in the latter *corriagh*.

during the day they mutually attempted to amuse each other with negotiation.

It is stated by the family of Kundè* Row, that regular reports were brought to him of all Hyder's preparations; that Hyder in his messages recognized in the services of Kundè Row all the success that had attended him in life; represented that without his counsel he was helpless, and was now ready to be guided by his commands; and deprecated in terms of the utmost humility his proceeding to extremities. That Kundè Row, in reply, acknowledged in his turn the benefits which he had received from Hyder, and disclaimed the intention of personal indignity; but stated that he was now the servant of the Raja, whose orders he must obey; that all he required from Hyder was to retire for ever from the service of Mysoor; and on receiving his promise to that effect, he would withdraw the guards from the opposite bank; and advised him to escape that night; as, on the morrow, he should be compelled to act decisively against him. I should hesitate to ascribe to Kundè Row the remnant of virtuous feeling which could dictate a conduct so politically imprudent if it were possible in any other manner to explain the known fact, that Hyder found the ordinary landing-place of the northern bank without a guard of any description. However this may be, he made a distribution of as much money and jewels as could be conveyed among his hundred horsemen, six officers, and two camel hircarras; all men of tried fidelity; and embarked immediately after the close of the day, swimming over the camels and

* Particularly by Butcherow, who was then sixteen years of age, and distinctly remembers the particulars.

horses, and loading them on the opposite bank with the proportion of treasure allotted to each: about twenty spare horses accompanied, for the purpose of replacing those which should first drop from fatigue: and thus equipped, Hyder left to their fate the whole of his family, and all his infantry; fled with all possible speed from the capital, and long before the arrival of the Mahrattas on the following morning he was far beyond the reach of their pursuit. At the dawn of day Kundè Row proceeded to the quarters deserted by Hyder, for the purpose of securing the remainder of the treasure, the stores, and cumbrous valuables. The infantry attempted no resistance: and Kundè Row gave orders for the immediate removal to the fort of the whole of Hyder's family, whom it is certain that he treated with kindness. Among them was Tippoo, then in his ninth year, and Kereem Saheb, born prematurely, in consequence of fright, on the preceding day.

The route of Hyder was to the north-eastward. Anicul and Bangalore are each distant from Seringapatam about seventy-five miles; the same road leads to each for near sixty miles, and then branches off to the east to Anicul, and to the north to Bangalore. The latter place was commanded by Kubbeer Beg, an old comrade and faithful friend. But the treachery of Kundè Row, who was the very last person that Hyder would have suspected, made him doubtful of the extent of the defection: and although Bangalore was his direct object, he was certain of Anicul, which was commanded by Ismaeel Ali, his brother-in-law: and there also he was certain of finding a small detachment of horse, preparing to march to the province of Arcot. He arrived at Anicul before day-light, forty horses out of one hundred and twenty having

1760. been left behind from fatigue, and their loads distributed among the remainder. Ismaeel Ali was instantly despatched to Bangalore for the purpose of ascertaining the fidelity of Kubbeer Beg, and conveying Hyder's directions for his conduct. He arrived at an early hour, and found Kubbeer Beg true to his trust. The garrison was chiefly composed of Hindoo Peadas, and a smaller proportion of regular infantry, all Mohammedans: it was probable that the former would obey any orders they should receive from Kundè Row; and it was therefore deemed necessary to exclude them from the fort. It happened to be the usual period for pay and muster; and Kubbeer Beg issued, as a matter of ordinary detail, an order for the Peadas to assemble immediately for muster on the glacis; and the regular infantry to take the guards of the gates. This arrangement was scarcely completed, and the gates closed, when the orders of Kundè Row arrived, directing the Peadas to seize the Killedar, and preserve the fort for the Raja. It was too late: and Ismaeel Ali sent the requisite information to Hyder, who, attended by the detachment of horse which he found at Anicul, entered Bangalore on the evening of the 13th of August, having performed on horseback a journey of ninety-eight miles in twenty hours, the first seventy-five on the same horse.

Hyder was now left, as it were, to begin the world again, on the resources of his own mind. The bulk of his treasures and his train of artillery and military stores all lost: the territorial revenue at the command of Kundè Row: and the possessions on which he could rest any hope for the restoration of his affairs, were Bangalore at the northern, and Dindegul at the southern, extremity of the territories of Mysoor; with Anicul and the fortresses of Baramahal. The sole foundation of a new army was the corps of Mukhdoom Ali; and its junction was nearly a desperate hope. He had, however, despatched from Anicul positive orders for them to commence their march without an hour's delay; withdrawing altogether the garrison of Thiagar, and every man that could be spared from the posts of Baramahal: and similar directions were sent to the smaller detachments abroad. Mukhdoom Ali received these orders at Pondicherry on the 16th of August; and immediately communicated their general import to M. Lally. On the 13th of September he delivered the fort of Thiagar to a French detachment; and entered Baramahal through the pass of Changama, about the end of that month: retarded by the mass of plunder which had been collected in the province of Arcot.

In the mean while Hyder augmented his little military chest by a loan of forty thousand pounds on his personal credit from the soucars of Bangalore*. Some of the smaller detachments had joined, and that of Yaseen Khan † was of importance: individual

* The Petta, protected by separate defences, is a large and opulent manufacturing town.

† Surnamed "Wunta Cooderi, single or unique horseman," from his personal exploits. He was formerly in the service of Mohammed Ali, which he left in disgust in 1757: and came over to Hyder at Dindegul, with seven hundred sepoys, twenty horse, and two light guns. The number of his horse was now increased to five hundred. The blunt manners and genuine bravery of this man soon made him a personal favourite and associate of Hyder; who, although of courtly and insinuating address when the occasion demanded, was, in his ordinary habits, of coarse and vulgar manners, and a master in the low slang which is peculiar to India; the character of which may be conjectured, by fancying the union of considerable wit with the volubility of Billingsgate, and the obscenity of a brothel. Hyder and Yaseen Khan were rivals in this obscene eloquence; and the former was in the habit of amusing himself with the foul-mouthed wit of Wunta Cooderie, which he sometimes retorted with keen severity on his master.

CHAP. XI. 1760. soldiers attached* to his fortunes were also daily coming in, who had either deserted from the hostile army or escaped from the small posts occupied by his troops, of which Kundè Row was daily getting possession: and soldiers of fortune of every description were invited to his standard. Among the persons whom he engaged in his service at this time was Fuzzul Oolla Khan, descended from a family of high rank at the court of Delhi, himself a soldier of distinguished reputation, and son-in-law of Dilaver Khan, the late Nabob of Sera. The Mahratta Balajee Row, on the conquest of that place in the year 1757, had assigned as a personal jageer to the family of Dilaver Khan a small district, including the town of Sera, which, according to the uniform practice of that people, had already been circumscribed preparatory to its gradual extinction. Fuzzul Oolla Khan, little disposed to be satisfied with a larger and undivided jageer, although affecting

It was some years after this period, that conversing on the subject of the battle of Chercolee, Hyder said it had been lost by the *nemuc haramee* of the army (literally being false to one's salt, properly treachery, or ingratitude, but also, figuratively, put for cowardice), and that he did not know the man who had done his duty on that day. "You are right," said Wunta Cooderie, "and I ran away with the rest; but (turning up towards him the socket of an eye, which he had lost by the wound of a sabre in that battle) eo die, cujus matris in vulvam hic oculus iniit?" On the occasion of another defeat, Hyder was pronouncing another philippic on *nemuc haramee*, and looked towards Jaseen Khan. "Why do you look at me?" said he: "you had better consult Nunjeraj on the subject of *nemuc haramee*." This dreadful jest would have cost the head of any other person: but Wunta Cooderie was a privileged man.

It was the practice of Hyder to take the musters of cavalry, by sending persons, without previous notice, to count the horses in the lines. The grooms and grasscutters of Wunta Cooderie's command were instructed how to comport themselves on such occasions: and the muster-masters, pelted with clods, and bedaubed with horse-dung, were generally happy to escape before the grooms began with the reserved ammunition of stones. The muster-masters complained: but Hyder laughed at all the jokes of Wunta Cooderie: and it became well understood that his corps was exempted from muster.

retirement, kept a small corps embodied for the ostensible purposes of police and security in these days of commotion. He was secretly surrounded by a considerable number, also affecting retirement, of his former companions in arms; and held constant communication with the adherents (scattered in various directions) of his own family and that of his father-in-law, in the expectation of some turn, in the course of events, more favourable to their union and future enterprize.

The accession at this period of Fuzzul Oolla Khan, an experienced officer and a man of high rank, to the service of a person but just emerged from the obscurity of a Naick, gave great reputation to the cause of Hyder; and by the rapid augmentation of his numbers was also of substantial importance. The terms of his engagement evince the high value at which his services were rated, and furnish another feature in the character of the Mohammedans of India. The primary condition was the regulation of his place and rank at court (or in public durbar), and on this head he stipulated, that whether on a saddle-cloth *, a carpet, or a musnud, his place should be on the same seat with Hyder; his officer, but his equal: and that he should have the distinction of two honorary attendants standing behind him, holding fans composed of the feathers † of the humma, according to the practice of his family.

* To persons whose habitual seat is exactly that of an English tailor, a chair is an useless annoyance, and the large double or quilted cloth which covers the saddle is a commodious seat for one or two, and a relief from fatigue always ready without a moment's preparation.

† I am not certain what the feathers really were; they are described to have been white and of a downy appearance. The humma is a fabulous bird. The head over which its shadow once passes will assuredly be encircled with a crown. The splendid little bird suspended over the throne of Tippoo Sultaun, found at Seringapatam in 1799, was intended to represent this poetical fancy.

Mukhdoom Ali, on entering the Baramahal, had necessarily consumed some time in disencumbering himself of his plunder, and collecting the disposeable troops of the garrisons. Kundè Row directed his chief attention to the destruction of this corps, and for this purpose placed the best of his troops under the command of Gopaul Heri, the officer who commanded the six thousand Mahrattas; and was now joined by four thousand more detached by Vesajee Pundit, who was himself encamped at the summit of the pass of Cudapanatam, which leads directly to Vellore. Mukhdoom Ali was strenuously opposed by these troops, and after some severe fighting found himself compelled to take post under Anchittydroog; which is situated about forty-eight miles S. by E. of Bangalore, near the verge of the descent into Baramahal. Here he was effectually blockaded by the superior numbers of the enemy, and reported to Hyder his absolute inability to advance without reinforcements. The whole of the force which could be spared from the defence of Bangalore, amounting to scarcely four thousand men and five guns, was accordingly placed under the command of Fuzzul Oolla Khan; who threw himself by night into Anicul, distant only twenty-five miles from Anchitty, and was instructed to watch an opportunity of breaking through the blockade and forming a junction with Mukhdoom. The attempt was made with considerable gallantry and skill, but many of the raw troops threw down their arms, and escaped into the woods at the moment that a farther effort would have forced the junction; he was accordingly repulsed with severe loss, all his guns were captured, and he retreated with the utmost difficulty to Anicul. Mukhdoom was now closely besieged and reduced to great extremities; and the career of Hyder seemed again to be approaching its close, when a negotiation, which had been for some time open, with Visajee Pundit, was adjusted with a degree of facility and moderation which Hyder received with equal astonishment and delight. The conditions of the immediate departure of the Mahrattas were, the cession of the Baramahal, and the payment of the trifling sum of three lacs of rupees. The comparison of a few dates and facts will enable us to explain this unusual moderation.

So early as the month of April Visajee Pundit had offered to aid both the French and the English; and in the latter end of November, the bishop of Halicarnassus was in his camp negotiating for the service of his troops; of which the cession of Ginjee was, among other conditions, to be the chief price. M. Lally was then blockaded in Pondicherry by Colonel Coote; and a primary condition was the payment of five lacs of rupees when this Mahratta army should appear in sight of Pondicherry*. Mohammed Ali, seeing in the advance of this corps an insurmountable obstacle to the success of his English allies against Pondicherry, concluded an agreement with Visajee Pundit, early in the month of January, 1761, for the large sum of twenty lacs, to be paid at distant instalments, on the condition of his marching towards Poona with the least possible delay. This fact alone would sufficiently explain the apparent moderation of Visajee Pundit; his retreat was already purchased, although not yet paid for. Like a true Mahratta, he had first sold himself to Kundè Row, and then to his opponent Hyder: and he had made a shew of selling himself to the French, in order that he might sell him-

* It appears by an intercepted letter from M. Lally to M. Raymond, French resident at Paliacate, that he continued so late as the 2d of January to expect the arrival of seventeen thousand Mahrattas on the 6th of the same month.

self to the English and Mohammed Ali at a better price. But another cause of still greater urgency accelerated his departure. On the 7th of January, 1761, the Mahratta army of Hindostan,
1761. drawn by the Abdalli into a situation in which it was compelled to fight, was defeated at Paniput with circumstances of disaster and destruction which seemed to be nearly irretrievable. The Mahratta forces from every direction were ordered to concentrate as if the Abdalli (who thought only of returning to the Indian Caucasus) were already at the gates of Poona; and Visajee Pundit, among others, had just received his secret orders of recal. Hyder's three lacs were paid; Mukhdoom Ali, relieved from his critical blockade, proceeded to Bangalore; and Visajee Pundit marched in haste to the northward. All this was inexplicable at the moment; but Hyder, although not yet aware of the exact causes of his good fortune, perceived symptoms of precipitancy which determined him to delay the delivery of any part of the Baramahal; and the intelligence of the defeat of Paniput, which public rumour soon afterwards conveyed, decided his plain and direct refusal, and confirmed the favourite doctrine of the fatalist, which teaches him ever to procrastinate when under the pressure of misfortune.

In the mean while, Kundè Row had written in his own name, and that of the Raja, letters to the government of Madras and all the neighbouring powers, explaining the expulsion of Hyder as an usurper, and disclaiming the hostilities which, at the same time that Mukhdoom was detached to Pondicherry, had been commenced in the vicinity of Madura and Trichinopoly. The frontier fort of Caroor, forty miles west of Trichinopoly, had been in retaliation besieged by a detachment from that place;

and the government and military officers of Fort St. George not knowing what they were to understand by the various and contradictory reports which they received, permitted the Mysorean commandant of Caroor to retire with his garrison on delivering up the possession of that place, and refrained from farther hostility until the English should be satisfied with regard to the actual state of the government of Mysoor. This officer was really a servant of Kundè Row; who had, with the greatest activity and intelligence, possessed himself of the whole of the lower country from Baramahal to Dindegul, that single fortress alone excepted.

Hyder, on the very day that he was joined by Mukhdoom Ali, pitched his own standard in the field, with a force so superior to that of Kundè Row, who had numerous detachments abroad, that he also ventured to make a considerable detachment into the lower countries of Salem and Coimbetoor, for the purpose of recovering the country and revenues wrested from him; which were to be his chief resource in the impending contest. He marched in a south-western direction, crossing the Caveri below its confluence with the Capilee near Sosilla, for the purpose of covering the operations of his detachment, and preventing Kundè Row from sending reinforcements through either of the passes of Caveriporum or Gujjelhutty. This detachment rendered the force under Hyder's immediate command inferior in numbers to that of Kundè Row, but he relied with confidence on its superior quality; for a French detachment, which was in the field between Thiagar and the hills for the purpose of collecting and covering supplies, had, on ascertaining the probable fall of Pondicherry, drawn farther to the westward; and on receiving

1761. intelligence of its actual surrender on the 16th of January had joined Hyder at Bangalore. It consisted of two hundred cavalry and one hundred infantry, all Europeans, under the command of M. Alain and M. Hugel, and some scattered detachments of natives. Kundè Row, who saw the consequence of this judicious movement, determined to give him battle, and came in sight of the troops of Hyder in the neighbourhood of Nunjendgode, about twenty-seven miles south of Seringapatam.

The troops which were to decide the fate of a kingdom were reduced by detachments to the small number, on the side of Hyder, of six thousand horse and five thousand foot, with twenty guns; and on that of Kundè Row to seven thousand horse and six thousand foot, with twenty-eight guns. For several days the two bodies rather manœvred than fought, with some loss on both sides, but no decisive result, and, in the opinion of many officers who were present, with very superior skill as well as uniform advantage on the part of Kundè Row; who, early in February, brought on a more decisive action. Hyder in vain attempted to avoid this decision with the view of obtaining reinforcements, which too late he perceived to be necessary. The favourite object of Kundè Row in his various encounters was to compel Hyder's infantry to change its front, and to charge it when in the act of performing that evolution. On this occasion his success was considerable, and Hyder was defeated with very heavy loss, but retired in tolerably good order towards Hurdanhelly.

Nothing but a confidence in powers of simulation, altogether unrivalled, could have suggested to Hyder the step which he next pursued. With a select body of two hundred horse, including about seventy French hussars under M. Hugel, he made a circuitous march by night; and early on the next morning, unarmed, and alone, presented himself as a suppliant at the door of Nunjeraj at Cunnoor, and being admitted, threw himself at his feet. With the semblance of real penitence and grief, he attributed all his misfortunes to the gross ingratitude with which he had requited the patronage of Nunjeraj; entreated him to resume the direction of public affairs, and take his old servant once more under his protection. Nunjeraj was completely deceived; and with his remaining household troops, which, during the present troubles, he had augmented to two thousand horse and about an equal number of indifferent infantry, he gave to the ruined fortunes of Hyder the advantage of his name and influence; announcing in letters dispatched in every direction his determination to exercise the office of Serv Adikar, which he still nominally retained, with Hyder as his Dulwoy, or commander-in-chief. Hyder, on leaving his army, had given directions for hanging on the rear of Kundè Row in the event of his making a movement towards Cunnoor; which, on receiving intelligence of the above stated facts, he of course considered to be his primary object. Hyder attempted by various movements to form a junction with his army, which Kundè Row, by more skilful evolutions, prevented, and pressed forward with such vigour, that the destruction of Hyder and his new friends appeared to be inevitable, when he was extricated by one of those instances of his talent for intrigue and deception which seems to have constituted the leading feature of his character, and to have influenced, more than any other, the whole tenour of his eventful life.

The movements to which we have adverted brought Kundè Row to Kuttè Malwaddy, twenty-six miles S.W. from Seringapa-

CHAP. XI. 1761. tam, about the 20th of February: and Hyder, closely pursued, was about ten miles in his front, when he prepared in the *name* and with the *seal* of *Nunjeraj* letters addressed to the principal leaders of Kundè Row's army: these letters adverted to a supposed engagement which they had made to seize Kundè Row and deliver him to Nunjeraj; they promised, on his part, to perform the conditions of the stipulated reward; and concluded with the observation, that nothing now remained but that they should immediately earn it.

The bearer of these letters departed duly instructed, and falling purposely into the hands of the outposts was carried to Kundè Row; who, entertaining not the least suspicion of the artifice, conceived that he was betrayed by his own army, and, seized with a sudden panic, instantly mounted his horse, and escaped at full speed to Seringapatam, without any previous communication with the suspected chiefs. The flight of the commander-in-chief being quickly known, a general agitation ensued; the more dangerous as the motive was utterly unknown: and every person began to provide for his safety by flight, without any one being able to communicate to the other the cause of his alarm. Hyder's light troops brought him early intelligence of the state of the enemy; and at this instant his army, by a preconcerted movement, appeared in the rear of Kundè Row's, while he moved his own corps to attack the front; and by falling upon it with his whole force, in this state of dismay and confusion, he obtained a complete and decisive victory, capturing the whole of the enemy's infantry, guns, stores, and baggage. The horse alone had by an early flight provided for their safety, and the infantry were incorporated without much reluctance into the army of the victor.

Hyder, by another stratagem, affected not to pursue his success; and halting four or five days at Cuttee Malwaddy, under pretence of being occupied in making detachments for the collection of revenue, found, by means of his spies, that the fugitives, deceived by this demonstration, were encamped in a disorderly manner, along with some infantry which they had begun to collect, on the island of Seringapatam, between the south bridge and the Mysoor gate. Hyder made a silent and unsuspected march with a select body, and falling upon this rabble at midnight put the greater part of them to the sword, and retired before the garrison was prepared to disturb his retreat, carrying off upwards of seven hundred horses and a large booty.

Hyder did not consider it advisable to prosecute his ultimate operation at Seringapatam until he had secured the whole of the resources of the lower country, which continued to oppose his detachments. He therefore descended the pass of Gujjelhutty, took the fort of Erroad, and all others which had been seized by Kundè Row or had declared for him (Caroor alone excepted, which remained for the present without discussion in the hands of the English), and levied a large contribution on his partizans. By the time that these arrangements were finished he had completed also the levies of his army, and had called in all his detachments. Every thing being now ready for the execution of his plan, he ascended the Ghauts in force, and early in the month of May arrived at Chendgâl, on the south bank of the Caveri opposite the centre of the island of Seringapatam; where, affecting to deprecate farther hostility, he appeared to be entirely absorbed in negotiations with Kundè Row; the remnant of whose cavalry, chiefly Mahratta, and still amounting to between five

CHAP. XI. 1761. and six thousand, were encamped with a corps of infantry on the island, south of the fort, and partly under the guns: Hyder, on the opposite bank of the river, which was then fordable, made every evening a shew of exercising his troops till after sunset. On the eighth day of this tacit armistice, instead of dismissing them as usual, he made a sudden dash across the river as if in the performance of an evolution of the parade, and carried destruction into the enemy's camp by complete surprise, capturing the whole of their heavy equipments and most of their horses. This enterprize completed the ruin of Kundè Row's field force; and Hyder, with the air of a conqueror already assured of his object, encamped, more in the style of a triumph than a military operation, across the island, on the ground now occupied by Sheher Gunjaum.

From hence he dispatched a message to the Raja, intimating in substance, "that Kundè Row was the servant of Hyder, and ought to be given up to him: that large balances were due to Hyder by the state, and ought to be liquidated. After the payment of these arrears, if the Raja should be pleased to continue him in his service, it was well; if not, he would depart, and seek his fortune elsewhere."

Such were the terms of his formal communication to the Raja. To the persons holding public offices he conveyed the object of his demands, and the consequences of rejection, in a more distinct manner. Many of these persons had long held the most important offices of the government, and had benefited largely by the laxity and corruption which had prevailed: they were accordingly more occupied with the means of securing their private fortunes than by considerations affecting the fate of Kundè Row, the rights of the Raja, or the safety of the state. Such principles opposed but slender impediments to the designs of the conqueror, who had signified his pleasure that the full extent of his meditated usurpation should, in the last bitterness of mockery, appear to be the spontaneous act of the Raja himself: that unfortunate personage was readily made to understand that the danger was imminent, that no means existed of paying the balances, or making any appropriation of funds for their speedy liquidation; and that one only arrangement remained which could afford the hope of averting more dreadful calamities. A proposal for carrying that arrangement into effect was, in this moment of terror, transmitted to Hyder in the name, and with the concurrence, of the Raja; namely, 1st. That districts to the amount of three lacs should be reserved for the Raja's personal expences, and one lac for Nunjeraj: 2d. That Hyder should assume the management of the remainder of the country, and charge himself with the responsibility of defraying the arrears, and providing for the pay of the army and public charges of every description; and 3d. That Kundè Row should be given up to him.

This heavy load of care and responsibility was of course most reluctantly but dutifully undertaken, and Hyder waited on the Raja about the beginning of June with all the forms of mock submission and respect; and from this moment his usurpation was complete. The solemn, affecting, and well-acted interview with Nunjeraj at Cunnoor was consigned to convenient oblivion, or revived in ridiculous forms for the amusement of his convivial hours; and that weak and credulous man, after the first impressions had subsided, seemed scarcely to have expected any other result.

CHAP. XI. 1761.

Kundè Row was given up, and confined: and his official servants, as well as himself, were of course plundered to the utmost extent of their means. Before it had been determined that Kundè Row should be surrendered, a joint message was sent to Hyder from the Raja and the ladies of the palace, praying for mercy towards that unfortunate man as a preliminary to the adjustment of public affairs. Hyder replied, that Kundè Row was his old servant, and that he would not only spare his life, but cherish him like a parroquet; a term of endearment common in conversing with women, from that bird being a favourite pet in the harams of the wealthy. When he was afterwards gently admonished of his severity to Kundè Row, he ironically replied, that he had exactly kept his word; and that they were at liberty to inspect his *iron cage*, and the rice and milk allotted for his food; for such was the fate to which he had doomed Kundè Row for the remainder of his miserable life.

The arrangements consequent on the usurpation occupied upwards of two months, and Hyder, having appointed his brother-in-law, Mukhdoom Aly Khan, Killedar of Seringapatam with a garrison of his most trusty troops, took leave of the Raja with the usual formalities early in September, and proceeded towards Bangalore, where other events demanded his presence.

CHAPTER XII.

FROM 1761 TO 1766.

Circumstances which led to the march of Basalut Jung to the south—and induced Hyder to move to Bangalore—Basalut Jung is foiled in the siege of Ooscota—Negotiation by which Hyder is invested with the office of Nabob of Sera: its ludicrous circumstances—Title of Hyder Ali Khan Behauder—Capture of Ooscata—Hyder's revenge for an outrage sustained in his infancy from Abbas Couli Khan—kindness to his family—United armies move to Sera, and after its capture separate—their respective motives and objects—Hyder moves to Little Balipoor—spirited defence—Morari Row moves to its relief—is defeated—Capitulation for the ransom of Balipoor—broken by the Poligar, who retires to Nundidroog—Balipoor is garrisoned by Morari Row's troops, and carried by assault—Hyder extends his conquests over the territory of Morari Row—returns to Sera—receives the submission of the Poligars of Raidroog, Harponelly, and Chittledroog—Singular impostor from Bednore—engages Hyder to invade that country—its description—Hyder's proceedings and progress—conquest of the capital—immense plunder—capture and imprisonment of the Queen, the young Raja, and the impostor—Design of making Bednore his capital—arrangements with that view—Conspiracy detected—characteristic punishments—Conquest of Soonda—Arrival of Reza Ali, the son of Chunda Saheb—Military improvements—public etiquette—Embassies to Poona and Hyderabad—objects and result—Designs regarding Savanoor—invasion of that province—defeat of the Nabob—military contribution—Hyder returns to Bednore—his general extends his conquests to the north—Proceedings of the Peshwa Madoo Row—his advanced corps defeated—advance of the main army—relative force—and plans of operation—Action of Rettehully—entrenched camp at Anawutty—Defeat of a detachment commanded by Hyder in person—Operations suspended by the monsoon—renewed—Madoo Row compels Hyder to abandon his entrenched camp and fight at a disadvantage

—signal defeat—and retreat to the lines of Bednore—discovers his injudicious choice for a capital—Peace with Madoo Row—views of the parties regarding its conditions—Insurrections in the eastern provinces—detachments to quell them—capture of the Poligar of Little Balipoor—Hyder prepares for the conquest of Malabar—Communications with Ali Raja, a Mohammedan chief—Notices of these Mohammedans—Military character and habits of the Nairs—Hyder's successful progress—Negotiation with the Zamorin—deception—Extraordinary suicide—Arrangements for securing the conquest—moves to Coimbetoor—General insurrection in Malabar—Hyder returns—dreadful executions—forcible emigration—apparent restoration of tranquillity—returns to Coimbetoor—Intelligence of a confederacy of the Mahrattas, Nizam Ali, and the English to invade Mysoor—Hyder proceeds to Seringapatam—Death of the former Raja and succession of his son—Harsh treatment and farther restraint—Causes of the war of 1767 to be explained in the ensuing chapter—Previous observations on the treaty of Paris.

CHAP. XII. 1761.

We left Basalut Jung, in December 1759, at Kurpa, distinctly unfolding, in his negotiation with Monsieur Bussy, his views of independent sovereignty in the south, and his desire, if he could effect that object without compromising his independence, of obtaining the aid of the French to oppose the better fortunes of his brother Nizam Ali, who had supplanted him as the minister and general of their elder brother Salabut Jung, still pageant Soubadar of the Deckan, but destined in 1761 to be imprisoned, and in two years afterwards to be murdered, by Nizam Ali. In the year 1760 Nizam Ali was engaged in a defensive and unsuccessful campaign against the Peshwa Balajee Row, between the rivers Kistna and Godaveri: and as Basalut Jung could scarcely move in any direction beyond the limits of his personal jageer without coming in contact with some Mahratta territory, dependency, or army, and he found it expedient to maintain an amicable intercourse with the actual opponents of his rival, the early part of that year was passed by him in a state of inaction at Adwanee. The great efforts which were made by the Mahrattas in the middle and end of that year to collect forces for the impending contest, which terminated on the 7th of January 1761 in the disastrous battle of Paniput, seemed to leave a more open field for his exertion: and in the month of August 1760 he began, in the ordinary process of eastern sovereignty, to draw within the circle of his own possessions the most convenient and accessible fragments of the shattered states around him. The success of this his first independent campaign was in its commencement encouraging: although occasionally checked, he had considerably enlarged his limits, and about the month of June 1761 had planned the reduction of Sera *, then in the possession of the Mahrattas, but formerly the capital of a Nabob or provincial governor, dependent on the Soubadar of the Deckan. He reconnoitred the citadel, but thought it most prudent to pass it. His military chest required more rapid supplies than were promised by its siege; and he moved farther south, over an undulating country, alternately strong and open: the plainer parts having been fortified against sudden incursion by walls and towers of kneaded clay, which surround every village.

It was the approach of this force which called Hyder from Seringapatam, immediately after the completion of his usurpation; and on his arrival at Bangalore he found that Basalut Jung was engaged in the siege of Ooscota. This place, which had be-

* A pavilion on a diminutive scale, but exhibiting considerable taste, built by the last Nabob Dilavar Khan, is still standing at Sera, and is the model followed in the erection of those splendid palaces built by Hyder and Tippoo at Bangalore and Seringapatam.

longed, as we have seen, to the Mahratta house of Shahjee, had afterwards passed into the possession of the Patan Nabob of Kurpa, and in 1757 had been captured by Balajee Row, in the same campaign in which he made the conquest of Sera. The fortifications were in the rude style of the village bulwarks, but it possessed the advantage from nature of being unassailable on one face, and was defended by a garrison which defied and derided the attempts of Basalut Jung to subdue them. The mortification of being thus foiled was extreme; the military chest was empty, and the period was favourable to Hyder's views. Ooscota is distant only eighteen miles from Bangalore in a north-eastern direction: the first communications were rapidly arranged, and Fuzzul Oolla Khan was sent as Hyder's ambassador to the camp of Basalut Jung. The distress of this chief, and the whole character of the negotiation, may be inferred from the fact that for a nezer of three lacs of rupees, he agreed to invest Hyder with the office of Nabob of Sera; an office, a country, and a capital, which were yet to be conquered! The alleged rights which Hyder acquired from this instrument of investiture have been gravely discussed and defended. The right of the grantor seems to have been inferred from the act of granting, for no other source of right can be readily discovered: the right of the sword, to which most political claims may be ultimately traced, was absolutely wanting in this case; and the decision of this arbiter, pronounced three years afterwards by Nizam Ali, de facto Soubadar, or ruler of the Deckan, shewed his sense of the authority of Basalut Jung, by restricting him by force of arms to the single district of Adwanee*. An incident

* He was besieged in Kurnool in 1764, and capitulated on these conditions.

occurred during the communications with Basalut Jung, which furnishes an additional feature in the character of Hyder, and illustrates the ludicrous turn which was given to the whole transaction. In the course of the negotiation, Basalut Jung proposed, with a view of obtaining a larger sum from Hyder, to honour him with a title of the order distinguished by its terminating Persian word "*Jung*" (war). Among the lowest vulgar this word is pronounced *Zung*, which also signifies the tinkling circular kind of bell, commonly strung round the necks of camels and oxen; and Hyder, among other remains of the society of his youth, retained this faulty pronunciation. When Fuzzul Oolla Khan came with this proposition, Hyder laughed in his face, and repeating four or five times the word *Zung*, "Let me have nothing to do with your ornaments of a beast of burden," said he, "but if the great man insists on giving such a decoration, you may take it to yourself." Fuzzul Oolla, who loved a title, and was not fastidious in scrutinizing authorities, took Hyder at his word; and returning to Ooscota did receive the title of *Hybut Jung* (terror of war), which he ever afterwards retained.

The sunnuds, or deeds of investiture, were however executed in due form, and the title of *Nabob*, and name of *Hyder Ali Khan Behauder*, by which he was designated in those deeds, were certainly thenceforth assumed by Hyder. On receiving these honours, he in October united his army to that before Ooscota, and in a few days gave to the great Basalut Jung the honour of being the reputed captor of a mud fort *.

* "*Mud fort*," from the usually imperfect construction of the village defences, is a term of contempt in India, although the substance itself (kneaded clay) resists the effects of cannon-shot better than any other material.

An object of personal revenge, which the impressions of infancy * and youth had strongly fixed in the memory of Hyder, next engaged his attention. Basalut Jung had, in the course of negotiation, wished to exclude from the enumerations contained in the deeds Great Balipoor, the jageer of Abbas Cooli Khan; but Hyder broadly answered, that his honours were worthless if they excluded a full and a deep revenge: that he accepted and paid for the sunnuds as a mutual accommodation, not from any diffidence of being able to achieve his own objects without them; and that another syllable indicating the exclusion of Balipoor should terminate the negotiation. Abbas Cooli Khan was anxiously attentive to Hyder's late proceedings; and on hearing of the junction of the two armies he distinctly saw his peril, and fled with the utmost precipitation to Madras, a distance of 220 miles, leaving his family to their fate †. Hyder's conduct to the family of Abbas Cooli Khan is among the very few examples in the history of his life, of any remote tendency towards the amiable feelings of human nature. On entering without opposition the fort of Balipoor, and hearing that the object of his vengeance had escaped, he presented himself at the gate of the dowager, the widow of his father's lord, but the mother of the fugitive. In a message, full of gentleness and delicacy, he shewed a remembrance of kindnesses conferred in the days of his infancy, and assured her of his gratitude and respect; and although he appropriated, without hesitation, every thing that for political purposes

* For the incident alluded to, see p. 246.

† Such was his terror, that when Hyder in 1769 presented himself at the gates of Madras, he embarked in a crazy vessel, and did not venture to land until Hyder's army had reascended the passes of the mountains.

might be considered as public property; he entirely verified his assurances to the dowager, and continued through life to treat the unoffending branches of her family with distinction and generosity. CHAP. XII. 1761.

From Balipoor the united armies moved to Sera, which made but a feeble resistance. Hyder achieved, without much delay, the conquest of his new dignities and capital, and the allied chiefs took leave of each other about the beginning of the year 1762. During the inefficient operations of Basalut Jung in the south, Salabut Jung had been imprisoned on the 18th July, 1761, by Nizam Ali, who openly assumed the office of Soubadar: it was then no longer the indirect influence, but the actual power of that chief, which was to be guarded against by Basalut Jung; and the vigorous preparations of his brother made it expedient that he should be nearer home, to attend to the eventual defence of Adwanee; he therefore departed, little enriched, to the north, while Hyder moved in a south-eastern direction, where other objects demanded his attention. 1762.

The dominions of Morari Row, the Mahratta chief of Gooti, were situated to the north-east of Hyder's new acquisition; their southern extremity was bounded by the small territory of the Poligar of Little Balipoor. This capital of his little state, and the usual residence of the Poligar, is situated fourteen miles to the eastward of Great Balipoor, recently acquired by Hyder, and twelve miles to the north of Deonhully *, his former frontier sta-

* The mention of this place leads me to notice a sect in this neighbourhood, so singular in their habits that I subjoin a description of them which I gave in a letter to a friend in the year 1805. This legendary tale will furnish an example of the wild mythology which the attentive Indian traveller will find luxuriantly strewed on every step of his progress.

CHAP. XII. 1762.

tions. The conquest of Little Balipoor had been long and anxiously desired by Hyder. The Poligar of Deonhully had, on

"In passing from the town of Silgut to Deonhully in the month of August last, I became accidentally informed of a sect, peculiar, as I since understand, to the north-eastern parts of Mysoor, the women of which universally undergo the amputation of the first joints of the third and fourth fingers of their right hands. On my arrival at Deonhully, after ascertaining that the request would not give offence, I desired to see some of these women, and the same afternoon seven of them attended at my tent.

"The sect is a subdivision of the *Murresoo wokul* *, and belongs to the fourth great class of Hindoos, viz. the Souder. Every woman of the sect, previously to piercing the ears of her eldest daughter, preparatory to her being betrothed in marriage, must necessarily undergo this mutilation, which is performed by the blacksmith of the village for a regulated fee, by a surgical process sufficiently rude. The finger to be amputated is placed on a block: the blacksmith places a chisel over the articulation of the joint, and chops it off at a single blow. If the girl to be betrothed is motherless, and the mother of the boy have not before been subjected to the operation, it is incumbent on her to perform the sacrifice.

"After satisfying myself with regard to the facts of the case, I enquired into the origin of so strange a practice, and one of the women related with great fluency the following traditionary tale, which has since been repeated to me with no material deviation by several others of the sect.

"A Rachas (or giant), named *Vrica*, and in after times *Busm-aasoor*, or the giant of the ashes, had, by a course of austere devotion to *Mahadeo* †, obtained from him the promise of whatever boon he should ask. The Rachas accordingly demanded, that every person on whose head he should place his right hand might instantly be reduced to ashes; and Mahadeo conferred the boon, without suspicion of the purpose for which it was designed.

"The Rachas no sooner found himself possessed of this formidable power, than he attempted to use it for the destruction of his benefactor. Mahadeo fled; the Rachas pursued, and followed the fugitive so closely as to chase him into a thick grove, where Mahadeo, changing his form and bulk, concealed himself in the centre of a fruit then called *tunda pundoo*, but since named *linga tunda*, from the resemblance which its kernel thenceforward assumed to the *ling*, the appropriate emblem of Mahadeo.

"The Rachas having lost sight of Mahadeo, enquired of a husbandman who was working in the adjoining field, whether he had seen the fugitive, and what direction he had taken. The husbandman, who had attentively observed the whole transaction,

* *Murresoo*, or *Mursoo*, in the Hala Canara signifies *rude, uncivilized—wokul, a husbandman.*

† *Siva.*

the surrender of that place in 1749; capitulated on the condition of being permitted to retire in safety to his relation at Little Ba- CHAP. XII. 1762.

fearful of the future resentment of Mahadeo, and equally alarmed for the present vengeance of the giant, answered aloud that he had seen no fugitive, but pointed at the same time with the little finger of his right hand to the place of Mahadeo's concealment.

"In this extremity * Vishnou descended in the form of a beautiful damsel to the rescue of Mahadeo. The Rachas became instantly enamoured: the damsel was a *pure* bramin, and might not be approached by the *unclean* Rachas. By degrees she appeared to relent; and as a previous condition to farther advances, enjoined the performance of his ablutions in a neighbouring pool. After these were finished, she prescribed as a farther purification the performance of the *Sundia*, a ceremony in which the right hand is successively applied to the breast, to the crown of the head, and to other parts of the body. The Rachas thinking only of love, and forgetful of the powers of his right hand, performed the *Sundia*, and was himself reduced to ashes.

"Mahadeo now issued from the *linga tunda*, and after the proper acknowledgments for his deliverance, proceeded to discuss the guilt of the treacherous husbandman, and determined on the loss of the finger with which he had offended, as the proper punishment of his crime.

"The wife of the husbandman, who had just arrived at the field with food for her husband, hearing this dreadful sentence, threw herself at the feet of Mahadeo. She represented the certain ruin of her family if her husband should be disabled for some months from performing the labours of the farm, and besought the deity to accept two of her fingers, instead of one from her husband. Mahadeo, pleased with so sincere a proof of conjugal affection, accepted the exchange, and ordained that her female posterity in all future generations should sacrifice two fingers at his temple as a memorial of the transaction, and of their exclusive devotion to the god of the ling.

"The practice is accordingly confined to the supposed posterity of this single woman, and is not common to the wholesect of Murresoo wokul. I ascertained the actual number of families who observed this practice in three successive districts through which I afterwards passed, and I conjecture that within the limits of Mysoor they may amount to about two thousand houses.

"The hill of *Seetee*, in the talook of Colar, where the giant was destroyed, is (according to this tradition) formed of the ashes of Busmaasoor: it is held in particular veneration by this sect, as the chief seat of their appropriate sacrifice; and the

* Dignus vindice nodus.

CHAP. XII. 1762. lipoor: the family had since that period been engaged in incessant plots to recover that place, and Hyder conceived the reduction of Little Balipoor to be indispensable to the safety of this part of his frontier. He approached the place, and the Poligar, who had the free option of retiring to the impregnable rock of Nundidroog, distant only three miles, thought proper to await the attack, in the nearly open town of Little Balipoor, which is provided with a weak citadel, so placed, that an assailant must previously possess himself of the town. Regular science, in its legi-

fact of its retaining little or no moisture, is held to be a miraculous proof that the ashes of the giant continue to absorb the most violent and continued rain. This is a remarkable example of easy credulity. I have examined the mountain, which is of a sloping form and composed of coarse granite.

"The name of *Seetee* is stated by the bramins of the vicinity to be an abbreviation of *Sree-puttee-Shweragerree*, or the hill of the husband of *Sree* * and *Ishwara*†.

"Siva's adventure with the giant of the ashes is stated by these bramins to be related in one of the Puranas‡, with some change in the circumstances, which does not seem to improve its merit as a tale. The flight of Siva is continued through the seven lower and seven upper regions to *Vicunta*, the paradise of Vishnou, who there appears in the form of a young Bramin, and with the aid of *Maya* (delusion) persuades the giant that Siva never yet uttered a truth, and that the boon was fallacious, as he might easily ascertain by placing his right hand on his own head.

"Swatadry, or Belacul (the white mountain), a temple near the south-eastern frontier of Mysoor, claims, in common with many other places, the honour of possessing the ashes of Busmaasoor; and I am informed that the descent of Vishnou in the form of a damsel, as stated by the *Murresoo wokul*, is related in the Sthalla Purana, or local history of the origin of that temple; but the bramins whom I have consulted have not been able to trace in any document the incident of the husbandman and his wife, nor the existence of any written authority for the sacrifice practised by this extraordinary sect.

"It is not a little remarkable, that neither the Dewan of Mysoor, nor any of his suite, nor of the bramins belonging to the resident's office, had ever heard of this singular practice, or were acquainted with the existence of this subdivision of the sect of Murresoo wokul."

* Letchmee, the wife of Vishnou. † Siva, or Mahadeo. ‡ Bhagvat.

timate application to the defence of places, is calculated to protract resistance, but in its practical effects it seems more frequently to have excused or accelerated their fall. This Poligar verified the better doctrine that all places are impregnable, so long as the moral energies of its defenders can be upheld. He contested every inch of ground in this open town; every successive house became a fortress; and at the expiration of two months Hyder could scarcely yet be said to have commenced the siege of *the citadel.* The spirit of the defenders was kept at its stretch by the expectation of relief from Morari Row, whose aid had been previously secured, and who was now approaching the place. Hyder's superior numbers enabled him to leave a strong corps for the maintenance of his ground, and by an unexpected movement of the remainder of his army against Morari Row, to give him a signal defeat. The Poligar was now left to his own resources; the place was completely invested; and the spirit of enterprise and defiance which the garrison had hitherto maintained was succeeded by despondency. Negotiation ensued, and an agreement for ransom was concluded for the sum of nine lacs of rupees. It was not expected that so large a sum could be paid down without some time for its realization; and Hyder, not unwilling to draw off from the pestilential consequences of the close conflict in the town, encamped on the plain near Deonhully to wait the arrangements for payment. The Poligar had no sooner got rid of his presence, than, in conformity to a previous agreement, a body of Morari Row's troops was thrown into the place, and the Poligar, with his family, ascended the impregnable rock of Nundidroog, distant only three miles, and overlooking the whole country. It was his project to leave Hyder to

CHAP. XII. 1762. waste himself anew in a contest with fresh troops; and when the garrison should begin to flag, to descend once more with his select followers, and by a vigorous effort finally compel his enemy to raise the siege.

Hyder was enraged at finding himself the dupe of this deception, and returned with renewed ardour to the attack. The spiritless defence of a mercenary garrison did not long protract the fate of the place: in about ten days it was carried by assault, and its future defence was committed to Budr u Zeman Khan, a nevayet officer of reputation from Arcot, who had entered the service of Hyder in the course of this campaign. Hyder made no immediate attempt on Nundidroog, but left a light corps under his maternal uncle Ibrahim Saheb, whose head-quarters were at Bangalore, with orders to destroy the surrounding country, and, in communication with the garrisons of Deonhully and Little Balipoor, to cut off the access of supplies. With the double view of furthering this object, and retaliating on Morari Row, he extended his conquest over a considerable sweep of country to the northward of this recent acquisition, and to the eastward of his former frontier, including Coodiconda, Penconda (the former capital of Carnatic), and Merg Sera. Morari Row acknowledged the decisive nature of the defeat which he had sustained by retiring to his capital of Gooti; and Hyder now considered his arrangements to be in a proper state for revisiting the capital of his new dignities, profiting by its direct territorial possessions, and by the submission of its reputed dependants. The chief of these were the Poligars of Raidroog, Harponelly, and Chittledroog, situated to the north and north-east of Sera. The former, on Hyder's approach, came spontaneously to offer submission and allegiance, and for this conduct he was ever afterwards distinguished by Hyder above all his Hindoo dependants. Harponelly obeyed the first summons: but the Poligar of Chittledroog* attempted to evade and procrastinate. Hyder met this attempt by overrunning his whole country with his cavalry; and in a few days the Poligar found it prudent to compromise for a fine of two lacs of pagodas, besides the regulated payments, after the ruin of a considerable portion of his country. He was then most graciously received at the camp of his new Nabob, and in the course of conversation mentioned the arrival at his own camp of a singular visitor, whose history opened to Hyder new objects of ambition.

Buswapa Naick, the last actual Raja of Bednore, had died in 1755, leaving as his heir an adopted son named Chen Busveia, about seventeen years of age, under the guardianship of the widow until he should himself attain sufficient experience. The widow had formed a connection of shameless publicity with a person named Nimbeia. The notoriety and public scandal† of

* This is one of the Boya or Beder race, and the early habits of the tribe are evinced in the relation of an exploit of one of their ancestors, as given in the manuscript history of the house, with something, perhaps, of embellishment. During the rule of the first of the family who attained the dignity of Poligar of Chittledroog, the place, it is said, was besieged by his sovereign of Vijeyanuggur. The Poligar determined to give him a specimen of the danger which he enceuntered, by stealing his favourite horse from the head quarters of his camp during the night. The horse shewed uneasiness at the approach of a stranger, and by moving about displaced one of his pickets and wakened the groom: the Poligar quickly concealed himself among the litter, and the groom in replacing the picket drove it through the hand of the Poligar, who bore the pain without flinching. When the groom had fallen asleep, the Poligar, finding it impossible to remove the picket without noise, drew out his knife, amputated his own hand at the wrist, and in this state mounted the horse and carried him off.

† It was so public as to be noticed by an European traveller, *Anquetil du Perron*, who passed through Canara in 1757.

CHAP. XII. this attachment had drawn animadversions from the young Raja, and in 1757 the lovers had found it expedient to remove

1762. this rude observer, by employing a jetti* while shampoeing† him in the bath, to dislocate his neck and destroy him; and they selected an adopted infant to fill the vacant throne. The visitor, whose history was related to Hyder, had announced himself as Chen Busveia, saved by an artifice of the jetti, concealed in the house of his preserver for five years, and now escaped to implore the protection and aid of his neighbours in the recovery of his patrimony, The youth was introduced to Hyder: the plan was quickly arranged of an expedition to reinstate him in his supposed rights, and to remunerate the services to be thus rendered by Hyder and the Poligar. The troops commenced

1763. their march towards Bednore about the close of January 1763, moving in four parallel columns, and preserving a distance from each other of from five to fifteen miles according to circumstances, for the purpose of reducing and occupying all the fortified places situated in the open country before they should attempt the fastnesses of the woods.

The district of Bednore Proper is situated on the summit of that range of western hills which overlooks the provinces of Canara and Malabar. These mountains, elevated from four to five thousand feet above the level of the sea, present to the west

* The athletæ too often added this employment to their other pursuits. The process alluded to in the text has been described to me to be performed by a sudden twist of the head, which dislocates one of the vertebræ of the neck; another twist in the opposite direction completes the destruction of the spinal marrow, and finishes the work of death.

† Shampoeing may be compared to a gentle kneading of the whole person, and is the same operation described by the voyagers of the Southern and Pacific ocean.

a surface in many places nearly perpendicular to the horizon, and by their height intercept the clouds of the south-western monsoon: nine rainy months in the year are usually calculated in this climate; and for six of that number it is the practice of most families to make the same preparatory arrangements for provision (water only excepted) as are adopted for a ship proceeding on a six months voyage. This extraordinary moisture* is not only favourable to the growth of the peculiar products of that rich province, but covers the face of the country with timber of luxuriant stature, with underwood scarcely penetrable, and a foliage which, added to a cloudy sky, has rendered it proverbial among its Mohammedan visitors, that a man may pass the greater part of the year in Bednore without a sight of the sun. The capital and fort of Bednore are situated in a bason encircled by hills, the crest of which, distant from the town from three to six miles, had been fortified in the weakest parts by lines which, with the woods and natural protection of the hills, constituted its only strength; the fort itself being from its position obviously incapable of a good defence. The dominions of this state not only embraced the mountainous range which has been described, but extended to the west over the maritime province now named Canara, and to the east over a tract of more open country stretch-

* Colonel Mackenzie, who watched the approach of a monsoon on the summit of this range, distinctly observed the clouds, in rolling along, frequently to diverge from their direct course apparently attracted by some hills, more powerfully than by others of equal or superior height; and every successive cloud diverging in the same line. This phenomenon appears to merit farther investigation, and may be found to explain the reason why places similar in situation have unequal proportions of rain.

CHAP. XII. 1763.

ing to Santa Bednore, and Hoolulkera, within twenty miles of Chittledroog, the residence of its constant rival and enemy.

On entering the province Hyder issued proclamations in the name of Chen Busveia, inviting the inhabitants of Bednore to return to their allegiance. At Simoga, a fort on the skirt of the woods, and distant forty-three miles from the capital, which fell without material resistance, he found a lac of pagodas*, of which he distributed a lac of rupees to the troops as a stimulus to their energies and hopes: at this place also he received and rejected a proposal from the Ranee to purchase his retreat by four lacs of pagodas. At Coompsee, distant thirty miles, he found a more important treasure, namely, Lingana, the prime minister of the late Raja, who had long been imprisoned at this place; this personage undertook to instruct Hyder respecting every branch of the resources of the country, and to guide him through a secret path by which the city might be approached without encountering any of the works which have been described. At Eitoor, a trifling post occupied by one hundred men, the garrison had the audacity to fire at the troops; they were surrounded and taken: Hyder ordered their noses and ears to be cut off; and in that state they were dismissed to spread terror before him. At Anantpoor, distant twenty-five miles, the Ranee offered twelve lacs of pagodas, and at his arrival before the first barrier of the works of the capital, eighteen lacs †; all which offers the information communicated by the captured minister induced him to reject with-

* The pagoda of Bednore is four rupees, that of Mysoor three, that of Fort St George three and a half; that of Masulipatam is also four rupees.

† Seventy-two lacs of rupees, or 864,000l.

out a moment's hesitation. The army of Hyder having advanced to this formidable position with unexpected celerity, had thrown the Ranee and her paramour into the greatest consternation; and on the rejection of the last offer, terrified at the prospect of an immediate attack, they fled to the fort of Bellalroydroog, situated on the summit of a hill in the continuation of the same range, but seventy miles to the southward. Orders were left for the expeditious removal of all the treasure; but to provide for the possible event of the place being carried before that should be practicable, persons were stationed with positive orders to set the palace and treasury on fire, whenever the danger should appear to be imminent.

Hyder, on the instant of his arrival at the barrier in the beginning of March 1763, ordered a noisy but feigned attack to be made on the posts in his front; while he placed himself at the head of a column formed of his most select troops, and, following the path pointed out by his guide, entered the city before an alarm was given of his approach.

The Ranee's servants set fire to the palace in different places in conformity to their instructions. The inhabitants of this rich and populous town had hitherto been exempted from the alarms and miseries of war; a felicity rare in India, and everywhere least appretiated by those who have most enjoyed it. They fled in all directions, with a dismay and astonishment embittered by its contrast with the stupid and insolent security of their former habits. The terror of such minds, outstripping the ordinary effects of fear, drove the whole mass of the inhabitants to concealment in the woods and mountains which touch the very confines of the city: and the immense property of the most opulent commercial town of the East, eight miles in circumference, and full of rich dwellings, was thus left without a claimant.

Hyder's first care was to extinguish the flames of the palace, in which he personally assisted; and his second, to put an end to the plunder of the troops, in order that he himself might become the exclusive possessor of the booty. His arrangements for this purpose were so skilfully combined, that in a few hours his official seals were placed on the doors of every public and private dwelling above the condition of a hovel, and safeguards were stationed to enforce respect to the only plunder which was deemed to be legitimate. The available property of every description, including money and jewels, which he realized on this occasion, is variously stated, but it may without the risk of exaggeration be estimated at twelve millions sterling; and was throughout life habitually spoken of by Hyder as the foundation of all his subsequent greatness.

The occupation of the rest of the country was rather a business of arrangement than of conquest. The two principal detachments possessed themselves of Bussoo Raj Droog, (fortified island) Honaver, (Onore) and Mangalore on the coast; and a third, of Bellalroydroog, where the Ranee capitulated on the general* assurance of due consideration for her rank and dignity.

* Budr ù Zeman Khan states that she capitulated on the condition of being reinstated in her sovereignty on her conversion to Islam; that she accordingly went through the form of renouncing her cast by eating beef, and after this wanton degradation was sent to Mudgherry. I have no doubt of the main facts of the case, but I conclude that my respectable informant must have forgotten some of its circumstances. Hyder seldom adhered to the spirit of an inconvenient engagement: but he professed never to deviate from its letter, and the oracle of Delphos was not more skilful in framing ar equivocal sentence. But a conversion to Islam certainly was never blended with his political views, and must have been the sponta-

On the arrival of the army at Coompsee, the fraud of the pretended Chen Busveia is understood to have been discovered, if indeed we are to suppose that Hyder at any time believed the tale; but until the capture of the Ranee he continued to treat the impostor with all the forms of distinguished external respect, not, however, concealing a smile at the jests of the soldiers, who amused themselves by saluting him with the title of Ghyboo Raja, or the Raja of the resurrection; a name which became the standing joke of the camp.

Whatever may have been the conditions understood by the Ranee, or the stipulations adjusted with Ghyboo Raja, it is certain that Hyder despatched to one common prison, on the fortified rock of Mudgherry, one hundred and eighty miles to the eastward, not only these two personages, but Nimbeia the Ranee's paramour, and Somasakur, her adopted son and sovereign. Their confinement was intended to be perpetual, and there they remained until liberated on the capture of the place by the Mahrattas in 1767.

Hyder formed the design of intrusting to the civil servants of the former government the detailed administration of the affairs of Bednore, to which he gave a distinct minister; and throughout the whole of his arrangements, affected to treat it as a separate kingdom: Seringapatam and its dependencies he on all occasions professed to consider as belonging to the Kerter (sovereign), or pageant Raja of Mysoor; Bednore, to which he gave the name

neous offer of a woman to whom disgrace was familiar: the expectation may have been inferred, but it is probable that Hyder never made a promise on such a condition.

of Hyder Nuggur*, he avowed to be his own. It is not intended to intimate that he ever seriously designed to alter the condition of that personage, but it is certain that he formed the deliberate determination of transferring to Hyder Nuggur the seat of his general government; and of blending Seringapatam, with all its remembrances, among the general mass of his minor possessions. Hyder could never have intended to establish his capital, his family, and his treasures, at a place of no military strength; the determination, therefore, in itself, confirms a suspicion to which we have before adverted, of his deficiency in an important branch of military judgment; a deficiency which is the more remarkable in a mind distinguished in other respects by a degree of sagacity and penetration which has seldom been exceeded. He gave orders for the removal of his family, the erection of a splendid palace (which was never finished), the establishment of a mint, in which, for the first time, he struck coins† in his own name, and the preparation of a dock-yard and naval arsenal on the western coast for the construction of ships of war; the latter under the direction of Lutf Ali Beg, a brave and excellent officer of cavalry, but eminently ignorant of every thing connected with his new duties of naval engineer and lord high admiral.

The rains commenced in June with their usual violence: few strangers escape their influence: and about the month of September the endemic disease had made such havoc on Hyder's

* It was a few days after its capture that some person, speaking of its population, said, that it had been intended by the former dynasty to augment the houses to ninety thousand, the distinctive number which constitutes a nuggur. "We will not mar the project," said Hyder, "and it shall be named Hyder Nuggur.

† Hydery Pagodas, of the same value as the former currency.

constitution, that he was no longer able to transact business in the public durbar. The servants of the former dynasty considering the opportunity to be favourable for the emancipation of their country, entered into an extensive conspiracy for the assassination of Hyder and the recovery of the capital. Some obscure suspicions were conveyed to him by a trusty servant; and he directed an investigation to be made by a commission composed of some of his oldest, and, as he conceived, his most trusty civil officers; who happened to be all accomplices in the conspiracy. The report of this investigation was read to Hyder while reclining on his couch, and shivering in a paroxysm of ague; but, even in this state, his keen perception penetrated the veil which they had attempted to throw over the few facts which were known to him. He dissembled, however, for the present, and detained the commissioners in feigned consultation, until the hot fit was succeeded by a slight remission; he then arose, and entering the durbar (or hall of business) re-examined the witnesses, and completely discovered the whole plot. He ordered the commissioners to be instantly hanged in his presence, in front of the hall of audience: the requisite arrests followed with rapidity, and before the close of the same day, upwards of three hundred of the chief conspirators were hanging at the different public ways which issued from the city. This done, he retired to rest with the same serenity as if he had only been discussing the ordinary business of the day, and arose on the following morning visibly recovered by the consequences of the unusual exertion to which he had been compelled. Bednore was thenceforward the most tranquil and obedient of all his possessions: but it was from this period that he began those improvements in the organization of his system of police which afterwards raised it to such horrible perfection.

As soon as the weather admitted, Fuzzul Oolla Khan* was detached about December, 1763, for the conquest of Soonda; a country of small extent, situated immediately to the north of Bednore Proper, and partaking of the same peculiarities of climate and produce. This conquest was achieved with the same facility as that of Bednore, and replenished the coffers of Hyder with a corresponding proportion of treasure. The Raja fled, after a feeble resistance, from his more elevated possessions to Tuccolighur, near Goa in lower Soonda; and in consequence of his distresses surrendered to the Portuguese the whole of his territory below the Ghauts, in consideration of receiving from them a fixed stipend; an arrangement which has been continued with his descendants to the present time.

The French Nabob Reza Ali Khan, the son of Chunda Saheb, had escaped from Pondicherry on ship-board during the siege which terminated in its capture in January, 1761; and after residing for some time in Ceylon for the purpose of watching the progress of affairs, landed in Canara in November, 1763, and came to claim the protection of Hyder. The talents of this officer appear to have deserved a greater degree of estimation than they had obtained from the French: he was received with distinction by Hyder, presented with a jageer of a lac of rupees, and, in the services in which he was afterwards employed, cer-

* I consult the convenience of the English reader in continuing this name instead of Hybut Jung.

tainly acquitted himself with a very creditable degree of spirit and military skill. From the long intercourse of Reza Ali with the French, he was enabled to assist Hyder in the arrangements which were now undertaken for the improvement of his army, and particularly in the discipline and interior economy of his regiments of infantry, now for the first time clothed in an uniform manner, and classed into *Avvul* and *Duum*, first and second, or grenadiers and troops of the line: the first was in conformity to the suggestion of Reza Ali, a distinction not exclusively regulated by stature and physical strength, but by tried steadiness and courage, and was rewarded by a superior fixed pay.

He now also established a regular order in forms of procession, a new splendor in the equipments of his retinue, and a more dignified etiquette in the ceremonials of public audience. The conquest of Bednore, in short, seemed to form a new æra in the history of this extraordinary man.

It will not have escaped the observation of the attentive reader, that the acquisition of Sera, which Hyder deemed it convenient to receive in the garb of a formal investiture from a Mohammedan lord, was, in point of fact, a conquest from the Mahrattas. Hyder was perfectly aware that this people would regard the fact alone; and that the fictitious part of the transaction would only give offence to the Soubadar of the Deckan, of whose supposed authority it was a direct usurpation. He accordingly despatched Apagee Ram as a vakeel to Hyderabad, charged with public gifts, and fortified with Soucar credit to an amount considerably exceeding the consideration paid to Basalut Jung. These means produced their usual effect at the court of the Soubadar, who was the more easily appeased from his incapacity,

CHAP. XII. 1763. at the moment, to resent the affront. To Poona, Hyder sent for the same purpose, and provided in the same manner, Mhedi Ali Khan; but here the injury was more direct and substantial. Madoo Row, the third of those chiefs under the title of Peshwa who had usurped the regal authority from the descendants of Sevajee, and had succeeded on the death of Balajee Row in 1761, was little disposed to acquiesce in the conquest of any part of his dominions; and it became necessary for Hyder to provide against an invasion, certainly more formidable, as well from the number and quality of the troops as from the talents of their leader, than he had anticipated from his former contests with Mahratta armies.

By the annexation of the dependencies of Sera, the frontiers of Hyder had been carried to the river Tombuddra, and by the conquest of Bednore and Soonda they stretched far to the north-west of that river. A slight inspection of the map will shew that the province of Savanoor forms a deep indentation into the territory then possessed by Hyder; who formed the design of attaching to his interest not only the Patan Nabob of that province, but those of Kurnool and Curpa, with a view to establish a sort of defensive cordon along the whole extent of his northern frontier, and acquire three corps of hardy Patan cavalry to serve with his armies.

We have already had occasion to explain * the cause which had compelled the Nabob of Savanoor to bend to the interests of the Mahrattas, and the arguments of Hyder's envoy had not succeeded in convincing him of their insufficiency: as soon,

* See page 380.

therefore, as Fuzzul Oolla Khan had completed the service in Soonda, he was directed to enter Savanoor, but to abstain from hostility while any prospect should remain of inducing the Nabob, by the joint power of terror and persuasion, to embrace the alliance of Hyder. Abdul Hekeem Khan, then Nabob, determined to risk the consequences of a positive refusal; and Hyder moved to form a junction with his advanced troops, accompanied by the body of his army from Bednore.

The actual situation of the Nabob of Savanoor had rendered it equally unnecessary and impracticable for him to maintain a large body of troops; and he moved out with between three and four thousand horse, and a rabble of irregular foot, rather for the credit of not shutting himself up in the town without an effort, than with any rational expectation of success against the overwhelming force of Hyder. The foot were spread over the plain so as to make a demonstration of greater numbers, and the Patan horse were reserved in a compact body to take advantage of events. Hyder, holding these demonstrations in contempt, made a disposition which was intended to envelope the whole, and to cut off their retreat. Abdul Hekeem charged the principal column when in the act of deploying, cut through it with considerable slaughter, and with great coolness and judgment prepared to overset the infantry, already formed in line, by a charge on their flank. At this moment a reserve of artillery opened with effect on this close and compact body of cavalry, and produced a degree of confusion which compelled the Patans to disperse and retire. Hyder seized with promptitude this favourable moment for a charge with his own cavalry; the fugitives were pursued to the very gates of the city, and a small remnant only

1764.

of the infantry, who stripped and passed as peasants, escaped the sabre on the plain. The immediate consequence of this gallant but imprudent effort was the unconditional submission of Abdul Hekeem to all the demands which Hyder had previously made, and to a farther military contribution of two lacs of rupees. Hoarding treasure is not among the propensities of a Patan, nor among the practices which escape the observation of a Mahratta; and as the Nabob had unfortunately little credit with the Soucars, or money-lenders, he was obliged to make payment in shawls, silks, muslins, gold cloths, carpets, and other valuables, equal in Hyder's forced estimation to the stipulated sum, but in actual value to four times the amount.

This object being accomplished, the arrangements of Hyder's recently acquired kingdom recalled him to Bednore, and he left Fuzzul Oolla Khan with a considerable division of the army to establish and extend his conquests to the northward. This able officer was active and successful in the execution of his orders. The apprehension of attack from the south had never entered into the contemplation of the Mahrattas; the places of strength were unprovided with the means of defence; and the important fortress of Darwar, with a multitude of minor posts, fell into his hands almost without an effort.

Madoo Row was not inattentive to the course of the late transactions. During the two last years he had been engaged in active hostility against Nizam Ali Khan, who, in the early part of his administration, exhibited a considerable degree of enterprize and military talent. In 1762, this chief had acquired by treaty the restitution of the fortress of Dowlutabad, which had been wrested from him by the Mahrattas on a former occasion;

and in a new campaign in 1763, he had carried his arms to the capital of the Mahratta dominions, and reduced the city of Poona to ashes. Another accommodation succeeded this event; and Nizam Ali being now engaged in hostility against his brother Basalut Jung in the direction of Kurnool, Madoo Row had leisure to attend to the operations of Hyder. The rapid and astonishing increase of the army and resources of his enemy rendered it necessary for the Peshwa to provide with corresponding care for the augmentation and equipment of his own force. During the delay which these preparations had occasioned, Fuzzul Oolla Khan had extended Hyder's northern frontier across the rivers Werda, Malpurba, and Gutpurba, nearly to the banks of the Kistna*. Gopaul Row the Mahratta chief of Meritch, immediately to the northward of that river, was furnished by Madoo Row with a considerable reinforcement, and ordered to cross the Kistna and check the progress of the enemy until the main army should arrive. Gopaul Row finding himself superior in numbers † to Fuzzul Oolla Khan, determined to give him

* These rivers are fordable excepting from June to November.

† I have found it proper to distrust my manuscripts in statements of numbers more than in any other case. In no country, and in no circumstance, is it safe to trust to any statement of numbers that is not derived from actual returns. Even Sir Eyre Coote, whose keen and experienced eye might be considered a safe guide, and whose pure mind never harboured a thought of exaggeration, states the force of Hyder in the battle of Porto Novo, first July, 1781, to have been from one hundred and forty to one hundred and fifty thousand horse and irregular infantry, besides twenty-five battalions of regulars; when it is certain that the whole did not exceed eighty thousand. I wish to be understood that when I have not been able to satisfy my own mind regarding numbers, I prefer the sort of relative statement adopted in the text; which may generally be determined with great probability where an opportuity has been obtained of examining the representations of both parties.

CHAP. XII. 1764.

battle, but was defeated with great loss in the month of April. Early in the ensuing month, the immense army of Madoo Row crossed the Kistna; Fuzzul Oolla deliberately retreated as he approached, and Hyder, recalling all his detachments, advanced towards Savanoor, and took up a position near Rettehully. There, encamped on an eminence which overlooked an extensive plain in front, he was secured by the vicinity of the woods in his rear, which afforded a cover for his infantry against the very superior numbers of the enemy's cavalry, from their commencement to the town of Bednore. On this ground he mustered twenty thousand horse, twenty thousand regular infantry, and twenty thousand irregular foot or peons chiefly armed with matchlocks, and a respectable train of artillery *. The force of Madoo Row was reputed at sixty thousand cavalry, Mahratta, Rajpoot, and Mohammedan, the same description of individuals which composed that of Hyder, their quality as troops not materially different, and therefore exceeding the same branch of Hyder's army in the proportion of three to one; but, as estimated numbers are always exaggerated, although in different degrees, from thirty to forty thousand may be considered in this case as a nearer approach to the fact. The infantry and artillery of Madoo Row were superior in number to that of Hyder in about the same degree as his cavalry: his regular infantry was composed of a better description of men, but in point of discipline was inferior. Of his irregulars a large proportion of the matchlockmen were Arabs, and superior to the same description of troops in the service of his opponent; but

* I cannot state its number or quality with confidence; but at this time twenty-five pieces was about the probable number of his field guns.

the Mahratta pikemen were decidedly inferior to those of Chitledroog, who (though as yet reluctantly) served in the army of Hyder.

The Mahrattas approached in their usual manner, covering the whole country with cavalry, and thereby concealing the movements of the rest of their army: the superiority was so decided as to enable them to invest Hyder in his camp and to intercept his supplies. His position however was purely defensive; and the object of assuming it was frustrated by the simple determination of his enemy to decline attacking it. His whole force from its relative inferiority was necessarily concentrated, while Madoo Row's detachments were actively employed abroad in recovering all that had been wrested from him by Hyder. That chief soon penetrated the design of the judicious plans which rendered useless all his dispositions; he determined to bring on a general action, and if possible still to lead the enemy by pursuit to attack him in his chosen position. With this view he confided the command of the camp to Fuzzul Oolla Khan, and moved out on the plain with a select corps of twenty thousand men. His manœuvres, however, terminated in his becoming the dupe of his own design: being drawn to the distance of six or seven miles, the irregular swarms of horse assumed a more fixed distribution, and discovered to him the whole army of Madoo Row closing upon him in every direction. The dispositions of Hyder for regaining his position were made with steadiness and skill; he forced the corps which was posted to intercept his retreat, and retired, hard pressed for a time, towards Rettehully, expecting to terminate a hard fought day by drawing the enemy to the ground which he had chosen for action. Madoo Row had

CHAP. XII. 1764. too much penetration to be so deceived; and Hyder, after sustaining a severe loss in the flower of his army, was foiled in all his objects. Distressed for supplies, he fell back the next day to Anawutty, where he had prepared an entrenched camp, and where the thick woods commence, which secured a communication with his supplies. To this position Madoo Row did not decline to follow him, and a few days afterwards appeared to be moving columns in different directions to invest the camp. Hyder imagined that he perceived an opportunity of cutting off one of these columns. He moved out for this purpose with two thousand regular infantry, one thousand select horse, and four light guns; he was again inveigled to advance too far, and completely surrounded. Hyder and about fifty of his cavalry escaped by the fleetness of their horses; the remainder of the corps was completely destroyed.

These operations were protracted beyond the middle of June. The south western clouds which had long been blackening in the distance, began to form along the crest of the hills that thick impenetrable gloom which it is necessary to have seen to be able to conceive; and the torrents of the monsoon commencing in a few days after this affair, compelled Madoo Row to retire to a situation less exposed to their violence. He cantoned his troops for the rains to the eastward of Savanoor.

Long before the rains had abated on the hills, Madoo Row passed considerable detachments over the river Toombuddra, and employed himself in reducing the whole of the eastern dependencies of Bednore, and the adjacent parts of Mysoor: while Hyder's army, wretched, spiritless, and sickly, from the inevitable consequences of its situation, looked with apathy or aversion to the renewal of active operations. About the beginning of the year 1765, the weather began to admit an approach to the woods of Anawutty, and Madoo Row opened the campaign with the employment of a numerous corps of pioneers, which he had organized and equipped during the rains. His object was to cut, in the first instance, a wide opening through the woods, to the southward of Hyder's intrenched camp; and progressively to form a line of circumvallation, by felling the gigantic forests around it. Hyder, perceiving the inevitable destruction which awaited him if he should permit his communication with Bednore to be cut off, immediately abandoned his intrenchments and commenced his retreat. The close and vigorous pursuit of the enemy necessarily impeded the celerity of his movement, and compelled him frequently to halt his whole force to sustain their attacks on his rear-guard. On the third day of these slow and retrograde movements, ground, comparatively open, afforded to Madoo Row the opportunity of moving a column between the army of Hyder and the point on which he was retreating, and thus forcing him to a general action. It is admitted by all who shared in the contest of this day, that although the dispositions of Hyder were respectable, the conduct of his troops was destitute of firmness and spirit; and that the action terminated in a disorderly rout in which he lost in killed alone three thousand horse, and double that number of infantry; the shattered remains of his troops escaping in dismay to the depth of the woods. The despondency of the army was communicated to the garrisons; the intermediate posts of Eekairee, Anantpoor, and Compsee, made but a feeble resistance; and Hyder, before the end of January, was reduced to occupy those lines surrounding Bednore which

CHAP. XII. 1765.

have been formerly described. In approaching this situation he began for the first time to reflect that the means by which he had himself achieved the conquest of this capital were also open to his enemies: that woods, although a protection to men individually animated in their defence, are equivalent to the concealment of night for troops who are not forward in the performance of their duty*: and that he had made the worst possible selection for the capital of an empire. Before he assumed this position his family was despatched by a route through the woods to Seringapatam, and detachments with treasure successively followed. In the mean time he had made private advances for negotiation through the medium of Ragonaut Row†, the uncle of Madoo Row, which terminated in an adjustment of extreme moderation, considering the desperate circumstances in which Hyder was placed.

1st. He engaged to restore all the districts and places which he had wrested from Morari Row.

2. To relinquish all claims on Abd-ul-Hekeem Khan, and the country of Savanoor.

3. To pay thirty-two lacs of rupees, on receipt of which Madoo Row engaged to retire, and did actually commence his march on the day after the payment was made, viz. about the end of February, 1765.

* Neither Hyder nor Tippoo, after this period, ever attempted to occupy a jungle (wood), although many opportunities occurred when they might (if not diffident of their troops) have done so with infinite advantage.

† Naroo Shenker was the person sent by Ragonaut Row to Hyder for the final adjustment of the terms; and among them were without question some secret articles which were the foundation of that good understanding which ever afterwards subsisted between Hyder and Ragonaut Row.

Hyder's occupation of Sera appears to have been tacitly admitted in this negotiation, and all discussions relative to the Poligars of Chittledroog, Raidroog, Harponelly, &c. seem to have been studiously avoided by both parties. Madoo Row had other contributions to levy during the open season from February to June; and by a proper understanding with these Poligars and with Morari Row, he considered the recovery of the posts wrested from the latter to furnish the certain means of regaining Sera, and the countries to the south-east of that capital, whenever he should find leisure to repeat his visit. While Hyder from an opposite consideration of the very same reasons determined to evade these retrocessions altogether.

During this unfavourable aspect of Hyder's affairs to the west, the whole of his recent acquisitions to the east were in a flame of rebellion. His brother-in-law Meer Ali Reza (usually called Meer Saheb), was therefore sent with a respectable force to Sera, and directed, after the re-establishment of Hyder's authority in that quarter, to co-operate with the corps at Bangalore, Deonhully, Ooscotta, and the two Balipoors; which had for several months been compelled by a general insurrection of the military population of those countries to adopt a cautious and defensive plan of operation. These insurrections were quelled without material difficulty; and the Poligar of little Balipoor being at length reduced to extremity from the want of supplies on the rock of Nundidroog, surrendered on one of those equivocal capitulations for personal honour and security, which are always interpreted according to the convenience of the conqueror. In the present instance the Poligar with his family was sent to Bangalore, and from thence to perpetual imprisonment in the distant fort of Coilmootoor (Coimbetore).

CHAP. XII. 1766.

Another corps under Fuzzul Oolla Khan was in the mean while employed in restoring order and levying revenue and contributions farther to the south-east; for the unprosperous aspect of Hyder's late situation had rendered necessary the presence of troops in every part of his dominions. These reverses appear however to have made but a temporary impression on the mind of this extraordinary man. His enterprising spirit and restless activity seem on all occasions to have converted unfavourable events into lessons of future conquest; and now impelled him to contemplate the condition of his southern possessions on the western coast, and of the contiguous province of Malabar.

The immemorial intercourse between Arabia * and Malabar had reciprocally induced many natives of each country to form temporary establishments for commercial speculation on the coasts of the other. The peculiar manners † of Malabar had produced an extensive intercourse between the females of that coast and their Arabian visitors; and in process of time had formed a separate class in the community, which retained the religion of their Arabian progenitors, blended with many of the local customs of Malabar. The access of new visitors and settlers from Arabia continued to preserve their bias towards that country; and soon after the appearance of their national apostle, the

* Arabia was formerly the emporium from which Europe was chiefly supplied with Indian commodities by a tedious coasting navigation. The accidental circumstance of a Roman having been blown to sea from the Arabian coast and driven to Ceylon, in the first century of the Christian æra, and the consequent discovery of the periodical winds, opened the first direct communication by sea between Egypt and India. See the interesting account of the discovery of Hippalus, in Dr. Vincent's dissertation on the Periplus of the Erythrean sea.

† The description of these manners will be more conveniently postponed until we have occasion to relate the characteristic efforts and *sermons* of Tippoo Sultaun for their reformation.

whole of this class embraced the religion of Mohammed. Ali Raja, one of these Mapilla (a term of doubtful etymology * by which they are distinguished), had in the progress of events obtained possession of the fort of Cananore †, with a small district on the coast, subject in the loose manner of such dependencies to the Raja of Colastri, or Chericul. Aiming at a greater degree of power and independence, he had sought the friendship of Hyder, as a power united at least by the ties of religion, when his frontier on the coast, by the conquest of Bednore and its dependencies, had approached within a short distance of Cananore. By means of this person, Hyder obtained a competent knowledge of the state of the northern districts of Malabar, and was enabled to add considerably to the information regarding the southern portion of that country which he had derived from the expedition of Mukhdoom Saheb in 1757. We have had occasion, in tracing the history of the landed property of Malabar, to notice ‡ the subdivision of that country into petty districts under the authority of chieftains comparatively independent, with subordinate proprietors of land, generally of the military class; and although the power and extent of these little clanships was subject to incessant revolution, the general aspect and condition of

* Two Malabar words, of which the name may be compounded, signifying "sons of their mother," would be the most probable etymology, if the difficulty of determining the father had been peculiar to these births in Malabar.

† It was a Portuguese fort and settlement so early as 1502, and was taken by the Dutch in 1663.—(Valantyn.) To enumerate the incessant revolutions of that coast, from internal quarrels, from the wars of the Dutch, Portuguese, French, and English, and from invasions by the armies of Bednore, would lead too far from the direct object of this narrative, and I have not attempted to trace the rise and progress of this little Mohammedan chief, who from an opulent trader became lord and merchant monopolist of Cananoor.

‡ Page 156 to 161.

CHAP. XII. the country was at this period so nearly the same as to demand no fresh description.

1765. The greater part of the year 1765 was employed by Hyder in repairing the disasters of the late campaign; in restoring his authority in the rebellious provinces; and in establishing such arrangements as should insure their future tranquillity. These objects being provided for, he left a corps of observation, consisting of three thousand horse, four thousand regular infantry, and ten thousand peons, at Buswapatan, to the eastward of Bednore; and with the remainder of his disposable force descended into
1766. Canara about the beginning of the year 1766, with the avowed intention of achieving the conquest of Malabar.

Passing southward by Mangalore, whither Ali Raja had come forward to meet him, he crossed at Nelisuram the boundary of Malabar, and proceeded with the guidance and aid of Ali Raja to the direct objects of the expedition: his second in command, Ali Reza Khan, the son of Chunda Saheb, had the chief direction of the subsequent operations, and commenced them (of course under authority) by a general instruction to grant no quarter.

The Nairs, or military class of Malabar, are, perhaps, not exceeded by any nation on earth in a high spirit of independence and military honour; but, like all persons stimulated by that spirit without the direction of discipline, their efforts are uncertain, capricious, and desultory. The military dress of the Nair is a pair of short drawers, and his peculiar weapon is an instrument with a thin but very broad blade, hooked towards the edge like a bill-hook, or gardener's knife, and about the length of a Roman sword; which the weapon of the chiefs often exactly resembles.

This hooked instrument, the inseparable companion of the Nair whenever he quits his dwelling on business, for pleasure, or for war, has no scabbard, and is usually grasped by the right hand, as an ornamental appendage in peace, and for destruction in war. When the Nair employs his musquet, or his bow*, the wea-

* The bow and arrow was the ancient missile weapon of India, but has been successively replaced by the matchlock, and more modern musquet; the latter, of European manufacture, was, at the period of Hyder's invasion, in general use on the coast of Malabar, in consequence of the long established intercourse of strangers with the people of that coast. The supposition that the use of gunpowder was known in India before its discovery in Europe appears to me to be not sufficiently supported. Mr. Halhed, in his preface to the Code of Gentoo Laws (page 57), adverts to a passage in Quintus Curtius, which mentions missile fire having been employed in the defence of a place attacked by Alexander. I have not been successful in my search for this passage either in Quintus Curtius, or Arrian. Philostratus, lib. ii. ch. 14, introduces in a dialogue between king Phraotes and Apolloneus Tyaneus, an account of the Oxydraci: "of which nation were the wise men who conversed with Alexander:" "they inhabit," says Phraotes, "the country between the Hyphasis and Ganges, which Alexander never penetrated, and would never have been able to conquer, for they fight with prodigious tempests and thunderbolts, being themselves accounted sacred and beloved by the gods". Hercules and Bacchus, it is added, were both repulsed by that people, who allowed them to approach their fortress, and then beat them back with thunders and fiery tempests. Arguments are also drawn from the names of the ancient instruments described in the Indian poems, *agnee aster* (the instrument of fire), &c. If I have been rightly instructed regarding the passages scattered through the Ramayan, which describe the action of these instruments, they are entirely fabulous. The *agnee aster*, the fire of which cannot be extinguished, may, plausibly enough, be put for the Greek fire, but the *brama aster*, or *astrum*, a weapon formed by magical process from a blade of grass, when once discharged cannot cease motion until it has hit its object. The baunum (*arrow* in some of the spoken dialects at this time), is also the name for the modern Indian war-rocket; but however various and fabulous, the twang of Rama's bow always announces the flight of the baunum. The argument amounts to this, that the effects of gunpowder may have been the foundation of these fables; but to this are opposed the following considerations. 1. No vestige of fire-arms, or of instruments discharged by gunpowder, is to be found in the Indian sculptures (to be seen in every part of India) which represent the war of the Ramayan, or any other war: the bow and arrow, the spear (the Indian bullum and Latin pilum) and sword, being

CHAP. XII. 1766.

pon which has been described is fixed in an instant by means of a catch in the waist-belt, with the flat part of the blade diagonally across his back; and is disengaged as quickly whenever he drops his musquet in the wood, or slings it across his shoulders for the purpose of rushing to close encounter with this terrible instrument. The army of Hyder had not before engaged so brave or so formidable an enemy: their concealed fire from the woods could neither be returned with effect, nor could the troops of Hyder be prevailed on to enter the thickets, and act individually against them. In every movement through the forests, with which the country abounds, bands of Nairs rushed by surprise upon the columns of march; and, after making dreadful havoc, were in a moment again invisible. On one occasion they were so imprudent as to depart from their characteristic warfare, and openly defended the passage of one of those rivers with which the province is everywhere intersected to discharge the mountain torrents. Hyder, by passing a column of cavalry at a higher ford, and combining their charge on the flank of the Nairs with a heavy discharge of grape in front, made a dreadful carnage among them. As he advanced to the southward he secured his communications by a series of block houses*; and the Nairs, perceiving the object of these erections, impeded his progress by the

the only weapons described. 2. The Persian and Tartar conquerors of later periods, and particularly Chingeez Khan, whose operations are minutely detailed, make no mention of a circumstance which would necessarily have excited the greatest astonishment; and so far as I have been able to examine the question, there is no direct evidence of the use of gunpowder in India, until a period long subsequent to its introduction in Europe.

* *Block-house* is a literal translation of the term which generally distinguished these posts, viz. *Leckerycota*.

defence of their own small posts. One of these, which my manuscripts name Tamelpelly, was surrounded by Hyder in the following manner: first, a line of regular infantry, and guns with an abbatis; second, a line of peons; third, of cavalry. This disposition was made for the purpose of striking terror by not allowing a man to escape destruction. The Nairs defended themselves until they were tired of the confinement, and then leaping over the abbatis and cutting through the three lines with astonishing rapidity, they gained the woods before the enemy had recovered from their surprise. Such was the character of the warfare in which Hyder was daily engaged; and in this manner continuing his progress through the territory of the five northern chiefs, he approached Calicut. Maan Vicran Raj, the Samoree (Zamorin), perceiving that resistance would be ultimately unavailing, and having heard of the peculiar favour which the Poligar of Raidroog had secured by an early submission, opened a negotiation, and proposed, if a safe conduct should be assured to him, to pay his respects to Hyder for the purpose of adjusting the terms of submission. This proposal being acceded to, the Raja proceeded to camp, where he was received by Hyder on the 11th of April 1766, with marks of particular distinction, and presented with valuable jewels. The terms adjusted at this interview were the confirmation of the Raja in his actual possessions as the tributary of Hyder, on his payment of four lacs of Venetian sequins as a military contribution. This arrangement being made, the army moved forward towards Calicut, accompanied by the Raja; but at the very moment that Hyder was receiving him with the honours which have been stated, a column was in motion by a circuitous route to seize the post of Calicut: the garrison rea-

1766. sonably concluding from this movement that the Raja was a prisoner, considered defence to be unavailing, and evacuated the place on the same night. Hyder had adopted this precaution from his experience of the deception practised by this Raja regarding the military contribution of 1757; and the Raja apprehended from this virtual infraction of the present agreement, measures of farther circumvention on the part of Hyder. After the expiration of a few days, Hyder intimated his expectation of receiving the stipulated contribution: and the Raja consulted with his ministers regarding the proper measures for its realization. But whether from inability, or design, they appeared to make but little progress in its collection. As the monsoon was not distant, Hyder, suspecting deception, placed both the Raja and his ministers under restraint; and applied to the latter the customary Indian methods of extorting treasure. The Raja, apprized of the cruelties and indignities offered to his ministers, determined to anticipate the possibility of a similar disgrace to himself; and having barricadoed the doors of the house in which he was confined, set fire to it in several places, and was consumed in the ruins in spite of all the exertions made by Hyder's command to extinguish the flames*. In the remembrance after a lapse of years of so extraordinary a scene as that which has been related, and even in the confusion of such a moment, a spectator

* The credibility of this circumstance is strengthened by a variety of instances of similar desperation on the part of other military classes of the Hindoos. The well known case of Ranga Rao of Bobilee, related by Mr. Orme, and the more recent occurrence at the capture of Gawilghur, are prominent examples; and occurred where the assailants were commanded in the former case by a French officer, and in the latter by an English general, both as eminently distinguished by their humanity as by the most brilliant military talents.

may have misconceived what he saw; but I have been assured by more than one eye-witness, that several of the Raja's personal attendants who were accidentally excluded when he closed the door, afterwards threw themselves into the flames, and perished with their master.

Even a scene of this nature was not calculated to operate on the impenetrable nerves of Hyder: the tortures of the ministers were continued without the least intermission, but the treasure which they at length produced fell far short of the stipulated sum.

While Hyder was occupied in these plans of exaction, the military arrangements for securing the conquest were also pursued with vigour: the fort of Calicut was enlarged and improved; additional posts were erected in different parts of the country, and stored with ammunition and provisions for their ample garrisons. A disposable column of three thousand regular infantry, aided by his newly acquired adherents, the Mapillas, was stationed at Calicut, and the civil government of the province was committed to an experienced officer of revenue named Madana. At the expiration of about a month employed in these arrangements after the death of the Raja, Hyder moved towards Coimbetoor, but was overtaken by the monsoon on his fourth day's march: he received however, in his progress, the submission and tribute of the Rajas of Cochin and Palghaut; and, after a difficult and dreary march, in which a heavy loss of horses and cattle was sustained, he passed through the woods of Animally, and distributed his army for refreshment and forage in the temperate and fertile province of Coimbetoor.

The civil governor to whom Hyder had entrusted the fiscal ar-

CHAP. XII. 1766.

rangements of Malabar, viewed its resources through the medium of the practices of exaction in which he had been educated; but was too little versed in the study of human nature to consider the habits and prejudices of a conquered people among the elements of his system of revenue. A quiet acquiescence in foreign subjugation was not to be expected under any circumstances from the natives of Malabar, but the imprudent measures of Madana precipitated their rebellion: and three months had not elapsed after Hyder's arrival in Coimbetoor, before intelligence was received that the Nairs had risen in all quarters; and attacked the block houses, which the swelling of the rivers had cut off from all reinforcement, either from each other, or from the moveable force at Calicut. Hyder collected his army without delay, and when the violence of the rains began to abate, moved with a light equipment of eight days' provisions by forced marches to Munjera. Hence, as a central station, he sent detachments in various directions. The troops now acted upon better information, and surprised and slew the insulated bodies of Nairs, whose insurrection had been made without any head to direct or arrange a general combination of their efforts. The prisoners taken in the first attacks were either beheaded or hanged; but as their numbers increased, Hyder conceived the plan of sparing them for the use of his former territories. This cure for rebellion in one province, and for defective population in another, of which such numerous examples occur in the Jewish history, was not successfully practised by Hyder. In a forcible emigration of a multitude of human beings, it would be inconsistent with the barbarous nature of the design that the arrangements for the subsistence of the captives should be made with scrupulous care:

the diseases to which all Indians, and particularly the natives of Malabar, are subject on a sudden change of climate, were superadded to hunger and mental misery; and of fifteen thousand who were removed, it is supposed that two hundred did not survive the experiment*.

After this example Hyder proclaimed an amnesty to such of the remaining inhabitants as should immediately submit to the conqueror: considerable numbers of those who had taken refuge in the woods returned to their habitations, and a deceitful calm succeeded the terrors of the late agitation. Hyder supposed that he had established an effectual and permanent tranquillity, and returned to Coimbetoor. On his route he gave orders for the erection of the present fort of Palgaut (Palicacherry), a pesition judiciously selected as an advanced post and depot, and for securing at all times an easy communication between the new conquests in Malabar and his fixed resources in the province of Coimbetoor, from the capital of which it was distant only thirty miles.

A body of four thousand cavalry, which his emissaries had been sent to engage in the territories of the Mahratta state of Najpoor, were reviewed at Coimbetoor, and seemed to arrive at a proper season to oppose a more formidable confederacy than Hyder had ever sustained. Madoo Row had issued from Poona; Nizam Alee, aided by an English corps, was approaching from Hyderabad; and all were confederated, according to report, for purposes hostile to Mysoor. The approach of these powers was

* We shall have occasion hereafter to describe more extensive experiments of this nature, followed by results as horrible.

CHAP. XII.

1766. certain; but the nature of their concert or ultimate designs was not accurately known to Hyder. In every event it was necessary to proceed without delay to Seringapatam for the purpose of making the most vigorous preparations. He arrived at that
1767. capital about the commencement of the year 1767; and while the military preparations were in progress, a civil arrangement, which now had sunk into a very subordinate degree of importance, also engaged his attention.

In April, 1766, the pageant Raja Chick Kishen Raj Wadeyar died; and Hyder, while occupied in Malabar, had sent orders, with all the indifference attached to an affair of ordinary routine, to go through the usual formalities of establishing as his successor his eldest son Nunjeraj Wadeyar, a young man then about eighteen years of age. Hyder, on his arrival at the capital, went through the ceremonial, from which habit and public opinion had not yet exempted him, of paying his public respects as a subject to his sovereign: he had, however, discovered that the youth since his mock elevation had betrayed some of those feelings of human nature which the habitual degradation of a splendid imprisonment had not absolutely extinguished; and these feelings Hyder deemed it necessary to crush before they should gather strength. It will be recollected, that districts to the annual amount of three lacs of pagodas had been allotted for the personal maintenance of the Raja; these were now resumed, and the palace was plundered of all the cash and valuables which had been saved from that income, with the single exception of the ornaments which the women had actually on their persons at the time that Hyder's myrmidons entered to execute his orders. A new and reduced arrangement of the household was enforced, which left none but Hyder's spies within the palace gates; and these precautions for internal security were adjusted without any interruption to the singular defensive measures against external attack, which we shall have occasion to describe, or to the most active preparations for an efficient military equipment.

The eventful war which commenced in 1767 and terminated in 1769, involved the interests and exercised the arms of all the principal powers of the south of India: and a clear and connected explanation of its causes shall be attempted in the succeeding chapter. The history of the British policy in India is not the direct object of the present work; but its intimate connection with the affairs of Mysoor may render it necessary to premise, that the treaty of Paris, which terminated the war between France and England on the 10th of February, 1763, *acknowledged Salabut Jung as lawful Soubah of the Deckan*, at a time when that office had, for upwards of a year and a half, been publicly and formally assumed by his brother: for Nizam Alee*, who murdered Salabut Jung in September, 1763, had imprisoned him, and ascended the Musnud on the 18th of July, 1761. By the same article† of the treaty of Paris, Mohammed Ali was acknowledged by the two powers *as the lawful Nabob of the Carnatic;* and the competition of English and French Nabobs having thus ceased, we shall henceforth distinguish Mohammed Ali by this his acknowledged designation.

The literal import of this title, namely, " the lawful deputy

* There was no affectation of ruling in the name of his brother. In his letters to Madras, Nizam Alee announces that the *king of Delhi* had displaced Salabut Jung for misconduct.

† Eleventh Article.

of a superior not named, in the government of a country mis-called and undefined," is only noticed for the purpose of illustrating the revolution of words and things, to which we have formerly adverted. The political meaning of the title must be sought in the intention of the contracting parties, who profess these acknowledgments to be made *in order to preserve future peace on the coast of Coromandel and Orixa.* Without stopping at present to enquire whether the acknowledgment of Mohammed Ali ought to be interpreted simply as a renunciation of future support to other candidates, or, in the construction afterwards assumed, as a direct recognition of sovereign authority; it would seem to be unquestionable that a measure apparently intended to compose the agitations in which this Nabob was concerned, tended only to stimulate an ambition too large for his talents, a corruption too prodigal for his means, and a combination of foreign and domestic intrigue, tending to objects of which he had probably never formed a distinct conception, profitable alone to the instruments employed, and to himself productive of nothing but misfortune.

Whether the peace of 1763, which delivered the English Company from serious impediments to the prosecution of their commercial concerns, left them also free to abstain from views of political aggrandizement, is a question which applies with the same force to every subsequent period of the British history in India, as to the short and important interval from 1763 to 1765, which placed the revenues of Bengal at the uncontrolled disposal of the English Company. To generalize and resolve this difficult and important question is, in effect, to determine whether human affairs can be rendered stationary by human wisdom.

The wisdom and virtue of political moderation, and the inexpediency and injustice of aggressive wars, are among those propositions familiarly denominated *truisms*, which more frequently pass through the ear than the understanding, and extend themselves over so large a surface as scarcely to be any where distinctly tangible. Nature has erected no visible boundaries to mark the proper extent of political power; and moderation, that word of amiable sound, which changes its meaning in the concerns of private life at every step from one hundred to one hundred thousand, is as perfect a Proteus in the political vocabulary: while in the very act of applying its ever varying form, ambition will not fail to whisper, that the fundamental principles and proportions which regulate a smaller scale remain precisely the same in the construction of a larger. We can scarcely conceive that the great and enlightened statesman who directed the affairs of Bengal in 1765, and seized with his characteristic penetration and promptitude the combination of circumstances, which, without previous design, led to an aggrandisement of unexampled rapidity and extent, intended to arraign the past by condemning its application to the future; nor can we in justice to his memory suppose, that in retiring from the scene of his past glory, and deprecating an extension of the British dominions, he contemplated any other than the existing condition of his own and the surrounding states, or meant to inculcate the expediency of the same measures under every possible variation of circumstances. To determine the evanescent line which separates moderation from ambition would seem to be a problem beyond the reach of general rules, and to require a consideration of the facts of each individual case, for its solution. The lights to guide our opinion on a question

1767. which appears simple to those only who confine their examination to its surface, must therefore be derived from a close attention to the progress of events. Without presuming to instruct the reader, the means of forming or revising his own judgment will be found in the series of more tardy steps which, from the year 1765 to 1799, tended with considerable fluctuation to a similar aggrandisement of the English power in the south of India. The principal events of these thirty-four years belong to the direct scope of our future narrative; and if precarious health should admit, and public opinion should not discourage the design, an attempt shall be made to relate them with fidelity.

APPENDIX.

No. I.

SINCE writing this passage*, I have obtained from the copy of Menu, in the possession of the Pundit of the court at Seringapatam, a transcript of these texts, for the purpose of being collated and examined by Mr. Ellis; and I subjoin, without farther observation, the ingenious and learned note with which he has favoured me, leaving the passage as originally written, for the satisfaction of those readers who may think proper to prefer the copy and translation of Sir William Jones.

Note, by Mr. Ellis, on the 239th and 243d Verses of the Eighth Chapter of Menu.

Menu, in his ninth chapter, see verse 41, 52, 53, &c. makes frequent mention of the land-owner, and in such terms as to leave no doubt that when this ancient work was written, private property in land existed in India. Besides these, the only two texts relating to this subject are verses 239 and 243 of the eighth book, the latter of which is so translated as not only to render doubtful what in the preceding sentence I have stated to be without doubt, but entirely to destroy the notion that private property in land obtained among the primitive inhabitants of this region of the earth.

* Page 128 to 133.

THESE TEXTS ARE,

239.—" Let the owner of the field inclose it with a hedge *of thorny plants*, over which a camel could not look; and let him stop every gap, through which a dog or a bear could thrust his head."

243.—" If land be injured by the fault of the farmer, *(as, if he fails to sow it in due time)*, he shall be fined ten times as much as the *king's* share *of the crop that might otherwise be raised;* but only five times as much if it was the fault of his servants without his knowledge.

The words in Italics do not occur in the text, but are the gloss of Culluca Bhutta.

In the first of these texts an " *owner*" of land is mentioned; in the second a "*farmer*" only; but on reference to the original, the same word appears to be used to express what is here so differently translated: this word in both texts is *Cshetra Carta*, literally, landlord, the first member of the compound Cshetram being understood in the first text on account of its occurring in the verse immediately preceding. It appears, therefore, according to the 243d verse, and its gloss, as translated by Sir William Jones, that the *Cshetra Carta*, the primitive Indian landholder, was subject to the continual controul and interference of the officer of government in the cultivation of his lands: wherever these, from ignorance or caprice, thought proper to find fault with his mode of conducting agricultural labour, he was liable to be fined, reckoning the "king's share" one-sixth, according to verse 130, chap. 7; in one instance, four-sixths more than the whole produce; in another five-sixths of it: the *Cshetra Carta*, in defiance of the positive meaning of the word, cannot therefore be considered as the lord of the land, the proprietor of the soil; and these considerations, probably, induced Sir William Jones in this text to render the word "*farmer*," though he had before translated it "*owner*." "Farmer" even is a term too independent for such a wretch.

There are some reasons, however, which would lead to doubt both of the correctness of the gloss and of the translation. It is in the first place to be observed, that the division of the chapter in which these texts are found is in the original called *Swamipalana pracaranam*, the division respecting the protection of masters or owners of cattle: this pracaranam commences with verse 229, and ends with verse 244; and the introduction of these texts, therefore, in this place is altogether incidental. Menu, in this place, certainly does not intend to prescribe rules for the conduct of cultivation, or to regulate the mode in which government should proceed towards the cultivator for the security of its interest in the produce: this must necessarily have had place in the preceding chapter, if the legislator had chosen to notice it all. Having in the commencement of the pracaranam stated the extent of the responsibility of the hired servant in case of loss, accruing to the cattle entrusted to him, he proceeds to lay down rules respecting damages done by the trespass of cattle on land. As a general security against such damage, in which thes tate, which by law is to receive a share of the increase, is interested as well as the proprietor, he directs, in verse 339, that fields liable to trespass from their neighbourhood to pasture lands shall be sufficiently enclosed. Verses 240 and 241 contain the law as relating to herdsmen and owners, when damage is committed either in inclosed or uninclosed fields. Verse 242 excepts certain descriptions of cattle from any fine; and verse 243, the text in question, proceeds to prescribe the punishment to be inflicted on the proprietor of the land, if damage be sustained by it, and consequently by the interest of the state in the crop upon it, if he disregard, or permit his servants to disregard, the law as prescribed in verse 239. Under this view of the context, the introduction by the commentator of the first sentence in Italics *as if he fails to sow it in due time)* is manifestly founded on misconception, as Menu makes no reference whatever to *loss sustained from neglect in sowing*, but *damages sustained by the trespass of cattle from neglect in enclosing lands:* this meaning is corroborated by reference to the original, in which the word *layam*, which, as a legal term, should be translated *damage*, means literally *damage by positive injury, destruction by violent means*, and never mere loss from accident or neglect, which the legislator would have expressed by the appropriate term *nashtam*, had he meant what his commentator attributes to him.

Still, however, a great difficulty exists in considering the Cshetra Carta as absolute proprietor, while he is subject to the enormous fine directed by the text itself to be imposed on him. In verse 232 of this pracaranam, the herdsman, when neglect has caused the loss of a beast, is only liable to make it good; but here the landholder for similar neglect not only makes good the loss sustainedby the state, but forfeits the actual produce of his land, and is fined nearly as much again—a punishment preposterous under any mode of land tenure, but absolutely precluding the idea that the holder so liable can be proprietor of the soil.

A reference, however, to the text as it exists in the southern copies, obviates this difficulty, and affords a clue by which the error which misled Sir William Jones in the translation of this text may be detected. The following translation, compared with the original and Sir William Jones's version, will explain this.

ORIGINAL TEXT.

Cshétra Carta	laye	dandah
The Land Lord	on account of damage	is to be punished.

[1] Bhógad	[3] dasa	[2] guno	bhavet
from the produce	a tenth	rate	be it

Iad	árdáhá	dándó	bhreyánam
of that	half the	punishment	of the negligencies

Agnyanát	Cshâitricasya tu
from ignorance	of his labourer.

(1) *Bhogam.*—This word signifies, primarily, enjoyment: secondarily, the produce of land, or of any thing that can be enjoyed: it may mean here the entire enjoyment, the whole produce, the *portion enjoyed* by the Cshetra Carta, or the *portion enjoyed* by the state. The grammatical construction appears to favour the former meaning, though the word may stand in apposition with Cshetra Carta, which occurs in the former part of the sentence; but it cannot bear any connection with Raja, which is no-

where expressed or understood; the remainder of the gloss, therefore, namely, the word "kings," and the words "of the crop that might otherwise have been raised," is wholly irrelevant. Bhogat is the fifth or ablative case, called by Sanscrit grammarians ayádánam, *the taking from*. (2) *Guno* signifies, primarily, quality, here *rate;* it is in the singular, and governs the verb *bhavet.* (3) *Dasa*, in composition, has as often an ordinal as a numeral signification. The correct translation of the text therefore is:

"The landlord is to be punished in case of damage by *a fine equal to* a tenth part of the produce, or half of that, if from the negligence of his labourer, unknown to him."

On comparing this with Sir W. Jones's translation, it is evident that he must have read this text differently, or he could not have written "ten times as much as the share," instead of "a tenth of the produce;" but this discrepancy is easily reconciled, by supposing the word *bhága* to be substituted in the northern copies for bhógàt, and the second line of this verse to be read

Bhaga dasa guno bhavet
As much as the share, a tenth rate, be it,

which would afford some colour for his translation, though it would not explain why he rendered *guno*, in the plural, "times," while the verb *bhavet* is in the singular. There can, however, be little doubt that he thus read it; and this substitution of *bhaga* for *bhoga* must have taken place in the northern copies, previously to the time of Culluca Bhutta, as appears by his endeavouring to render the term *bhága, share*, precise, by introducing the word "kings," without perceiving that he makes the whole nonsense by the enormous fine to which he subjects the landholder. This substitution, and the mode of commentary, evince that the northern government had long before the Moslem conquests encroached on the rights of the subject; and that they found, as other instances also prove, no lack of legal quibble, and perhaps legal forgery, among the interpreters of the law, when they wished to sanctify these usurpations in the eyes of the people, by adducing the authority of the ancient books in support of them.

No. II.

The first of these is an inscription on stone found at Canchi or Conjeveram, written partly in *Ellacanun* the ancient, and partly in the modern *Tamul.*

It begins with the usual invocations, and recites that it was written during the government (probably provincial) "of *Bookana Wadeyar*, and *Veera Cambana Wadeyar*, *after* the Sahabdam, or year of Salivahan, 1222, in the year of the Hindoo cycle *Plava*, viz. A.D. 1301, the sun being in the sign of Aquarius, in the first fortnight of the moon, on the eleventh day, being Thursday, under the star *Poonur pooshum*."

"In the land of victory, *Chola Mundalum*" (Coromandel)—then follows a detail, shewing the division, the township, and the quarter of the township—"*Moodeliar Nacheyar*, otherwise called Yellantalayal, daughter of Tomoondi Achachè, the slave of Peroomal among the Dasicul, dancing women, (announced) "of my own consent my own *Canyatchi*, two manas situated"---Here follows a detailed account of its boundaries, the property being a small patch within the town.—" These two pieces of ground of mine, in the midst of these four boundaries, I consent to sell. Who will buy? Thus she proclaimed; which being heard, then answered *Ayapaningar*, son of *Anna Coopaningar*, of the tribe, &c. &c. If you sell at my price I will buy." Then the said woman (repeating her names) and the purchaser Aayapaningar, both said, we consent and agree for current money without blemish, pannums * twenty-seven.—" These two grounds, with their groves, trees, shrubs, and parasitical plants, all these I have sold and have received the money without objection, and have delivered my original bills of sale; there is no doubt with regard to (the title of) these grounds: if any doubt should occur, I will stand up and remove it. These grounds he may sell or grant in charity to any one, and alienate at his pleasure; and their price being fixed at auction at twenty-seven pannums, which I have received without balance, they are hereby transferred to Ayapaningar, son, &c. with full consent, by Nacheyar, &c. in the presence of Aroolala Veejayaramum.

(Signed) AROOLALA VEEJAYARAMUM.

The second, an inscription on copper, begins with the usual invocation; and after reciting the praises of the king (Deva Raya of Vijeyanuggur), in thirty-three extravagant compound epithets, proceeds:

" When he was ruling the kingdom in the year of the Cali-Yoog, 4517, of Salivahan†, 1349, (A. D. 1416) after the year (of

* What the value of the pannum of that day may have been, I do not know.

† There has probably been some error in copying or engraving one of these dates. A learned paper by Mr. Davis, in the 3d volume of the Asiatic Researches, p. 16, traces astronomically the source of an increasing error, amounting in 1791 to eleven years, between the reckoning of the Deckan and that of Benares; and the date of this document, according to the year of Salivahan, differs to that exact ex-

the cycle) *Plava*; the 21st of Maasee; the 5th of the increasing moon under the star Rogany. On that auspicious day was written this bill of sale.

"In the land of victory, Tonda * Mundalum, in (here follow the divisions and subdivisions) the village or township of *Coom Mungalum*, situated, &c. &c. *Mootoo Naig*, the son of *Andiapa Naick*, of the cast, &c. &c. who resides in the village of *Velloda*, situated near the said *Coom Mungalum*, he and his relations *Oam*, agreed or united (proclaimed).

"The village of Velloda, half of which is my *Canyatchi*, will any body buy my half village? thus he proclaimed. These words being heard were answered in the said Mundalum, in the said division, in the said Naad. *Cota, Perria Broomoo Setty*, of the village of Wopaulakum, of the Vyasa cast, he and his kindred with one consent answered, We will buy. Then the said parties (repeating their names) agreed and fixed the price in the presence of the bramins of *Coom Mungalum*, at one

tent from the reckoning of the Deckan, which would bring the two modes of reckoning, viz. the Cali Yoog, and Salivahan, to coincide in A. D. 1416; still, however, the year of the cycle Plava would differ six years from the coincidence of the other two. But exclusively of the probability of error in the copy, it appears to me that farther investigation is necessary for unravelling some variations of reckoning in different parts of India, which do not seem to depend on astronomical errors. For example, the astronomers of the Deckan reckon the commencement of the æra of Salivahan in the year *Pramadee*, or the 13th of the cycle of sixty: while those of Mysoor reckon its commencement in the preceding year *Bhoudanià*, or the 12th of the cycle, and this difference of one year appears to be invariable in all inscriptions ancient and modern of those two countries.

* *Tonda Mundalum* was the portion of *Chola Mundalum*, which corresponded nearly with what is named at this time the province of Arcot. It extended along the coast, from Cheddember (Chillumbrum) to Paliacate, and westward to the first range of hills. It received this name from the *son* of the Chola Raja, who subdued it.

hundred and twenty-five new Varaha (Pagodas)*." Here follows the measurement of the lands, which I cannot reduce for want of a knowledge of the value of the ancient measures. "We have sold our part, and received the consideration or value fixed. This is the price: twice: thrice: the said *Canyatchi* of ours you may enjoy while the sun and moon endure. There is no doubt (in the title) of the said *Canyatchi*. If any doubt occurs we are ready to remove it.

"In consequence of the agreement of Mootoo Naig and his kindred with *Cota Broomoo Setty*, we have thus confirmed it, and granted this bill of sale of our *Canyatchi* land."

"This is the hand-writing of
"Mootoo Naig,
"of the village of Coom Mungalum."

Subscribed by eight witnesses from the above recited and other neighbouring villages.

* *Pagoda*, or *Pagod.*—I can offer neither information nor satisfactory conjecture regarding *this name*, which we find applied by Europeans to *a gold coin* and to *the Indian temples;* and can only affirm that the name is not, as stated in the Encyclopædia Britannica, applied to either of those objects by *the Indians*, nor known to them in any sense whatever. The Persian etymologies which have been attempted come no nearer than *But-khana* and *But-kedda*—the *house*, and the *place* of idols; but neither of these terms approach the sound given to the word Pagoda in any of the European languages.

Varaha, the boar, one of the incarnations of Vishnou, was the emblem which the Rajas of Vijeyanuggur adopted as the impression on their gold coins, and the coin itself *was* and *is* named *Varaha* in consequence, in the Hindoo languages of the south. The ignorant Mohammedans believed that the figure of this abhorred animal had been adopted as a mark of defiance or derision towards them.

Hun, or *Hoon*, is the name which Persians, Moguls, Usbecks, Afghans, and natives of Hindostan, continue to give to this and similar gold coins of the south. It is the Canarese name for *gold*, and the plunder of the capital of Carnatic carried with it this name through Hindostan to the plains of Tartary. Hunna, henna, munna, say the Canarese (gold, woman, land), are the three objects from which it is most difficult to withdraw our attachment.

The third is a bill of sale in the Mackenzie collection, of which I have before me two translations, and adopt that by Mr. George Hughes, a native of India, perfectly conversant with the Tamul language, in which the original is written; and well-informed on the general subject of Indian agriculture, in which he at one time carried on considerable speculations.

Be it propitious!

On this fortunate day, Monday the 16th of the month Ahvany, of the year (of the cycle) Kahlyuktee, in the year of *Salinahan* 1720, and of the *Cali Yug* 4899, being the third day of the increasing moon, under the auspicious conjunction and happy influence of the constellations Ashanattee and Magarum: *Kistna Sawmey Pilla* of Cunnatoor, the son of *Vencatachelum Pilla*, for himself and his house executes this deed of sale of land to *Cumana Sawmey Pilla*. That is to say: Of the twenty-eight established shares of Cunnatoor, I have made a full and complete sale to you of my own two shares therein for one hundred chuckrums; and you having paid, and I having received the said one hundred chuckrums for the said two shares: therefore, possess the nunja, punja (wet and dry lands), trees, groves, gardens, hillocks, water, wood, stone, and treasures; the well that points beneath, the tree that points above, *together with all property belonging in common thereto* within its four boundaries. Your children from generation to generation are free to bestow, to exchange, or to dispose of it at their pleasure. Possess and enjoy it as long as the sun and moon, the earth and its vegetation, the mountains and the river Cauvery, exist; and all prosperity attend you. Thus it is subscribed by me *Kistna Sawmey*

Pilla, with my full consent to *Cumana Sawmey Pilla.* This deed is written by *Mootoo Sawmey*, the village Conicopoly.

Witnesses, (Signed) KISTNA SAWMEY.

ARNACHELUM,

SUNKALINGUM,

SHUMMOGUM.

A few days before I left Madras I had the satisfaction to know, from a judgment pronounced in the Supreme Court, that the rights of which I am the humble advocate are capable of being substantiated by direct proof in a regular court of law.

The revenues of the village of *Tondiarpet*, near to the black town of Madras, were formerly received by the collector of the jageer, who, like other collectors before the establishment of the Zilla, or provincial courts, had also a certain jurisdiction within the limits of his collection.

Dissentions had arisen between the *Vellalers*, *Meerassdars*, or *Canyatchikars* of that village and the *Pyacarees* (or *Graminy*, as they are sometimes called in the proceedings), which had more than once been carried into the mayor's court; but the points at issue do not appear ever to have touched the direct question of the proprietary right of the land.

In the year 1794, for some reasons which are not distinctly known to me, the *Vellalers** were forcibly ejected from the village under the authority of the collector, and possession was given to the *Pyacarees.* The suit was an ejectment brought by the Vellalers to recover the village.

A complete body of evidence was adduced, entering into

* For the meaning and etymology of this term, see page 168.

many of the details which I have stated, and establishing, to the entire satisfaction of the court, the hereditary right of the Vellalers to the landed property of the township. Owing to an error in point of form, viz. the want of proof of present possession in the defendants of that which the action was brought to recover (for the possession had much changed since 1794, and perhaps while the suit was pending), a verdict was given for the defendants on the 26th of September, 1808. But the proprietary right of the *Vellalers* was recognized without reserve by the court; and as I understand, they will now bring separate ejectments against the several possessors of the different parts, and obtain verdicts as a matter of course.

No. III.

Of the actual system for the administration of justice to the native subjects of British India I wish to speak with respect, because it originated and has been continued in the purest intentions. On the political question I presume to risk but one short observation. It is impossible to separate the political tendency of laws from the genius of the government from which they emanate. The spirit of the English constitution assigns to the mass of the people an extensive control over the exercise of public authority; and deems the executive government to be the representative of the public will. This spirit pervades the whole body of its laws; these laws necessarily reflect back, and reproduce the principles from which they spring: and it is matter for grave reflection, that if this species of reaction should ever be produced in India, from that moment it is lost to this country for ever. The efficient protection of our native subjects in all the rights which they themselves consider to be essential to their happiness, is certainly the most sacred and imperious of all our duties; and it is on this express ground that our present regulations, considered as a system of jurisprudence for the south of India, appear to me to require a radical reform.

To apply the *criminal law of Arabia*, the most defective on earth, and the least capable of correction, to the Hindoo subjects of Great Britain under the government of Fort St. George, is just not quite so absurd as to import the criminal law of Japan. If it were even admitted that the principles of the *Koran* are more susceptible of improvement than the law of the Hindoos, the absurdity would still remain of governing that people by a *foreign bad code*, when we may with equal facility govern them by a *foreign good code;* namely, the English law, which even in point of prescription* had a local existence before the scourge of Mohammedan conquest and Mohammedan law had yet reached the plains of Coromandel.

In the *civil code* we profess to administer justice according to the laws of the parties. This subject requires a more ample discussion than can be given in the compass of a note. The essen-

* The first establishments of the English on the eastern coast of the peninsula were at Masulipatam and Armagon; the latter was founded in 1626. The first grant from *Sree Rung Rayeel* of territory at Madras is dated in 1639. The first invasion of the territory, now improperly named the Carnatic, by the Mohammedan forces of Vijeyapoor and Golconda, occurred in 1646.

tial nature and objects of justice are everywhere uniform: the end is the same, the means are various. The principles of law in different countries do not materially vary; particular laws or regulations consist less in declaring principles, than in applying them to existing customs, and not unfrequently in a bare enunciation of the forms of legal proceeding. With a people like the Hindoos, among whom religion, and law, and the forms of legal proceeding, are all of equal sanctity, and considered to have the same divine origin, the substitution of the forms of Westminster Hall for the forms prescribed in their sacred codes, or rendered equally venerable by immemorial usage, if not a subversion of an important part of their legal system, is at least a violation of customs which we profess to respect. Principles in all countries are understood by a number sufficiently small; forms by every one: and if we can condescend to govern the Hindoos by their own forms, we may (I do not affirm that we ought) correct the principles of their law without its being generally observed or opposed. But holding in constant recollection the character of the people to be governed, it is incontestable that we may introduce Mohammedan or English law, both, or either, directly, or covertly, without the most distant chance of any influence, immediate or remote, in ameliorating the morals of the people, or changing their opinions, in any other way than that of producing disgust at our rule.

Exclusively of forms, I fear that some fundamental errors of principle have been committed. Imprisonment for debt, for example, which is considered by all philosophical reasoners as one of the most defective institutions of European jurisprudence, is unknown to the ancient codes, or to the common law of the south of India, and is repugnant to all the habits which so peculiarly separate that race from the rest of mankind. But this terrible and most offensive innovation has been introduced into the English civil code, which professes to govern the Hindoos by their own laws. The distinction of casts, which is absolutely the key-stone of Hindoo law, has unfortunately either not been recognized at all in our laws and regulations, or indirectly treated with contempt; thus insulting the higher, without gratifying the lower classes; and, added to the novelty of our forms, exciting in both the apprehension of farther change. It would be absurd and unjust to impute to the authors of this system the intention of proselytism; and it can only be lamented that it has contributed, among other causes, to produce the belief of such an intention. But if, as some publications* give reason to believe, such views have really been entertained by other persons, it will be incumbent on sober thinkers seriously to consider that, exclusively of the excess of visionary folly, it is a most unmanly, ungenerous, and unchristian deception to veil this object under the pretext of respecting the civil and religious customs and prejudices of the people; for all their prejudices, all their opinions, and all their customs, from the most trifling to the most important, are absolutely incorporated with their religion, and ought all to be held sacred.

The founder of a philosophical Utopia would certainly reject with abhorrence a system which tends to enslave the human mind, and to entail hereditary degradation on a large portion of his citizens. But we are not here discussing a speculative theory.

* The reader who may desire farther information regarding these views will find them described and discussed in the Edinburgh Review, vol. xii. p. 151.

The objects in our contemplation are not metaphysical entities to be moulded into ideal forms; but human beings, already fixed in stubborn and immoveable prejudices, to which any system founded in wisdom and humanity must necessarily conform. It is not the question, it never can be a question, whether the English or the Hindoo code of religion and jurisprudence be entitled to the preference: but whether the Hindoo law and religion, for they are one and the same, are, or are not, to be maintained, or whether we are at liberty to invade both. If we profess to govern the Hindoos by their own laws, let us not falsify that profession by tearing them up by the roots on the pretence of pruning and amending them. They are no longer Hindoo if they are subject to innovation. Before quitting this branch of the subject, it may be useful (for the sake of illustration) to examine the reasonableness of interfering with the most exceptionable of all their institutions. It has been thought an abomination not to be tolerated, that a widow should immolate herself on the funeral pile of her deceased husband. But what judgment should we pronounce on the Hindoo, who (if any of our institutions admitted the parallel) should *forcibly* pretend to stand between a Christian and the hope of eternal salvation? And shall we not hold him to be a driveller in politics and morals, a fanatic in religion, and a pretender in humanity, who would *forcibly* wrest this hope from the Hindoo widow? To return to the question of cast. To equalize them is impossible; to attempt it, offensive beyond all endurance to those whom we would exalt, as well as to those whom we would debase; and if we possessed the power, to exercise it would be a gross and intolerable oppression. That our regulations, where they do extend, and where they have not yet reached, are considered with terror as the instruments of a foreign rule, and that the Hindoos neither do nor can feel that they are governed by their own laws, seems to have been distinctly foreseen by the able and learned officer* who aided in the first compilation of the judicial regulations of Fort St. George. In a preliminary report he deprecates the idea of sudden innovation, and observes, "that the system ought rather to grow out of the first germ, than start at once, full grown, like Minerva from the head of Jupiter, shaking a lance and ægis at the astonished native. They will arise gradually, as the best laws ever have done, out of the manners and habits of the people, meliorating and reflecting back the principles they have derived from them."

In framing a new and full grown system (since, however, exceedingly enlarged), the excellent and able men who were employed naturally referred to the system of jurisprudence which we are all habituated to revere, for their rules, their forms, and modes of proceeding, down in many instances to the very technical terms. Fixed judges and magistrates have been established, and courts of appeal, of circuit, and gaol delivery, with all their English appendages; and a superior Hindoo court, with a Perso-Arabic title, administered by Englishmen; and it has already become a difficult study to be able to understand the voluminous code which has been framed. Of all this I should wish to speak with reverence; but really an enormous amount of technical labour, and skill, and expence, and the application of most respectable talents, terminates in performing the proposed ope-

* The Judge Advocate General, Major Leith.

ration very ill, or not at all: the component parts are clogged by their own complexity and misapplication; the machinery of an Arnold's chronometer has been applied to perform the work of a smoke-jack.

If Anglo-Indian legislators would throw off a little of that which they somewhat too largely ascribe to the natives of India, namely, the prejudice of education, they would find the rules of proceeding prescribed by the Hindoo code (with all its numerous imperfections on its head), combined with the local customs, or common law of India, not ill adapted to the state of society to which it is intended to apply; and in the *Panchaiet* or *Indian jury* *, which is (or rather was) universally established in the south as the common law of the land, an admirable instrument of practical decision. The Hindoo character, like all others, is of a mixed nature, but it is composed of strange and contradictory elements. The man who may be safely trusted for uniformly unfolding the whole truth to an European in whom he reposes confidence, may be expected to equivocate, and even to contradict every word he has said, if called on to repeat it in presence of a third person whom he either fears or suspects; and in one of these descriptions he usually includes all strangers. The same description of man, sometimes the same individual, who from pique, and often without any intelligible motive, will perjure† himself without shame

* An institution so entirely neglected or misunderstood, that I believe its existence is now, for the first time, presented to the notice of the English public.

† The branch of Hindoo law which refers to this object is dreadfully objectionable, but the practical rules of evidence are calculated to correct it. I feel that the reproach of English prejudice applies in a certain degree to some of my observations on this subject in 1804: and I regret having made them at all, because they have been misapprehended; and I have been quoted in courts of law for what I have not written.

or compunction at a public trial, is faithful, kind, and respectable in the intercourse of society; and the single but notorious fact of habitual lending and borrowing of money and effects, among the husbandmen, without bond, or note, or witness, abundantly proves, that this people, apparently so destitute of morals in one view of their character, are in another habitually honest and true in their dealings; that they mutually trust, and deserve to be trusted. The more intimately they are known, the more favourable is the judgment of every good and humane European on the character of this interesting people; but fully to understand them, requires to have lived and been educated among them, as one of themselves; and I conscientiously believe, that for the purpose of discriminating the motives of action, and the chances of truth in the evidence of such a people, the mature life of the most acute and able European judge devoted to that single object would not place him on a level with an intelligent Hindoo Panchayet.

To govern the Hindoos in reality, and not in pretence, by their own laws and customs, civil and criminal, would admit of extensive aid in judges and juries (panchaiets) from among the natives themselves, checked without material danger of corruption by a reduced scale of European controul. The new establishments of police, on which large sums have been unnecessarily expended, might be entirely retrenched by putting in activity the admirable institution of village officers, and directing, instead of attempting to destroy, this excellent instrument of police; of which I speak, not from vague tradition of what it has been, but from a close observation of what it is. If theory required that the judicial functions should be rendered distinct from the fiscal, it seemed equally to demand the separation of the duties of magistrate and judge, which have been united in the new system with the most obvious practical inconvenience. There may have been a real propriety in preventing the fiscal officer from being the judge in a contested case of fiscal demand (although we do not see this propriety practically acknowledged in England), but beyond this there seems to have been little necessity for the cumbrous establishments to which we have adverted.

These suggestions, however imperfect, are not the result of loose or solitary remarks, but the consequence of deliberate discussion, with some of the most able and efficient instruments of the present system; of a careful and vigilant observation of the conduct and practical operation of a Hindoo court, which has been established within the last five years at Mysoor; and of a coincidence with the mature judgment of regular English lawyers, free from the trammels of their profession. The names of some of these, if I were at liberty to adduce them, would give irresistible weight to the opinions which I have attempted to sketch.

No. IV.

From conversation with some intelligent Jungum priests, I learn that they derive the name from a contraction of the three words, junnana, to be born; gummana, to move; murrana, to die. The word jungum thus constantly reminds them of the most important dogma of the sect, namely, that the man who performs his duties in this world shall be exempted from these changes in a future state of existence, and shall immediately after death be re-united with the divine spirit from which he originally emanated. This doctrine, not altogether unknown to the braminical code, is pushed by the jungum to the extent of denying the metempsychosis altogether. This sect condemns as useless and unmeaning the incessant detail of external ceremonies, which among the bramins of every persuasion occupies the largest portion of their time, and forms the great business of their lives. The jungum disclaim the authority of these gods upon earth, as they impiously and familiarly call themselves. The priests of the jungum are all of the fourth or servile cast, and habitually distinguish the bramins by the opprobrious appellation of dogs; yet, strange to tell, in some districts, by reciprocal concessions, and a coalition of religious dogmas with temporal interests, they have descended to receive as their spiritual preceptors the cast of which they have been successively the martyrs and persecutors, and are consequently considered as heretics or renegadoes by the genuine jungum.

The religion which inculcates what is real, in preference to the observance of form, is, according to this sect, of great antiquity; and they consider Chen Bas Ishwur, a native of Callian in the Deckan, the reputed founder of the sect in the eleventh century, to have been only the restorer of the ancient true belief; and in spite of the most sanguinary persecutions, they are found scattered in considerable numbers over the Concan, Canara, Deckan, Mysoor, and every part of the south of India, and constitute a considerable portion of the population of Coorg, the

Raja himself being of that persuasion, as were the former Rajas of Mysoor, Bednore, and Loonda.

The fanciful notions of internal and external purity and uncleanness (the former having a twofold division of bodily and mental) are the foundation of most of the distinction of casts which seem so absurd to Europeans. To the question of what is the difference between such and such a cast, the first answer will certainly be to indicate what they respectively can and cannot eat; but when we consider the plausible dogma not altogether unknown in Europe, that a regular and abstemious life (which they would name the internal purity of the body) contributes to mental excellence, we may be disposed to judge with more charity of the absurdity of these distinctions. The Jungum priests and the elect among their disciples abstain altogether from animal food; while the Sheneveea bramins of the Concan and the Deckan indulge in fish; and many of Bengal, Hindostan, and Cashmire, eat the flesh of fawn, of mutton, and whatever is slain in sacrifice: the bramins of the south abhor these abominations, but the latter at least is distinctly authorized by Menu and all the ancient Smirtis, as the most bigoted are compelled to admit.

In the leading traits of the doctrine of the Jungum which have hitherto been noticed we recognize the hand of a rational reformer. The sequel is not so favourable. The Jungum profess the exclusive worship of Siva; and the appropriate emblem of that deity in its most obscene form, enclosed in a diminutive silver or copper shrine, or temple, is suspended from the neck of every votary as a sort of personal god; and from this circumstance they are usually distinguished by the name of *Ling-ayet* or *Lingevunt*. They profess to consider Siva as the only God; but on the subject of this mode of devotion they are not communicative, and the other sects attribute to them not very decent mysteries. It is however a dogma of general notoriety, that if a Jungum has the mischance to lose his personal God, he ought not to survive that misfortune.

Poornia, the present minister of Mysoor, relates an incident of a *Ling-ayet* friend of his who had unhappily lost his portable God, and came to take a last farewell. The Indians, like more enlightened nations, readily laugh at the absurdities of every sect but their own, and Poornia gave him better counsel. It is a part of the ceremonial preceding the sacrifice of the individual, that the principal persons of the sect should assemble on the bank of some holy stream, and placing in a basket the lingum images of the whole assembly, purify them in the sacred waters. The destined victim, in conformity to the advice of his friend, suddenly seized the basket and overturned its contents into the rapid Caveri. Now, my friends, said he, we are on equal terms: let us prepare to die together. The discussion terminated according to expectation. The whole party took an oath of inviolable secrecy, and each privately provided himself with a new image of the lingum.

Mr. Ellis considers the Jungum of the upper countries, and the Pandarum of the lower, to be of the same sect, and both to deny in the most unequivocal terms the doctrine of the metempsychosis. A manuscript in the Mackenzie collection ascribes the origin of the Pandarums, as a sacerdotal order of the servile cast, to the religious disputes which terminated in the suppression of the Jain religion in the Pandian (Madura) kingdom, and the influence which they attained, to the aid which they rendered to the bramins in that controversy; but this origin seems to require confirmation. In a large portion, perhaps in the whole, of the braminical temples dedicated to Siva in the provinces of Arcot, Tanjore, Trichinopoly, Madura, and Tinnevelly, the *Pandarum* is the high priest of the temple, and has the entire direction of the revenues, but allows the bramins to officiate in the ceremonial part according to their own good pleasure, as a concern altogether below his notice. He has generally the reputation of an irreproachable life, and is treated by the bramins of the temple with great reverence; while on his part he looks down with compassion at the absurd trifles which occupy their attention.

These facts seem to point to some former revolution in which a Jungum government obtained the superiority over the braminical establishments, and adopted this mild mode of superseding the substantial part of their authority. It is a curious instance of the *sooder* being the spiritual lord of the *bramin*, and is worthy of farther historical investigation. A dynasty of *Beejul Rai* ruled at *Callian*, but the extent of their dominions, and the duration or exact æra of this dynasty, is at present uncertain. I find it placed in my notes from the Mackenzie manuscripts between the Cadumba and the Chola.

No. V.

Jqin.—For a particular account of this singular sect the ninth volume of the Asiatic Researches may be consulted. The following abstract is the result of several conversations with Dhermia, a Jain bramin far advanced in years, whom Lieutenant Colonel Mackenzie has discovered and taken into his service since that essay was written; and corresponds in what relates to their doctrines, with the notes of similar discussions taken by Pere Dubois, a worthy and intelligent missionary who has lived for seventeen years among the Hindoos as one of themselves.

The ancient religion of India, and, as Dhermia supposes, of the whole world, was uniform: namely, the *worship of one God*, a pure spirit, indivisible, without form, or extent, or any corporeal attribute, omniscient, all powerful, possessing infinite wisdom, and *infinite happiness*. Absorbed in the contemplation of his own perfections, he interferes in no respect in the government of the universe, or in terrestrial concerns. Having originally given to all things their appointed order and course of action; having rendered punishment the inevitable result of vice, and happiness after death the sure reward of virtue; he leaves mankind to the consequences of their actions, and considers with indifference the complicated effects of good and evil upon earth which necessarily arise from the operation of free will.

After death the virtuous go to *Hoordwaloga* (Paradise), and the wicked to *Ashdaloga* (Hell), for a determined number of years, according to the measure of their actions upon earth; at the expiration of that period they return again on earth to a new state of existence, determined also by their conduct in the last; and thus to circulate though various transmigrations. But a superior degree of sanctity purifies the soul from the grossness of corporeal contact, and causes it to be reunited for ever with the divine spirit. The twenty-four Teerters, or saints, of this religion have thus been deified, and they are worshipped accordingly, as being intimately and inseparably united with God.

Although the fourfold division of casts prevails among the Jain, and they, like the ordinary Hindoos, have their bramins, we are obliged for want of more convenient terms to discriminate the sects, by calling the doctrine of the latter that of the *bramins*, and the former that of the *Jain*. To the bramins the Jain attribute all the corruptions of the present state of religion; the fabrication of the four vedas; the eighteen *Pooranas;* the blasphemous doctrine of the Trimourty, or three Gods, and the monstrous fables which relate to it; the Avatars of Vishnoo; the obscene worship of the lingum, of cows and snakes, of the sun, the stars, the planets, and the elements; the sacredness of the waters of the Ganges, and other rivers; and the whole catalogue of modern superstition. These corruptions, as the Jain affirms, did not take place at once, but have been gradually introduced; and among them the crime of murder, in the sacrifice of animals, which though less frequent now than at some former times, is still practised in the Egniam.

Even the remnant of the Jain which had survived the repeated persecutions incited by the bramins has not escaped the corruption of the times; and the rites of their religion in the temples formerly most sacred (as those of Canara, Baligola, and Mudgery) are now performed by unqualified persons of the third cast; whom Dhernia considers as heretics. I have myself conversed with the *Gooroos* of the two former places, mentioned by Major Mackenzie and Doctor Buchanan in the ninth volume of the Asiatic Researches; and they have acknowledged to me that they are Vaysias. The Jain bramins appear to have been the select objects of persecution; and in all Mysoor not more than fifty or sixty families now remain. I have heard of none in any other part of the south, and the only temple where the rites of the religion are duly performed is in the small village of Maleyoor, of which Dhermia is one of the officiating priests.

The bramins relate with exultation the *lacs* of Jain who have been destroyed at different periods, in persecutions which appear to have been more sanguinary than any recorded in the western world: and the following brief notice of these persecutions is taken chiefly *from the bramins*, and from documents in the Mackenzie collection. The earliest persecutor of the Jain of whom I have received any distinct account is *Bhutt Acharya*, who lived about or before the commencement of the christian æra. This person had become the disciple of a Jain Gooroo* for the express purpose of learning the philosophy of that sect (in which the bramins admit that they excelled), and thus defeating them with their own weapons. He betrayed what he found exceptionable in their doctrines; and after having excited against them the most active persecution, finally condemned himself to perish by a slow fire, as an expiation for the crime of *having betrayed his Gooroo*. In the act of sustaining this punishment at *Hurdwar*, where the Ganges enters Hindostan, he was visited by the celebrated *Sancara Acharya*, a native of Kerala or Malabar. In the midst of his sufferings *Bhutt Acharya* instructed this apt disciple, and exhorted him to continue the holy work of persecution; an injunction which Sancara Acharya effectually observed in his travels through every part of India. The Jain religion however continued to flourish to the south, to the extent of being professed by several dynasties of kings, among whom

* Spiritual preceptor.

we may enumerate with some certainty a very ancient dynasty which ruled at or near Conjeveram before that part of Drauveda was conquered or colonized by the Chola dynasty, and assumed the name of Tondamundelum, from the name of the son of the Chola king who commanded the expedition; the Pandian ruling at Madura; and a branch of it in Canara; and the Hoisala or Bellals who ruled at Doorasummoder, now called the Hallabede, near the western range of the hills of Mysoor. In 1133 *Ramanuja* or Ramanjacharee, the famous Vishnavite reformer, flying from the persecution of a king of the *Chola* dynasty in Tanjore of the sect of *Siva*, who exacted a confession of faith from all his subjects, ascended to Mysoor, and converted to the Vishnavite religion the reigning king of the last mentioned dynasty, named Veera Narsa Bellal, who thenceforth assumed the name of *Vishnoo Verdana;* and it is to the persecution of this period that the bramins exultingly refer for the final extinction of the Jain, by the most extensive slaughter and unheard of torments, one of which was that of grinding them in an oil-mill.

The relative antiquity of the Jain and the bramins cannot perhaps at present be decided: there is little room to doubt that they were originally the same, and the question would relate to the doctrine which each of them pretend to have preserved unpolluted. But it appears to me incontestable, that the distinction of doctrine and separation of sects had taken place before the expedition of Alexander. On asking Dhermia the reason of prefixing the popular term *Sravana* to the names of all their temples, he tells me that the word is a corruption of *Sramana*, the most usual term for the sect, or rather for the holy persons belonging to it: he enumerated six other distinctive terms which are indiscriminately applied to them, viz. Arhata, Digumbera, Jenna, Jaina, and Pramâna. It will not probably be questioned that the *Sramana* are the *Sarmanes*, *Germanes*, *Samanes*; and *Pramana* the *Pramnæ* of the ancient authors of the west. Strabo would seem to consider the *Germanes* and the *Pramnæ* as distinct sects; but both are said to be opponents of the *Brachmanes*, and the latter particularly to ridicule their study of astrology. It may be noticed as a confirmation of the distinction of doctrine at this period, that Philostratus and Pliny speak of the *Brachmanes* as worshipping the sun; but although some obscurity may be expected in the imperfect information of the ancients, I do not find this worship any where attributed to the *Sarmanes* or *Pramnæ*, who to this day hold it in abhorrence. The *Zarmanochagas*, noticed so much by ancient authors for having publicly destroyed himself at Athens, was probably a Jain. In a note on Strabo lib. 15—1048, on this name, we are told that old manuscripts (*Veteres libri*) have two distinct words, *Zarmanas* and *Chagas*, and Dion Cassius names this person Zarmanes without any addition. *Sramana-ganna*, as Dhermia informs me, is the usual form of speech to indicate the *sect* of Jain.

The following substance of an extract from a Jain Pooranam in the Mackenzie collection is at least curious. The last of the Teartees named *Verdamanna*, studied along with his sister's son *Parswa Butarick*: the latter becoming jealous of the superior progress of his relative in the established studies, sought another path to distinction by the invention of a new religion, chiefly supported by *magical illusions*. He converted by these means many kings, and chiefly extended his religion to the west, from whence (the Jain very strangely imagine that) after suffering many subsequent corruptions and changes it returned to India, under the form of the Mohammedan religion. This person commenced the promulgation of his new religion when he was thirty-three years of age: the æra of his contemporary *Verdamana*, the last of the Teartas (but whether his birth, death, or sanctification I do not find in my notes) is the conclusion of the fourth age, according to the chronology of the Jain; of the fifth 2466 had elapsed in 1807, which places its commencement in 659 B. C.; a period sufficiently near to the supposed æra of Zoroaster to render the coincidence very remarkable. In a curious but mutilated manuscript history of Persia formerly in the possession of Colonel Close, but now I fear irrevocably lost, I recollect the narrative of a war between Iran and Turan in consequence of the king of the former having embraced the *new religion* of *Zerdusht*, which the king of Turan in a letter full of reproach terms the *foolish doctrines of a stranger*.

If the other circumstances of coincidence should appear to be satisfactory, the difference of name will be found to furnish no objection. Zerdusht or Zeradusht, the person whom we name Zoroaster, probably assumed that fanciful title (signifying the *leader* of a flock of those descriptions of birds which observe a regular order of flight) when he became the founder of a sect.

Whatever in other respects may be the state of science in the ancient books of the Jain; Dhermia is a proficient in logic, and a very acute metaphysician. This intelligent and venerable old man is preparing a history of the sect, which may probably throw some faint lights on ancient history; but I fear that the lapse from the only true religion, with which the bramins are so rudely charged, may be retorted in many instances on the minor doctrines of the Jain themselves.

The Jain are very commonly confounded with the worshippers of Bhoud by the bramins and Hindoos of every cast. But it is only necessary to state that the Jain have, and the Bhoudists have not, a distinction of casts, to prove that the two religions must have been at all times irreconcilable. The Jain assume to themselves the merit of having expelled the worshippers of Bhoud from the southern peninsula at the conclusion of a violent religious war. We have already adverted to a dynasty of Jain kings which ruled at Conjeveram at a very early period; and Colonel Mackenzie has also found at the same place many incontestable remains of a Bhoudist establishment, but no authority for determining the date of their alleged expulsion.

No. VI.

List of the Purgunnahs that appear to have been in the possession of Chick-Deo-Raja of Mysoor, at the time of his death in 1704.

No.	MYSOOR.	Revenue.
		Canty. Pagodas.
1	Puttun Astagram	10,000
2	Mysoor Astagram	11,500
3	Mysoor Tallook	14,000
4	Hardanhully	15,000
5	Periapatam	6,200
6	Muddoor	13,200
7	Heggadavancotta	8,000
8	Bettadapoor	7,000
9	Tāyoor	8,000
10	Yellandoor	10,000
11	Mallavelly	9,000
12	Tālcad or Sosilla	8,100
13	Narsipoor	10,200
14	Yedtora	7,200
15	Bailoor	15,700
16	Arcullgode	4,300
17	Chinnapatam	12,100
18	Hassun	7,900
19	Honawully	9,400
20	Nagamunglum }	4,700
21	Bellore }	3,100
22	Maharajdroog	10,000
23	Gram	3,500
24	Ramgherry	7,400
25	Turkanamby	7,400
26	Cuddaba	12,000
27	Toorvykeira	9,000
28	Coonygul	5,008
29	Hoolioordroog	4,000
30	Hickairee	4,065
31	Chewrayputtun	9,138
32	Noogyhully	3,000
33	Mailcottah }	6,100
34	Kishnrajpoor }	
35	Suckroyputtun	6,200
	Carried over	281,411

No.	MYSOOR.	Revenue.	
		Canty. Pagodas.	
	Brought up -	281,411	
36	Banawar		
37	Gurradungeery	10,000	
38	Harunhully		
39	Boodihall	7,000	
40	Hagulwādy	12,000	
41	Bangalore	55,000	
42	Māgry	8,400	
43	Mudgerry	36,000	
44	Cortekeirah	4,000	
45	Cankanhully	8,900	
46	Nellamunglum	16,000	
47	Dodabulla		
48	Anicull	10,300	
49	Byrandroog	4,000	
50	Hebboor	7,000	
51	Ootradroog	5,000	
52	Chenroydroog	8,000	
53	Toomkoor	18,000	
54	Deoroydroog		
55	Nidjigull	16,000	
56	Māklydroog		
57	Cundykurah	16,000	
58	Chickanaighully		
59	Chicka Moogloor	8,134	4
60	Cuddoor	7,129	7¼
61	Burra Ballapoor	44,000	
62	Settigall		
63	Codahully	15,200	
64	Allambaddy		
65	Denkanicotta	14,000	
66	Ruttingerry		
67	Ossoor	18,096	
68	Ankusgeery	4,000	
69	Solageery		
70	Bāgloor	3,000	
	BARRAMHAL.		
1	Barramhal	64,000	
2	Caveriputtun	10,000	
3	Verabuddrdroog	8,000	
4	Raycottah	8,000	
5	Kangoondy	6,000	
6	Darampoory	8,000	
7	Pennagra	10,000	
8	Tingrycotta	12,000	
9	Caverypoor	8,000	
10	Ahtoor Anuntgeery	18,000	
	Carried over	788,571	1¼

No.	MYSOOR.	Revenue.
		Canty. Pagodas.
	Brought up -	788,571 1¼
11	Purmutty - - - - - -	14,000
12	Shendamungul - - - -	20,000
13	Womloor - - - - - -	16,000
14	Sankergeery - - - - - -	40,000
15	Namcall - - - - - -	16,000
16	Koosh - - - - - - -	8,000
17	Salem - - - - - - -	24,000
	COIMBETOOR.	
1	Coimbetoor - - - - - -	80,000
2	Danaikencotta - - - -	35,000
3	Cheoor or Sheoor - - - - -	27,000
4	Chingeery - - - - - -	27,000
5	Darapooram and Chuckergeery -	64,000
6	Cangium - - - - - -	20,000
7	Sattimunglum - - - - -	30,000
8	Undoor or Andwor - - -	8,000
9	Perindoora - - - - - -	14,000
10	Vizimungle or Arravacourchy -	20,000
11	Errode - - - - - - -	20,000
12	Caroor - - - - - - -	41,000
13	Oodgully - - - - - - -	15,000
14	Caverypooram - - - - -	4,000
	Total.	1,331,571 1¼

END OF VOL. I.

ERRATA.

Page 33. Note, for *Kalla Canara* read *Holla Canara*.
45. Second line from the bottom, for *conquest* read *conquests*.
49. 7th line from the bottom, for *laid* read *lay*.
55. Note, 7th line from the bottom, for *Dad* read *Dua*.
82. 7th line from the bottom, for *awakening* read *awaking*.
90. Note, for Appendix *No. VI.* read *No. V.*
95. 15th line, for *ama* read *Rama*.
97. Note, 3d line, for *expelled* read *expected*.
113. Note, last line, between *regarding* and *landed* insert *the*.
144. Note, last line, place *d. l.* after *Cicero* instead of after *Livy*.
152. Note, 11th line, for *Chalde t* read *Chaldesh*.
153. Note, 2d line, for *Madaveeun* read *Madaveeum*.
166. Note, 9th line from the bottom, for *Jollâlehoo* read *Jellâlehoo*.
183. 6th line from the bottom, between *tract* and *which* insert *in*.
189. Note, 3d line from the bottom, for *Major* read *Lieutenant-Colonel*.
190. 7th line, place the inverted commas at the beginning of the line.
215. 2d line from the bottom, strike out one *e* in *Chittledroog*.
241. Note, for 1729 read 1720.
293. 2d line from the bottom, for *Jamedar* read *Jemmadar*.
334. Last line, for *detached* read *detailed*.
405. 1st line, for *county* read *country*.
422. Note, for *Jaseen* read *Yaseen*.
435. Heading of Chapter XII. for 1766 read *to the commencement of* 1767.
465. Margin, for 1764 read 1765.
477. For *Najpoor* read *Nagpoor*.
493. The year of Salivahan 1720, corresponds with A.D. 1798.
505. 2d line, for *Loonda* read *Soonda*.
511. 7th line, between *called* and *Hallabede* expunge *the*.
512. 7th line from the bottom, for *Teartees* read *Tearters*.

PREFACE.

xx. For *Ooner* read *Omer*.